The Contingency of Necessity

New Perspectives in Ontology
Series Editors: Peter Gratton and Sean J. McGrath, Memorial University of Newfoundland, Canada

Publishes the best new work on the nature of being

After the fundamental modesty of much post-Heideggerian Continental philosophy, the time is now for a renaissance in ontology after the rise of the new realisms and new materialisms. This new series aims to be an interdisciplinary forum for this work, challenging old divisions while borrowing from the ontological frameworks of post-humanism, ecological studies, critical animal studies, and other post-constructivist areas of endeavour. While often working within the Continental tradition, the books in this series will move beyond the stale hermeneutics and phenomenologies of the past, with authors boldly reopening the oldest questions of existence through a contemporary lens.

Editorial Advisory Board
Thomas J. J. Altizer, State University of New York at Stony Brook
Maurizio Farraris, University of Turin
Paul Franks, Yale University
Iain Hamilton Grant, University of the West of England
Garth Green, McGill University
Adrian Johnston, University of New Mexico
Catherine Malabou, Kingston University
Jeff Malpas, University of Tasmania
Marie-Eve Morin, University of Alberta
Jeffrey Reid, University of Ottawa
Susan Ruddick, University of Toronto
Michael Schulz, University of Bonn
Hasana Sharp, McGill University
Alison Stone, Lancaster University
Peter Trawny, University of Wuppertal
Uwe Voigt, University of Augsburg
Jason Wirth, Seattle University
Günter Zöller, University of Munich

Books available
The Political Theology of Schelling by Saitya Brata Das
Continental Realism and Its Discontents edited by Marie-Eve Morin
The Contingency of Necessity: Reason and God as Matters of Fact by Tyler Tritten
The Late Schelling and the End of Christianity by Sean J. McGrath

www.edinburghuniversitypress.com/series/epnpio

The Contingency of Necessity

Reason and God as Matters of Fact

TYLER TRITTEN

EDINBURGH
University Press

Edinburgh University Press is one of the leading university presses in the UK. We publish academic books and journals in our selected subject areas across the humanities and social sciences, combining cutting-edge scholarship with high editorial and production values to produce academic works of lasting importance. For more information visit our website: edinburghuniversitypress.com

© Tyler Tritten, 2017

Edinburgh University Press Ltd
The Tun – Holyrood Road
12(2f) Jackson's Entry
Edinburgh EH8 8PJ

Typeset in 11/13 Adobe Garamond by
Servis Filmsetting Ltd, Stockport, Cheshire

A CIP record for this book is available from the British Library

ISBN 978 1 4744 2819 4 (hardback)
ISBN 978 1 4744 2821 7 (webready PDF)
ISBN 978 1 4744 2822 4 (epub)

The right of Tyler Tritten to be identified as the author of this work has been asserted in accordance with the Copyright, Designs and Patents Act 1988, and the Copyright and Related Rights Regulations 2003 (SI No. 2498).

Contents

Acknowledgements vii

Introduction: An Attempt at a Speculative Ontology or an Alternative to Possible-God Theologies 1

Part I Critical and Constructive Preliminaries: Meillassoux, Boutroux and the Early Schelling

1 Meillassoux against the Principle of Reason: An Ontology of Facticity 17
2 Boutroux's Alternative: An Ontology of the Fact 44
3 On the Primacy of Matter: Neoplatonism Right-Side Up 75

Part II Contingent Reason and a Contingent God: The Late Schelling and the Late Heidegger

4 Reason as Consequent Universal: On Thinking and Being 103
5 Decision and Withdrawal: On the Facticity and Posteriority of God 136
6 Event and De-cision: Towards an Appropriation of Heidegger's Last God 167

Part III Application and Concluding Remarks

7 A Response to Old Riddles and a New Typology: On the Euthyphro Dilemma and Theomonism 205

Afterword   239

Bibliography   248
Index   256

Acknowledgements

This book would not have come to fruition, at least not in this decade, without the generous financial support and flexibility of the Alexander von Humboldt Foundation. In this context, I wish to my express my sincere thanks to my hosts in the departments of philosophy and theology respectively at the Albert-Ludwigs-Universität Freiburg, Lore Hühn and Andrzej Wiercinski. Without Andrzej, who first invited me to apply for the fellowship, I would scarcely be connected to the philosophical community. He is a great scholar, facilitator and friend. In my time at Freiburg, I also benefited from the companionship of Alexander Bilda and Philipp Schwab. Their knowledge of Schelling far surpasses my own.

I am extremely grateful that Edinburgh University Press has patiently stuck with me throughout the writing of this book. They are first-class publishers. Carol McDonald requires thanking in particular, whose expertise and advice I probably did not always follow as closely as I should have. The editors of the series in which this book appears, Sean McGrath and Peter Gratton, also merit special mention for their help throughout this process. Inevitable disagreements notwithstanding, I was enthused to learn that Sean and I may be philosophically kindred spirits.

All of my colleagues in the department of philosophy at Gonzaga University, who took a risk on me and my 'upside down metaphysics', have been steadfastly supportive. David Calhoun and Kirk Besmer in particular have endured philosophical discussions about many of the themes that appear in this book. I doubt I have yet convinced David of its basic theses . . . but I would like to think I am close. Duane Armitage, a former colleague and present friend, has been there to educate me about all things Heidegger. Where my interpretation of Heidegger runs afoul, even if intentionally so, it cannot be said that he did not advise me of a more appropriate reading.

The editing and proofing of this book was greatly aided by Christopher 'Tof' Chapin, Edward Butler, Daniel C. Barber, Vladimir Titkov and Annalee Ring. I thank them for their patience.

Finally, friends in philosophy without whom this text could not have come to be include Daniel Whistler, who carried me as we co-edited a special edition of *Angelaki* as I was completing the draft of this project; G. Anthony Bruno, who has provided stimulating exchanges on Meillassoux, Schelling and Heidegger; Jason M. Wirth, who has supported me personally and professionally throughout the years in more ways than I can name here; Marcela García, who is one of the friendliest and most approachable scholars I know; and Kyla Bruff, who, though at the beginning of her philosophical journey, undoubtedly has a great future ahead of her.

All acknowledgements, however, truly begin and end with my wife, Danielle A. Layne, who continued to thrive as a scholar and educator of ancient philosophy even as I made her into a single mother to complete this book, as I twice left her alone with our two sons for eleven months combined to work on this project in Freiburg, once as she was starting a new job. Not only did her academic career continue to thrive, but she remained a gracious wife and mother throughout. Her sacrifices have not gone unnoticed. In addition to all this, she has also served me in every professional function imaginable, from sounding board to dialogue partner to teacher to proofreader. Her philosophical genius shines brightly.

My eldest son, Simon, despite being the most precocious eleven-year-old I know, has not yet had the penchant to ask philosophical questions taught out of him. I hope this never changes. My youngest, Felix, always has the ability to retrieve me from my ivory tower (or maybe it is only a well) in order to pull me back into the real world of people and things. I love them both.

Finally, I cannot omit to mention the support offered by my parents, sister and grandparents. They have all made great sacrifices for me, even when they have not known or understood what I am doing. I wish I saw them more frequently.

If this book has a voice, it is a symphony of the voices just mentioned and of others that have remained unnamed. Nevertheless, I take responsibility for this symphony, particularly its faults, as its orchestrator. Perhaps one should no longer speak of the death, but rather of the *inspiritus*, of the author, in whose breath many voices are heard.

Introduction

An Attempt at a Speculative Ontology or an Alternative to Possible-God Theologies

This book is unapologetically ontological and speculative rather than epistemological, ethical, political or 'scientific'. The programme is not first to ground the possibility of knowledge as such by securing epistemic access to being before commencing with ontology proper. There is a deliberate refusal to concede to epistemology any pre-eminence over ontology. The pitfall of modernity was that it deluded itself into thinking that epistemology was first philosophy and that it could be practised apart from ontological decisions. Modernity fell into this trap because it began with the artificial doubt of Cartesianism and so immediately found itself delivered over to 'the fundamental presupposition of scepticism, namely the primacy of the epistemological'.[1]

The thesis of this book is that all necessity is consequent; or, no necessity is absolute. At bottom, all necessity is based on the utter contingency of being as a *factum brutum*, the fact that there is something rather than nothing. This book hopes faithfully to elaborate the ramifications of this, specifically arguing (1) that reason itself, the domain of necessary truths, is being's eternally contingent and consequent universal and (2) that God, while necessary according to essence, is contingent with respect to existence. The thesis, then, is that both reason itself and God are contingent, albeit eternal, necessities. In general, then, this book deigns to answer the question: How does a necessary essence, for example, rationality, regularity, order and lawfulness, supplement utterly contingent, that is, chaotic, irrational, disordered, unregulated and lawless, existence, the brute fact that there is something instead of nothing?

Contemporary ontology and the possibility of speculative theology

This introduction has been written twice, once to inform the author of his own intentions and once, after writing the book, to inform the reader about what the author has actually done, except in a disingenuous future tense. What, then, has been done or, rather, what will be done in this book? It is, much to the author's own surprise, a book on logic. It is also, against the author's own desires, a book on the late philosophy of F. W. J. von Schelling.[2] It is not, all the same, a commentary or secondary resource, and nor is it a book exclusively about Schelling. There are entire chapters dedicated to the thought of Quentin Meillassoux, Émile Boutroux and Martin Heidegger respectively, with large sections of chapters devoted to Plato, Proclus and Alain Badiou. Embedded throughout one can also find a book-long conversation with C. S. Peirce, and ambivalent or quasi-polemical interactions with Markus Gabriel. Aristotle, Immanuel Kant and G. W. F. Hegel also play subterranean roles.

Although arranged according to both constructive and critical confrontations with authors, this remains a book on logic or, more precisely, the ontology of logic. Given that logic is a supposed universal science, valid for all irrespective of time and place (which is not meant to deny that there is a history of logic or even an Indian logic as opposed to Western logic), it would seem that the logician should disappear from view. Further, a central thesis of this book is that knowledge is not an autonomous construction of a subject, be she philosopher, natural scientist or mathematician. Instead, knowledge is the construction of being itself. For these reasons, the author, even if he cannot entirely disappear from the reader's view, ought not to presume possession of the knowledge generated through 'his' research. At the risk, then, of failing to stand by one's work, of failing to take responsibility for what has been/will be said, this book has omitted the use of the first person.

The absence of the first person should not suggest that the train of thought consists in an anonymous chain of propositions, each derived from the foregoing and implicating the following, in an attempt to camouflage the decisions that have been made. There are, in fact, a fair number of decisions, rather than just a string of inferences, made throughout, but one of those decisions is itself that most decisions are not made by an autonomous author in full transparency and self-mastery. There are many decisions in this book; they are everywhere, but it is uninteresting and, more importantly, philosophically impoverished to psychologise an author and her decisions away. What is interesting is, as Socrates suggested, 'to follow the argument where it leads'.[3] What is interesting is not to uncover the psychological motivations of an author's decisions, but to inquire whither certain decisions lead, to ask what decisions can do, what they can create. Even to inquire about the topic of a book is already to attempt to become clear about its most basic decision. So, what is this book about? What decisions has it made?

As mentioned, modern philosophy, beginning with the epistemic, became deaf to questions and phenomena not easily accommodated by prevailing epistemic schemas. Philosophy, however, begins in curiosity, wonder or astonishment, and what is more astonishing than rogue phenomena that refuse annexation into prevailing views, for example, God, the miraculous,[4] freedom or the fact that there is something rather than nothing? Perhaps nothing inspires more awe and wonder (θαυμάζειν) than freedom, which results in unexpected consequences for which no account could ever be given in advance of its actuality, lest freedom be nullified as freedom. That freedom, more than anything else, provokes the awe constitutive of a philosophic disposition is one of the wagers of this book. Accordingly, the objective is not to defend contingency from the encroachment of various types of necessity, especially metaphysical necessitarianisms, in order to preserve freedom, but, inversely, by first acknowledging freedom as an incontrovertible fact of experience one is compelled to posit being as pure contingency, as that which calls for, nay, demands free decision. This book, then, attempts to think not only the status of being *qua* being as chaos or pure contingency, but also the manner in which the contingency of being demands that the equipoise or utter contingency of all possibilities be decided. The task is to exhibit how the decision of being results in the consequent construction of reason, in logical space or being's supplementation with thinkability and rationality, as well as to expose this same decision as the withdrawal of God, as holiness and divinity.

This task will seem absurd to many, due to their own metaphysical commitments or the (misguided) conviction that they lack metaphysical commitments, but the core of this book, Chapters 4, 5 and 6 on Schelling and Heidegger, will hopefully render this mystification sober. For now, let it be stated that by thinking of being *qua* being as contingent rather than necessary, the attempt is to think otherwise than 'metaphysically', to think being without resorting to the presuppositions of ontotheology. In this respect, one should note Gert-Jan van der Heiden's recently published *Ontology after Ontotheology: Plurality, Event, and Contingency in Contemporary Philosophy*, where he remarks,

> One may understand this 'core' of ontotheology to consist in the metaphysical quest for (or presupposition of) a unifying reason or ground . . .

> Therefore, I propose to consider contemporary ontology in light of its efforts to offer an alternative to unity as well as to reason or ground.[5]

While sympathetic to his point of departure, which refuses to presuppose a reason or ground of being, it remains the case that for him the surpassing of ontotheology entails more than is required, namely 'ontology after ontotheology, that is, an *ontology without theology*'.[6] To think otherwise than ontotheologically should not necessarily preclude theology any more than it precludes ontology. If there can be ontology after ontotheology, there should also be theology after ontotheology. This book differs from Van der Heiden's in two substantial ways. First, while he provides an overview of ontologies of contingency in the twentieth century, namely Heidegger and after, this book does not offer a comprehensive historical overview but has as its aim the construction of an ontology of contingency or an 'ontology of the fact'. Second, while he declines theology, convinced that this enterprise is antithetical to 'post-metaphysical' thought, this work operates under the assumption that a speculative ontology is inseparable from an equally speculative theology. This book's use of Schelling's late philosophy of mythology and revelation, which consists largely in a critical response to the logocentrism and rationalism of Hegel as well as, more obliquely, to the anti-historical transcendentalisms of Kant and Fichte, stems from this conviction.

Concerning Schelling's departure from Kant and Fichte, Iain Hamilton Grant writes, 'Schellingianism is resurgent every time philosophy *reaches beyond the Kant-inspired critique of metaphysics, its subjectivist-epistemological transcendentalism* . . .'[7] Schelling's latest thought, although it retains an ontological account of God, that is, a speculative theology, radically calls into question and reorients in a way relevant for contemporary ontology the nature of the a priori and the nature of ground, namely the principle of reason. It opts against the transcendentalisms and 'correlationisms' of critical philosophy and its phenomenological heritage, instead espousing a new kind of empiricism, which Schelling sometimes termed 'metaphysical empiricism'[8] and which this book explicates as 'narrative empiricism'. Demonstrating that the act of grounding, and thus also the absolutely a priori, is only explicable *per posterius* or through the posterior, Schelling's approach is also explicable as an empirical apriorism, as a speculative and experimental construction of reality, the being of reason and God included, from the absolute *prius* forth. Such an unabashedly speculative construction is also the objective of this book, which attempts to explicate the contingency of necessity as the consequent or posterior construction of necessity or lawfulness from out of the contingency or lawlessness of chaos as being *qua* being, as absolute *prius*. The method is thus inductive in the sense of letting the empirical order emerge before one's very eyes. The method is progressive, genetic or historical insofar as it reconstructs the genesis of being from the ground up, from the *prius* forth, as opposed to Heidegger who rather attempts to retrieve the meaning of being through a nostalgic return to philosophy's origins before its metaphysical entrapments.

The prevailing assumption is that Schellingianism names a possibility for contemporary thought. Karl Jaspers judges of Schelling, particularly *apropos* of his late philosophy, that 'he had radical thoughts in a conservative form'.[9] In his latest philosophy, Schelling elaborated an ontology that denied any a priori governance to the principle of (sufficient) reason and thereby also denied absolute necessity in all its forms. Strikingly, he accomplished this not by denying that God is the *ens necessarium*, but by offering a radical reinterpretation of the same, thus retaining the rhetoric of traditional metaphysics but surpassing its basic concepts. Schelling uncompromisingly constructed an ontology of God. Such a speculative endeavour, as one commentator has phrased it, requires no more justification except to realise that genuine thinking consists in 'the projection of possibilities'.[10] This work, Schellingian at heart, will offer reasons for affirming God not simply as a possibility for thought but as a matter of fact, yet without lapsing into natural theology and its decision to presuppose the efficacy of a principle of reason.

Kant's criticisms of the traditional arguments for the existence of God had seemingly closed the book for anybody still wanting to speak of the 'being' of God. Prohibiting constitutive assertions about God, Kant left room for God only as a regulative ideal or as a postulate of purely practical reason. Subsequently, post-Kantian continental philosophy, dominated largely by phenomenological approaches, refraining from following Kant in postulating the existence of God for the purposes of the *summum bonum*, that is, for morality, has instead heeded his theoretical strictures. (Process and proto-process thinkers like Peirce, Samuel Alexander and Alfred North Whitehead, who find difficulties fitting in with the continental tradition as much as with the analytic tradition, represent peculiar exceptions.) Consequently, contemporary thinking about God, at least from the so-called continental perspective, has generally abandoned any possibility of elaborating an ontology of God, relegating itself instead to phenomenological or hermeneutical descriptions and analyses of religious experience, for example, the meaning and existential structure of faith as well as phenomenological descriptions of encounters with alterity. Post-Kantian philosophy has confined itself to a philosophical description of experiences that might rightly pass as 'religious', regarding as antiquated any efforts to speak of the being of God. There are signs, however, that contemporary thought is on the precipice of a change. Authors like John Caputo or Richard Kearney, who argue for a God who might possibly exist in the future or a God who might exist presently, although as possibility (or *possest*) rather than as *actualitas*, have done much to reinvigorate an ontological rather than merely existential-phenomenological approach to the question of God. Additionally, Meillassoux's inexistent God who may-be, in contradistinction with the militant atheism of other authors loosely identified with 'speculative realism' or 'new realism' movements, offers an especially provocative alternative.

This introduction, then, before providing a synopsis of the book as a whole, will first detail how its approach differs from the possible-God theologies of Kearney and Caputo. Meillassoux will be treated in detail as the focus of Chapter 1. Caputo and Kearney, although breaking from the phenomenological tradition of post-Heideggerian theology[11] insofar as they seem willing to speak of the being of God, yet remain indebted to phenomenological hermeneutics, permitting, in Caputo's case, only a weak or possible-God rather than an actual God. They (perhaps interminably) postpone God for a future date. By contrast, this book does not speculate on a possibly future God but on a God who is actual and eternal, yet who could also eternally never have been. This is not a possible-God but a contingent God, God neither as future possibility nor as necessarily existent, but as an eternally contingent fact. This book thus hopes to revive the prospects that contemporary philosophy of religion, which, since Heidegger, has consisted, by and large, in a phenomenological hermeneutics of religious life, can again embark upon an ontology of God, but now as a post-metaphysical thought that begins neither by presupposing the principle of sufficient reason nor by instantiating the same as a *causa sui* first cause. Reason and God are contingent, yet eternal, consequents.

To recapitulate, this book contains two principal theses, one general and one particular. The general thesis, epistemo-ontological in nature, concerns the facticity of reason, arguing that reason itself, as a consequent emergence from pre-rational being, is a contingent facticity. The question thus concerns epistemo-genesis or the ontological emergence of the epistemic domain, including the cardinal laws of logic. While the general thesis concerns the contingency of necessity as such, the contingency of reason, the particular thesis argues for God as the paradigmatic exemplar of the contingency of being. It argues for an unexplored option in the field of the philosophy of God: a contingently necessary God. While Meillassoux, Kearney and Caputo propose a possible-God who does not yet exist but may in the future, this book argues for a contingent God who exists eternally but nevertheless could just as easily eternally never have been. The proposal is for a contingently necessary God, an eternal contingency according to existence who is nevertheless necessary according to essence, just as the essence of reason constitutes the domain of necessary truths while the existence of this domain remains a contingent matter of fact.

Against possible-God theologies

Although Kearney and Caputo are examples of those who are returning to an ontological account of God, this is not as clearly the case with them as it is with Meillassoux. Kearney, for example, is still able to write, 'This return to the religious remains for us philosophers a hermeneutic exercise rather than a theological dogma. It is not apologetics.'[12] While Kearney's intention is not to deny ontological import as such but only to defend his view from dogmatics, he nevertheless remains a hermeneuticist. While hermeneutics certainly does not exclude forays into ontological speculation, neither does it permit a clean break with the phenomenological tradition, which certain speculative realists require. In any event, the objective is neither to espouse nor to denounce a return to the religious – this book has nothing to say about religious experience or religion as a social practice – but the objective does entail a rejection of accounts of God that are only phenomenological or hermeneutical in nature. Claims about the religious state of a subject who feels gripped by something 'more' or something 'out there' – whatever that means – is not the concern.

Kearney summarises his possible-God theology, which he baptises anatheism, in the following:

> Anatheism differs from dogmatic atheism in that it resists absolutist positions *against* the divine, just as it differs from the absolutist positions of dogmatic theism *for* the divine. It is a movement – not a state – that refuses all absolute talk about the absolute, negative or positive; for it acknowledges that the absolute can never be understood *absolutely* by any single person or religion . . . It respects agnostic atheism that remains just that – *agnosis*, not-knowing . . . what anatheism opposes is militant antitheism, which . . . is just as pernicious as triumphal theism.[13]

Anatheism, so-named because it purports to operate above the dichotomy between theism and atheism, represents, as Kearney phrases it, a *via tertia* between the two, placing its hope in 'The God Who May Be'. That this *via tertia* signifies a rejection of the principle of excluded middle, affirming the possible as the not-to-be-excluded middle between God's existence and non-existence, is commendable. That this may drag his position down to the 'weakness', not just non-absolutism but even anti-absolutism, of Caputo's thought is regrettable. Contrary to Meillassoux, Kearney's and

Caputo's positions deliberately refrain from the task of thinking the absolute; they remain theoreticians of finitude. Kearney, for example, remains convinced 'that the absolute can never be understood *absolutely* by any single person or religion'. This 'weakness' – which is Caputo's term – presupposes a position of finitude that forecloses knowledge of the absolute. This book, however, while, like Kearney, also endeavouring to refuse the absolute provenance of the bivalency of truth or the principle of excluded middle by affirming the possible as a *via tertia*, nevertheless repudiates the diplomacy of compromising middling positions. The limbo of middling positions – as regrettable in ontology as in politics – and agnosticisms is rejected in favour of a return to the absolute. Agnosticism, as a sceptical counterbalance of propositions, can only emerge if things are approached epistemologically anyway. In this regard, both militant antitheism and triumphal theism can be superior to the indecision of agnosticism. As critical as the reading of Meillassoux in Chapter 1 will be, his brazen attempt to think the absolute is laudable.

The weakness of Kearney's position is admittedly not as weak as Caputo's, whose corpus is littered with statements like: 'In a strong theology, the name of God has historical determinacy and specificity – it is Christian or Jewish or Islamic, for example – whereas a weak theology, weakened by the flux of undecidability and translatability, is more open-ended';[14] and, 'The weakness of this theology . . . has to do with the undecidability of the name.'[15] To the contrary, this book contends that God cannot be the God of the undecided, but God only is God if decisive. God is not the undecided but the deciding of the undecidable, the separation of wheat from chaff: justice. God is not indiscernible and unnameable; he is the one who raises himself to the highest degree of individuality and discernibility. Divinity, that which makes God God, only occurs in decisiveness rather than in the impotence or weakness of undecidability. A weak God, by contrast, does not even raise itself above the plight of Buridan's Ass, because this God eternally hovers in the limbo of the possible, eternally ambivalent between being and non-being, deciding for neither.

Caputo glosses that Kearney's 'God is the excess of *posse* beyond *esse*'[16] or, as Kearney gleans from his readings of Nicholas of Cusa, God is *possest*. For Kearney, this can either mean that God is not actual but possible or that God is the being, that is, the actuality, of the possible. Kearney, perhaps unsurprisingly, ambiguously oscillates between these viewpoints. This work pursues the suggestion that 'God is the excess of *posse* beyond *esse*' as meaning that *posse* is an unforeseeable and posterior supplement of *esse*. It argues that *posse* ensues from the decision, but does not precede it.

In opposition to Kearney, Caputo views possibility as the possibility of some thing or of some event. He speaks of 'the possibilities harbored in events – by the fragile "perhaps" in things'.[17] Caputo finds possibility to be latent within an event, something already given as possible in advance of the event's actuality. This book rather argues that events are not undecidable or unnameable, although only specifiable *post factum*, because events do not pre-contain possibilities. Possibilities are not latent within events, but they are an event's supplement. Possibility or *posse* is not given within an event but it is only ever consequent upon an event, posterior to its actual eventuation, hence why events are only nameable after the fact. Caputo instead conceives of the event as something already harbouring possibility within it, yet also as something that never actually decides between its possibilities, hence why his event never emerges from undecidability and unnameability/anonymity.

This book, which argues not for a possible-God but for a contingent God, also differs from the theses of Kearney and Caputo insofar as the possible advent of their God very much rests in the hands of human beings. Their God is actualisable only as a consequence of the proper moral comportment of all, the possible actualisation of social and political justice. William Desmond, for one, justly criticises that

> a God who could not be God without us is hardly a God of possibility, more an impossible God, or not a God at all. If God possibilizes, God possibilizes us; but if God could not be God without us, somehow we possibilize God. Would it be so, then, that the God who may be would be impossible if *we* did not possibilize God? But if God possibilizes us, how can we be said to possibilize God? Either God is possibilizing Godself in and through us (Hegel), or we are possibilizing ourselves in God and through God (Feuerbach and sons).[18]

Caputo's position, if not Kearney's as well, is but an inflationary account of Feuerbach's, in which humanity as a whole not only projects God as an image but creates the reality or being of God as such (hence why it can never be exclusively named or annexed by a part of humanity only). Desmond, here critiquing Kearney rather than Caputo, correctly notes that the passivity and impotence of any God who is neither pure possibility nor pure act, but a possibility awaiting its actualisation by human hands, is as much the created as the creator, the (perhaps impossible) limit-term of human praxis.

One commentator seems to have extricated Kearney's God from human dependency, imploring that 'meaningfulness arises as an *eschatological theogony* from out of *chaos* (confusion *and* openness)'.[19] The promise to explain the emergence of meaning from a chaos thought as the very opening of being as such resonates with one of this book's theses, but this author continues by adding that meaning is '"generated" by the deconstructive, or "forensic", analysis of the textual corpus, or "corpse", of the onto-theological God'.[20] With this addendum he immediately drags God back down into the hands of human critique. Consequently, this is not real theogony but, along the lines of Feuerbach, (critical) anthropogony projected on to a divine screen.

It is rather Jeffrey Bloechl who offers the most promising interpretation of Kearney's possible-God. He states that

> it is not the logical 'maybe' by which we suppose that a thing may possibly exist but also possibly does not. It is also not the 'maybe' by which . . . the past moment and condition in which an event that is now present was once only possible.[21]

He breaks both from logical possibility – as this more radical account of the possible even places the being of logic or reason itself in question – and from a conception of possibility as something pre-contained in the foregoing, either a prior substrate or a past event. If the present is not big with its future, but it is still to be affirmed that God consists in the surplus of possibility or *posse* over being or *esse*, this is because *posse* is not contained in *esse* but advenes upon it, because *posse* supplements *esse* as something completely novel that was not there before. This reading affirms possibility as a novel consequent or supplementation; being precedes possibility, yet without presupposing some actuality/*actualitas* as the prior substrate or bearer of these possibilities. Only in this way can God be thought absolutely without prior conditions or foregoing possibilities, such that logical modality too becomes God's consequent rather than his antecedent. This is first a God who will be who he will be, not a possibly future God but an actually futural God, God not as future possibility but the God of the future, a God not yoked to possibilities pre-contained in past events or social conditions. That God is or is not is not just a speculative possibility, but a contingent fact consequent upon the pre-godly decision of being itself. That this decision is to be named Godly rather than ungodly can only be done after the event, *post factum*, but it can be named. An event that remains in the limbo of pure possibility is an event that never takes place, an event which is not. This book, however, will argue for a God that can be named as a matter of fact, an event not possible but affirmed, while also recognising the contingency of God, the fact that this decision/event could have never taken place/eventuated.

Synopsis

The fundamental decision is to avoid ontotheology, the presupposition of a first cause as the sufficient reason for why there is being rather than nothing at all, while still constructing a speculative ontology of reason and of God, but as eternal consequents rather than as presupposed antecedents. This book thus follows Van der Heiden's characterisation of the ontotheological tradition: 'the two motives that hold ontotheology together: the primacy of unity as well as the primacy of ground or reason'.[22] This characterisation of ontotheology, however, does not entail a rejection of unity, reason and ground as such, only the rejection of their absoluteness or antecedence. They can, of course, advene as contingent supplements, even as eternally contingent consequents.

Part I, that is, the first three chapters on Meillassoux, Boutroux and the early Schelling, respectively, functions as a propaedeutic to the actual ontological construction. Chapter 1 argues against Meillassoux's thesis for the necessity of contingency, retaining his rejection of the principle of reason as absolute but combatting his retention of the principle of non-contradiction as something obtaining even in chaos. Meillassoux, a self-proclaimed rationalist, logicises being, ultimately reducing it to quantification, as he calls for the reintroduction of the primary qualities of modernity. This permits him to follow Badiou in equating mathematics with ontology. The primary criticisms, then, are directed against his conception of the nature of contradiction and, as the kernel of his thesis for the necessity of contingency, against his conception of factiality.

Chapter 2 presents Boutroux's ontology of the fact as an alternative to Meillassoux's ontology of factiality, but it does not follow Boutroux to the letter. Boutroux's position, particularly his conception of habit, will be radicalised as a full-fledged ontological thesis instead of as a merely epistemological or psychological thesis. Boutroux explains why one must regard the logical, the mathematical, the transcendental and the laws of nature as contingencies that could have never been, while simultaneously affirming them as facts or domains operative according to a necessary modality. They are thus consequent necessities or contingent necessities. Consequently, Boutroux not only serves to expose the contingency at the basis of disciplines typically thought to be dealing with necessary truths, for example, logic and mathematics, but he also makes plausible the possibility that necessity, for example, the uniformity of the laws of nature, is nothing more than the habit of being's decision viewed from the outside.

Chapter 3, which completes the propaedeutic portion of the book, begins with Schelling's early reading of Plato's *Timaeus* and then demonstrates its effect on his mature period, finally contrasting Schelling's Plato with the more traditional and canonical reading of the Neoplatonists, Proclus in particular. In this way, it will be seen how Schelling is actually able to construct an ontology of contingency, as Boutroux had only paved the way for the possibility of an ontology of contingent necessity.

The basis of Schelling's ontology lies in the convictions that quality precedes quantity, the unlimited precedes the limited, the erratic precedes permanence, and lawlessness precedes law. These convictions support and structure Schelling's thesis concerning the contingency of necessity. This Platonist beginning to Schelling's thought also turns canonical Platonism upside down insofar as Schelling's Platonism does not begin with a descent from the perfect (πρooδoς) to be followed by a return ascent (ἐπιστροφή), but it begins with the inferior and ascends to superior levels of unity and order.

Part II, consisting of Chapters 4 and 5 along with Chapter 6 on Heidegger, comprises the heart of the book because these chapters, through a close reading of the later Schelling, reconstruct the ontological emergence of reason (Chapter 4) and God (Chapter 5). Reason and God emerge from chaos by means of the decision of being itself. The decision or the event can only be named or identified by means of its consequents or *per posterius*. The decision bears a distinctive *modus operandi*, namely a Godly rather than ungodly *modus*. God, in his propriety, is not to be identified with the decision as such, but with the withdrawal or reserve of the decision, its abysmal remainder. Reason too is not synonymous with the rupture of the decision as such but with its consequent or emergent essence, namely with the regularity and lawfulness that ensues from the decision. More precisely, the decision brings about possibility as its consequent, something only even seen to be possible after it is actual. Accordingly, Kant's transcendental Ideal or totality of all possibility can now be viewed realistically. The totality of what is possible and thinkable, the laws of logic included, constitutes the essence of reason itself. God, he who recedes in the decision, he who is set apart or the 'Holy', is thereby equally consequent to the decision, but this consequent belatedly supplements the decision with its identity. No longer anonymous, the decision acquires its name *post factum* as the will or act of 'God'.

The last chapter of Part II and the penultimate chapter of the book is devoted to Heidegger and his *Auseinandersetzung* with Schelling, particularly concerning the need to think that from which the decision of being leaps. Heidegger's 1936–38 *Beiträge* proves particularly pivotal, as here, in the same years he is writing and reading on Schelling (as well as on Friedrich Nietzsche and Friedrich Hölderlin), he offers his most sustained thoughts on the decision and the last God, which is more helpfully rendered as the most extreme or most decisive God. The event of beyng, which, as Heidegger contends, is 'needed' by the gods, will be demonstrated as a reciprocal need. Beyng also needs the advent or passing by of the gods insofar as the passing by of Godhood is the very motion, the transitive occurrence, that draws the fissure, cleft or opening in beyng. The passing by of the gods and the last God is the event of divinisation; the event of divinisation is the decision of beyng itself.

Part III contains only the final chapter, Chapter 7, which is followed by some concluding remarks in the form of an Afterword. Chapter 7 accomplishes three aims. First, it applies what has been learned from the book as a whole to the Euthyphro Dilemma, offering a creative, and what this author believes to be novel, solution to this classic problem in a way that shows the inextricable relation between the question of the ontological status of reason (eternal truths) and the ontological status of God (divine will). Secondly, a new typology for conceiving of God's existence is drafted: theomonism. Contrary to traditional understandings of monotheism, theomonism does not posit one God, rather than zero or two plus, but it posits that that which is God is the same as that which is One. Theomonism understands that that which is divine only is so because it is One; it understands that oneness is the necessary *modus operandi* of divinity, a position which can only be meaningful if one has first posited a chaos or non-identity, as well as a multiplicity of mythological gods, in advance of the God who is One. Thirdly, this final chapter illustrates certain homologous similarities between the logic outlined in this book and Badiou's philosophy grounded in set theory. Materially, Badiou's formalism is completely at odds with the thesis of this book, but structural, that is, homologous, affinities abound.

Notes

1. Hodges and Lewis, *Thinking in the Ruins*, p. 20.
2. See the author's first book, Tyler Tritten, *Beyond Presence: F.W.J. Schelling's Criticism of Metaphysics* (Boston: De Gruyter, 2012).
3. Plato, *Republic*, 394d.
4. Hume's rejection of miracles epitomises modernity's impotency to deal with alleged events that, even were they true, could find no place in the epistemic system and the prevailing account of the lawfulness of nature. For an attempt at a method capable of accounting for such rogue or miraculous phenomena, see Tritten, '*Per Posterius*: Peirce and Hume on Miracles and the Boundaries of the Scientific Game'.
5. Van der Heiden, *Ontology after Ontotheology*, pp. vii–viii.
6. Ibid., p. 9.
7. Grant, *Philosophies of Nature*, p. 5.
8. Schelling, 'Einleitung in die Philosophie der Offenbarung oder Begründung', *SW II/3*, p. 114.
9. 'hatte er radikale Gedanken in konservativer Gestalt' (Jaspers, *Schelling*, p. 7).
10. 'Entwerfen von Möglichkeiten' (Frank, *Auswege*, p. 364).
11. According to Christina M. Gschwandtner, in his early article 'Phenomenology and Theology' (1927) Heidegger held that 'theology is not speculation about the existence of God, does not seek to ascertain God's nature, but instead describes faithfully the way in which Christians experience life within the world of faith' (Gschwandtner, *Postmodern Apologetics?*, p. 24). Contemporary theology should rather limit itself to

analyze and describe the actions and words that arise out of the faith of the life believers live, instead of engaging in arguments about abstract propositions about the divine . . . not speculate about God's existence (an activity rejected almost unanimously), but describe the life of faith as it actually takes place. (ibid., p. 24)

Not only is this all-too-severe limitation to be rejected, but it is not clear that Heidegger himself stringently adhered to this stricture. Note, for example, his comments on the last God in the *Beiträge* of 1936–38.

12. Kearney, 'Epiphanies', p. 13.
13. Kearney, *Anatheism*, p. 16.
14. Caputo, *Weakness of God*, p. 9. In opposition to this indecisiveness, the risky claim has been ventured, by means of Schelling's Christology, that the God of which this book speaks could only be the Christ-God or no God at all. See Tritten, 'Christ as Copula'.
15. Caputo, *Weakness of God*, p. 11.
16. Caputo, 'Richard Kearney's Enthusiasm', p. 312.
17. Caputo and Vattimo, 'Spectral Hermeneutics', p. 51.
18. Desmond, 'Maybe, Maybe Not', p. 76.
19. Nichols, 'God Who May Be', p. 116.
20. Ibid., p. 116.
21. Bloechl, 'Christianity and Possibility', p. 129.
22. Van der Heiden, *Ontology after Ontotheology*, p. 262.

Part I
Critical and Constructive Preliminaries: Meillassoux, Boutroux and the Early Schelling

Chapter 1

Meillassoux against the Principle of Reason: An Ontology of Factiality

Quentin Meillassoux[1] has recently incited both excitement and unease within the philosophical community with his scandalous thesis for the necessity of contingency. His argument appears in *After Finitude: An Essay on the Necessity of Contingency*, but it has also been gradually and carefully elaborated, arguably in more detail, in articles and public talks. Through a critical engagement with these texts, the following will argue for the possibility of the inverted thesis, the contingency of necessity.

The task, epistemo-ontological in nature, is to elucidate the ontological status of the epistemic, particularly reason itself. The assumption is that epistemology should not precede but follow ontological reflections because the epistemic domain, rational and logical space, contingently emerges from and supplements pre-rational and absolute being. Meillassoux, however, a self-proclaimed rationalist, argues for the necessity of contingency, versus the contingency of necessity, by already presupposing one of the cardinal laws of reason, the principle of non-contradiction, despite rejecting the principle of reason. On the basis of the principle of non-contradiction, he argues that contradictory beings are necessary beings. More exactly, given that contradictory beings cannot be and given his argument that contradictory beings are necessary beings, Meillassoux thus offers a kind of proof against the *ens necessarium*. He subsequently concludes, however, not simply that only contingent beings can be but also that they must be, that contingency is necessary. The principal way of combating Meillassoux's provocative thesis will be to expose reason itself, inclusive of the principle of non-contradiction, as a contingent fact. While this would still permit the consequent necessity of the truths of reason, it would oppose all a priori necessity for the existence of reason, including the aforementioned principle of non-contradiction. This alternative to

Meillassoux's rationalism could be called a 'narrative empiricism', which treats the facticity of reason like any other fact, namely something only to be narrated but never to be derived through a law of formal logic. The fact that there is reason rather than unreason can never be proved a priori but only narrated *post factum* as a consequent necessity.

This opening chapter does not yet narrate the actual emergence of reason and its laws from pre-rational chaos. Its more propaedeutic purpose is to create a critical distance from Meillassoux's argument for the necessity of contingency in order to pave the way for a more positive foundation for the contingency of necessity, which will be the task of the following chapter. The first two sections of this chapter will detail the significance of metaphysics for Meillassoux, sketch his vision of non-metaphysical speculation, define correlationism and explain what it means to absolutise the facticity of the correlation rather than the correlation itself. After this has been accomplished, the remainder of the chapter will no longer consist in a simple reconstruction of Meillassoux's arguments, but it will elucidate a possible alternative to the conclusions he draws on the basis of his critique of metaphysics and correlationism. Taking, then, a more critical position with respect to Meillassoux, the bulk of this chapter will discuss his distinction between facticity and factiality, ultimately rejecting the notion of factiality as Meillassoux understands it in order to reveal that his espousal of factiality rests upon a misapplication of the principle of non-contradiction. Meillassoux's use of the principle of non-contradiction relies on the unjustified presumption that the principle of excluded middle holds in what he terms 'Hyper-Chaos'. Finally, the chapter will conclude by offering a brief discussion of time in Meillassoux, gesturing towards a conception of time that permits one to surpass Meillassoux's purely logical or rationally determined chaos. Ultimately, this initial chapter will function as a scaffolding to be deconstructed by the two central theses of this book, namely that reason can be thought as a consequent and contingent – rather than a priori and necessary – universal, and that God too can be thought as contingent with respect to existence but necessary with respect to essence.

Metaphysics and necessity

In *After Finitude* Meillassoux clarifies the normally blurry distinction between metaphysics and whatever is meant by the 'post-metaphysical'. His definition of metaphysics differs from those provided by Heidegger or Derrida, according to which metaphysics is a thinking of presence, a kind of foundationalism that seeks a basis in a fixed entity, a stable point of presence, for example, God, transcendental subjectivity or an absolute signifier. Heidegger, for instance, contends that metaphysics, as a philosophy of presence, becomes manifest in the God of ontotheology, namely God as first cause. This definition, however, is too vague for Meillassoux, because it would allow figures like 'Heraclitus, Nietzsche or Deleuze' to escape metaphysics too easily.[2] These thinkers refrain from substance-based metaphysics, but on Meillassoux's account they still posit a necessary structure of becoming in its stead. According to them, becoming, Meillassoux laments, must occur according to some prescribed set of laws and no others. Everything repeats, for example, according to the necessities of πόλεμος (Heraclitus), will to power (Nietzsche) or repetition (Deleuze). Additionally, Meillassoux does not even follow his predecessor, Alain Badiou, to the letter, who defines metaphysics as 'the enframing of Being by the One'.[3] Rather, the defining characteristic of metaphysics is not presence or the enframement of being by the One, but any recourse to necessity stemming from the principle of (sufficient) reason.

Heraclitus,[4] Nietzsche and Deleuze theorise difference without recourse to substance-based ontologies and without privileging the One; yet all three remain metaphysicians. Metaphysics, while not excluding its appearance 'as the enframing of being by the One' or a grounding of all entities by a first substance and first cause, is rather 'defined by its belief in the determinate necessity of entities *or* processes'.[5] Theoreticians of difference – including perhaps process thinkers – have thus not yet extricated themselves from metaphysical thinking. Metaphysics, for Meillassoux, is more precisely determined through the principle of sufficient reason, which can hold both if things are static or in process. The principle of sufficient reason is always able to elucidate why (static) things are the way they are or why processes change the way they change. The principle of sufficient reason states that an adequate explanation requires that reasons (causes or laws) be given not only for why something is as it is or changes the way it does, but also for why something is not otherwise than it is and does not change according to different laws than it does. Simply put, the principle of reason is a generator of necessity and, hence, for Meillassoux, the lynchpin of metaphysics.

The primary effect of the principle of sufficient reason is to render things, structures or laws necessary, and in so doing to efface all vestiges of contingency. Accordingly, any thinking that does not succumb to the metaphysical tradition must somehow depart from the principle of sufficient reason; it must break with all forms of absolute necessity (whether necessary beings or necessary laws of change). Not even contemporary philosophy – primarily, phenomenology and post-structuralism – breaks sufficiently from the principle of sufficient reason. Phenomenology still makes recourse to the transcendental ego (Husserl), the existentials of Dasein and the event of appropriation (Heidegger),[6] the hole in Being (Sartre) or the chiasmus/flesh of the world (Merleau-Ponty) as necessary structures, relations or comportments. Similarly, variants of post-structuralism (loosely construed) insist on necessary operations of repetition/differenciation (Deleuze), the play of signifiers/*différance* (Derrida) or the rules of the game (Wittgenstein). By contrast, Meillassoux radically insists – although he will eventually argue the opposite – that 'the project of non-metaphysical speculation would be established thus: our inability to prove why there is something rather than nothing . . .'[7]

The Leibnizian question of why there is something instead of nothing does nothing if not betray the utter contingency of the world, its facticity. Even if one accepts Leibniz's answer, which too facilely resorts to the principle of sufficient reason, a series of questions concerning the ground of sufficient reason itself remain: Why must every entity be resolvable into a 'why'? Why must nothing emerge *ex nihilo* but rather be secured by a ground? Why must things be grounded in reason? It seems that no sufficient answer can be offered in response to this family of questions. This is the case whether one proceeds religiously or philosophically. If there is something rather than nothing because God created it, then whence came God? If there is something rather than nothing because thinking and being belong together, then is it not the case that this co-belonging is only necessary if, only given the fact that, there is something instead of nothing? Is this not, at bottom, factical rather than necessary? In other words, there is evidently no reason why thinking/reason and being could have just as easily never belonged together, in which case there would have been nothing instead of something, unthinkability rather than conceptuality, chaos rather than order and identity. At any rate, the contention of this book, and Meillassoux would agree with this point, is that the co-belonging between thinking and being can only amount to conditional necessity, namely factical necessity. To repeat Meillassoux, 'The project of non-metaphysical speculation would be established thus: our inability to prove why there is something rather than nothing . . .'[8] Only a thought that radically pursues the implications of the utter contingency at the basis of everything can evade the principle of sufficient reason and, concomitantly, metaphysics.

Correlationism and the accidental

To assert that being and thinking are co-originary is, according to Meillassoux, a variant of correlationism. Correlationism is the view that 'there are no objects, no events, no laws, no beings which are not always-already correlated with a point of view, with a subjective access'.[9] Although correlationism overcomes naive realism, Meillassoux insists that it remains metaphysical because the correlation itself is thought as necessary. The subsistence of the correlation – variously articulated as a correlation between Being and beings (Heidegger's *Ereignis*), subjectivity and objectivity (German Idealism), *noesis* and *noemata* (transcendental subjectivisms), *être-en-soi* and *être-pour-soi* (Sartre), or intentionality and object of intention (Husserl) – is thought as a necessary structure or necessary relation between beings which are known and beings which know. Meillassoux does not critique correlationism as a naive realist but as a 'speculative materialist'.[10] He seeks something – which he has famously termed 'the great outdoors'[11] – that exists prior to the correlation. For the correlationist, however, everything is given only within the correlation. Objectivity does not subsist outside of or in advance of the correlation – what Meillassoux terms the 'ancestral' – but only as one of its poles, the objective correlate, regardless of how non-subjectivistically the other correlate is conceived (for example, Heidegger's *Dasein*).

Meillassoux's desire to break from the tradition of metaphysics is commendable enough, but this does not require the affirmation of a speculative reality 'outside'[12] the correlation: an uncorrelated reality, the ancestral, 'the great outdoors'. The correlation can be preserved without relapsing into metaphysics. Meillassoux himself contends,

> Strictly speaking, correlationism as I define it is not anti-realism but anti-*absolutism*. Correlationism is the modern way of rejecting all possible knowledge of an absolute ... There are *two* main forms of the absolute; the realist one, which is that of a non-thinking reality independent of our access to it, and the *idealist* one, which consists on the contrary in *the absolutization of the correlation itself*.[13]

Rather than absolutising the correlation itself, as the idealist does, Meillassoux absolutises the facticity of the correlation. This results in at least three important entailments.

First, to absolutise the facticity of the correlation rather than the correlation itself does not necessarily entail a denial of the existence of the correlation. Meillassoux arguably leaves open the possibility that the correlation is something like the original accident or original fact: *der Urzufall*. In this way one can preserve the correlation without absolutising it as such but only its facticity.

Second, Meillassoux shows that one can retain the correlation as a fact without that entailing anti-absolutism, because the absolute would thus appear as the facticity and, ultimately, contingency of the correlation. As

Meillassoux himself argues, contingency is only ever the contingency of some fact, hence why he will ultimately argue that it is necessary that something, contingent being, exists rather than nothing at all. Meillassoux's position would only constitute a rupture with the tradition of absolutism if the absolute were synonymous with the *ens necessarium*, but nothing precludes that absoluteness is compatible with the simple affirmation of the correlation as the *ens realissimum*, at least if the existence of the *ens realissimum* is thought as something factical[14] rather than necessary.

Third, the correlation is thought realistically rather than idealistically if it is thought as a fact, an accident that just as easily could have not been, a contingent fact. As Graham Harman has noted, the fear of idealism is obviated

> when it is observed that the correlationist would slip into idealism if not for relying on an absolutization of facticity rather than an absolutization of the correlate. Our supposed ignorance of the true nature of things is converted into a *knowledge* of the absolute contingency of all that exists.[15]

By absolutising the facticity of the correlation (realism) rather than the correlation itself (idealism) one now knows as a tenet of ontology that the correlation could have not been and thus, by extension, that knowledge itself or the domain of ideality could have never been.

Nothing precludes one from preserving the correlation by thinking of it as absolutely 'primordial contingency [*das Urzufällige*]' or as 'primal accident [*der Urzufall*]'.[16] This would strip the correlation neither of its facticity nor of its contingency so long as it is understood as an accident. The term 'accident' does not here designate a secondary quality inhering in a substance. On the contrary, the term is intended – against traditional philosophical usage – as that which constitutes the 'substantiality' of being as such. The accidental results from no necessity whatsoever; it is pure contingency. Whatever is necessary, however, cannot be a fact but only a ground or a relation that cannot remain unposited, something necessarily to be presupposed as the prerequisite or a priori condition, the sufficient reason, for a consequent. The accidental, however, apart from any necessity, only offers itself as something to be thought if it gives itself to be thought at all. It gives itself only as a matter of fact, never as a truth of reason, and this holds even for the facticity of reason itself. To understand the facticity of reason as accidental is therefore not an idealist absolutisation of the correlation; it is instead an absolutisation of contingency, the absolutisation of the contingency of the correlation and the contingency of reason. Already to intimate towards a criticism of Meillassoux, this manoeuvre makes the correlation between reason/thinking and being, *qua* contingent, into the paradigmatic fact *par excellence*.

Meillassoux remarks, in seeming accord with the explication just provided, 'I call "facticity" the absence of reason for any reality . . . We can only attain conditional necessity, never absolute necessity.'[17] Meillassoux does not, then, banish necessity *tout court*. Perhaps against his own intentions, he admits the possibility of conditional or factical necessity, of subsequent rather than prior necessity, namely contingent rather than absolute necessity. Although the correlation necessarily exists if and only if there is to be something rather than nothing, this imputes only conditional necessity to the correlation insofar as the correlation is hereby viewed as the sufficient reason for the existence of the world as its consequent. The facticity of the correlation, however, the fact that it exists, is not necessarily there for the sake of the world and so it is, in this respect, ab-solute or uncorrelated. In other words, one can speak of the existence of the correlation as a necessary condition only subsequently, only *post factum* or from the viewpoint of the consequent. In itself, however, the correlation is not necessarily existent but the paradigmatic and contingent fact, the primordial accident. Actually, to refer to it as a contingent fact is superfluous because, *per* Meillassoux, facts are facts precisely because they 'lack a reason for their reality', because they are not grounded in the necessity of a reason. If the correlation is a fact, it is contingent; therefore, to affirm the correlation as an uncircumventable fact is to think against the metaphysical principle of reason. Meillassoux himself remarks that '*if* the correlation is factual, we can no longer maintain, as does the subjectivist, that it is a necessary component of every reality'.[18] It follows that if one affirms the correlation not by making it necessary but rather by confronting its lack of reason, its brute facticity, then one has not only avoided subjectivism and idealism, but metaphysics as such, thinking according to the principle of sufficient reason.[19]

Facticity, factiality and law

If one does not think metaphysically according to the principle of sufficient reason, then reason can at most acquire only conditional necessity, posterior necessity. That there is reason at all is not necessary because reason is not self-grounding; there is no sufficient reason for the existence of reason itself. Prior to the subsequent necessity of reason, one finds no further conditions, reasons or grounds, but only the absence of reason. As Meillassoux controversially hypothesises, 'The irrationality of things thus discloses to us being qua being, and this being of all things consists in a chaos subordinate to no reason whatsoever.'[20] Despite this claim to have disclosed being without reason, one should remember that Meillassoux remains a rationalist who presupposes the principle of non-contradiction. All the same, he posits that being *qua* being consists in a chaos devoid of the principle of reason and that from this it follows that contingency is itself necessary. He writes, 'Contingency, and *only* contingency, is absolutely necessary; facticity and only facticity, is not factual, but eternal.'[21]

Despite his claim that non-metaphysical speculation could only be established by the inability to answer why there is something rather than nothing, to the contrary, he does offer an argument for the necessary existence of contingent beings, a proof for why it is necessary that there is something rather than nothing. Pitting contingency against necessity, he makes contingency the new necessity, but in so doing he fails to consider the possibility of a contingently eternal existent (although he sometimes muses playfully on God as an everlasting fact).[22] Meillassoux conflates eternity and necessity so that the necessary means as much as that which must exist at all times.[23] Could it not be that reason is eternal and universal, yet without its own reason? Is it not possible for reason to be contingent yet still eternal, contingent yet still universal? Why must the eternal be something necessary? Why must the universal be something necessary? Why can there not be an eternal fact? To understand the full weight of these critical questions that one could pose to Meillassoux, it is first important to understand Meillassoux's motivation.

Meillassoux does not simply argue that to posit a necessary, that is, metaphysical, entity is in error, but he also wants to offer a proof against the very possibility of necessary beings so that nothing non-contingent, nothing necessary, may be. Evidently, therefore, primal chaos – what he calls Hyper-Chaos – is not a fact after all, because its contingency necessarily holds sway; it is necessary that there is no necessity. Even when he speaks of a God to come or a God that 'may-be',[24] this God neither necessarily exists nor exists necessarily, namely in a necessary manner.[25] He thinks the necessity of contingency as the necessity of facticity, which he terms factiality: 'Factiality is not facticity, but the necessity of facticity, the essence of facticity.'[26]

Transitioning, then, to an explicit criticism of Meillassoux's position, although he is right to affirm that the co-belonging, the correlation, between thinking/reason and being is not necessary but absolutely factual, his thesis that facticity itself is not factual, but factial, remains unconvincing. Even if all facts must necessarily be contingent facts rather than 'necessary facts', which is a contradiction in terms for Meillassoux, that does not preclude that there could have been nothing at all. None of this leads to the conclusion that contingencies are necessarily existent. Meillassoux is only able to argue that contingency is necessary, namely necessarily existent, because he understands contingency only as the possibility that actual entities could exist in a different manner than they actually do and not also as the possibility that they could have never existed at all. Contingency, for Meillassoux, is only ever the contingency of some actual entity, hence his infidelity to his original tenet that non-metaphysical speculation could only be established by the inability to determine why there is something rather than nothing. Quite the contrary, Meillassoux renders the existence of contingency necessary, only permitting that whatever exists could have been otherwise. An entirely different set of contingent entities or laws could have existed than the ones that actually do, but it is not possible that none could have existed.

Facts are admittedly contingent, but by no means should that preclude the possibility that there could have been nothing instead of something and, as Meillassoux had seemingly admitted, by no means should that preclude the possibility of the subsequent accrual of necessity as a contingent accident, a subordinate or conditional necessity: contingent necessity. Against Meillassoux's argument that 'to be is to be factual – and *this* is not a fact',[27] there is good reason to doubt that facticity is factial and instead affirm that to be is to be factical – and this is a fact.

The present critique of Meillassoux stems from that fact that he does not merely argue that absolutely necessary beings cannot be, but he fallaciously concludes too much from this argument, namely that, therefore, contingent beings are necessary. This constitutes the core of his argument for the necessity of the fact that there is something rather than nothing. 'It is not a fact but rather an absolute necessity that factual things exist',[28] Meillassoux bluntly declares in stark opposition with his other assertion that 'the project of non-metaphysical speculation would be established thus: our inability to prove why there is something rather than nothing . . .'[29] As one commentator glosses, 'If the correlationist affirms the possibility that the correlate could be wholly other than it is (absolutely contingent), then he must admit that we know that facticity is necessary . . .'[30] But, does this follow? Does this conclusion not rest on a false dichotomy introduced by Meillassoux's presupposition of the principle of non-contradiction, illegitimately employed without first justifying the principle of excluded middle? Can one, by knowing that necessity cannot exist (~N), therefore know that contingency (C) must exist? Formally, this would look very strange indeed, ~N ∴ C, which would only follow if one were in a position to equate non-necessity (~N) with contingency (C). The question of this equivalency will be taken up in more detail later, but let it suffice for the moment to suggest that the being of contingency may not have to consist in a given *actualitas* – as Meillassoux thinks – but in the ambivalence between being/something and non-being/nothing. This would avoid the false dichotomy between necessary and contingent existence by holding that it was, originally, possible that there could have not been any existents at all. Even if necessary beings were impossible, it would not follow that at least one contingent being must be existent. As will be seen, Meillassoux's illegitimate presupposition of the operativity of the principle of excluded middle as already operative in what he calls Hyper-Chaos prematurely precludes the option that nothing is actual, neither the necessary nor the contingent, and that everything is only possibly or, better, virtually being.

There is good reason to assert, against Meillassoux, that if contingent beings exist, this is not because contingency is necessarily existent but because contingency is only factically or accidentally existent. According to Meillassoux's own principles, only the lack of absolute or a priori necessity – and nothing more – is necessary. In other words, from the simple absence of necessity, due to the inoperativity of a principle of reason, the operativity of the principle of unreason does not necessarily follow, as if one or the other must be operative, either the principle of reason or the principle of unreason. Meillassoux prematurely excludes the middle option that neither reason nor unreason are operative as principles. Both principles can be deactivated or suspended at once. The necessary lack of a priori necessity does not entail the necessity of contingent beings unless one unjustifiably presupposes, as Meillassoux does, that the principle of excluded middle and hence also the principle of non-contradiction are already operative in Hyper-Chaos. Instead of Meillassoux's chaos, which is already rationally or logically determined by the principles of excluded middle and non-contradiction, chaos could instead be defined as that in which the principle of excluded middle and thus too the principle of non-contradiction do not hold, at least not yet.

On the one hand, Meillassoux, rationalist that he is, presupposes the existence of reason – not in terms of the principle of sufficient reason but in terms of the principle of non-contradiction – but, on the other hand, he does not seem to want to admit that reason could be efficacious as a consequent principle. For him, reason is reduced to one of the basic and timeless laws of formal logic. In short, it seems that Meillassoux posits the principle of non-contradiction as eternal and, hence, as necessary. What happens, however, if the hypothesis that reason itself, including the principle of non-contradiction, could have not been and, therefore, only factically – rather than factially – exists is pursued to its most radical consequences? If facticity itself is not factial, but factical, then one could argue that reason itself is not just any fact but the primordial and paradigmatic fact. The simple lack of reason, which is the defining characteristic of facticity, cannot prescind the subsequent supplementation of a sufficient, albeit belated, reason. Contra Meillassoux, the thesis here is that necessity, namely the principle of sufficient reason and the law of non-contradiction, only advenes upon the facticity of being after the fact.

To argue for the facticity, rather than factiality, of facticity and for the contingency, rather than necessity, of contingency requires a more radical account of contingency than Meillassoux's because his position renders contingency necessary and facticity factial. The critical alternative to Meillassoux's thesis for the necessity of contingency, which would not prematurely presuppose the efficacy of the principle of excluded middle, affirms that contingency is so contingent that it does not even exclude its contrary – necessity – at least as a consequent, as *posterius* rather than as *prius*. All that is excluded is absolute or a priori necessity.

Would this really constitute a radical break with Meillassoux though? Believing he has thought contingency as radically as can be done, he designates his contingency as Hyper-Chaos. Yet he comments, 'Hyper-Chaos: its contingency is so radical that even becoming, disorder, or randomness can be destroyed by it, and replaced by order, determinism, and fixity.'[31] Despite his argument that contingency is necessary because necessary beings are logically impossible, it also seems that Meillassoux's wellspring of contingency – Hyper-Chaos – does not preclude its opposite, namely the subsequent supplementation with necessity, order or permanence. He affirms, '[i]f facticity is the absolute, contingency no longer means the necessity of destruction or disorder, but rather the equal contingency of order and disorder . . .', something only describable as 'surcontingence, supercontingency'.[32] To understand this more clearly and to determine whether it marks an inconsistency or impasse in his thought, it will help to observe a criticism that Graham Harman has already levelled against Meillassoux concerning the laws of nature.

Harman's most damaging critique of Meillassoux hinges on the question of why he permits any order, stability or permanence – in short, necessity – at all, and particularly why he does so in the form of stable – even if only temporarily so – laws. Harman's proposal is that Meillassoux cannot affirm disorder or contingency to the exclusion of order, as then the very thing he wishes to affirm, contingency, would no longer be a possible part of experience. Harman explains,

> Laws do exist, and for the most part they do function. But precisely through this admission that laws exist, Meillassoux concedes that the principle of sufficient reason is operative much of the time . . . And this means that laws are binding, or necessary; the fact that a new necessity might someday arise without reason to replace the current one does not change the necessity of the relation here and now. Only when rising to the level of the laws themselves, which can always change for no reason, does the principle of sufficient reason collapse.[33]

Harman's claim is not that the principle of reason is absent but that it falters or 'collapses'. Such collapsing obviously presupposes that the principle of reason exists and is operative, against Meillassoux's own intentions. Contingency has in fact not excluded necessity, namely necessarily operative, albeit temporary, laws, because it cannot exclude necessity, namely the permanence and identity of a thing and/or laws. This is the case, at least, if there is to be something rather than nothing and, for Meillassoux, contingency is always only the contingency of something that exists. By contrast, if one conceives of chaos differently than Meillassoux's logical and rational chaos, if one rather thinks of chaos as bereft of the principle of excluded middle and non-contradiction, then the principle of identity would not hold. This is for two reasons: (1) because something would immediately pass away in the exact same instant in which 'it' came into being; and (2) because the principle of identity can only be in effect if the principle of non-contradiction is also in effect, insofar as it is the principle of non-contradiction that first necessitates that something be one thing and not another, either A or ~A but never both. Some form of necessity – regularity, stability, continuity, order and so on – must accrue in order for any specific and determinate something to be possible, let alone actual. Only in this way is it possible for a thing even to be the thing that it is rather than its negation. This, in fact, is precisely Meillassoux's motivation for presupposing that the principle of non-contradiction is always already in effect. Had he, however, taken seriously the possibility that there could have been nothing, hence no identities at all, instead of something, he would have been able to deny the necessity of the principle of non-contradiction's operativity, instead being able to consider that this too is contingent, at most a consequent necessity.

This all means that if a contingent being – let alone a necessary being – is to be, if anything is to be rather than nothing, then chaos must be supplemented with identity and the necessity of law for at least the faintest flickering of time. As Harman criticises:

> To say that 'the laws may change over time' is certainly radical, but it does not allow for complete contingency. For rather than being contingent, as Meillassoux promises, things are tied to necessary laws now as much as ever, but simply to laws whose character might change suddenly for no reason. Here once more, Meillassoux seems entirely focused on *diachronic* contingency, and does not seem bothered if the principle of sufficient reason continues to operate in a single instant.[34]

Laws exist, laws which necessarily govern happenings and changes, but their existence remains contingent. They can cease to exist and be replaced by new laws. There are here at least two distinctions to be made. First, laws have a necessary *modus operandi*, but their existence remains a brute contingency. There is a difference between the necessity or contingency of something's essence, its *modus operandi*, and the necessity or contingency of its existence. Second, concerning the contingency of the existence of laws, Meillassoux only allows one to admit that any law can become otherwise, another law, but he fails to ask why there are laws at all rather than none whatsoever. This, however, is not surprising given his peculiar adherence to the necessity of contingency, which means the necessity of there being something rather than nothing at all, for which lawfulness is a concomitant requisite.

Meillassoux never questions lawfulness as such, but he only provides a curious sort of response to Hume's repudiation of miracles. Laws can, are and must be broken, so long as one understands that the broken law is always replaced by a new continuity, new regularity or new necessity, that is, a new law. What this presumes and what Meillassoux fails to think to its end is that laws there are and laws there must be – again, if and only if there should be something rather than nothing. This is indeed an odd conclusion considering that it is, as Harman insists, highly questionable

> why Meillassoux needs any concept of *laws* at all [because] advent in Meillassoux's universe always comes from the top, through the sudden change of laws for no reason, not from local rogue incidents in which specific billiard balls would violate the general rule by weeping or exploding when struck.[35]

If anything could happen merely according to chance and therefore not necessarily by means of determinate interaction with other beings through the necessity of a causal link, then the need to posit any law or regularity in the first place would seem superfluous. There would be, as it were, but one causal relation required in Meillassoux's occasionalistic universe: straight from the contingency of Hyper-Chaos to the concrete events themselves. Beings could remain, as it were, windowless, without causal relation. Meillassoux, at any rate, cannot deliver on his own promise: far from abolishing the principle of reason – and with it the principle of causal connection between things – he rather assumes this as an edifice to be broken in order to show the disruption, not inefficacy or inoperativity, of this same principle. What Meillassoux fails to address, because he simply assumes it, is the question of efficacy and operativity as such. Harman confirms, 'The more radical step of denying the existence of laws altogether is not attempted, nor apparently even desired.'[36]

Meillassoux's Hyper-Chaos, then, cannot exclude its opposite, namely order, stability, permanence or the subsequent efficacy of the principle of reason. Against factiality, the necessity of contingency, Meillassoux's Hyper-Chaos cannot definitively exclude non-contingency or necessity.

Chaos and non-contradiction

Meillassoux argues that Hyper-Chaos – which is for him a merely logical chaos regulated by the principle of non-contradiction – can render compatible the principle of factiality and the fact that the opposite of contingency, hence necessity, is permitted by means of the principle of non-contradiction. He proclaims, 'Non-contradiction is a condition of contingency, for a contradictory reality couldn't change since it would already be what it is not.'[37] Whatever is contingent can be otherwise, even the negation of itself – for example, a red chair can be painted yellow or refashioned into a table in order to become a not-red chair – whereas the principle of non-contradiction states that something absolutely cannot be its negation, at least not at the same time and in the same respect.

Admitting that a contradictory reality cannot be and that whatever is not a contradiction can be or is logically possible, it is still difficult to see how Meillassoux draws the further inference that a contradictory reality is a perfectly necessary being. He reasons, on the basis of merely logical possibility, that only a contradictory reality – were such a thing possible – must necessarily be its negation to be what it is, namely a contradiction, and so only contradictory beings are necessary beings, which, given that contradictions cannot be, also entails that necessary beings are impossible. To rephrase, contradictory realities are necessary beings because they are necessitated to 'already be' their negation and they cannot exist because contradictions cannot be, hence necessary beings cannot be and only contingencies can exist, or, as Meillassoux illegitimately concludes, contingencies necessarily exist. The problem is that Meillassoux's leap from the conclusion that only contingencies can exist to the further conclusion that contingencies must exist, that contingency is necessary, only holds either if there is a metaphysical law that says everything that is possible must become actual, which Meillassoux decisively rejects, or if there is no middle option between contingent and necessary existence because the principle of excluded middle is already in effect, with the result that the denial of both contingent and necessary existence, namely the possibility that there could have been nothing instead of something, is already excluded.

Meillassoux's inference is fallacious because he wrongly presupposes that the middle has already been excluded in Hyper-Chaos and because he forgets his tenses. Something is only a contradiction and, therefore, impossible if one affirms that this something both is what it already is and what it already is not. In other words, something is contradictory only when its existence is affirmed and negated at the same time. As Albert Franz comments,

> If it were possible [to assert the negation of something at the same time and in the same respect], then τὸ αὐτό would no longer be identifiable as such; as internally contradictory it would have lost its identity and nothing could any longer be said of it with truth. This is why for Aristotle the principle of non-contradiction is also demonstrated as a law of being.[38]

Contradictions are impossible only when an actuality and its negation are announced as being 'at the same time'. Nonetheless, it remains possible that something may 'already be' in the present the negation of what it 'may be' in the future. Meillassoux would seem to acknowledge this point when he explicates Hyper-Chaos along the lines of the possible, the 'may-be' (*peut-être*).[39] His account of Hyper-Chaos as the domain of what may-be, rather than of what is actual, thus makes his forgetting of tenses – his collapse of possible (or virtual) contradiction into the domain of actual contradiction – all the more striking. Certainly, as Schelling has said, 'The calmest and deepest sea is also the one that can most greatly incite itself, but the still sea and the one capable of inciting itself are not two seas, but only one and the same sea.'[40] Similarly, the boy who is presently sick is the same boy who in the future can be or 'may-be' healthy, that is, not-sick. The principle of non-contradiction, contra Meillassoux, only precludes that something cannot be its opposite *in actu*, only that it cannot 'already be' what it is not, but it does not preclude the possibility that something simultaneously 'may-be' its negation.

Meillassoux's *peut-être* literally translates as 'perhaps', indicating, for him, supercontingency or Hyper-Chaos, a contingency that apparently cannot even preclude that necessity may-be. Admitting that a contradictory being, were such a being possible, would have to be that which is A and ~A, being and non-being, at the same time and in the same respect, Meillassoux errs in concluding that contingency must be. As one commentator remarks, 'To account for being in terms of contingency means also that it is approached in light of possibility or potentiality; this means that being is understood as *that which can be as well as that which can not-be*.'[41] One must only be careful here not to understand 'possibility' in the standard Aristotelian sense as a potentiality given in the nature of a thing, merely awaiting its actualisation *a potentia ad actum*; it is not the potency of a pre-given οὐσία. The virtuality of the may-be indicates that middle between 'already being' and 'already not-being' that should not yet be excluded in chaos; it is the possibility to be or to not-be prior to any determination of specific potencies. This 'not yet' here indicates that one is operating (1) in advance of being at a point from which being is still something futural, something which will only perhaps come to be (or not), and, therefore, (2) outside of a merely logical or formal account that excludes all temporal determinations. Chaos should rather be conceived as the futural *par excellence*. Meillassoux, however, is misled by his rationalism. Assuming a merely logical rather than ontological chaos, he is only able to understand the law of non-contradiction as an a-temporal law that establishes logical possibility rather than material possibility. Meillassoux's logical approach compels him to say everything in a timeless moment and thus to consider all contraries, necessity and contingency included, as if they were timelessly antithetical contradictories. Meillassoux knows no tenses but only the *sub specie aeternitatis* operative in merely logical investigations.

If one is speaking not of what already actually exists but only of what may-be, then one finds oneself, in Meillassoux's terms, in the domain of the 'virtual',[42] but the principle of non-contradiction only regulates the domain of actuality insofar as it prohibits not that something 'may-be' its negation but only that something is 'already being' its negation. In opposition to Meillassoux, given that nothing has actual being in a virtual domain, in Hyper-Chaos, the principle of non-contradiction cannot therefore be operative in this domain. In other words, since the contradiction between possibly being A and possibly being ~A is not actual, but only the virtual counterbalance of dense-possibles, the principle of non-contradiction, which says only that these disjuncts mutually and actually exclude each other, is inoperative. Nothing is actually excluded in Hyper-Chaos and so everything is possible, albeit a possibility destitute not only of actuality but also of potency in the Aristotelian sense insofar as nothing is actually already positively included as a determinate potency either. The co-possibility of contraries, contra Meillassoux, cannot be excluded in Hyper-Chaos. All that is excluded is that something's contrary might be co-factical, that is, co-actual. Unlike contradictories, contraries, and this is the significant point, can both be false, namely not yet actual or not yet factical. Contraries can be co-possible or co-virtual, just never co-actual, never 'already' at the same time. Meillassoux's principle of non-contradiction can in no way exclude the possibility of necessity, which remains co-possible with contingency in Hyper-Chaos, and therefore this principle cannot possibly ground the necessity of contingency.

The virtual, that which chaos has not yet precluded, is not yet possible in the sense of being an actual potency of some entity, but it is, for Meillassoux, only what has not been excluded as logically impossible. The only thing that is precluded is that Hyper-Chaos would 'already be' an actual, rather than virtual, contradiction. Τὸ αὐτό, moreover, can only be τὸ αὐτό if its negation has been excluded in fact, that is, *in actu*, and this holds even for the being or identity of Hyper-Chaos itself. Contrary to Meillassoux, then, even Hyper-Chaos first is 'itself' only if it emerges from that virtual duplicity in which nothing, not even non-chaos or order, has yet been excluded, that is, only if it emerges from undecidability. Meillassoux, however, says, 'Now, the only necessity proper to chaos is that it remain chaos . . .'[43] Meillassoux urges that chaos must remain undecided, yet he also believes that it cannot persist in contradiction, in the simultaneity and equal possibility of order and disorder. Simply put, Meillassoux determines chaos both as that which must remain undecidable and as that which must not persist in contradiction given that it is already governed, for him, by the law of non-contradiction.

Meillassoux, then, seems ultimately ambivalent about whether the principle of excluded middle is or is not operative in Hyper-Chaos. If, however, instead of having to remain in this ambivalence, this equipollence of virtualities *sub specie aeternitatis*, chaos first actually accrues its identity as chaos by excluding the non-chaotic – identity, permanence, order, necessity and the like – from itself, then all that would remain for Hyper-Chaos after this exclusion of its negation is non-identity, impermanence, disorder, contingency and so on. In short, what if chaos only is chaos in an indicative sense – according to which it must be thought ontologically rather than simply logically – once its negation, not-chaos, has decisively been excluded? Prior to this exclusion, even chaos itself is nought or a merely virtual chaos; beforehand, it signifies only the virtuality of the 'may-be'. The contention, then, is that the virtual or 'may-be' is precisely that not yet excluded middle that prevents actual contradiction, because contradiction, and with it the principle of non-contradiction, only actually emerges once the possible or 'may-be', namely the middle between being and non-being, has actually been excluded.

Meillassoux's Hyper-Chaos denotes a merely logical chaos in which all virtualities are considered *sub specie aeternitatis*; things are merely logically but not actually opposed. Consequently, it seems that only logical possibilities and impossibilities can take shape here, never actual or material possibilities and impossibilities. Employing the principle of non-contradiction to speak only of what is logically impermissible, of what never may-be, Meillassoux has not produced a set of what is actually possible, that is, potent. Meillassoux is right to conclude, then, that virtuals or dense-possibles cannot be totalised by any set; they cannot constitute a material ground of possibility, namely Kant's transcendental Ideal as the *ens realissimum*, at least if that is to be understood as a completed set of all possible predicates. Meillassoux comments, 'We will retain the following translation of Cantor's transfinite: *the (quantifiable) totality of the thinkable is unthinkable.*'[44] With this he not only exposes his dependence on Badiou's set theory, the equation of mathematics and ontology, but he simultaneously rebuffs the notion that Kant's transcendental Ideal could ever be construed as the totality of all possibilities, as a complete set, which makes Adrian Johnston's critique of Meillassoux all the more pertinent. Johnston incisively asks,

> Why should the de-totalization of the totality posited in connection with chance, a de-totalization supposedly requiring the replacement of chance with contingency, make the flux of inconstancy less rather than more likely? How does this solve the problem of frequentialism raised against the speculative materialist thesis of hyper-Chaos?[45]

Chance is operative only where there is a totalisable set of possibilities, for example, when one flips a coin. Probability applies in this case, whereas the virtuality of Hyper-Chaos, which operates not by chance but rather by 'supercontingency', precludes probability. Probability is precluded by the virtual because probability rests upon the assumption (1) of physical laws and (2) of a totalisable set. Probability, in short, is still a remnant of metaphysics and the necessity generated by the principle of reason. Johnston asks how detotalising the set operative in probability, thus rendering it infinitesimally larger without limit, could possibly circumvent the problem of frequentialism rather than exacerbating its improbability? Although the possibility of a law-governed world, as has been seen, cannot be positively excluded by Hyper-Chaos, neither can it be positively included as an actual potency. The virtual acknowledges only dense-possibles; it cannot acknowledge material possibility, namely potentialities.

Van der Heiden, addressing the conjunction between Meillassoux's analysis of the difference between contingency and probability as well as his admission that laws do in fact exist (despite being occasionally overturned), remarks that this

> only shows that this empirical stability *does not offer us a decisive argument* for either the principle of reason or the principle of unreason (since the empirical stability of physical laws is perfectly compatible with the principle of reason). This analysis leaves the issue of 'principle of reason' or 'principle of unreason' *undecided*.[46]

Meillassoux, due to his strict adherence to the prior operativity of the principle of non-contradiction (which itself is a result of his blindly presupposing the principle of excluded middle), believes that because the principle of reason is rejected that the principle of unreason must be affirmed. This, however, treats the principle of non-contradiction and the principle of excluded middle as if they had the same content. The principle of non-contradiction states that something is either true or false, presupposing the principle of excluded middle, which states that the options of true and false are exhaustive. While the principle of non-contradiction states that truth is bivalent, the principle of excluded middle is what first ensures that something must have truth-value at all, because it excludes the middle option between truth and falsity, namely that which is neither true nor false, but the possibility (the may-be) of both. The principle of excluded middle is what first grants provenance and universal governance to the principle of non-contradiction, which means that the application of the principle of non-contradiction presupposes the prior establishment of the principle of excluded middle. If the principle of excluded middle is inoperative, then so too is the principle of non-contradiction (and if the principle of non-contradiction is inoperative, then so too is the principle of identity, which states that something must be itself and not something else). Where something is neither true nor false – because the middle possibility that it may-be either has not yet been excluded – one does not yet find oneself in a domain in which contradictions could actually occur. For something actually to be both necessary and contingent in the same respect is indeed impossible, but the possibility of both, which is neither of the two *in actu*, is permissible. In short, and against Meillassoux, the principle of non-contradiction only presides over actuality and not over possibility, not over a virtual domain. Meillassoux collapses contrariety into the contradictory, which he understands as something which holds irrespective of temporal determinations, overlooking the fact that actuality can be denied of two contraries even if both cannot be simultaneously affirmed. Just because hot is negated does not mean cold must be affirmed, and so, in Meillassoux's case, just because reason has been suspended does not mean unreason must be activated. Hyper-Chaos, prior to its becoming decided through the exclusion of the middle, could instead be thought as that domain in which neither reason nor unreason are efficacious. Just because necessary beings cannot be, that does not mean that contingent beings must be. Instead of the necessity of contingency, the impossibility of a priori necessity spells no more than the possibility, the may-be, of both posterior necessity and contingency. If one does not presuppose the principle of excluded middle in order prematurely to render the principle of non-contradiction operative, as Meillassoux does, then one can remain with the possible, namely the virtual or the neither/nor. Nothing has to become actual; there could have always been nothing instead of something.

The middle of the merely virtual contradiction is not something already excluded in chaos but rather that which demands de-cision and hence exclusion. Demanding that one side ought to be excluded, the principle of excluded middle describes nothing, but rather prescribes decisiveness. It is thus not a formal or logical law, but an ethico-ontological imperative. Meillassoux, in his desire is to attain absoluteness, hastily affirms that where the principle of reason is inoperative, there must unreason operate as a principle. Yet, as Van der Heiden insists, 'since the concept of a principle or *arché* refers back to a ground and a reason for thought, the thought of contingency does not seem to allow for any principle'.[47] Meillassoux, failing seriously to ask why there is something rather than nothing, convinced that he has already proved the necessity of contingent beings, fails to take the more radical step before grounds and principles altogether, before the principle of non-contradiction and hence also before the principle of excluded middle. This step behind the operativity of all principles would have permitted him to regard Hyper-Chaos as the domain of undecidability that nevertheless prescribes decisiveness. He would have found himself before, that is, in advance of being, at a vantage point from which being only appears as a something (possibly) futural.[48]

Meillassoux would only be in a position to offer a reply to the problem of frequentialism if he were able to show how the 'time' of Hyper-Chaos, the 'time' of the may-be, namely its futurity – which he seemingly precludes insofar as he thinks the law of non-contradiction timelessly or *sub specie aeternitatis* – could bring about contingently, but nevertheless in fact, a necessary correlation, namely a lawful order. In this way probability and lawfulness as such might be a-probably founded; reason and the correlation itself might eventuate as facts 'without why', something only to be empirically narrated but never something whose possibility has already been rationally grounded by the principle of non-contradiction. The correlation between thinking and being would thus emerge as an unforeseeable and 'unprethinkable' possibility, as a 'factical necessity'. The correlation would be factical and not factial, a contingent and accidental fact that happens to operate in a necessary manner. In other words, the correlation's existence would be completely contingent, but its *modus operandi*, its essence, would be necessarily operative according to necessary laws as the 'uniformity of nature'.

The question, then, is whether time, as Meillassoux conceives it, can really bring all this about. It would seem that it cannot because, at cross-purposes with himself, he ultimately conceives of Hyper-Chaos through the lens of an a-temporal logic as the timeless co-virtuality of everything that is not contradictory. In his Hyper-Chaos, everything is thought *sub specie aeternitatis*. With Meillassoux the question remains unanswered because it remains unasked: Whence the impetus to movement, to real and actual succession, to a real and actual ordering and potentiation of pre-potential virtualities? In short, what conditions the movement of time? Failing to uncover the imperative of the decision, he misses the real *momentum* of time.

The time of the may-be

What Meillassoux desires is a time that renders all laws – save the law of non-contradiction – contingent. Meillassoux exclaims, 'This is not a Heraclitean time, since it is not the eternal law of becoming, but rather the eternal and lawless possible becoming of every law.'[49] The virtuality of Meillassoux's Hyper-Chaos contains only dense-possibles, the virginal future or the time of the may-be. He writes,

> I accord to time the capacity to bring forth new laws which were not 'potentially' contained in some fixed set of possibles . . . *which were not at all contained in precedent situations* . . . We must then understand that it follows that such cases irrupt, properly speaking, *from nothing*, since no structure contains them as eternal potentialities before their emergence . . .[50]

Neither a state of potency nor of actuality, virtual time, for Meillassoux, indicates more than the simple transition by which already existent potentialities or already actual things are altered or changed; he wants time to function as that by which potentialities and actualities first come into being *ex nihilo*. This suggestion, however, is difficult to square with his primary thesis, which he believes to have rationally proved, namely that it is necessary that there is something, contingent beings, rather than nothing at all. If Meillassoux's conception of time as a force which may, but must not, bring forth something from out of nothing is true, then, contrary to Meillassoux's proof that contingent beings must exist, it seems that it should be possible that neither potencies nor actualities must necessarily eventuate *ex nihilo*; there could have always just been the *nihil*. In this way, whatever irrupts, in fact, would be something that could only be narrated[51] as a contingent happening rather than as something derived from the necessary unfolding of time. Now, virtual or chaotic time, in Meillassoux, cannot function as the contradiction of eternity – since, of course, he thinks the virtuality of Hyper-Chaos itself *sub specie aeternitatis* – but nor can time operate as the unfolding of the virtual as a prior substratum of reality or constitute a substratum itself, as this would signify a relapse into metaphysics and its *ens necessarium*. Can it rather be concluded that Hyper-Chaos is not some substratum of reality exhibited in time but that chaotic time constitutes the being of Hyper-Chaos itself? Moreover, would this concomitantly mean that ordered time – succession, seriality or the countable – would name that which supplements chaos with identity?

Time, Meillassoux urges, is the condition of chaos and not vice versa. If time were the unfolding of chaos, then one would be inadvertently positing chaos as a substrate and time as the necessary law of its presencing.

Meillassoux confirms that one finds 'time underwritten by no superior order ...'[52] Time, in Meillassoux, is thus neither the measurement of before and after nor the measurement of an already ordered series, but the event of randomness, the capacity for events to advene *ex nihilo*. To argue inversely would be to posit chaos as an a priori substratum, to transform Hyper-Chaos into the necessary ground of time, thus relapsing into metaphysical thinking. Tychistic time, however, as it might be called after C. S. Peirce, neither presupposes chaos as a substrate nor successiveness or seriality, namely Aristotle's countable. On the contrary, tychistic time is the condition of both Hyper-Chaos and orderedness because it presupposes neither. Chaos as well as the uniformity and necessity of succession are, *per* Meillassoux, products of mad, virtual, pre-potential, densely possible time. This time, however, is something only thinkable in terms of the nought, the non-actuality of the virtual. This time could only be thought as something capable of bringing forth something from nothing, consequents without precedent/antecedent, if its possibilities would exceed the domain of simply logical compossibility, namely Meillassoux's rationally determined chaos. Should time in Meillassoux really be able to bring forth something *ex nihilo*, then he must abandon his merely logical chaos; he must learn to think before the operativity of the principles of excluded middle, non-contradiction and identity.

Towards the possibility of the *ens necessarium*

This critical reading of Meillassoux has shown that it is possible to agree with his own critique of metaphysical necessity while still affirming an account of reason as a subsequent or contingent necessity, as a future advent that is really possible rather than just not yet logically excluded. While reason's existence, its brute facticity, would be necessarily contingent, reason's essence, its manner of existing or *modus operandi*, would be necessary and uniform. The existence of reason, an *ens necessarium* according to essence, is impossibly precluded from hyper-contingency. By making plausible the possibility of reason as a fact, which thus escapes the metaphysical principle of sufficient reason, the inversion of Meillassoux's thesis becomes possible. Instead of his concern to render contingency necessary, one can now argue for the contingency of necessity: the consequent construction of ordered, serial time from chaotic and tychistic time, or the emergence of necessary law, the uniformity of nature, from radical contingency. Primarily, however, the thesis for the contingency of necessity refers to the fact that there is something rather than nothing and to the fact that there could have also been nothing.

While this chapter has provided only a critical or negative propaedeutic, the following chapter will positively lay the constructive groundwork for an ontology of contingent or consequent necessity by means of the philosophy of Émile Boutroux. Chapters 5 and 6 will argue that God's existence as the necessary being is contingent, specifically that God's existence, understood absolutely, is synonymous with the rupture or event that is time itself, the event of ordering or serialisation. It will also be argued, however, that God's essence is necessary and uniform. The existence and essence of God are thus homologous to the existence and essence of reason. The existence of both is contingent even though the manner of existing or *modus operandi* is necessary.

Furthermore, it will be argued that although God's existence is contingent, God's manner of being is not capricious and arbitrary. This God is not like the one in whom Meillassoux has placed his hopes, a God who may advene at an unknown date in the future, only perhaps to pass away five minutes later. Concerning Meillassoux's God – who may (or may not) irrupt *ex nihilo* at any given time and for no reason whatsoever – Peter Gratton incisively questions, 'It is not clear why this outcome would come over any other: why not life born by a Demiurge who resurrects us only to provide us with greater evils?'[53] Meillassoux might reply that one cannot know that this God, rather than some other God or no God at all, will arrive, but that this is a speculative possibility for which one should hope. Nonetheless, Gratton's question pinpoints the source of a recurring uneasiness: Meillassoux seems to elevate the *ad hoc* to a principle; or, for Meillassoux, there is only a principle of errancy, the errant cause! Even granting that Meillassoux is speculating on a God who would provide a solution to the problem of evil and suffering, as outlined in 'Spectral Dilemma', the uneasiness remains unassuaged.[54] This is because, ontologically considered, the advent of this God would irrupt without a real connection to other events, an event emergent not just *ex nihilo* but also as *ad hoc*.

In this respect, Meillassoux comes close to falling prey to the very thing he wishes to avoid with his criticism of metaphysical thought: contemporary fideism. He comments, 'In leaving the realm of metaphysics, the absolute seems to have been fragmented into a multiplicity of beliefs that have become indifferent, all of them equally legitimate from the viewpoint of knowledge . . .'[55] Yet, given that new orders of being in Meillassoux can always eventuate *ex nihilo*, it seems that a kind of fideism is still at play in the (ontologically capricious) event of God's arrival. Meillassoux's fideism, however, is, in his own words, 'a fideism that is "fundamental" rather than merely "historical" in nature . . .'[56] One of the tasks of this book will be to find a way of articulating a God contingent according to existence and necessary according to essence without falling prey either to the fideism of historicism or to the *ad hoc* fideism of post-metaphysical thought. This can be achieved by means of a being-historical philosophy, a *post factum* or narrative philosophy, which – although dispensing with the pretension of concluding to a necessary entity by means of a proof – does not discard all forms of reasoning whatsoever. At any rate, Meillassoux's fundamentalist fideism seems as unfounded, if not also as pernicious, as the historicist variety.

While Meillassoux's philosophy only speculates about a possible God, the remainder of this book will attempt to formulate a narratival ontology capable of affirming God as actual. As one commentator has phrased it, 'Meillassoux . . . rather than affirming any event . . . aims to think what *can* take place, and all that is – the world as well as thought – may be otherwise.'[57] On the contrary, it is possible to affirm what is or what has been without rendering it necessary. It is possible to affirm something as a contingency, as factical rather than as factial. Meillassoux, describing his approach to speculation, remarks:

> We have two ways out of the correlationist circle: either by absolutizing the correlation, or by absolutizing facticity . . . This is precisely what we obtain by absolutizing facticity – we do not maintain that a determinate entity exists, but that it is absolutely necessary that every entity might not exist.[58]

Meillassoux thus speculates in a manner dismissive of the recognition of the actual. By contrast, this book contends that it is possible to 'maintain that a determinate entity exists', while also acknowledging, to paraphrase, 'that it is absolutely necessary that every affirmed entity, or even *all* entities as a whole, could have not existed'. Maintaining that certain things do exist, namely reason itself and God, should not obscure the fact that they just as easily could have not existed. Instead of affirming factiality, the absolute necessity that contingent beings must exist, it is possible to affirm the absolute necessity that whatever actually exists could have never existed, which means there could have been nothing instead of something.

Finally, the contingently necessary God espoused by this book is not absolute in the sense of being absolved from any correlation to time or the necessity of thought. Instead, as the very timing of time or the event of the ordering of time (and chaos), God is the unprecedented, uncircumventable and thus absolute facticity of the correlation between thinking and being, but not the correlation itself. God is neither one of the correlates nor even their absolute coincidence. God is not *Indifferenz* but the copula, the copulating act. In opposition to the Absolute of German Idealism, God is not the indifference of subject and object, but the very facticity of the event of differentiation and correlation. God unites only by differentiating subject and object as a temporal difference between prior and posterior, while the Absolute merely names the a-temporal coincidence of opposites that one finds in Meillassoux's Hyper-Chaos. As of yet, however, these theses are only promises and the hope is that the remainder of the book will provide their corresponding *apologia*.

Notes

1. This chapter includes less than six pages that have been greatly revised and readapted since their original publication in Tritten, 'After Contingency', pp. 24–38.
2. Meillassoux, 'Time without Becoming', p. 10.
3. Badiou explains, 'It is because the One normatively decides on Being that the latter is reduced to what is common, reduced to empty generality. This is why it must also endure the metaphysical preeminence of beings. Metaphysics can be defined as follows: the *enframing* of Being by the One' (Badiou, *Briefings*, p. 34).
4. Meillassoux states that 'Heraclitus, according to me, is a terrible fixist. His becoming must become, and persist eternally as becoming' (Meillassoux, 'Time without Becoming', p. 10).
5. Meillassoux, 'Time without Becoming', p. 10.
6. Markus Gabriel writes that 'it is absurd when Meillassoux presents his own thinking of chance and his renunciation of the principle of sufficient reason as a critique of Heidegger. This is absurd because Meillassoux's basic ideas in *After Finitude* can be understood as a well-grounded interpretation of Heidegger' (Gabriel, 'Heidegger's "Turn"', p. 60). While Meillassoux's critique of the whole of phenomenology and Heidegger in particular is unfair, it is not because Meillassoux fails to do anything different than Heidegger and instead only provides a well-grounded interpretation of him. If, as will be argued in Chapter 6, Heidegger espouses the contingency of necessity and Meillassoux, of course, the necessity of contingency, then the difference between them is great, if not insuperable.
7. Meillassoux, 'Immanence', p. 446.
8. Ibid., p. 446.
9. Meillassoux, 'Time without Becoming', p. 1.
10. Ibid., p. 6.
11. Meillassoux, *After Finitude*, p. 7.
12. The rhetoric of 'outside' or 'outdoors' is misleading. Meillassoux is not looking for a type of transcendence; he is an internalist or philosopher of immanence. For him, transcendence can only name an otherworldly reality that would necessarily ground this one, a metaphysical reality, be it religious transcendence or Kant's noumenal as the ground of the phenomenal. All post-Kantian philosophies, he contends, are but variants of correlationism. It is with pre-Kantian Hume, however, that one last finds an author capable of pointing beyond Kant, because Hume is audacious enough to think the contingency of all laws of nature.
13. Meillassoux, 'Time without Becoming', p. 7.
14. The term 'factical' has appeared a few times when it might seem that the term 'factual' would have sufficed. 'Factual', however, will be reserved for empirically falsifiable facts. Accordingly, not all facts are factual.
15. Harman, *Quentin Meillassoux*, p. 84.

16. Schelling, 'Einleitung in die Philosophie der Offenbarung oder Begründung', *SW II/3*, p. 464.
17. Meillassoux, 'Time without Becoming', p. 8.
18. Ibid., p. 8.
19. It is striking that the same figure credited with formulating the question, 'Why is there something rather than nothing at all?' – which one might already venture to formulate as, 'Why is there a correlation between thinking/reason and being rather than unthinkability and unreason?' – is the same philosopher credited with the formulation of the principle of sufficient reason. Nevertheless, although Leibniz first explicitly formulated the question, Karl Jaspers has stated, 'While, with Leibniz, this issue is quickly processed with logical operation and occurs incidentally only once, the question has first become an actual question through Schelling. [Während bei Leibniz die Sache mit der logischen Operation schnell erledigt ist und beiläufig einmal vorkommt, ist die Frage durch Schelling erst zur wirklichen Frage geworden.]' (Jaspers, *Schelling*, p. 124). Jaspers correctly identifies Schelling, rather than Leibniz or Heidegger, as the first to pose the question in its proper profundity. Furthermore, Schelling is also the first to think the facticity of the correlating ground as an unground, as something without reason, an utterly contingent fact, the primordial accident (*das Urzufällige*). For Schelling, Leibniz's question becomes: 'Why is there reason rather than unreason? [Warum ist denn Vernunft und nicht Unvernunft?]' (Schelling, 'Die Philosophie der Offenbarung: Erster Theil', *SW II/3*, p. 247).
20. Meillassoux, 'Immanence', p. 446.
21. Meillassoux, 'Time without Becoming', p. 9.
22. Meillassoux writes, 'We could certainly envisage the emergence of an entity which, *as a matter of fact*, would be indiscernible from a necessary entity, viz., an everlasting entity, which would go on existing, just like a necessary entity' (Meillassoux, *After Finitude*, pp. 65–6). Meillassoux, while admitting that this entity may never be surpassed by another, would not admit a fact without beginning, without an initial irruption into being *ex nihilo*. In other words, he refuses to admit that there could be eternal facts if for no other reason than his conflation of an eternal fact with a necessary one.
23. This is similar to how Kant sometimes conflates necessity with universality so that necessity means that which holds as a structure universally present in the mind of all rational agents.
24. See Meillassoux, 'Spectral Dilemma', and his forthcoming *L'Inexistence Divine*.
25. The difference between necessarily existing and existing necessarily is homologous to the fact that a unicorn does not necessarily exist but, should it exist, would exist necessarily as a one-horned horse. Its manner of being would be necessary despite the fact that its existence remains contingent.
26. Meillassoux, 'Time without Becoming', p. 9.
27. Ibid., p. 9.
28. Meillassoux, *After Finitude*, p. 75.
29. Meillassoux, 'Immanence', p. 446.
30. Sparrow, *End of Phenomenology*, p. 99.
31. Meillassoux, 'Time without Becoming', p. 10.
32. Ibid., p. 10.
33. Harman, *Quentin Meillassoux*, p. 62.
34. Ibid., p. 40.
35. Ibid., p. 142
36. Ibid., p. 64.
37. Meillassoux, 'Time without Becoming', p. 11.
38. 'Wäre dies möglich, dann wäre das τὸ αὐτό nicht mehr als solches identifizierbar, es hätte als innerlich Widersprüchliches seine Identität verloren, und es könnte nichts mehr mit Wahrheitsanspruch von ihm gesagt werden. Damit ist für Aristoteles das

Widerspruchsprinizip auch als Seinsgesetz erwiesen' (Franz, *Philosophische Religion*, p. 164).
39. Meillassoux, 'Time without Becoming', p. 11.
40. 'Das stillste und das tiefste Meer ist auch das am meisten sich empören könnende, aber das stille und das sich empören könnende sind nicht zwei Meere, sondern nur ein und dasselbe Meer' (Schelling, 'Die Philosophie der Offenbarung: Erster Theil', *SW II/3*, p. 221).
41. Van der Heiden, *Ontology after Ontotheology*, p. 8.
42. The term 'virtual' indicates neither that which is not actual nor that which has no reality at all, but a middle domain between actuality and non-actuality.
43. Meillassoux, *After Finitude*, p. 66.
44. Ibid., p. 104.
45. Johnston, 'Hume's Revenge', p. 104.
46. Van der Heiden, *Ontology after Ontotheology*, p. 269.
47. Ibid., p. 270.
48. This move, which would uncover the imperative for the decision as such, as Chapters 5 and 6 will demonstrate, is first to be found in Schelling and Heidegger, not in Meillassoux.
49. Meillassoux, *After Finitude*, p. 64.
50. Meillassoux, 'Potentiality and Virtuality', p. 72.
51. Necessary truths of reason are timeless; they operate *sub specie aeternitatis*, but facts, which cannot be known in advance of their actuality, can only be narrated. In this sense facts are inherently mythological. One can only narrate them; one can only say that they have happened in this way, but one cannot rationally ground their actuality.
52. Meillassoux, 'Potentiality and Virtuality', p. 74.
53. Gratton, 'Meillassoux's Speculative Politics', p. 14.
54. Meillassoux, 'Spectral Dilemma', pp. 261–76.
55. Meillassoux, *After Finitude*, p. 47.
56. Ibid., p. 46.
57. Van der Heiden, *Ontology after Ontotheology*, p. 268.
58. Meillassoux, *After Finitude*, p. 60.

Chapter 2

Boutroux's Alternative: An Ontology of the Fact

Émile Boutroux, a severely underappreciated philosopher, advanced a philosophy of contingency more than a century prior to Meillassoux. Engaging the scientific discoveries of his time, Boutroux lamented the loss of freedom that arose at the hands of the doctrines of determinism or necessitarianism. This chapter will show how he combated necessity in the following possible forms: logical, mathematical, physical and transcendental. He actually undersells the scope of his thesis by entitling his first book – a dissertation defended in 1874 at the Sorbonne – *On the Contingency of the Laws of Nature*, because it is far more than the laws of nature that he reveals to be contingent.

Boutroux's primary achievement is to show that the laws of nature – far from indicating the necessary ordering of the world by a transcendental ego and far from following the necessity of some logical or mathematical formula – portray nothing but the habit of being itself. This, at least, is a way of reading Boutroux's thesis ontologically. His thesis is relevant for the argument of this book for two principal reasons: (1) he argues that the quantification of mathematics is merely the abstract ordering of pure quality (this thesis will be taken up in more detail in the following chapter); and (2) he contends that all forms of necessity are abstractions or only external observations of habit, which – when viewed from the inside – appear as the consequence of a free deed, of decisiveness. Habit, in other words, presupposes a foregoing act of freedom or spontaneity, but, all the same, when viewed only externally or abstractly, habit appears as the lawfulness or necessary uniformity of nature.

Logic and mathematics

Commenting on logical forms of inference, Boutroux writes, 'Analysis and syllogism demonstrate only derivative necessity, *i.e.* the impossibility of a certain thing being false if a certain other thing is admitted to be true.'[1] It is imperative, in view of this claim, to distinguish between first-order and second-order necessity. Second-order necessity, for example analysis and syllogistic inference, corresponds to what Boutroux here names derivative necessity, namely necessity that only holds if one first grants certain other axioms, premises or hypotheses. First-order necessity, however, would refer to the presumed necessity of these very axioms, premises or hypotheses. It is this type of necessity that Boutroux aims to expose as illusory and as actually contingent. In modus ponens, B certainly follows, it is necessarily derived, but only insofar as one first grants the conditions (1) that B is consequent upon A, which the syllogism cannot demonstrate but only contingently accept, and (2) that one in fact posits that A is the case, which is at best a matter of fact to be corroborated empirically and at worst a non-instantiated premise.

Markus Gabriel, a contemporary philosopher who is highly critical of Meillassoux, can be read as an augmentation of Boutroux's thesis. Gabriel, delimiting necessity to the domain of logical space, asks, as an explicit result of his readings of Schelling, the first-order question of why there is logical space at all rather than chaos, now conceived in opposition to Meillassoux as that which lacks logical structure. Gabriel's philosophy counters both Meillassoux's assumption that the logical law of non-contradiction holds even in chaos and his claim to have proved why there must be something rather than nothing. By contrast, Gabriel proclaims, 'There is no *ratio determinans* for the existence of logical space . . . logical space could have not come to be: it is sensu stricto contingent, because its other, that which it would be otherwise, cannot be a priori ruled out.'[2] It will be argued that the other of logical space, chaos, has contingently, but in fact, been decided against or 'ruled out'. While an account of the decision by which the other of logical space has been ruled out, namely excluded or 'extained', must be delayed for following chapters, for now it should suffice to observe that Gabriel too has not only hinted at the fact that first-order necessity, namely the necessary existence of logical space as such, is an impossibility, but he has also transformed the question from a merely logical one into an ontological one. To ask the first-order question of why there is logical space or reason at all, instead of chaos or unreason, is to have departed from a merely logical and epistemic domain in order to ask an ontological question.

Stated more exactly, the question to be asked is epistemo-ontological in nature. What is the ontological status of the epistemic? What are the ontological conditions of logic, reason, mathematics, set theory and the transcendental? Whence do they originate? Gabriel, influenced by Wolfram Hogrebe's reading of Schelling's ontology as a theory of predication,[3] depicts the question in terms of

> the dynamic by which something is determined *as* something. The question of why anything at all takes place, therefore, is not solely an ontological issue (and certainly no cosmological or ontic quest for the actual origin of the universe), but it is rather the logical-ontological *ur*-question.[4]

While Gabriel's theses are more deflationary than the thesis proffered in this text, which does have something to say about the origin of the universe, his point retains its validity. The question of the existence of logical space as such is, properly speaking, a logical-ontological[5] question because it concerns 'the dynamic by which something is determined as something'. In other words, as has been explained in Chapter 1, for an entity to be an entity, rather than a house divided against itself, the principle of excluded middle must first hold. It is this principle that first demands that a thing either be or not be; this first renders the principle of non-contradiction operative. If a thing must either be or not be, this means that contradiction cannot remain: a thing cannot persist as A and ~A. This further means that A=A, that the principle of identity now also holds. As Boutroux himself succinctly states, 'All [logical laws] do is to declare that if something is, it is.'[6] It is not, at any rate, necessary that the ontological provenance of these fundamental laws of logic, now conceived as laws of being, hold court. Their provenance is only a second-order necessity that holds if there is to be something rather than nothing at all, but that such is the case is a fact that concerns first-order contingency *par excellence*.

Both contingency and necessity, thought as modalities, are only operative as second-order predicates. It is therefore impossible to speak of the fact of logical space as such, the fact that there is something rather than nothing, as contingent or as necessary when these are only thought as modalities. This is because as modalities both contingency and necessity take their sense from the domain of logical space. Gabriel confirms,

> Contingency and necessity can only take place under the condition that there be domains. The rules that constitute the modalities of objects within a particular domain, such that it is distinguishable from other domains, do not necessarily apply to the domain itself.[7]

It should be noted, however, that Gabriel not only repudiates the necessity of any domain but also excludes the possibility of a universal domain.

He does not admit that logic's fundamental laws, or reason itself, could hold universally but still contingently. He repudiates the possibility of a contingent universal, a point which will be disputed throughout this book.

If logic itself is only derivatively necessary but not necessarily existent, then this is the case all the more so for mathematics, which progresses only by means of the construction of its objects from axioms or postulates. This remains true regardless of how one might attempt to clarify the sticky relationship between logic and mathematics, or regardless of how one might try to decide which is more fundamental. That said, one might here note a remark from Heidegger, particularly insofar as it addresses an assumption that Meillassoux inherited from Badiou. Heidegger comments, in a lecture course delivered in 1928, 'Contemporary logic shows a new distortion of the problem. Not only is metaphysics reduced to logic, but logic itself is reduced to mathematics. Contemporary logic is symbolic, mathematical logic, and thus a logic which follows the mathematical method.'[8] This comment is perhaps prescient of Badiou's claim – which Meillassoux then inherits – that mathematics, set theory in particular, is ontology.[9] Heidegger's comment also decries the dominance of quantification in contemporary logic. This predominance of quantification over quality or material implication is, as will be seen, precisely what Boutroux attempts to combat.

Boutroux regards the difference between logic and mathematics in the following way: '[Mathematical knowledge] proceeds from the simple to the compound, which logic does not do.'[10] He thus agrees with Kant that mathematical propositions, arithmetic at least, are synthetical, while logic, beginning already with the compound, consists in mere analysis, in the explication of elements logically contained in the compound. Logic, analytical in character, parses elements from a pre-given whole, while mathematics, synthetical in character, constructs its objects. Additionally, 'Philosophical mathematicians admit, either as coming from experience or from the intellect, given and inscrutable principles.'[11] Boutroux here aligns himself with Kant's view that mathematics contains intuition of some sort. Mathematics therefore requires postulates as the foundation upon which it constructs its objects, while logic analyses relations pre-contained in a concept. Furthermore, Boutroux claims the axioms of the mathematician are, at bottom, inscrutable, which means they are not necessarily grounded but merely contingent givens. As Gabriel remarks,

> Hence, even though 2+2 is necessarily 4, the rules of basic arithmetic might not be necessary, or, at least, not necessary in the same sense. We can always adopt a different arithmetical system. There is no over-arching rule of nesting one field of sense in another and, therefore, no infinite regress.[12]

Boutroux similarly comments, '[Mathematics] consists in imagining axioms and definitions that allow of the development of demonstrations with the utmost possible continuity and the fewest possible gaps.'[13] Yet this 'imaginative' process reflects neither a physical nor a metaphysical necessity. Mathematics is rather a free construction, the most autonomous of the special sciences that make the rules instead of following a pre-given set of rules.

Although mathematics is a priori, it is, Boutroux contends, not deductive. As a constructive method, it progresses from its *prius*, its axioms, definitions and postulates. It is a priori only insofar as its objects are constructed by the mathematician herself; these objects are not ready-made and present for empirical intuition, but they are available only for intellectual or pure intuition. As Boutroux definitively states, 'The philosophical analysis of principles and of mathematical methods reveals therein many a contingent determination, many an artifice accepted mainly because it is successful. And so mathematical necessity itself is no longer unconditioned in our minds . . .'[14] Two questions need to be answered: (1) If mathematical necessity is not 'unconditioned in our minds' – and this might already mark a decisive break from Kant's transcendentalism – but also surely not unconditioned in the world, then how does mathematics arise? (2) If mathematics is but an 'artifice accepted mainly because it is successful', what ensures its success?

In response to the first question, mathematics, *qua* imaginative, is a hypothetical method with only hypothetical or conditional necessity. Contra Badiou or Meillassoux, mathematics is not ontology, at least not if ontology seeks the absolute rather than the hypothetical. Mathematics neither reaches things themselves as mere primary qualities nor does it reveal being *qua* being. Whence arises mathematics, then, if neither from a reflection on the structure of being as such nor from a necessary structure of the mind, *à la* Kant? Boutroux's response concerns not only mathematics but also logic.

> Logic and mathematics are solely derived neither from knowledge *a priori*, nor from knowledge *a posteriori*: they represent the work of the mind which, incited by things to exert itself, creates a mass of symbols in order to subject these things to necessity and thus make them capable of being assimilated by itself.[15]

Boutroux's response to the first question, 'How does mathematics arise?' already hints at an answer to the second question, 'What ensures its success?' The success of mathematics lies in the fact that it subjects or regulates everything to necessity by fixing, stabilising and submitting to analysis and derivation a pre-given flux bereft of mathematical and quantifiable properties. Logic and mathematics are the tools of quantifiable assimilation. In response to the first question, then, logic and mathematics arise, for Boutroux, neither from mere reflection on the world nor merely as a construction of the mathematician; they arise from both. The mathematician does not reflect upon but operates upon the world, subjecting it to her constructions. There is, however, also a role played by abstraction. Boutroux asserts (explicitly with regard to logic but with obvious ramifications for mathematics), 'Logic, in spite of the indispensable part it plays in knowledge, is but an abstract science. It does not determine the degree of intelligibility presented by real things.'[16] In fact, he even offers the following equation of logic with abstraction: '[l]ogical order, or the subordination of facts to notion'.[17] Abstraction is an operation imposed upon the world in order to assimilate it into a constructed system.

Boutroux's critique of logic and modern mathematics is extremely illuminating. In condemning both as mere abstractions and tools of assimilation, however, it also seems that neither has ontological significance. How, then, can his project still be of service to the epistemo-ontological task of this book? Boutroux enacts a damning critique of logic as ontology, which is to say Hegelian logic, but he does not come as far as a positive restoration of logic. In other words, Boutroux seems only to be able to view logic and mathematics as artificial or negative, as an abstraction or movement away from the Real. Can one retain from Boutroux's critique the criticism that the function of logic and mathematics is to abstract a necessary artifice from the contingency of being, yet understand this imposition of necessity as a positive law of being? Can one understand this imposition ontologically rather than merely abstractly, regulatively or epistemically? Can one re-read his critique no longer as critique but already as ontological construction? What if logic and mathematics are indeed consequents rather than what is original, consequents that subjugate – not just for thought or the practicalities of life, but ontologically – chaos to thinkability, unreason to reason, quality to quantity? In this way, while still remaining derivative with regard to first-order contingency, logic and mathematics would 'determine' – in the transitive sense of the term – 'the degree of intelligibility' in real things.

Should the proposed ontological reorientation of Boutroux prove feasible, one would find that the answer to the second question concerning that which ensures the success of logic and mathematics would no longer require any appeal to the constructions of mathematicians and logicians themselves. The success in question would rather be ensured, because enacted, by being itself. What if being itself subjugates chaos as being *qua* being to logical and mathematical determinations, which would coordinate, partition and quantify chaos in order to bring about stability, permanence and order, namely lawful regularity or necessity. This speculative suggestion, at any rate, far exceeds Boutroux's own position, which seems to view the success of logic and mathematics only as something won by the scientist herself. He writes, 'Mathematics imparts to science, necessity; experience imparts conformity with facts. Such is the root of modern determinism. We believe everything to be necessarily determined, because we believe everything, in essence, to be mathematical.'[18] Boutroux is right to dispute the equivocation of mathematics and ontology, since being *qua* being is not mathematics or set theory but unquantified, unpartitioned chaos. This does not preclude, however, that chaos is quantifi-able or mathematis-able. Μέθεξις certainly remains possible, because in chaos no possibilities are excluded. In fact, mathematics, thought as consequent rather than as absolutely a priori, may be able to deliver being from modern determinism, as mathematical relations would then not determine being, but being would give itself over to μέθεξις. Mathematics would not determine being, but it would be the supplementation of being. Along these lines, one of the central aims of this chapter is to show that Boutroux, although he only provides a critical foundation, can be ontologised by means of his own suggestion that the lawfulness of being, both logico-mathematical and physical, is but the habit of being. Habit, which always ensues from a prior spontaneity, can be thought as the consequent execution of the decision of being itself to subordinate, that is, assimilate and appropriate, chaos to lawful regularity, that is, to necessity.

Transcendentalism and apriority

Traditionally, the principal product of the a priori is necessity, while contingency results from the a posteriori. If this is true, then aside from logic and mathematics, which one might simply dismiss as abstractions, there is also the necessity of the transcendental to combat. The transcendental even claims to annex both logic and mathematics as necessary components of the mind, hence Kant's transcendental logic. The overcoming of all forms of absolute necessity therefore requires a critique of the limits of transcendental reasoning. Yet this critique entails a question: is the transcendental itself a domain of being or is it the necessary pre-condition of all domains?

Iain Hamilton Grant warns,

> 'Necessity' cannot be straightforwardly concluded from apriority: while an earth is a necessary a priori for human history, nothing determines the

necessity of *that* history as opposed to any number of others. If the earth, therefore, has only a contingent apriority with respect to its dependents, nature itself, by contrast, has unconditioned apriority.[19]

Once more, one is forced to admit only derivative necessity for the a priori. If the a priori supplies the conditions for the possibility of something, namely transcendental conditions, then those conditions are only necessary given the fact that something actually exists, and this cannot be proved necessary by means of the a priori itself. Grant contends that all apriority is only conditional, except for nature, which alone would constitute unconditioned apriority. (Note that the unconditioned and the necessary are not identical.) What Grant terms nature can here be used as a synonym for the more neutral and non-committal term 'being'. Nevertheless, even if unconditional apriority is to be ascribed to being, which would mean that whatever is impossible for being is impossible absolutely, this still does not necessitate that being must be instantiated in any particular beings at all. Being itself, *qua* un-conditioned, should not be thought as a mere condition or ground for a consequent. To say that 'being is' is to utter an existential proposition. Furthermore, as Kant has rightly taught, all existential propositions are synthetical and all synthetical propositions are contingent, because the predicate of the proposition is not entailed by the subject as its a priori, necessary ground. This means that being itself – thought for its own sake as an unground rather than as a ground or a priori condition necessarily posited for the sake of its consequent – is factical. Considered for its own sake rather than retroactively from the perspective of its consequent, being is nothing a priori or transcendental as such but only to be regarded as sheer facticity. If the transcendental exists, if, in fact, being exists transcendentally, then it exists only as being's consequent and not as the a priori of being.

To think of being as antecedent to the transcendental is to think a variation of Meillassoux's ancestral or 'great outdoors', except without the limitations he imposed upon it. Meillassoux writes, 'To think science is to think the status of a becoming which cannot be correlational because the correlate is in it, rather than it being in the correlate.'[20] Taking the correlate, the conjunction of thinking and being, as the transcendental, it becomes clear that to think being in advance of the correlate as unconditionally prior or as absolute *prius* is also to think in advance of the transcendental. The transcendental, the correlation between thinking and being, resides in being; being does not reside in the correlation. If thinking (subjectivity) and being (objectivity) are correlated, then this conjunction must be thought objectively rather than subjectively. This breaks from traditional transcendentalism, which locates the transcendental in subjectivity, expressing instead an 'inverted transcendentalism'.[21] This is not an anti-transcendentalism, which would relinquish the transcendental. The transcendental, namely the epistemic domain or the pre-conditions of experience and thinkability/knowledge, remains, but only in being and not as antecedent to being. In other words, the conditions of thinkability, although non-empirical, although nothing that can become an object of sensible experience, are nevertheless not to be found in a *locus* transcendent to being itself. Epistemic conditions may not necessarily be ontically instantiated within nature as something empirically observable – hence, for example, not as neuroscience – but they are nevertheless ontologically founded within being as such as its internal consequent.

In opposition to the empirico-ontic ancestrality Meillassoux hopes to secure for science, the issue here concerns the ontologically ancestral. It is not because there is thinking or the transcendental domain that there is (the appearance of) being, but there is thinking/reason only because this is how being has eventuated, an event not to be grounded but only narrated. In short, the transcendental is not, as Kant thought, a universal domain, but it is local, something that takes place as being's posterior. Even as Meillassoux has remarked, '[The ancestral] concerns the space-time in which transcendental subjects went from not-taking-place to taking-place – and hence concerns the space-time anterior to the spatio-temporal forms of representation.'[22] The question, then, is how to think time and space, inclusive of the logical space of reasons, as ontological and real rather than as transcendental forms of representation. In short: How can philosophy move past Kant as a robust realism rather than as a phenomenology?

Gabriel outlines the task thus: 'In contrast to the "old realism," New Realism includes and integrates the conditions of its own truth within the region of what is real.'[23] The task with which contemporary realisms have been charged is to exhibit the production of the transcendental domain as an immanent occurrence. Post-Kantian realisms must take the form of monism; post-Kantian realisms can only exist as philosophies of immanence.[24] Epistemo-ontology[25] includes within itself an ontological explanation of the appearance of the immanent domain of knowledge and experience. This means that although one still thinks a correlation between thinking and being, one does so from the perspective of the ontologically ancestral, from the viewpoint of the absolutely prior. Furthermore, this means that one thinks the very eventuation of this correlation as a fact that could just as easily never have been. Gabriel can therefore surmise,

> This neither entails 'correlationism' nor 'finitude' in Meillassoux's sense. On the contrary, the reflection on the ontological constitution of finite objective knowledge turns out to be the absolute itself. The absolute is not opposed to

knowledge as an unattainable beyond, but identified as the very process of a subjectivization of being in the form of finite objective knowledge.[26]

The transcendental, as the consequent of being itself, its supplementation, cannot be derived from being but only acknowledged as a matter of fact; the transcendental is not a truth of reason but more akin to the very eventuation of reason, the fact of reason. Accordingly, it is not necessary to abandon Kant's critical philosophy to be post-Kantian or a full-blooded realist. One only needs to take a step before Kant, before the transcendental and its critical strictures. This is possible because, as Catherine Malabou justly contends, 'There can be no transcendental *deduction* of the transcendental. The a priori is just a presupposition. What Kant calls deduction is only a description.'[27] The fact that being is groundless does not mean that it cannot be auto-generative or *sui generis*, that it cannot, belatedly, generate its own grounds.

Philosophies of immanence teach nothing if not that grounds eventuate from the groundless itself and that reason immanently eventuates from unreason. In Kant, the term 'transcendental' signifies a domain removed from experience itself that satisfies the conditions for the possibility of experience. Philosophies of immanence or epistemo-ontology, however, render obsolete transcendental philosophy's pathological search for such conditions. They do so by denying that the ground of being (and thus too the ground of the experience of being) is produced anywhere except from within being itself. Being is generated as *autophysis* and so requires no conditions outside itself. As Meillassoux, like Malabou, perpetually insists,

> Kant maintains that we can only *describe* the *a priori* forms of knowledge (space and time as forms of intuition and the twelve categories of the understanding), whereas Hegel insists that it is possible to *deduce* them. Unlike Hegel then, Kant maintains that it is impossible to derive the forms of thought from a principle or system capable of endowing them with absolute necessity. These forms constitute a 'primary fact' which is only susceptible to description, and not to deduction (in the genetic sense).[28]

Kant begins with the fact of experience and then asks for its necessary conditions.[29] Transcendental necessity thus only functions conditionally, on condition of the facticity of experience. Yet if experience itself is a contingent fact, so too are its conditions. None of it is necessary; the conditions of possible experience are simply 'co-factical' with experience itself.

Transcendentalism could only be secured as a 'necessary fact' – which is an oxymoron if not a contradiction in terms – if Kant's transcendental Ideal, the embodiment (*Inbegriff*) of all possible predicates, were, ironically enough, necessarily incomplete. There would have to be at least one predicate – 'not-transcendental' – excluded from this 'totality', from the idea of *omnitudo realitatis*. Stated bluntly, for transcendentalism to be necessary, the negation of transcendentalism must already be excluded as a possible predicate; yet such an exclusion renders the transcendental Ideal incomplete and, therefore, not what it is. Transcendentalism, then, can only be necessary on its own terms if the transcendental Ideal is incomplete, excluding its negation, not-transcendentalism, as a possible predicate. The transcendental Ideal *qua* transcendental Ideal, however, impossibly excludes its negation from itself. Consequently, the following aporia ensues: if the transcendental Ideal is complete, then transcendentalism and not-transcendentalism are equally possible, but if transcendentalism necessarily holds, then not-transcendental must be absent from the transcendental Ideal, rendering this 'totality' incomplete. Consequently, if transcendentalism is in fact the case, then it could only have occurred as a possibility of being itself rather than the inverse. It is impossible that being would be possible only on the basis of the transcendental, that being would require the conditions of its possibility in advance of itself. It is not because there is thinking that there is being; it is because there is being that there can be thinking; it is because being is the absolute *prius* that logical laws are not merely formal laws of thought but ontological principles of being. The transcendental Ideal, when it retains the possible predicate 'not-transcendental', says nothing more than that it is actually the Real – and not the Ideal – that constitutes the sum total of all possibilities. The transcendental Ideal, in other words, demands to be thought as Real. Of course, all this amounts to nothing more than what has been gleaned from the remark by Grant above, namely that whatsoever is impossible for being itself is impossible absolutely. Being must be thought as the Real which is capable of Ideality, capable of generating thinking, reason and the transcendental as consequents, even eternal consequents. In this way, logic, mathematics, the transcendental and the epistemic as such are neither reduced to mere abstractions on the part of the thinker nor to a thinker's own construction; they are instead the constructions of being itself. Being mathematises and transcendentalises itself; being constructs its own domains.

Laws of nature and the *clinamen*

Of logic, mathematics and the transcendental, none contain absolutely necessity and all are to be thought realistically, that is, ontologically, rather than as mere abstractions employed for epistemic purposes. Nevertheless, by conceiving of the laws of nature as nothing more than an abstraction,

Boutroux also provides a rebuttal against physical necessity. Here, then, is the question and the task: How can Boutroux be turned around so that laws of nature can be thought realistically, yet without making them absolutely necessary and thereby reinstituting physical determinism? As Boutroux asserts, 'Natural law . . . is not a first principle but rather a result . . .'[30] He begins, then, by already intimating that natural law is itself another abstraction, which is what he here means by 'result'. The present task, however, is to let nature's lawfulness remain a 'result', a consequent, but not as a merely abstract result or ideal.

Anticipating the role of habit, which is of vital significance because it will offer a means of regarding the laws of nature positively rather than as mere abstractions, one might draw a comparison with one of Boutroux's contemporaries, Charles Sanders Peirce. In Peirce's philosophy, '*categorically* there is no difference between mental habits and natural laws. Arguing for a likeness of mind and matter, Peirce's point is that the difference between the rational mind and physical nature is of absolutely no categorical significance.'[31] If, as argued in the prior section, the mind (the transcendental domain) and nature (being) are not two separate orders, given that the former is only the consequent construction of the latter, then one should not expect them to follow two different sets of laws. Dualism is out. Physical laws or, as will be argued, 'inviolable habits' of the mind, far from abstracting from being, may rather mark the highest order of being.

Laws of nature, unlike those of logic and mathematics, are not constructed a priori, but induced a posteriori. Induction, however, can never lead to a definitive and universal conclusion, or, *per* Kant, 'to advance to absolute totality by the empirical road is absolutely impossible'.[32] Boutroux never tires of making this point, although he does so in a more historical manner than Kant, insisting that according to 'the ancient point of view . . . laws were only general and ideal'[33] and, 'in Aristotle's mind, no empirical knowledge, as such, might lay claim to universality and necessity. Experience was inevitably limited to the relative.'[34] Consequently, (1) one must either make recourse to accounts that can never attain more than varying degrees of probability; or (2) one can deceive oneself, persisting in the belief that the empirical road can lead to necessity and universality. The latter option, to Boutroux's mind, is the one pursued by abstraction, though with an important qualification: the scientist eventually forgets that she is only dealing with abstractions derived from reality and eventually turns the order of things around so that laws which are induced from the world and which appear to be universal and necessary come to be regarded as the motor behind all changes in the world.

Obviously, it is the first option that holds the most promise, although it too will prove problematic, hence why Boutroux, discontent with the mere probability offered by this option, searches for a conception that permits laws of nature to name something more than a simple abstraction of the mind. He thus hypothesises, 'Laws are the channel along which rushes the stream of facts: the latter have hollowed it out, although they follow its track.'[35] From this fascinating passage, at least two points are to be extracted: (1) Boutroux understands law not as a foregoing principle that dictates the movements and relations between matters of fact, but rather as consequent to a prior movement in matters of fact themselves; and, simultaneously, (2) he shows how laws are not merely abstract but indicate something – a channel – with a real ontological status, something with a constitutive rather than regulative operation, that, although consequent to them, still directs antecedent matters of fact. Should he prove to be able to account both for the fact that lawfulness is consequent and yet still able to direct the motion of things antecedent to it, then he has achieved an astonishing feat indeed. He will have found a way to preserve freedom by preventing a deterministic worldview while also allotting a real role to physical law. If Boutroux's metaphor is correct, then it can be posited that matters of fact are, initially at least, not guided by law but actually constitute the channels of law. One should thus attempt to understand the movement of facts in advance of law.

The original motion of things thus requires no external mover and no law to guarantee the preservation of this motion after the external mover has finished its work. The original 'motion' of things is rather presupposed as the play of quality in advance of the spatial motion, locomotion, of mere quantity. This presupposition was, in fact, already implied in Boutroux's claim that mathematics is an abstraction. If mathematics, or lawfulness in general, is only a consequent of being, this means being, as pure quality, only becomes quantified.

Before discussing the relation of quality and quantity in more detail, however, it will be helpful to consider how this primordial motion of things can be conceived along the lines of tychism (Peirce) or as the 'swerve', the *clinamen*, of the ancient atomists (Epicurus and Lucretius). In 'The Logic of Continuity',[36] Peirce even identifies his category of Firstness with the Epicurean notion of the 'swerve', raising the possibility that the swerve is not, as it is standardly conceived, something derivative but rather an originary motion. Such an account of tychism and/or the *clinamen* proves suggestive, because it insists that the originary motion of facts precedes law, a motion thus antecedent to the necessity and universality of law.

Boutroux, however, is not uncritical of the ancient notion of the *clinamen* and its concomitant atomism. He complains,

> Speaking generally, atomism can give a reason for everything, provided it endow the atom with the very thing that has to be explained. Now, this way of developing atomism contradicts its principle, which is essentially one of economy, in more precise terms, the idea of explaining the higher by the lower, the appearance of finality by mechanism, mind by matter.[37]

The issue for Boutroux is not that atomism presupposes everything in the beginning as such but that this runs counter to its own 'economy': if the higher is already entailed in the lower, the lower does not explain but already presupposes the higher. Should everything higher already be presupposed in the lower, then why not just begin with the higher, for which one is more easily convinced that it already contains everything to be explained, and then deduce the lower? Boutroux prefers the economy of explanation in atomism, which moves from the lower to the higher. His objection rather stems from the fact that he does not see the higher as something already entailed in and subsequently unfurled by the lower. For Boutroux, higher orders of reality are not entailed by or pre-endowed in lower orders, but they supplement lower orders without cause; higher orders are not unfolded from out of lower orders, but they eventuate as unforeseeable novelties.

In this respect, Boutroux is in agreement with Meillassoux: both view the advent of organic life and consciousness as the addition of something novel and unforeseen to the prior domain of lifeless matter. Consciousness and organic life are thus also understood as two different orders. Boutroux, like Meillassoux, accounts for the random supplementation of lower orders with higher orders not by positing everything to be explained as already contained within the lower but rather by conceiving of the basic level of reality – which is not yet an order of reality, because it is something chaotic – as radical contingency, capable of anything and everything without cause and without law. For Boutroux this contingency is always thought – and here he proves quite different from Meillassoux – not in logical terms but in close proximity with the freedom of being to do as it pleases. Along these lines, he states that in 'Epicurus, we find the *clinamen*, which, after all, is no more than an *ébauche* of free-will'.[38]

This *ébauche* or original figure of freedom cannot be thought as a way of pre-endowing the antecedent with its consequent. In such a case, the relation between consequent and antecedent would be fundamentally Spinozistic insofar as consequents would be pre-contained within the antecedent substance. One should rather think of this *ébauche* as pre-conscious ambivalence, as the contingency or undecidability of all possibilities. According to this interpretation, if one possibility would be chosen at the exclusion of others, this could only be stated as a matter of fact; regarding the chosen possibility, it could only be stated that things have in fact occurred thus, but certainly not that they had to occur this way or even that something had to occur at all. Interpreted in this manner, the *clinamen* allows one to move from the lower to the higher without having to endow the atom with everything that would merely appear later.[39] This can be done by retaining the economy of atomism but not its ontology. In other words, one can begin from a domain prior to the physical atom itself, namely from the *clinamen* thought not as a swerve or derivation from the already established order of things but as a contingent motion prior to the eventuation of order. In short, the *clinamen* can be thought as the pure spontaneity or undecidability of the contingency of chaos. This position would then be neither atomistic, materialistic nor idealistic, but it is a kind of realism. The Real in this realism corresponds neither to the objectivity of science, to what is given within experience as something falsifiable, nor to the subjectivism of Kant's transcendentalism, to the mere conditions for the possibility of experience.

Although this interpretation of the *clinamen* is historically inaccurate with respect to Epicurus and Lucretius, it is philosophically informative. In fact, such a heretical reading of the *clinamen* has already been indicated by Deleuze, who offers the following account:

> We must conceive of an originary direction for each atom, as a synthesis which would give to the movement of the atom its initial direction, without which there would be no collision . . . The *clinamen* or swerve has nothing to do with an oblique movement which would come accidentally to modify a vertical fall. It has always been present: it is not a secondary movement, nor a secondary determination of movement . . . The *clinamen* is the original determination of the direction of the movement of the atom.[40]

For Epicurus and Lucretius the *clinamen* most certainly was a derivative and oblique movement of atoms already subjected to the necessity of a downward movement or fall. The swerve was nothing more than a way of adding spontaneity or contingency to a prevailing necessity in an effort to save a quotient of indeterminism. Inversely, the thesis here will be that the lawfulness of movement is always only added on to contingent spontaneity. The *clinamen* will not designate some occult property of the atom, an accidental and inexplicable power inherent within the atom, but it refers to the primacy of tychism. Necessary movement – lawfully regulated and quantifiable movement – supplements purely contingent and purely qualitative movement.

Now, it is well-known, at least since Hume, that if laws regulate cause and effect relations in the world, then these relations are synthetical and never analytical in character. Boutroux is thus right to argue that the lawfulness of nature is nothing more than a matter of fact: 'Known by experience alone, the most general connexions between things remain, so far as we are concerned, radically contingent, as Newton said. Why are bodies attracted to each other in the ratio of their mass and not of the square of their mass? This is a fact, nothing more.'[41]

If, as Hume showed, causal relations are necessarily regulated neither according to resemblance nor according to contiguity in space and time, then what law of relation presides over causal synthesis? Boutroux flatly answers that no law regulates these connections,[42] at least not in advance of the originary movement of things. If it happens to turn out that causal relation corresponds to the ratio of the attracted bodies' mass and not to their mass squared, then there is no derivation of this 'law' but only the observation that this indeed has been and remains the case. Said otherwise, this 'law' itself, formed as the channel hollowed out by the antecedent motion of things, can be no more than contingent, as all synthetical relations are. Why does causality take effect according to the ratio of mass rather than according to a ratio of height or according to a hue of colour or some other way altogether? This is like asking why fish smell like fish or snozberries taste like snozberries. In other words, *qua* synthetic, the qualities of things, even of 'lawfully' regulated causal interactions, precede their quantification. In short, modern science's attempt, dependent as it is on the law of the conservation of energy, to measure or quantify the amount of force in an effect in relation to its cause, is misguided. Quality precedes quantity. There is no answer to the question why a quality is like the quality that it is, why, for example, vibration leads to the quality of sound rather than smell or light to that of sight rather than taste. This, at least, is the case when the attempt to explain such facts by appeal to the merely quantitative force operative between objects (thought as primary, mathematical properties free of quality in themselves) has been occluded. The claim, then, is not only that the primary qualities of modernity were a false abstraction but that this abstraction inverts the order of things: quantity is the secondary property and quality the primary.

To recapitulate, one can either regard lawfulness as mere probability or regard its necessity as a mere abstraction, or one can seek a new method that would account for things not in the abstract but as they really are. Boutroux, in other words, pursues a historical method.

> No longer is [experimentation] even the totality of the data amongst which induction discerns law, and which, once thus summed up in a general formula, renders new observations ineffectual: it is the eternal source and rule of science, in so far as this latter would know things in truly objective fashion, *i.e.* in their history as well as in their nature, which, after all, is but one of their states.[43]

If the fixity of something's nature is but a mere state of something actually fluid, dynamic and contingent, then the knowledge of something's present state or nature does not allow one to say that this something is known. Rather, to know an object objectively is to know the history of its states or natures, the historical genesis of its various crystallisations into points of fixity. Objects can only be known genetically because history is not the unfolding of a pre-constituted nature. The identity of a thing is but a congealment or point of ossification in that thing's history, or, in fetishised instances, the false abstraction of one moment that thereby artificially arrests the genesis of the object itself. This 'objective' method, at any rate – at least when it is able to avoid the temptation to fetishise – corresponds to what has already been designated as a 'narrative philosophy' or 'narrative empiricism'.

Two questions now emerge: (1) If laws are the consequent channels carved out by the motion of things and if this prior motion becomes subsequently habituated to these channels, then, as Boutroux suggests, can the lawfulness of nature be thought as the habit of being itself? Indeed, if it is the *ébauche* of freedom that first posits a habit of being, then the historical or genetic account must seek to uncover that first free act by which this habit was enacted. As a further elaboration of the historical approach to the nature of things, Boutroux explains, 'It is act that explains essence, far more than essence can explain act. It is not, then, the nature of things that should be the final object of our scientific investigations, it is their history.'[44] (2) What was the impetus to this act, which set the course, the channel, for the ensuing trajectory of the object? The following sections will attempt to provide answers to these two questions.

Law and habit

The question is not how freedom or spontaneity is possible but how the rational, causal totality has emerged, namely from what decision. Put differently, what requires explanation is not motion and quality, but fixity, order, continuity, seriality and quantity. Boutroux, among others sharing in his *Zeitgeist*, namely Peirce, William James and Félix Ravaisson,[45] has attempted to answer this question by appealing to habit. In other words, it is possible to read Boutroux (and his contemporaries) so that habit explains the permanence of law and rationality. This entails understanding habit ontologically rather than psychologically. Boutroux inconsistently pursues this ontological employment of habit himself, as he here ambivalently remarks:

> Habit is not a fact but rather the disposition to realise certain facts, and consequently can find no place in the formula of a positive law . . . The real

> positive laws are relations which spring, in the final analysis, from the nature of things, considered as constant. They do not precede beings, but simply express the consequences of their reciprocal action. Undoubtedly, in scientific demonstration, they may be considered as governing facts of detail, in so far as they are linked to the nature of beings, *i.e.* to general facts; but they really remain subordinate to general facts, which are their basis.[46]

This citation periodically lapses into the notion that laws, because they are consequent, can be no more than abstractions and so cannot be formulated as positive law. He determines positive law as something that springs from things considered as constant. Given this determination, he is thus right to remove habit from the domain of positive law insofar as 'positive' means empirically verifiable and/or falsifiable, but he is wrong to remove habit from the domain of positive law insofar as 'positive' means generative, rather than merely reflective, of states of affairs or natures considered as constant. What if positive law rather springs from the original motion of things by narrating the continuity that emerges from the history of these motions?

It would be correct to say that, for Boutroux, habit enacts the lawfulness of being so long as one adds that habit itself is always only the consequence of a foregoing act. Without the deed, without the act, there can be no habit. Boutroux occasionally acknowledges this with clarity, writing, 'The spontaneity of the lower beings ... animal instinct, life, physical and mechanical forces are, as it were, habits that have penetrated more and more deeply into the spontaneity of being ... Seen from without, they appear as necessary laws.'[47] In this context, he explicitly binds habit to the 'spontaneity of being'. Although Boutroux sometimes relapses into speaking of habit as having merely psychological valency, the more radical ontological thesis should be pursued. Only by means of an ontological, rather than psychological, employment of habit would Boutroux be able to offer a response to the perceived conflict between spontaneity and determinism, freedom and necessity. He maintains, 'In this way, freedom and necessity are mutually reconciled; being is free in the absolute, and the order of its manifestations is necessary ... we nowhere find necessity which is not added on to freedom.'[48] Nowhere, in other words, does one find necessity that is not added on to contingency; 'as necessity is absolute, on the side of phenomena, so freedom is infinite, on the side of beings'.[49] Boutroux's somewhat clumsy distinction between habit as freedom's inside and necessity as its outside parallels the Kantian distinction between freedom as noumenal and its appearance, the domain into which freedom's consequences fall and become subject to the necessary operation of the category of causality, as the phenomenal. Nonetheless, he is not Kantian insofar as he views spontaneity or freedom neither as regulative nor merely as practical, but constitutively. Boutroux does not delimit spontaneity to subjectivity alone; he, in principle at least, expands it to all of being.

Nature's lawfulness is but habit considered from the outside, and habit but the lawful ordering or internal regulation of irregular freedom. Said otherwise, it is only because a spontaneous act is allowed to develop in a consistent manner, rather than immediately being contradicted by the freedom to will the negation in the same moment, that something like habit, and thus lawfulness and regularity, can take hold. Otherwise, freedom, immediately retracting its will in every moment, could never actually lead to a consequent, and whatever lacks a consequent is not; to be is to have a consequent. Boutroux maintains, 'Our freedom spends itself in a single act.'[50] This cryptic comment indicates that freedom, in order to be freedom, cannot consume itself at every moment with the advent of a new freedom. This point is reminiscent of Meillassoux's admittance of an inevitable recurrence of the structure of lawfulness, whereby it became evident that even as he affirmed that laws are always capable of being replaced by new laws, he could not deny lawfulness altogether. Lawfulness must hold, even if only for a short time, for freedom to be more than sheer vapidity. An act not permitted to bring about consequences is nullified as an act. An act only is an act if it has a consequent; an act without a consequent is the same as never to have acted.

The necessity of habit, freedom considered only from the outside, or, in Kantian terms, only as something phenomenal, follows from a contingent act that preceded the habit, which thus functions as the inside of habit. Accordingly, one could say that necessity is but the mode or modality of a contingent, that is, free, act. Habit, as the *modus*, the *modus operandi*, of an act, is necessary, namely regular, uniform and continuous; yet this does not compromise the contingency of the existence of the act itself. Considered in advance of its consequent lawfulness and regularity, which constitutes a thing's nature or essence, the existence of the act is perfectly contingent. The fact that it occurs is perfectly lawless or unhabituated. As a result, necessity is the *modus essendi* of the modeless, a modality of pre-modal, first-order, contingency. Again, if an act that is inoperative is no act all, if acts, to be acts, require *modi operandi*, then necessity could be considered as the *modus operandi* of contingency itself, that which first constitutes something's *modus essendi*. To introduce, perhaps prematurely, a more speculative conclusion, habit, as the *modus* that permits an act to emerge at all rather than being perpetually consumed by a counter-act, functions as the grace that alleviates modeless ἀνάγκη from its fatality and self-bondage. This proposition, however, is premature. In order simply to develop an infrastructure that may support such a conclusion, the relation between an act and its consequent matters of fact must still be analysed in greater detail.

Possibility and act

Concerning the relationship of the possible and the actual, which should not be read in the sense of an existent actuality but should rather refer to act in a verbal sense, Boutroux expounds as follows:

> Being, reduced to the possible, remains purely ideal; to obtain real being, a new element must be admitted. Indeed, of themselves, all possibles lay equal claim to being, and there is no reason, along these lines, why one possible should be realized in preference to the rest. No fact is possible without its contrary being equally so. If, then, the possible is left to itself, everything will be eternally hovering between being and non-being, nothing will pass on from potency to act. Thus, instead of the possible containing being, it is being that contains the possible and something besides: the realization of one contrary in preference to the other, the act, strictly so called.[51]

Kant's transcendental Ideal depicts that domain in which 'all possibles lay equal claim to being' and, as has already been argued in Chapter 1, this Ideal must be thought as an Ideal of being, that 'instead of the possible containing being, it is being that contains the possible'. Instead of the Real resulting from the Ideal, it is the Real that contains the Ideal. Being does not follow from possibility; possibility, or potency, is a result of being, of the Real. Only in this way can possibilities be real possibilities instead of what is simply not logically excluded. Only because being precedes possibility is it conceivable that any possibility could ever be actualised. Inversely, if possibility preceded being, then possibility, in Boutroux's words, could only 'eternally hover between being and non-being', never being definitively decided for or against.

This is not a modern adaptation of St Thomas Aquinas's argument for God's existence on the basis of an inference from possible being to necessary being (the 'third way' or 'middle way'). Quite the contrary, it is an inversion of the Aristotelian understanding of the potency-act relationship on which Aquinas – among many others, including Hegel – depends. Boutroux's position (or this author's, for that matter) in no way presupposes an actuality already bearing potencies inclined towards actualisation or ἐντελέχεια by means of a movement *a potentia ad actum*. Boutroux's position is distinguished by the convictions that *actus* precedes *potentia*, that being precedes possibility, and thus that movement *a potentia ad actum* is impossible or, minimally, not a genuine, but perhaps only a logical, transition.

Although his distinctive account of possibility, potency and act is philosophically central, Boutroux's primary concern is nevertheless not to react against Aristotelianism. His primary target is rather the abstractionism of modern science. Nevertheless, the distinction between Boutroux's and Aristotle's accounts of possibility remains indirectly relevant, because Aristotle's account underwrites Hegelianism and Hegelianism may be understood as bound up with the modern abstractionism Boutroux repudiates. What is Hegelianism, after all, if not the intention to begin from the conceptually possible – the possibility latent in *der Begriff* – and from there to proceed to actuality, understood as the actualisation of the *Begriff* itself. It is this move, from the abstract or conceptual to the concrete and actual, *a potentia ad actum*, that Boutroux decisively negates as absolutely impossible. Boutroux's positive point is that possibility, in order to be real and not abstract or ideal, must be the consequent of *actus*. Possibility must stem not from an actuality (*actualitas*) but from an act, a deed. For possibles to be possible they must, *qua* possible, follow from act.

Recall that Meillassoux thought of the absolute not as *actus* but as the possible, what may-be or the *peut-être*. In conjunction with this, however, he offered a proof for the fact that there is something rather than nothing. Unfortunately, although he attempted to think absoluteness apart from an absolute entity, he nevertheless reaffirmed the primacy of the ontic, the primacy of actual entities, insofar as he thought absolute contingency always in terms of the contingency of some actuality. As Harman emphasised, for Meillassoux, 'Contingency can be thought only as the contingency *of something that exists* (this is the first Figure of the factial: a demonstration that there ought to be something rather than nothing).'[52] Although Meillassoux has not relapsed into substance metaphysics and its presupposition of some actuality in particular, namely God, he still regards the role of actual existents as necessary. By arguing for the necessity of contingency, Meillassoux thus ultimately finds himself arguing for the necessity of existent actualities rather than none whatsoever. Now, although one surely must not follow Meillassoux here, it is nevertheless telling that even he felt compelled to posit *actus*, if only as the *actus* of contingent beings. His error, therefore, is not that he posited *actus* but that he made it something actually existent, an *actualitas*, and, more precisely, something absolutely necessary. Now, if – and this 'if' marks a contingent but nevertheless factical condition – possibility is not to sway in eternal ambivalence between being and non-being, as Boutroux says it would if possibility were thought in advance of being, then one must affirm the act by which the possible itself is ontologically rather than merely logically grounded.

To espouse act before potency – or, perhaps better, the actuality of the possible – is not to return to the medieval doctrine of a first actuality (God as first cause). That would mark but another instance of Aristotelianism. Boutroux rather affirms that 'The possible . . . is not potency, which is and remains in being both before, during, and after the act . . . The act is not the change that takes place in potency when it creates an object, the transformation of potency into a generating cause.'[53] What is at stake is not the potency of a given substrate or entity but the generation of potency as such from the im-potent as an unforeseeable possibility. In this context, to affirm act prior to potency indicates no more than that what is possible can never be known in advance of its actuality. Something is only known to be possible after it is seen that it is actual. Boutroux asserts that

> It is not contrary to reason to admit that the possible should never pass into the act, or that the actual should exist from all eternity. Thus, not only can the knowledge of being, *qua* reality, be derived from experience, but it cannot have any other origin; it cannot be attributed to a synthetic judgement *a priori*. Experience cannot induce to attribute a necessity of fact to this passing.[54]

Because being is knowable only in its actuality, Boutroux is able to denounce all forms of apriority, even the transcendental. That which can be known only if it is actual is a fact, namely that which can never be known through reason alone precisely because it lacks a sufficient reason for its existence. Consequently, being – including the possibility of being – is knowable only as a fact. In turn, neither the actuality nor the possibility of facts can be known a priori; they can be known only via experience; their actuality can only be factually narrated. The astounding thesis Boutroux actually espouses, then, is that even truths of reason are only first-order matters of fact, or that the existence of truths of reason is not a priori, analytical and necessary, but a posteriori, synthetical and contingent. All truths are synthetical matters of fact that are not simply the unfolding of a substance/subject unto its attributes/predicates. Against Spinoza, who says that all truths are analytical, Boutroux (and eventually Schelling) will argue that existential propositions at least can only be synthetical. Even, or especially, the fact that there is something rather than nothing is a synthetical proposition known only as an item of experience, namely *post factum*. To begin with the a priori, which supplies the conditions for the possibility of existence and is, in this respect, synonymous with the transcendental, is decisively rejected. To begin, however, in advance of the possible – which is, to repeat, not a return to a medieval doctrine – is what it means to affirm *actus* prior to *potentia*.

The ontology of logic and ground

The purpose of this section is to draft a speculative construction of the logical and causal as such, of the very eventuation of reason and ground from out of chaotic unground. While this constructive project is foreign to Boutroux's explicit aims, the endeavour is not excluded by the basic principles of his thought. This is because his philosophy affirms that order and stability are not original. In his own words, 'It is unintelligible that absolute permanence should give rise to change. Change, then, is the principle; permanence is but a result; and so things must admit of change, even in their most immediate relations.'[55]

Permanence is consequent to impermanence, a novel supplement, which is only possible because all truth is synthetical. In other words, the relation between *antecedens* and *consequens* is not primarily a logical relation, but it is always a synthetical relation, a causal synthesis. Boutroux glosses,

> Indeed, how can we imagine that the cause, or immediate condition, really contains all that is needed to explain the effect? It will never contain that wherein the effect is distinct from itself, that appearance of a new element which is the indispensable condition of a relation of causality.[56]

Whenever a consequent adds something novel, something not previously present in the antecedent, the relation is causal and synthetical rather than logical and analytical.[57] Causality, as it were, is always a relation of supplementation; effects do not follow from but rather supplement their cause. Now, if logic itself eventuates from, that is, supplements, a chaos precedent to logic, if reason eventuates from or supplements unreason, then logic too is a novel consequent, something not entailed in antecedent chaos. Hence the very existence of logic is synthetic, a novel supplement consequent upon pre-logical being, pre-logical *actus*.

Note the basic operations of logic: the law of excluded middle, the law of non-contradiction and the law of identity (which taken cumulatively may be said to constitute the principle of sufficient reason). Let it be asked – in a manner not unlike the hypotheses concerning the being or non-being of the One in Plato's *Parmenides* – whether in the antecedence of chaos these basic operations of logic do or do not obtain. These two hypotheses – logic obtains; logic does not obtain – can only be in contradiction if the truth or falsity of one of the hypotheses is exhaustive, only if the principle of excluded middle holds. This principle does not hold, however, since in chaos the laws of logic neither are nor are not; they occupy a middle position not yet excluded; they could hold, that is, they may-be or can-be as virtuals or dense-possibles. Because the law of excluded middle does not hold in chaos, the law of non-contradiction also impossibly finds traction. In turn, without the governance of the law of non-contradiction there is no rational imperative for something to be what it is rather than its negation – which is, of course, equally possible in chaos. In other words, things have no more reason to be A than ~A, and so the law of identity has also not yet been put into play.

Within chaos the basic operations of logic are inoperative. The virtual contradiction, which is but the virtuality of chaos itself, between the possibility of A and the possibility of ~A, between the possibility of being and non-being, presides only prescriptively but not descriptively, as it is not yet efficacious. In advance of the domain of actuality, in which these laws hold court descriptively, they can nevertheless prescribe. More precisely, they prescribe what ought to be if there will actually be something rather than nothing.

That these laws will actually hold sway, not regulatively but as operative principles of being, is contingent. The imperative has already been sounded, however, that they ought to hold sway if there should be something and not nothing, but nothing necessitates that they in fact do. The real issue first concerns neither logical, metaphysical, physical nor transcendental necessity, but the necessity of the proto-ethical word: Be one thing only; have an identity; emerge from duplicity; purity of heart is to will one thing! The ethico-ontological imperative and the logical laws of being are, insofar as the latter are thought prescriptively, one and the same. Thus, when Boutroux quips that 'when unity has vanished, concept is non-existent . . .',[58] he has put the cart before the horse. It would be truer to say that if conceptuality, namely lawfulness of thought, would be non-existent, then unity would fail to be called forth from out of chaos.

The laws of logic, as prescriptive principles of being, are what first permit something identical to eventuate from the non-identical, orderliness from flux; the laws of logic are what first permit the possibility of any emergence at all from an otherwise all-consuming chaos. Pushing the point, the laws of logic or laws of thought, namely the contingent and consequent fact that thinking and being are correlated,[59] ultimately allow for the eventuation of a consequent from a chaos that would first be posited as antecedent or as ground only by means of its novel and unforeseeable consequent/supplementation. Logical laws thus constitute the law of ground and, since ground is transitive and synthetical rather than analytical, logical laws as the prescriptive dictates of being itself lay the foundation of causal relation as such. This also means that causality does not just happen now and again to produce effects independent and different from their cause, but, *qua* synthetical and transitive, non-equivalence and disequilibrium is the very essence of grounding and causality. It is of the essence of causality to produce effects independent from and unforeseeable from the point of view of the cause.

Boutroux muses,

> Is it, then, in conformity with experience to admit of a proportionality, an equality, an absolute equivalence between cause and effect? No one regards this proportionality as constant if things are considered from the point of view of utility, of aesthetic and moral value, in a word, of quality.[60]

If an equivalency subsists between cause and effect, it can only ever be a quantitative equivalency of forces abstracted from their qualitative effects. It is not just that qualitative equivalence is never given as an empirical fact, that it is never 'in conformity with experience', but it is also that, on principle, one would never consciously enact a causal relationship if the effect, or consequent, provided nothing distinct from the cause. Just as exchanging a single one-dollar bill for another is useless,[61] so any causal interaction that produces no alternative qualities is empty transference.

Quality is always a novel consequence, which is to say that it is never dissolvable into the quantitative interaction of forces. Logical rule or logical space itself, for example, is but an instance of the accumulation of a quality not yet contained in chaos and thus a novelty unforeseeable in advance of its actual facticity. To repeat, there is thinking, including and primarily logical space, because there is being, but it is not the case that there is being because there is thinking. Boutroux, employing the term 'notion' instead of thinking, urges, 'It is impossible to affirm that, in addition to being, disciplined by notion, there does not remain a certain quantity of being, more or less ill-adapted to its ordaining influence . . .'[62] In this remark, which is eerily similar to Schelling's 'indivisible remainder [*der nie aufgehende Rest*]',[63] Boutroux maintains not only the priority of being over thinking but also the ultimately synthetical and transitive character of their relation. He explicitly states, 'The law of notion, then, is a synthetical proposition.'[64] Being and thinkability could have remained forever uncorrelated in the abysmal chaos of nothingness. Their transitive – read: temporal – synthesis is thus the original matter of fact. Every advent, every emergence of a novel and unforeseeable consequent, supplements the prior (1) with a novel or original quality, and (2) with its very identity as antecedent, ground or cause.

Quality and quantity

To affirm that quality supplements an antecedent without a sufficient and determining reason is, as the following chapter will show, to reject a certain reading of the ancient doctrine that 'like causes like', which is surely implicit in the more common dictum that 'like knows like'. Boutroux rejects this doctrine by repudiating any equivalency and similarity between cause and effect.

> It is generally admitted that great effects may result from small causes, and *vice versa* . . . Where are we to find a consequent which, as regards quality, is exactly identical with its antecedent? Would this also be a consequent, an effect, a change, if it differed from its antecedent neither in quantity nor in quality?[65]

To repeat, an antecedent only is an antecedent if it has a consequent and a consequent only is a consequent if it is more than a simple replication of – a quantitative equivalence of force in equal and opposite reaction to – the antecedent. Perfect replication does not indicate a perfect causal relationship but rather the very absence of a causal relationship, the very absence of synthetical relation. In other words, the law of identity is transitive, temporal and genetic rather than a law of equivalence or a law of conservation. This stance rejects not only a strict rendering of the ancient notion that like causes like but also the medieval or, more accurately, Neoplatonic notion that an effect can exceed the cause in neither being nor dignity. Boutroux permits both an increase and a decrease in being, but never equivalency.

Why, then, the belief in this ancient dictum? Whence the widespread conviction that causal relations can be sufficiently explicated by means of the quantitative equivalence of force? Boutroux conjectures, 'Hence, is it likely that the simple repetition of the same quality, a thing devoid of beauty and interest, exists nowhere in nature, and that homogeneous quantity is but the ideal surface of beings?'[66] As before, necessity – understood as a result of the conviction that things can be resolved into merely quantifiable properties – views things only from the outside, regarding only the surface of things. No matter how many times an object is cut, gutted, poked or prodded, one reaches only more surfaces. Alternatively, the inside of objects, their genesis and history, remains impenetrable or inviolable from the surface, from the outside. If one will permit a sensitive metaphor, approached from outside objects are impermeable or immune to rape because every penetration of surfaces only reveals more surfaces. Or, perhaps, it is precisely the reduction of nature it to its outside, to its superficiality, and the neglect of its inside, its genetic history, that one can name 'rape'. This reduction of things to the numerable bifurcates nature into that modern distinction between primary (mathematical) and secondary (qualitative) properties. The modern account of nature may, in effect, be nothing more than a violation of nature.

Boutroux's greatest gift to posterity is his insistence that the modern paradigm, its faulty division between primary and secondary properties and its concomitant adherence to the principle of the conservation of energy, be rejected. Against the ancients, one must recognise not only that like is capable of causing something unlike itself but that 'the like' first acquires its own identity or self-likeness only by virtue of the consequent that belatedly posits it as self-identical antecedence. Against the medievalists – or the Neoplatonism latent therein – one must admit that the causal chain does not entail the degradation of being but that the effect can also contain more being than the cause. Against the moderns, one must acknowledge that quantification is never primary but that all quantification is the quantification of a prior sphere of quality. Boutroux surmises, 'Whereas quality may very well be conceived as the substance of quantity, the latter, regarded as the substance of quality, is unintelligible; it acquires signification only as a limit . . . and all limit presupposes a thing that is limited.'[67] Causality, as a heterogeneous confrontation of quality against quality, never admits of the necessity that quantification deigns to provide.[68]

Rule and measure, in isolation from what is ruled and measured, dissipates as something ethereal. It is nothing in abstraction from unlimited quality. Rule and measure do more than describe a pre-given stretch of being in terms of number, but the proper ontological function of rule and measure is to limit, to erect boundaries around something, to make the very incisions between which a numerable quantity consists. Measure, if one has learned anything from Boutroux, must not remain abstract, but it can be reinterpreted as a positive ontological function, the function of πέρας, the task of which is to inscribe borders around ἄπειρον.

Boutroux, more empirically motivated and less 'metaphysical' than Schelling (who is the main focus of the following three chapters), is important for two reason, one critical and one constructive. Critically, he holds all forms of reductionism and their concomitant determinisms at bay. In this endeavour, he also extricates himself from the a priori in all its forms. Constructively, he demonstrates that all truths are synthetical in nature, positively preparing the terrain for an ontology that is free to suppose the contingency of necessity and that can genetically, which means historically, progress from the unbounded freedom of the absolute. In Boutroux one finds something like a de-rationalised and fully empiricised Meillassoux. If Meillassoux plays the role of counterfoil for this book, Boutroux provides the positive and constructive framework for an empirical ontology of contingency. It is still necessary, however, to first look at Schelling's historical method, which meets Boutroux's demand for an objective method.

The next chapter, with Boutrouxian principles in hand – (1) the critique of abstraction; (2) the aposteriority and synthetical nature of all truths; (3) the demand for an objective or genetic method; and (4) the affirmation of quality over quantity – contrasts Schelling's early reading of Plato's *Timaeus* with that of Proclus and Neoplatonism generally. It will be demonstrated that Schelling also affirms the primacy of quality over, or rather before, quantity; quantification is possible only if thinking has already advened upon, already supplemented, being. Although Schelling's interpretation of the *Timaeus* is greatly informed by Kant, he too, like Boutroux, departs from Kant by thinking the transcendental, the domain of epistemic conditions, only as being's consequent.[69]

Notes

1. Boutroux, *Contingency of the Laws*, p. 10.
2. Gabriel, *Transcendental Ontology*, p. 71.
3. See Hogrebe, *Prädikation und Genesis*.
4. Gabriel, *Transcendental Ontology*, p. 68.
5. This term would be roughly equivalent to what has been termed the epistemo-ontological question, which also asks about the conditions of identity or what makes a thing come to be as something. However, it is not clear that this question hews as closely to logical questions as Gabriel suggests, and it is less convincing that Gabriel's approach supplies an actual response to the question as to why there is something at all instead of nothing.
6. Boutroux, *Natural Law*, p. 29.
7. Gabriel, *Transcendental Ontology*, p. xxx.
8. Heidegger, *Metaphysical Foundations*, p. 106.
9. For a different account of the relationship (but perhaps one that still conflates logic and mathematics), a pair of commentators on Wittgenstein have asserted that there is 'a distinction between "describing methods of measurement" (logic) and "obtaining and stating results of measurement" (empirical enquiry). Thus the normative character of logic is not compromised, even though it . . . depends on the fact that we agree in making certain judgments' (Hodges and Lewis, *Thinking in the Ruins*, p. 39). Although this account claims that the normative character of logic is not threatened, it still suggests that logic's normativity relies on the arbitrary standards of mathematical measurement, reducing it to an empirical agreement among subjects. Even if logic's normativity somehow remains unscathed in this way, its apriority is certainly lost. Moreover, this makes logic prone to the same localisation as mathematics, since just as there can be more than one geometry depending upon the axioms with which one chooses to begin, so logic seems to lose any universality by being reduced to competing logics or to competing standards of quantification.
10. Boutroux, *Natural Law*, p. 209.
11. Ibid., p. 209.
12. Gabriel, 'Meaning of "Existence"', p. 83.
13. Boutroux, *Natural Law*, p. 209.
14. Ibid., p. 209.
15. Ibid., p. 47.
16. Boutroux, *Contingency of the Laws*, p. 44.
17. Ibid., p. 193.
18. Boutroux, *Natural Law*, p. 207.

19. Grant, *Philosophies of Nature*, p. 48.
20. Meillassoux, *After Finitude*, p. 22.
21. See Tritten, 'Against Kant'.
22. Meillassoux, *After Finitude*, p. 26.
23. Gabriel, 'Heidegger's "Turn"', p. 49.
24. Gabriel thus argues that transcendence, for contemporary realisms, can mean no more than the following: 'Transcendence depends on immanence; it is nothing but the failure of absolute theoretical closure. Transcendence is the very contingency of all ways in which the infinite withdraws in our efforts of grasping it. The infinite therefore depends on the finite' (Gabriel, *Transcendental Ontology*, p. 33). This is as misleading as it is helpful. The infinite depends on the finite only insofar as it is posited as transcendent to or as impossibly encapsulated by the immanence of the transcendental; however, the transcendental is, as it were, a domain of immanence hollowed out in the middle of the infinite by the infinite. Beginning from an outside not yet related to an inside, thus from an absolute outside or 'absolute outdoors', thus beginning from the infinite, everything appears as immanent and as productive of finitude.
25. Gabriel's name for epistemo-ontology is 'transcendental ontology', which '*investigates the ontological conditions of our conditions of access to what there is*' (Gabriel, *Transcendental Ontology*, p. ix).
26. Gabriel, *Transcendental Ontology*, p. 2.
27. Malabou, 'Can We Relinquish the Transcendental?', p. 243.
28. Meillassoux, *After Finitude*, p. 38.
29. There is a slight difference between the accounts of Malabou and Meillassoux. Malabou said that what Kant calls deduction is nothing more than description, while Meillassoux said that Kant himself claims only to describe and that it was Hegel who first tried to deduce the categories that make experience possible. It is preferable to grant the more charitable reading of Kant that views his own intentions as extending no further than describing the factical conditions of experience, which, while universal, are still not necessary, even if Kant does often seem to confuse necessity with universality. In any event, Slavoj Žižek's criticism of Kant is certainly misinformed.

> Kant, like a good compulsive neurotic . . . sets up the network of the conditions of possible experience in order to make sure that the actual experience of the real, the encounter with the thing, will never take place, so that everything the subject will effectively encounter will be the already gentrified-domesticated reality of representations . . . (Žižek, *Indivisible Remainder*, p. 75)

Whatever Kant's own stance actually was, he did not begin prior to the fact of experience, asking only how it could be possible rather than how it is actual and thus inadvertently insulating himself from the very thing whose possibility he was attempting to secure. On this reading, Kant would not only be neurotic but clinically mad. Rather, Kant begins with the fact of the experience of a thing and only subsequently describes what its conditions of possibility must have been. Whether, or in what sense, he views the conditions he provides as factical or as necessary is a question better left to Kant scholars.
30. Boutroux, *Contingency of the Laws*, p. vi.
31. Ejsing, *Theology*, p. 49.
32. Kant, *Critique of Pure Reason*, p. B656.
33. Boutroux, *Natural Law*, p. 12.
34. Ibid., p. 206.
35. Boutroux, *Contingency of the Laws*, p. 45.
36. See Peirce, 'The Logic of Continuity'.
37. Boutroux, *Natural Law*, p. 103.
38. Ibid., p. 102.

39. To view subsequent and higher stages as the mere appearance of the lower is, as Grant criticises, the Hegelianism by which 'the "ascending process of the phenomenon" (Goethe 1975: 396), eliminates time, or reduces it to the measure of organization . . .' (Grant, *Philosophies of Nature*, p. 132). Time thought as the capacity to bring about the novel, a future not already entailed by a past big with its future, is nullified by all such Hegelianisms.
40. Deleuze, *Logic of Sense*, p. 269.
41. Boutroux, *Natural Law*, p. 211.
42. A particularly fascinating aspect of Boutroux's philosophy is that it could be read as a way of treating Humean scepticism not as epistemological failure but rather as ontological affirmation. Whereas Hume seeks to assuage his scepticism psychologically by appealing to the custom or habit of the mind, Boutroux hints at an ontological employment of habit. (However, it should be mentioned that this is only a hint, and that at other times he too seems to regard habit only as a psychological form of inclination.) As a prime example of this, note: 'As regards causality, which, of itself, would never obtrude upon us, habit replaces the intuition lacking, makes association practically indissoluble, and so inclines us to look upon the laws of nature as really universal and necessary' (Boutroux, *Natural Law*, p. 17).
43. Boutroux, *Contingency of the Laws*, p. 166.
44. Ibid., p. 166.
45. Although they enter the scene only decades later, so-called process philosophers like Samuel Alexander and Alfred North Whitehead might also be added to this list. One commentator interjects, 'Whitehead, like James and Peirce before him, instead regards the so-called laws of nature to be descriptive of the widespread *habits* of nature' (Griffin, *Whitehead's Radically Different Postmodern Philosophy*, p. 63).
46. Boutroux, *Contingency of the Laws*, p. 108.
47. Ibid., p. 192.
48. Ibid., p. 168.
49. Ibid., p. 168.
50. Ibid., p. 169.
51. Ibid., p. 18.
52. Harman, *Quentin Meillassoux*, p. 165.
53. Boutroux, *Contingency of the Laws*, p. 19.
54. Ibid., p. 21.
55. Ibid., p. 31.
56. Ibid., p. 30.
57. This is akin to how Meillassoux insists, while discussing the facticity of the categories of the transcendental for Kant, 'Like Kantianism, strong correlationism insists upon the facticity of these forms, but differs from [Kantianism] by extending this facticity to logical form as well – which is to say, to the principle of non-contradiction' (Meillassoux, *After Finitude*, p. 39). Meillassoux assumes the law of non-contradiction as descriptive of Hyper-Chaos whereas this book has argued that it is preferable to elucidate the law of non-contradiction as something prescriptive, denying its prior governance in chaos where the principle of excluded middle does not yet hold.
58. Boutroux, *Natural Law*, p. 25.
59. This all differs from Meillassoux (1) insofar as this espouses the correlation of thinking and being only as consequent to a chaos first posited as antecedent by virtue of this consequent; (2) insofar as this does not presuppose the governance of the law of non-contradiction but it, along with the law of identity, does not hold in chaos because the principle of excluded middle does not hold in chaos; and (3) insofar as it does not posit the law of non-contradiction as a descriptive, that is, already operative, principle that forbids the existence of contradictions, but it rather thinks the law of non-contradiction as a prescriptive imperative that demands that contradiction cannot remain, not even virtual contradiction. In short, Meillassoux is a rationalist who has

already assumed the provenance of the laws of logic rather an empiricist who affirms them only as contingent and consequent matters of fact.
60. Boutroux, *Contingency of the Laws*, p. 28.
61. This is, of course, not true in the case of exchanging a crumpled one-dollar bill that the vending machine will not accept for a crisp and untattered one-dollar bill, but then the exchange is indeed qualitatively heterogeneous.
62. Boutroux, *Contingency of the Laws*, p. 39.
63. Schelling, 'Philosophische Untersuchungen', *SW I/7*, 360.
64. Boutroux, *Contingency of the Laws*, p. 40.
65. Ibid., p. 29.
66. Ibid., p. 29.
67. Ibid., p. 30.
68. Note also: 'Necessity can only consist in the quantitative relation of antecedent to consequent. Now, quantity can be conceived only as the measure of, and as subordinate to, quality . . .' (Boutroux, *Contingency of the Laws*, p. 156).
69. Daniel Whistler is thus too harsh when he speaks of Schelling's 'rejection of the post-Kantian search for grounds' (Whistler, *Schelling's Theory*, p. 83). Schelling retains the transcendental, but only as consequent. Whistler does rightly identify the defining characteristic of the transcendental, writing, 'A transcendental argument is one which discovers the universal and necessary conditions of experience. Its premise is that there are conditions of experience graspable in isolation from experience itself' (ibid., p. 83). He errs, however, in thinking that the conditions of possible experience further encapsulate the conditions of being itself; he errs in presupposing that the conditions for the possible experience of an object are the same as the conditions for the existence or being of an object. This error also leads him to this overstatement: 'In Schelling's universe, there is no such thing as the transcendental. There is nothing that is merely a condition of reality without in fact being that reality' (ibid., p. 83, n. 30). The transcendental certainly does not purport to harbour the conditions of reality; it articulates only the conditions of the experience or knowledge of reality, and these conditions are contained, as Whistler is right to emphasise, in reality itself. Yet this does not entail a denial of the transcendental but only an 'inverted transcendentalism', which affirms the transcendental only as consequent. See Tritten, 'After Contingency'. Undoubtedly, Whistler's response to this criticism would be more than brilliant.

Chapter 3

On the Primacy of Matter: Neoplatonism Right-Side Up

In 1830,[1] a few decades prior to Boutroux and on the precipice of his own positive philosophy of mythology and revelation, Schelling[2] bemoans that negative philosophies are those that begin only with something artificial, with something abstract,[3] adding that philosophy has suffered under the negativity of the abstract or the purely logical since Descartes.[4] Schelling's primary whipping boy, however, is not Descartes but Hegel. Hegel, he claims, can know no other movement than the 'refilling [*Wiedererfülltwerden*]'[5] of an empty abstraction, which, of course, would require no refilling had it not already been artificially emptied of content and transformed into an abstract formalism in the first place. Moreover, if the abstraction by which something was stripped of its content was artificial, then so is the 'movement' that refills it, a process that thus occurs only for thought and by thought. An abstract concept bears not only no necessity but not even the possibility of self-movement; it is only the abstract thinker who sees in this the requirement that empty form provide its own content. This constitutes the kernel of Schelling's critique of modern philosophy generally and Hegel in particular. This interpretation of Schelling then runs counter to that of Walter Schulz who argued that Schelling, far from posing an alternative to modern philosophy, did not even surpass German Idealism but was rather the culmination of this tradition insofar as Schelling purportedly espoused a philosophical system in which form generates its own content.[6] This chapter will show, however, that Schelling did quite the opposite. Schelling showed that it is rather content that precedes form, or that content stands in need of form and order. If Schulz was correct to identify the basic problem of German Idealism with self-determination as a dialectic between form and content,[7] then he was wrong to associate Schelling with this tradition, insofar as Schelling, both in his early essay on Plato's *Timaeus* and in his mature philosophy, affirms a reality in need of form and never a form capable of generating its own matter. This opening chapter on Schelling, then, will show how he systematically exhibited the insights that have been gleaned from Boutroux's critique of abstractionism and the relationship between quality and quantity, matter and form, the unregulated/lawless and rule/order – although it would be prudent to mention that Boutroux was probably influenced by Schelling and not Schelling by Boutroux.

In particular, this chapter contrasts the so-called emanationism of Neoplatonism, particularly Proclus', with Schelling's naturephilosophy,[8] which is here intended to designate more than the earliest period of this thought but rather something that is central to his thought in all its periods. The contention is that Schelling's philosophy, from early to late, stands Neoplatonism on its head by inverting its order of procession. Schelling agrees with Neoplatonism that matter is the lowest and most inferior of the hypostases – not even constituting a proper hypostasis itself because incapable of self-reversion – but he differs from Neoplatonism by viewing matter as cosmologically prior to Intellect, Soul, the demiurge and the like. The question does not concern the hierarchical but the ontological ordering of matter. For Schelling, procession is not a descent into being (and eventually non-being) from a One beyond being, but an elevation (*Steigerung*), intensification and potentiation of being, which precludes the need for return (ἐπιστροφή). This, in fact, is the trademark of Schelling's late distinction between positive and negative philosophy. Positive philosophy is progressive, beginning with the inferior as the most original in order to ascend to the superior through a consequent intensification of being, while negative philosophy is regressive, beginning with the inferior only as something already derived in order regressively to retrace its descent back up to the superior One. Being, for Schelling, however, is not constituted as an eternal circle but as the irretrievable temporality of the line, because no level of reality reverts upon itself without remainder. In order to elucidate how Schelling's early inversion of Neoplatonism forged his later distinction between positive and negative philosophy, this chapter begins with his reading of the role of 'matter'[9] in Plato's *Timaeus* and then offers an experimental reading of Proclus' *Elements of Theology*. The ultimate upshot of the chapter, however, with respect to the central thesis of this book, is that the groundwork for an ontology of contingent necessity, namely contingent reason and a contingent God, will finally be laid in its entirety.

Schelling's early reading of the *Timaeus*

Schelling's essay on the *Timaeus* was published in 1795 when he was nineteen, but this does not mean that it was uninfluential for his mature thought. This precocious teenager here translates the language of the intelligible/determinate and the sensible/indeterminate in the *Timaeus* into the Kantian language of the form of the understanding and the matter of sensibility, only to read the *Timaeus* against transcendental philosophy in a way prescient of his later thought.[10] A few authors have already shown how Schelling's early reading of the *Timaeus* is indispensable for the relation between *Grund* and *Existenz*, unprethinkable matter and intelligible form, in the 1809 *Freiheitsschrift* and beyond.[11] Werner Beierwaltes, for example, has argued that in the *Timaeus* essay Schelling wanted to show that physics, namely matter, generates the ideal, namely the transcendental, writing that (especially in Schelling's later thought) 'transcendental philosophy and naturephilosophy [*Naturphilosophie*] basically represent *one* science'.[12] Schelling reads Plato as a physicist or naturephilosopher who places matter, namely the unruly receptacle or the χώρα, as prior to order and form, prior to the intelligible and transcendental.

Schelling notes, in accord with the *Timaeus* itself, that

> the elements, insofar as they are *visible*, are to be wholly differentiated from the matter in which they are grounded and which as such never becomes visible, and that they are not properly *matter* itself, but rather *forms, determinations* of matter, which matter obtains externally.[13]

This begs the question concerning what the elements were prior to becoming visible by means of 'forms' or 'determinations' externally imprinted on matter. What stands outside of question for Schelling, at any rate, is that 'matter', so-called, is something for itself, apart from its relation to that which 'externally' imprints form and determination upon it; matter is not reducible to its empirical products. Schelling names this being-in-itself of matter 'ἀόριστον τί',[14] which he later terms, in a more Pythagorean fashion, simply '*Duas*' and 'the ambivalent Nature (*natura anceps*)'.[15] Matter may be considered in two distinct ways, as an empirical substrate/ὑποκείμενον or as potency/δύναμις.[16] As Plato writes in the *Sophist*, 'I hold that the definition of being is simply power [δύναμις].'[17] Dynamically considered, namely in terms of power/potency, matter only has being as ἄπειρον. Schelling proclaims, in opposition to canonical readings of Neoplatonism, that for Plato, matter, thought as ἄπειρον and as δύναμις, is not the last emanation from the One, but it is, despite its lack of self-sufficiency or inability to revert upon itself, the first procession from the One (albeit still the lowest in rank) insofar as it is to become the substance of the cosmos. Said differently, insofar as everything can be predicated only of substance, as Aristotle suggests, so the substance of the world is nothing but ἄπειρον; all that exists is ἄπειρον or quantitative determinations of ἄπειρον. Schelling remarks that 'all reality is ἄπειρον τι'. Everything emerges 'from out of the ἄπειρον and, according to its form, from out of the πέρας'.[18] Both of these, in turn, the unlimited and the limited or the indeterminate and the determinate, are bound together by the activity of the demiurge.[19]

Schelling does not read Plato according to the canon that suggests that because intelligible form, the definite and ruly, is superior to matter it is also ontologically prior to matter, the indefinite and unruly. This would be as if an attribute could bring about its own substance, that of which it is predicated. Schelling rather states that the demiurge 'saw these [form (πέρας) and matter (ἄπειρον)] (regularity and unruliness) as two things constantly striving against one another' and thus concludes that 'at this point the pre-existing original matter of the world is presupposed'.[20] Thought in terms of Neoplatonic procession, matter, as the indefinite and unruly, does not stand at the end as the final emanation. Matter is only last in terms of superiority, but it is ontologically more originary than rule, order and form.[21]

Beierwaltes explicates that, in his translation of Plato into Kantian terms, 'Schelling translates πέρας-ἄπειρον with "Grenze und Uneingeschränktes" (Limit and Unrestricted) and with "Regelhaftigkeit und Regellosigkeit" (Regularity and Irregularity)'[22] or, better, as the ruly/intelligible and the unruly/unintelligible. Their relation is such that the ἄπειρον/Indefinite/Unruly/Irregular constitutes the substantiality of πέρας/Limit/Ruliness/Regularity;[23] the latter is merely attributed. The former is the presupposed, ungenerated *subjectum*. Schelling here anticipates a possible criticism of his reading of Plato's *Timaeus*. What if, as a good Neoplatonist is quick to point out, ἄπειρον and πέρας are co-originary and mutually determinative? For in Neoplatonic thought, procession from the One, at least unto the point of the sensible reality of the cosmos and the concomitant emergence of time/becoming, is not to be thought as a temporal succession but as eternal procession. Matter, for example, would not be there before Intellect, but they are both eternal processions from the One. To this, Schelling offers the following rebuke:

> that the ἄπειρον first emerges through the communication of the πέρας. Fine! If what is at issue here is *empirical* existence, then in that case both are only present in their being bound together. However, Plato speaks of ἄπειρον to the extent that it is separated from πέρας and says . . . that the imitations of that which is most beautiful and most glorious, that is, the ideas, must also be found in the ἄπειρον as such.[24]

Plato, Schelling proclaims, speaks of ἄπειρον or matter in a way that Aristotle could never permit, namely as separate from form and determination, as χωριστόν. It is probable that most Neoplatonists, as most scholars readily admit, are not actually thoroughbred Platonists, but are heavily influenced by Aristotle's reading of Plato. At any rate, says Schelling, ἄπειρον, the matter of matter, cannot be consequent, not even eternally consequent, from the Ideas, from the realm of pure Intellect, because indefinite matter subsists even there. This too, namely the existence of intelligible matter, is something most Neoplatonists would readily admit, though perhaps not in these terms.[25] More scandalous, however, is that Schelling regards the matter of matter, which is also called χώρα, as an Idea itself. Or, to repeat, 'the ideas must also be found in the ἄπειρον as such'.

Aside from Kant, the other largest influence on Schelling's early reading of the *Timaeus* is his reading of the *Philebus*, in which one finds a discussion of all four kinds (γένη). Of this connection Grant writes,

> The Platonic gene: it is a phase space of the Idea in unlimited not-being, that is, the always-becoming, in which the Idea acts as the limit-attractor towards which becoming never ceases to become, the *auto* or absolute approximated but never realised in the generated particular.[26]

The ἄπειρον, as one of Plato's kinds, contains the Idea; the Idea exists within this kind as the attracted limit for the 'always-becoming'. The ἄπειρον, in turn, is the attractor of limit, of πέρας. As one of the causes of becoming, but yet not something that has itself become, ἄπειρον can be called an Idea or, better, a generator/attractor of the Idea, the determinate.[27] Schelling writes of these kinds, and particularly of that dark Idea or dark kind, ἄπειρον, generically called matter because it grants things their substantiality,

> One thus sees clearly the extent to which Plato is speaking of intelligible archetypes of every individual object, namely, not insofar as he believed that every individual object has its particular *individual* archetype, but rather insofar as each individual object stands under the universal form of all existence.[28]

In this intriguing passage Schelling explicitly associates the indefinite kind, dark and unruly matter, despite its indefiniteness or 'materiality', as an 'intelligible archetype', normally termed Idea. In what sense, then, the unruly and indeterminate is intelligible is clear. It is intelligible because it is a limit-attractor; it attracts definiteness and intelligibility to itself. It is to be called an archetype because it is a 'universal form of all existence'. Nothing exists that is not ἄπειρον; the Indefinite itself constitutes the substantiality of all that is. In this context Sallis writes, 'Schelling insistently reinscribes its [the receptacle's] name as *substance*, *substratum*, and especially *matter*.'[29] If something like this can be called an Idea even though it can never serve as an archetype for any particular individual whatsoever, then what does this mean for the so-called theory of participation and the corresponding doctrine of the Ideas? Schelling takes Plato to mean that there are, in fact, only four Ideas, the four kinds – γένη – which alone are universal forms operative in all existence and which are, accordingly, not models for participatory copies but genes, generators of all reality, including intelligible reality.[30] Matter or ἄπειρον, as the first of the kinds which must always be presupposed as that which attracts limit, order and intelligibility to itself, proceeds from no prior hypostasis. It is assumed as one of the four generators for all levels of reality. Grant is therefore able to state, 'Whatever therefore *appears* or *bodies forth* in nature is necessarily not an image of its original.'[31] Neither Plato nor Schelling divorces model and copies, form and matter. The two-world theory is wrong because matter is not antithetical to the intelligible; it is an attractor of intelligible form. Here, again, does the motif of epistemo-genesis or epistemo-ontology arise, namely the affirmation of intelligibility, of epistemic conditions, only as something consequent.[32] The Neoplatonist Proclus too agrees that matter is not antithetical to the higher, intelligible levels of reality and even the One itself, sarcastically commenting, 'The unlimitedness and measurelessness of matter must consist of the need for measure and limit. But how could the need for limit and measure be the contrary of limit and measure?'[33]

The Indefinite or Unlimited, as one of the four kinds, is an archetype and it is intelligible; it contains the Idea within itself – recall that 'the ideas must also be found in the ἄπειρον as such'[34] – insofar as ἄπειρον attracts πέρας to itself. It is the presupposition of limit and not vice versa, just as matter is the presupposition of intelligibility. Limit, however, does not act upon the Unlimited as something inert (unlike the matter of the modern period, which is utterly inert because completely de-potentiated as nothing more than the merely geometric matrix of extension). As Schelling comments,

> Now, insofar as the *form* that God imparted to the world refers only to the form of the movement of the world, the world must also have had its own *original* principle of motion, independently of God, which, as a principle that inheres in matter, contradicts all regularity and lawfulness, and is first brought within the bounds of lawfulness through the form (πέρας) that the divine understanding gave to it.[35]

The Indefinite, in Schelling, is to be equated with the unruly and so it is neither an inert substrate nor even a pre-partitioned grid. It is irregular motion but motion all the same. Form, the definite and intelligible, is static, but matter is δύναμις, a dynamism. 'The understanding (namely, the form of understanding) came to *dominate* over *blind* necessity'[36] – the not yet intelligible motion of the apeiratic – 'precisely because the pure form of the understanding is unchangeable and cannot take its direction from matter, but rather, on the contrary, matter makes itself subservient.'[37] Putting aside the Kantian rhetoric – which is quite obstructive in this passage – one can see that matter, which has a principle of motion within itself, only makes itself subservient to form by coming to a standstill for thought. This is how it attracts limit to itself; this is how it becomes intelligible. The domain of becoming comes to be by arresting rather than by initiating movement. The motion of becoming/time is, as it were, already provided through the substantiality or matter of that which becomes. It was rather stability that had to be added in order for becoming/time to come to be. The originary motion, that which is always presupposed, is the unceasing motion of matter itself – as Boutroux similarly argued – as the substrate and attractor of the formal and intelligible. Schelling does, however, at least reaffirm the Neoplatonic stance that intelligibility is superior to materiality, even if he rejects that intelligibility is more original. In so doing he also shatters any notion of matter as the Aristotelian idea of a merely logical substrate, which bears no powers, no δύναμις, except the passive potency of receptivity to predication.

A break with Neoplatonism?

Under Schelling's (Kantian) interpretation, Plato provides a physics of the transcendental; he provides the transcendental with its substance. There is a materiality even of the formal. While Neoplatonists have admittedly already spoken of an intelligible matter, nevertheless, when Plotinus, for example, thinks of matter as mere non-being and hence mere privation, his Platonist side has become dominated by Aristotle. In this vein, Grant has convincingly argued that Aristotle's philosophy brought about for later antiquity a 'desubstantialization of *ousia*'.[38] He argues that in Aristotle 'matter loses all substantial existence' by means of

> its reduction to logic, to a purely extensional *logos* . . . Aristotelian metaphysics is that science concerned with substance not insofar as this is particular, sensible or material, but insofar as it is a *predicable essence*, i.e. only insofar as it is the subject or *hypokeimenon* supporting a *logos*.[39]

For this reason, Aristotelian matter, which thought in itself is unlimited, cannot exist apart from a limiting form. Matter, in Aristotle, does not signify any sort of ontological or cosmological reality, a substantial reality, but only an indeterminate X as the logical subject of predication. Consequently, one finds Aristotle recoiling at the idea of attributing any sort of substantiality, any sort of ability to exist apart as χωριστόν, to matter in the *Metaphysics*. Immediately after seemingly granting to matter some substantiality, he recants: 'But this is impossible; for it is accepted that separability and individuality belong especially to substance. Hence it would seem that the form and the combination of form and matter are more truly substance than matter is.'[40] Ironically, it may be that Plato's insistence, at least upon the readings of Schelling and Grant, that matter can, in fact, exist apart is the very thing that saves Plato from a two-world dualism because, by this means, Plato is able to retain an ontological rather than merely logical status of matter. This matter is neither a logical nor inert substrate, but it bears a principle of (chaotic) motion within itself, which means that it is a principle. As Grant remarks, 'Platonic physics concerns the emergence of order from disorderly and unceasing motion, which creates a post-Aristotelian conception of Platonism: no longer a formal or moralising two-worlds metaphysics, but a one-world physics.'[41] Should one find this narrative plausible, then one cannot exclude that Neoplatonism, arguably as influenced by Aristotle as by Plato, has in part developed under Aristotle's misrepresentation of the role of matter, so-called, in Plato. In this vein, one finds Schelling lamenting that Plotinus, though a 'profound spirit, had already given up the Platonic pre-existence of a lawless entity striving against order, and adopted a certain viewpoint according to which it is assumed that all has begun from the most pure and perfect'.[42] One wonders whether Neoplatonism, in relegating matter to the most inferior, has also removed its ontological status as something pre-existent and thereby fashioned it as the most derivative, as last in the procession from the One rather than as a wet nurse even to the One. To approach this question, one must turn to Proclus and not Plotinus; for Proclus levels a criticism against Plotinus' account of matter and thereby attempts to restore, at least somewhat, the dignity of matter. Matter, for Proclus, is not evil and so, perhaps, it is also not degraded to nothing more than the last station on the descent from the One.

There are many reasons to suggest that Proclus recognised, the One aside, that matter is pre-existent to every hypostasis. He details in his own commentary on Plato's *Timaeus* and in obvious opposition to the more Aristotelian Porphyry and strikingly even Iamblichus, with whom he shares more affinities, that 'those around [those who side with] Porphyry and Iamblichus castigate this position on the grounds that it puts the disordered before the ordered, the incomplete before the complete and the unintelligent before the intelligent in the universe'.[43] That one does not find the term 'matter' in this passage has to do with the fact that Proclus is much more careful than Schelling to hold matter as such as something elemental, as a stuff and substrate, apart from the 'matter of matter', the substantiality of the substrate as the Indefinite or Unlimited, ἄπειρον.[44] This legitimate refusal to equate the two can be seen in the following lengthy passage of Proclus:

> [Plato] placed first unlimitedness, the [unlimitedness] which is prior to the mixed, at the summit of the Intelligibles and extends its irradiation from that point (*ekeithen*) all the way to the lowest [reaches of being]. And so, according to [Plato], matter proceeds both from the One and from the Unlimitedness which is prior to One Being, and, if you wish, inasmuch as it is potential being, from One Being too ... And [it is] devoid of form, on which account [it is] these prior to the Forms and their manifestation ... For just as Plato derived (*paragein*) two causes, Limit and Unlimitedness, from the One, so also did the Theologian bring Aether and Chaos into existence from Time, Aether as the cause of limit wherever it is found, and Chaos [as the cause] of unlimitedness. And from these two principles he generates both the divine and the visible orders.[45]

First, Proclus situates the Unlimited at the 'summit' of the Intelligibles and traces its influence from there down to the lower, more derivative levels of reality. Accordingly, the Unlimited cannot itself be the lowest procession, because its effect takes hold already at the level of intelligible reality and extends its influence from there down. Second, matter, here called by name explicitly and not just in terms of the Unlimited, 'proceeds from the One'. Matter is not last in the procession from the One, but it is an immediate procession from the One that does not first pass through the Intelligible, Soul and so forth. Third, matter proceeds 'from the Unlimitedness which is prior to One Being ... and from One Being too'. Here one sees how Proclus is careful to distinguish matter proper from its own substantiality, namely that from which it has proceeded: Unlimitedness, ἄπειρον. Moreover, he tantalisingly suggests that this matter of matter, Unlimitedness, is even prior to One Being, though he is careful to add that it proceeds from One Being too. What is not up for debate is that Unlimitedness (and Limit) is an immediate procession from the One and not a later, mediated procession. It could not be otherwise for it to retain its status as an originary kind. For the kinds are generators of intelligible Forms, and Proclus, too, asserts that the Unlimited is both 'prior to the Forms and their manifestation'. It is thus not just a condition of the appearance or manifestation of Forms in the sensible cosmos, but it is prior to Forms as such. Cosmologically considered, Limit and Unlimitedness are to be equated with 'Aether and Chaos', with the elemental substrate and its apeiratic substantiality. As a final word, Proclus notes that from these two kinds 'both the divine and the visible orders' are generated.

In addition to the lengthy passage just cited, one also finds Proclus asserting that the demiurge only 'took over' matter,[46] minimally ascribing to matter a pre-existence with regards to the sensible cosmos as such, and that

> the Paradigm takes over matter from the Good and informs it – for the forms *qua* forms are offspring of the Paradigm – and the demiurgic [cause], receiving the Forms from the Paradigm, regulates (*diakosmein*) them by means of numbers and imposes order upon them by means of proportions (*logoi*).[47]

Matter is thus explicitly stated to be pre-existent to the Forms and affirmed to be a procession ensuing immediately from the Good, itself the presupposition of all lower levels of reality, where lower is here understood not in terms of inferiority but in terms of ontological ordering.

Despite the evidence garnered from these passages, one probably still feels compelled to follow the more canonical reading of Proclus which allows him to fit more neatly into the Neoplatonic corpus as a whole. Neoplatonist and Procline scholar Radek Chlup preserves the canon here, informing his readers that 'most ancient Platonists were convinced that the image [of a primordial disorder] is not to be taken literally'.[48] According to the canon – and it is not the task here to rewrite the canon but merely to make plausible an alternative reading – Proclus, though he has a more positive account of matter than Plotinus, only regards matter as a passive rather than active potency, an end and not a beginning – which is to say that matter is not a principle that has its own motion, however chaotic it may be, within itself. Matter may not be mere privation, as it was for Plotinus (and also for St Augustine) but, unlike in Schelling, it cannot positively begin anything. Perhaps Chlup is correct and one is to take very little in the Neoplatonists, who were so fond of allegorical interpretations, literally.[49] Proclus himself will often speak of these issues in almost mythical fashion, or as if on a par with mere myth and allegory. He writes,

> in giving existence to the discordant and unordered ahead of the production of the cosmos [Plato] is copying the theologians. For just as they introduce wars and uprisings of the Titans against the Olympians, so too does Plato assume two starting-points, namely the unorganized (*akosmos*) and that which produces organization (*kosmopoios*).[50]

Whether his words are to be taken literally or figuratively, it should not be surprising that Proclus, arguably the most Platonist and least Aristotelian of the Neoplatonists, was the one to criticise the deflationary account of matter provided by Plotinus. This should also not be surprising if one finds any merit in the thesis that the true follower of Plato will accord to matter a genuine ontological status instead of relegating it to the shadows of non-being as Aristotle's merely logical presupposition. Whether Proclus truly adopted matter or the Unlimited as an unruly and, hence, ever-moving and actively dynamic (δύναμις) principle at the origin of things, or whether he relegated it to a mere passive potency as the final procession emptied of all being cannot here be decided. The attempt here is rather to offer an experimental reading of Proclus' *Elements of Theology*, altering one of his presuppositions in accordance with Schelling's reading of the *Timaeus* in order to see what might follow as a consequence for the rest of the propositions of the *Elements of Theology*. Finally, it must be asked if this bastard reading corresponds to what we find in the later Schelling. Did Schelling, in fact, develop his later thought as an outgrowth of reading Plato's *Timaeus* in the nineteenth year of his life?

An experimental reading of Proclus' *Elements of Theology*

If matter is the most incomplete, imperfect, discordant and inferior – concerning which Schelling and the Neoplatonists are in agreement – then should one assert that matter lies at the basis of everything, so the complete, perfect, ordered and superior could only be consequent, even if eternally so, and not original? If one begins with matter as the only cosmological pre-existent and progresses towards the more perfect and ordered, then one is denying the medieval doctrine that the effect cannot contain more being and dignity than the cause and also the ancient doctrine that like causes like insofar as order would be consequent upon a disorder which it is in no way like. This is precisely the proposition (#7) to be axiomatically denied in Proclus' *Elements of Theology*, which states, '*Every productive cause is superior to that which it produces.*'[51] Any further alterations of propositions in this experimental reading will ensue as a result of this first amendment. Substituting Proclus' premise with a more Schellingian one, one will be led to regard the procession of being as a possible gradation (*Steigerung*) of higher and higher levels of superiority and not as a descent according to which being is gradually lost until one hits rock bottom in the non-being of utterly inferior and derivative matter.

Now, proposition 8 reads as a direct consequence of proposition 7. '*All that in any way participates the Good is subordinate to the primal Good which is nothing else but good.*'[52] Proclus offers as an implication that 'all appetite implies a lack of, and a severance from, the object craved . . .'[53] How is this not the exact implication that causes Plotinus to regard evil as a mere privation, arguably the presupposition at the heart of Western metaphysics? Desire/appetite is, in this way, thought completely in terms of lack, apophatically rather than cataphatically. Desire or appetite thus has no being of its own but is only culled by the absent object, 'the object craved'. Desire is a consequence of having departed from the Good which can satisfy it, which raises Nietzsche's question: Why did the Good ever leave itself?[54] As one possible response, let the term 'Good' be reserved only for the One in return or ἐπιστροφή; for, only in return is the One desired as the missing object of desire. Procession, however, according to Neoplatonic thought, does not occur because of a missing or absent good, but on account of the effusiveness of the One (even if this effusiveness is still conceived in terms of apophatic theology as the negation of all inferior forms of being). By reserving the term 'Good' for the One only as the object reverted to in ἐπιστροφή, proposition 13 follows all the more tightly.

Proposition 13 reads: '*Every good tends to unify what participates it; and all unification is a good; and the Good is identical with the One.*'[55] Procession is a departure from the One or, as it were, diffusion, whereas the unity of all things is only constituted through their reversion to the One. The One only exerts a unifying operation and is thus only the Good proper in return or reversion, because 'all unification is a good' and because 'the Good is identical with the One' insofar as it is unity-bestowing. Proclus comments,

> For if it belongs to the good to conserve all that exists (and it is for no other reason that all things desire it); and if likewise that which conserves and holds together the being of each several thing is unity (since by unity each is maintained in being, but by dispersion displaced from existence): then the Good, wherever it is present, makes the participant one, and holds its being together in virtue of this unification.[56]

The Good is only good insofar as it is one-making or limit-giving. This means that the One is only to be called Good in return, not as the First but as the Last, not as the Origin but as Consequent. For this reason Aristotle's God, which Proclus criticises for its impotency to act as principle and begin any process, acting instead only as the end of movement, is to be called good only insofar as it is an end and not an origin, a culmination and achievement of unity and not a generator of difference. Like Aristotle's God, which is a perfectly self-enclosed circle or self-desiring desire that ensures that the object of desire is never absent, goodness is only intrinsic to that which can revert upon itself, to that which is self-sufficient by means of self-knowledge or self-reversion. This is why matter, for Plotinus, is at the end of the day still probably thought as a deficiency of goodness, a mere privation of the Good, that last procession in which all goodness has finally been dissipated, which is to be seen in the fact that it is essentially discordant, unable ever again to become one with itself. (It is, of course, always capable of receiving oneness or determination insofar as it is a one-attractor.) Proclus, for all his criticisms of Plotinus, thus far falls in line with Plotinus, viewing the Good as one-bestowing and desire as motivated by a lack of goodness, namely a deficiency or privation of oneness, insofar as Proclus too denies that matter can self-revert and acquire self-sufficiency.

Chlup notes in this context, 'The emanation can only stop at a level that is no longer capable of self-reversion.'[57] This level is, of course, the material world; thus only in matter has the One proved itself as effusive and perfect, albeit still not self-sufficient. The One, as effusive, is not self-sufficient because it is self-overflowing; it cannot suffice with itself. It ends not in sufficiency but in excess. Prior to matter – the excess of the One – has the One actually proved itself to be effusive? In other words, is the One effusive prior to the procession of matter? If not, then matter would not just be permitted but it would be required for the One to be identified as the effusive Good to which things ought to return, and thus matter, as Proclus wishes to affirm, could not be evil as such or even the source of evil. Matter is rather the posterior condition of the Good as the posterior proof of the One's effusiveness, its inability perfectly to revert upon itself. Matter itself would then not so much participate in the Good – which it clearly does not do insofar as, as the receptacle of limit, it lacks oneness and identity in itself – but it would consequently, that is, *post factum*, establish the One's effusiveness and thereby generate the need to return in order that things may become one and hence good. It would be the consequent condition of the One as the Good, as the absent object that bestows unity on that which has been disseminated. Only that capable of reversion is capable of oneness.

Now, in proposition 24, Proclus brings the discussion to its decisive juncture. He writes, '*All that participates is inferior to the participated, and this latter to the unparticipated.*'[58] Given this study's methodological rejection of proposition 7 and the insight that the consequent overflow of the One, matter, operates as that artifice by which the One proves itself to be more than One, more than itself or effusive, namely the effusive Good, so too must this proposition be denied. According to the experimental or even bastard reading offered here, this proposition must be rejected because the One too has acquired something extra, a supplement, namely its goodness, through its consequent: matter. The Good is only good because it is extra-one or more than one. The Good is good because it bestows oneness on the participating and reverting even though it itself, in the production of matter, surpasses oneness. It produces an extra, a supplement to the One.

The Good, consequently constituted through matter, which thus proves the One's effusiveness and generates the need for reversion, is accordingly superior to the One prior to the emanation of matter, superior to the One in its pre-processual or pre-lapsarian state. There is something more in the One as consequent, that is, as Good, as object of desire, than it had as pre-processual antecedent. What is to be affirmed in its entirety, at any rate, even if in a sense foreign to Proclus' own intentions, is proposition 26, which states, '*Every productive cause produces the next and all subsequent principles while itself remaining steadfast.*'[59] The suggestion of this experimental reading is to read μονή along the lines of Schelling's idea of 'the never presencing remainder'.[60] This too affirms that the cause or, stated in a more deflationary manner, the antecedent is never dissipated in its consequent, but rather heightened and greatened! The antecedent, the One, is now not just the One that begins a motion (procession) – a first cause simply – but also an end and object of desire, also the Good.

Proclus states in proposition 32, '*All reversion is accomplished through a likeness of the reverting terms to the goal of reversion.*'[61] Sense can no longer be made of this proposition, as the consequences of this bastard reading of the *Elements of Theology* has made the One to differ from itself in its pre-processual state, as it is only Good in a post-lapsarian sense as the object of return. In other words, it is now unlike itself as it was prior to the act of procession (even if such a pre-processual state is simply a moment for thought and nothing actual). There is thus a denial that like causes like precisely because there is also a denial that there cannot be more in the consequent than in the antecedent. The One as consequent has become unlike itself as antecedent by becoming superior to itself as antecedent, by becoming the Good, a bestower rather than diffuser of unity. This marks the break with the traditional understanding of the theory of participation. The One as antecedent, although it indivisibly remains (μονή), although it is not assumed and encapsulated by its consequent, is nevertheless altered by a change that occurs 'outside' it, the ex-cretion of matter. It is not a change in the One itself that alters it, but it is a change that occurs outside the One that alters it. This is the consequence of thinking the Good and desire for the Good in positive terms rather than as negativity, rather than as mere privation; the One now works to heighten and elevate itself to more superior domains, the domain of the Good. Neoplatonism operates from the top down while Schelling works from the bottom up. The former approach affirms that causes are superior to their effects – which always leaves one wondering why it should leave itself or eventuate in any effects at all (the notion of the effusiveness of the One aside)[62] – while the latter posits that causes are inferior to their effects. According to the latter option every creation is a heightening and intensification of being and not a diffusion and descent unto the inert non-being that is matter. On the former account, considered from the perspective of the One itself, there would be no need for reversion; reversion would leave the One as is. Reversion would be, so to speak, no good for the One on the traditional Neoplatonist reading. The latter Schellingian reading, however, recognises this and therefore drops the cyclical character of reversion altogether in order to think through the basic implication of linearity: historicality. This Schellingian reading suggests that a cause is only a cause if it brings about a consequent that is independent or no longer participatory precisely insofar as the effect inversely posits the cause as antecedent. As Proclus has stated, 'God brings all unlimitedness into existence, he also brings matter, which is ultimate unlimitedness, into existence. And this is the very first and ineffable cause of matter.'[63] Could this not be read as saying that God brings the Unlimited into existence as matter, as substrate and antecedent, and that God brings Limit into existence as consequent? In this respect, one can affirm both the historical nature of creation, that is, the division of times into before and after, antecedent and consequent, while still affirming the eternal nature of procession. Things proceed from the One always with an as-character. Matter or the Unlimited proceeds always as antecedent and pre-condition, always as past and *subjectum*, and Limit always as future consequent; for, a consequent can only be the consequent of a 'prior' antecedent. This historical process would not occur 'in' time because the positing of the Unlimited as antecedent/past and Limit as consequent/future is the very positing of the order of time itself. Time itself cannot be posited 'in' time just as Becoming cannot itself become, but time is timelessly or eternally posited. There is nevertheless a veritable prior and posterior, and not the Neoplatonist circle of simultaneity/eternity in which everything happens in one stroke. This reading, in concurrence with Proclus and Neoplatonism in general – although perhaps particularly in line with Damascius – preserves the ineffability of the One, because the effect, as no longer resembling or being like the cause, discloses nothing about the cause. (This is also how Aquinas departs from Neoplatonism and the doctrine of participation, requiring that God's causing be nonunivocal.) The effect is now no longer a mere predicate or attribute of the cause as fully participatory in it, but the effect is only an effect at all because of its independence from, its lack of participation in, the antecedent cause. This is precisely how it inversely posits the antecedent as antecedent rather than as simultaneous with itself as an eternal source of presence and participation. The antecedent, matter construed as a principle rather than just as a logical substrate of predication, is not/nought; it retains a relative non-being because, in not passing over into its effect, it remains distinct from that of which it is the principle, namely distinct from that which is. Accordingly, the antecedent is not self-predicating, not a pre-given subject that clothes itself with predicates, but self-constructing. The antecedent only is the antecedent, the same (το αὐτό) that it is, by means of that which becomes outside of it, the independence of the effect from the cause. Non-univocal or heterogeneous causing, in denying that like causes like, rejects that the effect remains in or participates in the cause, but it accepts that the cause remains in itself, never subsumed into the effect, its consequent become independent. Causality is thus not participation and unification, but independence, rupture and differentiation! Contra Neoplatonism, to be an effect is to be independent from the cause and to be a cause, as Proclus would want of the One, is thus to be unparticipated, an indivisible remainder. There is, in short, a transitive breach between cause and effect, antecedent and consequent, past and future, which spells the end of participation and reversion.

This bastard reading, then, also denies proposition 35: '*Every effect remains in its cause, proceeds from it, and reverts upon it.*'[64] It does, however, wholeheartedly agree with proposition 75: '*Every cause properly so called transcends its resultant.*'[65] Effects cannot encapsulate or exhaust their cause, not because they are always less than their cause but because they are more than and independent from their cause, which is inversely altered by this change in the effect that is now outside it or no longer participatory in it. The effect supplements the cause as the external condition of its very being as cause. To dispute what Proclus says in proposition 69, the effect is not a part participatory in the whole-before-the-parts and this constitutes a decisive break with participation as the doctrine that the participating retains only passive potency and so can have no inverse effect on the being of the cause. The One, for example, can indeed be altered into the Good by means of the independence of its effect/consequent, primarily matter, which is but the proof of the One's unparticipatedness, proof that the One can produce something supplemental in the sense of non-participatory and incapable of reversion to the One itself.

Standing Proclus on his head

Any judgement concerning the correct interpretation of the role of matter in Proclus shall remain an open question, but Schelling's reading of the *Timaeus*, at any rate, certainly sets the canonical interpretation of Neoplatonism (and Platonism at large) – which is probably more Plotinian and Aristotelian than Procline (and Damascian) – on its head by rejecting the idea that reality descends from superior originals to inferior copies. This chapter has attempted to explicate what would ensue if proposition 7 of Proclus' *Elements of Theology* concerning the inferiority of the effect with regard to its cause were methodologically denied in accordance with Schelling's reading of Plato. The contention is further that Schelling's later thought continues to build upon his early reading of Plato's *Timaeus* in such a way that it inverts the direction of so-called emanationism in Neoplatonism. Emanation (or, if one prefers, procession) descends from the superior to the inferior, but Schelling hopes to ascend, to repeat at a higher intensity, from the inferior to the superior.

Schelling remarked in the 1840s,

> The entire collection of his remaining works is thoroughly dialectical, but at the summit and point of transfiguration . . . in the *Timaeus* Plato becomes historical and breaks through, albeit only violently, into the positive, namely in such a way that the trace of scientific transition is scarcely to be detected or only with great difficulty. It is more of a breach from the foregoing (namely, the dialectical) than a transition to the positive.[66]

In Schelling's own estimation, then, the turn in Plato's later thought from a dialectical project to a historical and narrative method prefigures Schelling's own division between negative and positive, that is, historical, philosophy, namely his philosophy of mythology and revelation. Peculiar to the emphasis on history is that movement is linear and one-directional rather than cyclical, as must be the case if one adheres to a doctrine of ἐπιστροφή. Schelling's positive philosophy is a priori only in the sense that it proceeds from the *prius* forth,[67] while negative philosophy seeks to regress to a first cause, ground or being. It is the directionality of the method that marks the difference between negative and positive philosophy, namely regressive and merely logical philosophy, on the one hand, and progressive and historical philosophy, on the other hand. Now, the need for reversion in Neoplatonism was to bestow oneness and goodness on that which had proceeded from the One and was thus deficient in oneness, longing for the One as the absent but desired object. Reversion was needed because procession was a movement from the superior to the inferior. Beierwaltes acutely judges, however, that for Schelling, already in the middle period of his thought marked by his drafts of *Das Weltalter* (1811–15), 'The end of this processive self-revelation of God is – in opposition to the Neoplatonic procession of the One/Good – the "*Highest*".'[68] Schelling's is not a system of emanation or procession hinged upon notions of imitation and participation, but a theory of novel production and elevation. Schelling denies that reality has descended from superior originals to inferior copies, instead arguing that reality moves from inferior matter, a principle with its own discordant motion(s), to higher and more superior levels of order and organisation. Beierwaltes's gloss is then perfectly accurate:

> Schelling understands matter in his speculative physics as a process productive in itself, and in the *Weltalter* as the precondition of the dynamic process of an historical unfolding of the Absolute . . . Thus, in his ennobling of matter . . . Schelling departs decisively from Plotinus. This difference has less to do with the concept of matter as an element and basis of nature than it has to do with the *progressive weakening* or destruction (*Zer-nichtung*) of reality.[69]

Beierwaltes is correct to indicate that the issue does not concern matter as such as the basis of reality, as both Plotinus and Proclus themselves affirm an intelligible matter, but the *Zer-nichtung*, the bringing to nought or bringing to non-being of reality. Matter is considered as mere non-being, as reality emptied of being and δύναμις; this is the end of procession for the Neoplatonists, hence the need for reversion. For Schelling, however, there is no reversion, only re-potentiation. By conceiving procession as progression, as a heightening or intensification of being rather than as descent or emanation, Schelling is able to avoid the need for reversion, which returns to things their lost unity and goodness. By conceiving of procession as an escalation, Schelling also posits the whole process as an open-ended, one-directional line without any need to return or close itself into a circle. This, for Schelling, is positive, historical philosophy, the objective or genetic method Boutroux had sought. Matter is not the last emanation that proves the effusiveness and impossibility of self-reversion for the One, but it is first and it is a principle.

One may plausibly argue that for Proclus, contra Plotinus, matter is not the last but rather the first emanation, but it nevertheless does not seem to be a productive principle. First, regarding the possibility that Proclus views matter as the first emanation from the One, Chlup can state that, for Proclus, 'matter is paradoxically very close to the One, being produced by it only and bearing no traces of the lower levels (*ET* 72)'. Similarities between the One and matter abound; for example, both are simple, properly invisible, non-intelligible (though the One is higher than the intelligible as inscrutable and ineffable while matter is rather less than intelligible). Moreover, both are otherwise than being: 'the One is non-being in the sense of what is "superior to being", while matter in the sense of what is weaker than being'.[70] Regarding their shared non-intelligibility, Chlup adds, 'The lowest inanimate objects are thus particularly suited for manifesting the divine, for by being deprived of all traces of intelligence they symmetrically mirror that which transcends Intellect . . .'[71]

Given Chlup's foregoing consideration and his clear depiction of matter as a direct and immediate procession from the One, it is baffling to read a passage like the following, a passage which must be rejected by this work's attempt to stand Neoplatonism on its head. '[Plotinus] seems to grant (in common with Proclus) that in the end matter is the final link in a long causal chain whose beginning lies in the Good . . . It was the lowest offshoot of soul (i.e. Nature) which produced matter (*Enn.* V 2, 1.21).'[72] However true this judgement may be of Plotinus, it is surely dubious in Proclus, for whom Chlup elsewhere clearly suggests that matter is not 'the lowest offshoot' and not 'the final link in a long causal chain', but rather pre-existent for all other levels on the chain of being as the first, albeit most inferior, and direct emanation from the One. If Chlup is correct in aligning Proclus with Plotinus in this respect, then Schelling's reading of the *Timaeus* would stand in direct contrast with Proclus', standing Proclus on his head. If, however, Proclus does admit that matter is pre-existent for all other levels of reality, then the main difference between the two is simply that Proclus does not admit that matter acts as a principle of motion and so fails to admit that reality could ascend and potentiate itself. At the end of the day, matter is still an evacuation of dignity and rank,[73] which functions as proof of the impossibility of self-reversion for the One, rather than being the presupposed substrate that allows for potentiation, intensification and elevation.

Concerning Schelling's relation to Plato and Neoplatonism, Grant has argued that Schelling avoids two-world Platonising by holding to the idea of pre-existent and unruly matter, which Plotinus (and, perhaps, also Proclus) rejected. Recently Daniel Whistler has reiterated this point, writing, 'The model of emanation is grounded in the very "two-world" metaphysics Schelling rejects. The distinction between copy and archetype is brought about by the process of emanation. Pre-existing archetypes produce inferior copies of themselves.'[74] Accordingly, Schelling has no need for reversion; one-directional linearity reigns. This is precisely the point of Schelling's late, positive, historical philosophy, which progresses from the origin without the accompanying need for reversion because reality potentiates itself rather than emptying itself into degraded and imperfect copies. For Schelling, things must not revert to the One to acquire their oneness, but the One acquires its unity all the more intensely the more things progress towards greater degrees of unity yet unknown. The One is constructed, not emanated or disseminated. According to the canonical reading of Neoplatonism, procession always produces only failing and inadequate forms of the One itself, hence their need to revert to their source, while for Schelling no forms of unity are derivate copies but excessive intensifications of oneness. The produced is always more than the source of production; consequents exceed their anterior in rank and dignity. The world did not begin with the perfect, but it might end with it. It is precisely this aspect of Schelling, which lead to the speculative rejection of proposition 7 in the experimental reading of Proclus' *Elements of*

Theology, that turns Neoplatonism upside down, first placing it on its feet, firmly implanted in a material base.

With this chapter, all preparatory work has been completed. The position of the necessity of contingency has been critiqued, the possibility of contingent necessity grounded and the Schellingian presupposition of disorderly, radically contingent, lawless and unlimited chaos fully elaborated. Additionally, Schelling's historical or genetic method and his argument for the superiority of the consequent has also been explicated. The following two chapters on Schelling will build upon this foundation. Chapter 4 will exhibit the eventuation of reason as an occurrence without reason, something only beholden as a fact, while nevertheless showing how reason occurs as a universal consequence without exception, that is, lawfully. Chapter 5 will point to the facticity of God as an eternal consequent without why, while yet showing that God's resolve, in order to be God's resolve, must hold eternally and definitively. Both chapters, then, exhibit the same structure. They will argue for the necessity of a thing's *Wesen*, which when thought verbally means the necessity of a thing's *modus operandi*, while also arguing for the factical and, thus, contingent existence of this necessary essence.

Notes

1. A more streamlined version of this chapter has been published as Tyler Tritten, 'On Matter: Schelling's Anti-Platonic Reading of the *Timaeus*', *Kabiri: The Journal of the North American Schelling Society*. Inaugural Issue (2017).
2. Schelling is not only a precursor to contemporary philosophy but, via his late critique of Hegel, perhaps the first instance of many of the principal questions and themes of post-Kantian continental thought. Žižek finds the roots of Marxism, existentialist finitude and temporality as the horizon of being in Schelling's drafts of *Ages of the World* (Žižek, *Abyss of Freedom*, p. 4). He lauds Schelling for providing a better description of the Other than Emmanuel Levinas (ibid., p. 25), for critiquing not just the formalism of time but also the predominance of presence, which occludes ontological difference (ibid., p. 30), and he mentions Deleuze as a 'great Schellingian' (ibid., p. 61). Jason M. Wirth, who has done more than anybody to promote Schelling's philosophy in North America, praises Schelling, in the editor's introduction to the translation of Schelling's lectures entitled *Historical-Critical Introduction to the Philosophy of Mythology*, for his anticipation of the twentieth-century's questioning of time (*Historical-Critical Introduction*, p. viii) and, elsewhere, because 'Schelling, with his critique of presence and his unswerving protection of both the mystery of all origins and the unprethinkability of the future, is, in Arendt's sense, the sworn enemy of all ideology' (Wirth, *Conspiracy*, p. 239). Andrew Bowie, the most hyperbolic of them all, hails Schelling as a 'post-metaphysical thinker' (Bowie, *Schelling and Modern European Philosophy*, p. 68) who, although he retained the rhetoric of metaphysics, even pre-emptively surpassed Jacques Derrida insofar as Derrida's *différance* recoils from the question of why being is disclosed in the first place (ibid., p. 71). Finally, Schelling is also thought to have exerted an influence on Peirce. One commentator has spoken of 'Peirce's

strong, albeit not explicit, dependence on Schelling's metaphysics' (Ejsing, *Theology*, p. 15), and Peirce himself told William James of his debt to Schelling (from Schelling, *Grounding*, 21–2).
3. Schelling, *Einleitung*, p. 3.
4. Ibid., p. 5. In fact, already by 1809 Schelling had lamented that nature does not exist for modern philosophy (Schelling, 'Philosophische Untersuchungen', *SW I/7*, 356).
5. Schelling, *Einleitung*, p. 64.
6. Schulz, *Vollendung*, p. 81.
7. Ibid., p. 124.
8. Ian Hamilton Grant speaks of Schelling not as a practitioner of the philosophy of nature but as a naturephilosopher. *Naturphilosophie* does not merely take nature as its object of study as if it were to be ordered among the philosophy of the political, the philosophy of gender, the philosophy of religion and so forth, but naturephilosophy indicates the nature of philosophy as such and in its universality before it has been delimited to a specific domain of objects. Naturephilosophy does not signify one sub-branch of philosophy among others, but naturephilosophy is *philosophia perennis et universalis*.
9. The philosophical sense of ὕλη (matter) is not actually discussed in the *Timaeus*. Rather, one finds a discussion of ὑποδοχή (receptacle), χώρα (Space) and ἄπειρον (the Indefinite). Schelling, following the precedent of a number of Neoplatonists in reading Plato and Aristotle as complementary rather than as antithetical, spoke of all these under the common heading of 'matter'. Schelling also speaks of this as μήτηρ (mother), which Schelling relates to the Latin *mater* and *materia*. '*Mater* and *materia* are in principle the same word . . . [Mater und materia sind im Grunde nur ein Wort . . .]' (Schelling, 'Die Mythologie', *SW II/2*, p. 193).
10. John Sallis notes the novelty of this translation of the *Timaeus* into Kantian terminology, commenting that 'Schelling's Reinscription of the *Timaeus* in the text of modern philosophy, his Reinscription of the dialogue into a text that while belonging to modern philosophy also renders it radically questionable, perhaps for the first time' (Sallis, 'Secluded Nature', p. 71). 'For what Schelling rewrites within the text of modern philosophy is a discourse on nature, on nature in its capacity to withdraw, on secluded nature' (ibid., p. 73). This withdrawn or secluded nature that does not present itself empirically because it is the presupposition of all presentation is the receptacle, which Schelling customarily refers to simply as 'matter'.
11. Note Sallis:

> Schelling inserts [in the *Freiheitsschrift*] a decisive *indication referring this entire development* back to the *Timaeus* and broaching in effect a Reinscription. The originary longing, says Schelling, is to be represented as a moving 'like an undulating, surging sea, similar to Plato's matter' (*PU* 360) . . . the darkness from which understanding is born, that is, the secluded ground, that is, *die anfängliche Natur*, is similar to Plato's matter . . . Schelling's discourse on the unruly ground, on secluded nature, may thus be taken – at least in certain decisive moments – as reinscribing the Timaean discourse on the receptacle. (Sallis, 'Secluded Nature', pp. 74–5)

12. Beierwaltes, 'Legacy of Neoplatonism', p. 400. The translation was slightly revised, altering 'the philosophy of nature' into 'naturephilosophy'.
13. Schelling, 'Timaeus', p. 229.
14. Ibid., p. 229. It will be seen that this cannot be equated with Aristotle's χωριστόν insofar as Aristotle denies that matter has being-in-itself. He only regards matter as the substrate of predication.
15. 'die zweideutige Natur (natura anceps)' (Schelling, 'Die Philosophie der Offenbarung: Zweiter Theil', *SW II/4*, p. 142)

16. As much as this reading is already influenced by Aristotle insofar as the word 'matter' is used at all, and precisely in relation to substrate and potency, it will be seen that Aristotle probably only recognises matter in the sense of a logical substrate as the mere potency to receive predication. Matter loses, in this way, its ontological or substantial character in Aristotle. It is de-substantialised, whereas it retains its substantiality in Plato.
17. Plato, *Sophist*, 247e4
18. Schelling, 'Timaeus', p. 232.
19. Schelling thus identifies ἄπειρον with quality and πέρας with quantity. He writes, referring to the *Philebus*, that 'Plato maintains namely that the world arose through the combining of the elements, insofar as these are ἄπειρα . . . they only stand under the category of quality . . .' (Schelling, 'Timaeus', p. 223) and 'God (the world architect) presented *everything* in the world as *quality* (reality) determined through quantity . . .' (ibid., p. 232). Quality or the ἄπειρον is thus only 'presented', says Schelling, and not cosmically created. Quality is not created but it is presupposed insofar as everything already 'stands under the category of quality'. Similarly, in the *Freiheitsschrift* of 1809, Schelling writes that 'nowhere does it appear as if order and form would be original, but as if something primordially unruly would have been brought to order [nirgends scheint es, als wären Ordnung und Form das Ursprüngliche, sondern als wäre ein anfängliche Regelloses zur Ordnung gebracht worden]' (Schelling, 'Philosophische Untersuchungen', *SW I/7*, p. 356). Similarly, Peirce has written of quality, which he identifies with Firstness,

> [Quality] is not anything which is dependent, in its being, upon mind, whether in the form of sense or in that of thought. Nor is it dependent, in its being, upon the fact that some material thing possesses it. That quality is dependent upon sense is the great error of the conceptualists. That it is dependent upon the subject in which it is realized is the great error of all the nominalistic schools. A quality is a mere abstract potentiality; and the error of those schools lies in holding that the potential, or possible, is nothing but what the actual makes it to be. (Peirce, 'Logic of Mathematics', p. 422)

As an empirical description, he adds, 'Red, sour, toothache are each *sui generis* and indescribable. In themselves, that is all there is to be said about them' (ibid., p. 424). For Schelling, Peirce and Boutroux there is thus no answer to questions about why vibration leads to the quality of sound rather than vision or why tactility leads to the qualities of taste and touch rather than odour. Qualities are without why. They are brute givens.
20. Schelling, 'Timaeus', p. 209. Note also: 'Plato assumed, after all, a pre-existing matter, but one that had absolutely no determinate empirical form' (ibid., p. 213). Note 51b–52a of the *Timaeus* itself for Plato's word here on these two kinds. Only the elements – earth, air, water, fire – have a determinate form. If these, as something in some sense created, are to be called matter, then that pre-existent matter is, as it were, the matter of matter or the substantiality of the elements.
21. As Schelling still affirms in 1813, 'Priority stands in an inverse relation to superiority' (Schelling, *Ages of the World (2nd draft)*, p. 179).
22. Beierwaltes, 'Plato's *Timaeus*', p. 272.
23. Schelling informed his audience in an 1832/1833 lecture series that the second cause, which imposes limit, first posits number (Schelling, *Grundlegung*, p. 319). If the first is pure quality and quantity only accrues with the activity of limit upon the unlimited, then, contra Badiou and Meillassoux, who hold that mathematics is ontology, for Schelling being *qua* being precedes number and quantification.
24. Schelling, 'Timaeus', p. 236.
25. See sections four and five of Plotinus' Second Ennead as a prime example of a discus-

sion of intelligible matter.
26. Grant, *Philosophies of Nature*, p. 45.
27. Schelling explicitly refers to ἄπειρον and πέρας as kinds, remarking that the one kind is operative 'by means of the activity of the understanding' and 'the other which without understanding and orderliness acts according to chance (ὅσαι μονωθεῖσαι φρονήσεως τὸ τυχὸν ἄτακτον ἑκάστοτε ἐξεργάζονται [on the other side those which, bereft of prudence, produce on each occasion a disordered chance effect] (47e))' (Schelling, 'Timaeus', p. 224).
28. Schelling, 'Die Philosophie der Offenbarung: Zweiter Theil', *SW II/4*, p. 238.
29. Sallis, 'Secluded Nature', p. 84.
30. Schelling writes that 'matter was *thus* first determined that the elements became visible and, to the extent that the elements emerged through the intelligible forms or, expressed otherwise, to the extent that they are imitations, copies of the intelligible form, they present the intelligible form' (Schelling, 'Timaeus', p. 237). What can 'present' mean if not a manifesting or making real for the first time? This is a very strange sort of 'imitation' and 'copying' at play here, an imitation that is but the manifestation of the original, of the thing itself, in its emergence and first determination.
31. Grant, *Philosophies of Nature*, p. 55. Grant is, therefore, also able to write, 'Natural history does not have objects as its field of study, but rather kinds, *gene*' – what will eventually become Schelling's potencies – 'and their becomings, their *genneta* or *gignomena*' (ibid., p. 53). Also, 'History, according to Platonism, is necessarily *natural* insofar as nature is not *what* is, but is the "always becoming" (*Tim.* 27e–28a)' (ibid., p. 54). The idea that reality is fundamentally historical rather than merely logical or eternally intelligible will become thematic later, as this constitutes the division between positive and negative philosophy in Schelling's later thought. Positive philosophy is historical while negative philosophy is merely logical and eternal, denying any becoming to the order of intelligibility.
32. In this respect, Schelling speaks later in his career, in 1832/33, of understanding or intelligibility as the dominance of a foregoing *Wahnsinn*, which functions as *das Stoffgebende* to the understanding (Schelling, *Grundlegung*, p. 452). Far, then, from beginning with empty form rather than presupposing an unruly content in need of form – which, according to Walter Schulz, was supposed to be the primary operation of German Idealism – Schelling operates in an inverse manner. To begin otherwise, according to Schelling, would be to begin not with *Wahnsinn* but with *Blödsinn*, which offers no content to be understood.
33. Proclus, *On the Existence of Evils*, 32.16–18. Proclus continues by questioning, 'How can that which is in need of the good still be evil?' (ibid., 32.18–19). For Proclus, this is a question concerning the compatibility of matter and the One, and matter and evil. As will be seen, Proclus' position on this issue and the question concerning the ontological status of matter in general is closer to Schelling's than Plotinus'.
34. Schelling, 'Timaeus', p. 236.
35. Ibid., p. 210.
36. This 'necessity' over which understanding rules is neither a logical, physical, metaphysical nor transcendental necessity. It is rather what the Greeks called ἀνάγκη, the Germans *Verhängnis* and Heidegger *das Geschick*. This so-called necessity, traditionally translated as fate or necessity, could just as easily be translated as 'contingency' or, more clumsily, 'that which bechances'. It indicates nothing other than that of which nothing more is to be said except that it has happened because it has happened.
37. Schelling, 'Timaeus', p. 225.
38. Grant, *Philosophies of Nature*, p. 35.
39. Ibid., p. 34.
40. Aristotle, *Metaphysics*, 1029a27–30.
41. Grant, *Philosophies of Nature*, p. 41.
42. Beierwaltes, 'Legacy of Neoplatonism', p. 414.

43. Proclus, *Commentary on Plato's Timaeus*, 382.14–17.
44. Schelling writes,

> the *matter of the world* . . . is this constituted out of the elements? . . . that which is continually appearing in various forms but which appears usually as fire is not *fire* but rather always only something *fire-like*, nor is it water, but always only something *water-like*. Thus neither can we give a *determinate* name . . . The elements *flee from* every determinate designation. (Schelling, 'Timaeus', p. 226)

45. Proclus, *Commentary on Plato's Timaeus*, 385.10–14, 385.16–22.
46. Ibid., 388.1–2.
47. Ibid., 388.5–9.
48. Chlup, *Proclus*, p. 202, n. 5.
49. As an example of Neoplatonism's penchant for analogy and allegory, Chlup writes, 'Eastern Neoplatonists take a different course. In their metaphysical accounts they are able to speak of the One quite clearly and precisely, but at the same time they constantly stress that none of their statements actually capture the true One as such' (Chlup, *Proclus*, p. 55). This is to be read against the many analogies of the One offered by Plotinus, who apparently believes that the reality of the One as such can be reached by these means. Yet Chlup also asserts,

> Proclus postulates the 'henads' or 'gods' as the basic 'subunits' existing within the One . . . The incomprehensible One turns out to be really just a tiny point on the top of the pyramid of all things in which everything else is subject to apprehension. Although the henads are unknowable themselves, we can know them safely through their effects. (ibid., p. 61)

If the henads can be known through their effects it is because the Neoplatonist is also committed – in opposition to Aquinas – to a notion of univocal causing, which should not be surprising as this is a staple of participation. Participation, of course, affirms that there cannot be more being in the participating than in the participated, hence that the participating cannot assert anything other than what it has found in the participated. Yet if causing is univocal and if the participating cannot express something otherwise than that in which it participates, then the participating does – also contra Aquinas – reveal something about the unparticipated or that in which the participating participates. Accordingly, it seems that some statements, even if they must be analogical rather than literal statements, should actually be able to divulge something about the unparticipated itself.
50. Proclus, *Commentary on Plato's Timaeus*, 390.28–32
51. Proclus, *Elements of Theology*, prop. 7.
52. Ibid., prop. 8.
53. Ibid., prop. 11.
54. Deleuze interestingly remarks,

> Nietzsche correctly points out that if it were the One which returned, it would have begun by being unable to leave itself; if it were supposed to determine the many to resemble it, it would have begun by not losing its identity in that degradation of the similar. Repetition is no more the permanence of the One than the resemblance of the many. The subject of the eternal return is not the same but the different, not the similar but the dissimilar, not the one but the many, not necessity but chance. (Deleuze, *Difference and Repetition*, p. 126)

55. Proclus, *Elements of Theology*, prop. 13.
56. Ibid., prop. 15.

57. Chlup, *Proclus*, p. 75.
58. Proclus, *Elements of Theology*, prop. 24.
59. Ibid., prop. 26
60. 'ein nie aufgehender Rest' (Schelling, 'Philosophische Untersuchungen', *SW I/7*, p. 360). This phrase, following Žižek, is normally translated as 'indivisible remainder'. 'Never presencing remainder', however, though clumsier, intimates that it is the source or substratum of all presentation without itself ever occurring within what is presented. It is not so much subtracted from presentation, as in Badiou, but it adds one to itself, an extra, a supplement, +1. It is not the subtraction of being but the addition of being.
61. Proclus, *Elements of Theology*, prop. 32.
62. Chlup correctly remarks that, for Neoplatonists, 'the One is often compared to the sun, whose rays do not illuminate our world intentionally, being a natural result of the sun's hotness' (Chlup, *Proclus*, p. 63). Procession from the One occurs according to Neoplatonism because the One is effusive, which means that there is no intention or volition involved. The One could not have failed to process/create; it is not free not to do so. The One is free because self-determined, but it does not act freely but rather out of its overflowing perfection. It is necessitated to overflow itself. Schelling, beginning with the inferior instead of the effusiveness of the perfect, rather speaks of the origin as a 'decision', a free decision, and not a natural overflowing. Chlup provides the Neoplatonist rebuttal here: 'A perfect being needs no decisions whatsoever, being always capable of acting in the best way possible' (ibid., p. 69). Progression or amelioration is impossible if one begins with the perfect.
63. Proclus, *Commentary on Plato's Timaeus*, 385.1–4.
64. Proclus, *Elements of Theology*, prop. 35.
65. Ibid., prop. 75
66. 'die ganze Reihe seiner übrigen Werke hindurch dialektische ist, aber im Gipfel und Verklärungspunkt . . . im Timäos wird Platon geschichtlich, und bricht, freilich nur gewaltsam, ins Positive durch, nämlich so, daß die Spur des wissenschaftlichen Übergangs kaum oder schwer zu entdecken ist – es ist mehr ein Abbrechen vom Vorhergegangenen (nämlich dem Dialektischen) als ein Übergehen zum Positiven' (Schelling, 'Die Philosophie der Offenbarung: Erster Theil', *SW II/3*, p. 100).
67. 'vom Prius herleitend' (ibid., *SW II/3*, p. 249).
68. Beierwaltes, 'Legacy of Neoplatonism', p. 406.
69. Ibid., p. 415.
70. Chlup says that Proclus 'admits that matter is a kind of non-being, but . . . non-being for him is connected with potentiality . . . it is the necessary 'vacuum' element in each level of reality . . . It follows that non-being is to be found on all planes of reality, matter being but its lowest and most passive expression' (Chlup, *Proclus*, p. 223).
71. Ibid., p. 90.
72. Ibid., p. 206.
73. Chlup comments similarly of Plotinus, 'Matter is seen by Plotinus as total privation, deforming forms and preventing their full realization' (Chlup, *Proclus*, p. 77). The Schellingian position, however, views matter as that pre-condition without which the Good could not come to be, rather than viewing it as an impediment to the Good.
74. Whistler, *Schelling's Theory*, p. 87.

Part II
Contingent Reason and a Contingent God: The Late Schelling and the Late Heidegger

Chapter 4

Reason as Consequent Universal: On Thinking and Being

The objective of this chapter, which in conjunction with the following two chapters forms the heart of the book's argument, is to analyse how (virtual) contradiction constitutes the *conditio sine qua non* of freedom as the impetus for the decision of being. By focusing not on the terms of a contradiction but on the middle of the contradiction, on the disjunction, the supplementation of being with thinking, intelligibility, conceptuality or reason will be historically narrated. This expands upon one of the central theses of the previous two chapters, namely that being precedes law, whether physical or logical, and order; being is the *prius* of reason and not vice versa. Consequently, reason will also be shown to be a contingent, yet eternal, matter of fact, the essence of which consists in the contradictory.

Reading the later Schelling

The first difficulty one encounters when reading the later Schelling is his use of terms, which often oscillate in meaning. As Jaspers specifies,

> In Schelling, there is no fixed terminology. *Das Sein* and *das Seiende* can invert their reciprocal meanings, beyond or above being can again mean *Sein*, the word Spirit is used for the third potency as well as for that which is above being that encompasses all potencies, God can mean that which is above being or its first appearance. Yet, in the context the presentation is clear.[1]

Although terms oscillate in meaning, as long as one is attentive to the specific *momentum* of the train of thought, his terms contain almost analytic precision. Extracted from their proper place in the movement of thought, however, they lose their significance entirely. Accordingly, rather than designating fixed English terms for German terms, context and interpretation should take the lead. There are, however, a few terminological distinctions that should be noted, namely that contingency and necessity as well as potency and actuality not only invert meanings, insofar as something can be contingent in relation to one thing but necessary in relation to another, potential in one respect but actual in another, but sometimes these terms function as modalities and sometimes they are attempts to refer to the modeless.

A second difficulty is coming to terms with the sometimes subtle and sometimes radical shifts within Schelling's own thought. The focus here will be on a few texts written during Schelling's latest period, 1832 and later, although reference will be made to earlier texts when relevant. With regard to secondary literature, given that there is no consensus concerning Schelling's latest thought anyway, the more 'heretical' accounts often prove to be the most insightful, even when they are also the most implausible. Jaspers, for instance, errantly writes,

> Schelling is a gnostic ... because he accepts and appropriates the material of *gnosis* through the transmission of theosophy, because he, from early to late, views everything within the space of intellectual intuition without first finding the effective context between it, factual knowledge of the world and finite activity ...[2]

Although Schelling unarguably inherits material from modern theosophists, particularly Jacob Böhme,[3] that does not *de facto* make him a gnostic. He is very concerned that everything be made methodologically explicit and that nothing be introduced through merely gnostic means or even intellectual intuition, a notion that he has dropped by 1832.

Schelling's later thought, which can be viewed, as Axel Hutter argues,[4] as a continuation of the Kantian critique, exposes reason to such a radical critique that György Lukács has even branded Schelling's thought 'the first form of modern irrationalism',[5] but this too is simply wrong. He is neither irrational nor an anti-rationalist. He never surrenders reason, but he does show that reason is not self-grounding and that it must therefore be confronted with its own facticity or lack of reason, its own *Ungrund*. It is to be emphasised, however, that the late Schelling is a not a rationalist, neither in the Hegelian nor Meillassouxian sense, but an empiricist. With respect to Schelling's *Auseinandersetzung* with Hegel, this interpretation emphasises everything to which Deleuze appeals in his defence of Schelling against Hegel and Hegelianism when he wrote,

> The most important aspect of Schelling's philosophy is his consideration of powers. How unjust, in this respect, is Hegel's critical remark about the

black cows! Of these two philosophers, it is Schelling who brings difference out of the night of the Identical, and with finer, more varied and more terrifying flashes of lightning than those of contradiction: with *progressivity*.[6]

Later, he adds,

> Hegel criticized Schelling for having surrounded himself with an indifferent night in which all cows are black. What a presentiment of the differences swarming behind us, however, when in the weariness and despair of our thought without image we murmur 'the cows', 'they exaggerate', etc.; how differenciated and differenciating is this blackness, even though these differences remain unidentified and barely or non-individuated; how many differences and singularities are distributed like so many aggressions, how many simulacra emerge in this night . . . this illusion . . . that groundlessness should lack differences, when in fact it swarms with them.[7]

The present interpretation could be read as an amplification of Deleuze's brief remarks on Schelling.

Neutrality or that without presupposition

It is impossible to begin from nowhere. One can, however, seek a neutral starting point, which is neither arbitrarily to commit oneself to one hypothesis, postulate or axiom nor to another – and the term 'neutrality' only means as much as this 'neither/nor' or, literally, not (*ne-*) either (*-uter*), the neither. To begin neutrally is to begin with what one cannot avoid presupposing, the presuppositionless presupposition or the absolute *prius*. Schelling thus follows the spirit of Plato's *Parmenides*, which has as its task the discovery of the ἀνυπόθετος. It would be hasty, however, to think that just because the absolute *prius* cannot not be presupposed, that it is necessary with respect to itself. Rather, it only qualifies as an absolute rather than relative *prius*, as the ἀνυπόθετος, precisely on account of its contingency. That it is neither this nor that, and so the neutral contingency of everything that could be, is precisely what secures its absoluteness. This must surely be the case for that which is not a *Grund* – which is relative insofar as it is necessarily related to its consequent – but *Ungrund*, not a ὑπόθεσις with its necessary entailments, but the ἀνυπόθετος. To discover why this and only this constitutes a neutral and absolute point of departure is the initial task of this chapter. It will prove helpful, however, first to state the position to be avoided.

As Schelling lamented in his Erlangen lectures of 1821, the limitation of branches of knowledge like mathematics is that such sciences proceed from voluntarily posited hypotheses.[8] Far from philosophy aligning itself with mathematics, philosophy strives beyond voluntary hypotheses towards what cannot not be presupposed, the absolute *prius*. Philosophy does not even assume reason but asks instead why there is reason instead of unreason.

Schelling does not adhere to the Hegelian dictum that 'what is rational is real; and what is real is rational'.[9] Reason, for Schelling, should function as no more than a handmaiden, thinking everything that could be actual without being able to derive actuality from itself. Reason is only a deciphering faculty, a passive or receptive faculty, as Schelling derives *Vernunft* (reason) from *Vernehmen* (court hearing), which he also relates to *Verhör* (cross-examination).[10] Reason comprehends/examines what is actual, but it cannot fathom the actuality of the actual. As Manfred Durner remarks, 'The science of reason grounds the conditions of the possibility of experience but not the actuality of experience.'[11] Reason only comprehends what something is and not that it is. Purely rational philosophy – what Hegel's philosophy should have remained and what Kant's critical philosophy hoped to delimit – is only a negative rather than positive philosophy. It comprehends quiddity, but, prior to its grounding in a pre-rational reality, it is unable to affirm that what it comprehends actually is; it cannot comprehend quoddity.

Schelling agrees with only half of the Hegelian dictum, namely that what is actual must be rational, that is, thinkable. Even then, he agrees only to a certain degree, writing, '[The world] contains a preponderant mass of unreason, so that one can nearly say that the rational is only the accidental.'[12] It will be argued that pure act, as the *prius* of reason, is precisely what reason fails to comprehend. If reason cannot comprehend quoddity and *actus purus* is nothing but 'thatness', this is obviously where the principle of sufficient reason falters. Schelling admits that everything which exists exists in the logical Idea; the nonsensical exists nowhere.[13] This only treats the negative aspect of existence, however, that without which nothing could sensibly exist but not that by which something positively does exist. It ensures that something is thinkable if it would be, but not that it actually is. Everything could reside in, that is, be comprehended by, the logical Idea without anything actually being explained thereby. This is just as everything sensuous can be grasped by number and measure, but number and measure (πέρας) do not account for the fact that something is. The latter is only granted through ἄπειρον, which is precedent to quantification, hence why mathematics is not ontology. Schelling's famous quote here finds its traction: 'Why is there sense at all, why not nonsense instead of sense? . . . The whole world lies as it were caught in reason, but the question is: How did it come into this net?'[14] In this context, one could also note Kierkegaard in *The Concept of Anxiety*, written in 1844, only a few years after attending Schelling's lectures in Berlin where he delivered a scathing *Hegelkritik*:

> neither logic nor actuality is served by placing actuality in the *Logik*. Actuality is not served thereby, for contingency, which is an essential part of the actual, cannot be admitted within the realm of logic. Logic is not served thereby, for if logic has thought actuality, it has included something that it cannot assimilate . . .[15]

Reason, even as formal logic, cannot secure its own ground. A philosophy is thus required that begins before reason and progresses historically, rather than logically or deductively, as a way of narrating reason's consequent emergence from the *Ungrund*. This history of being, the genetic narrative of being, is provided by positive philosophy rather than by negative or purely rational philosophy.

Negative philosophy does not begin in advance of reason and so its movement follows the epistemological rather than ontological order of things. Realising, however, that it cannot reach the actuality of the actual, which is antecedent to the structures, categories and dialectics of thought, purely rational or negative philosophy comes to desire positive philosophy, which can attain the actuality of the actual, as something that it wants.[16] Positive philosophy is that towards which negative philosophy strives but, ensnared within the nets of reason, negative philosophy can never reach it. To begin immanent to reason and then to strive to transgress its borders is impossible, the very movement Kant condemned as dogmatising. Ecstatically to begin in advance of reason, however, in order to proceed to reason, Schelling contends, is possible.[17] Phrased differently, the pure science of reason merits its status as first epistemology but ontology remains first philosophy. Philosophy's task is epistemo-ontological because epistemology can never ground ontology, only vice versa. Nevertheless, the present exhibition of Schelling's philosophy will propaedeutically commence negatively, immanent to thought itself, and then – and this continues into the following chapter – retrace these steps positively as an event narrated as the history of being itself, from the absolute *prius*, the ἀνυπόθετος, forth.

Three moments of thought

This section closely follows Schelling's elucidation of the determinations of being (*das Seiende*) in his 1832 lectures, *Urfassung der Philosophie der Offenbarung*. The objective is to begin absolutely and neutrally, departing neither from the presupposition of reason nor even from the fact that there is being. One must begin prior to being. *Das Seiende* is thus not presupposed but approached as that which will be (*das was sein wird*). From the standpoint before being, being can only appear as futural, what will be, if it would be. The fact that there is being must be suspended from this viewpoint where being is not yet given. If it would be, then it must be determined as that which can be (*das Sein Könnende*), that neuter and neutral which neither is nor is not, but can be or may-be. Being is approached as the contingency to be and to not-be. Schelling aims to reveal that which will be as that which, as such, is neither being nor not-being, as that which is no more compelled to be than to not-be, hence as the freedom to be or not-be, which is not simply before being but also above being, sovereign over being and thus free to posit or to not-posit it.

The first determination of that which will be, which one cannot avoid admitting, is the possibility of its being,[18] that which can pass from possibility to actuality simply by virtue of its own will to be (and, for Schelling, all determinations of that which will be are forms of will, because willing is primal being, or *Wollen ist Ursein*). Concerning this first determination, Schelling comments, 'If this will is ever incited, then it is no longer will – it is no longer that which *can* be and not-be; it is now that which *was able* to be and not-be . . . the being of the contingent is transformed into necessity . . .'[19] If the first determination wills rather than remaining in repose, it loses itself as what can be and is reduced to what was able to be and not-be, what could have also never been but now, in fact, irrevocably is. Having willed, it cannot retract its will and so it now necessarily is, having forsaken its contingency to be or to not-be. The first determination of that which will be loses its being as contingency – again, only if its will is actually incited – and becomes, *post (f)actum*, something necessary. Schelling confirms, 'The contingent becomes necessary, because it, if it is, can no longer not-be.'[20]

That which will be, which as a whole constitutes the contingency of being, what can be or not-be, is to be distinguished from the first determination of the same, which, unfortunately, Schelling also designates as the primal contingency to will (or not). Moreover, both the whole and, concomitantly, its first determination are to be thought as prior to being because on both accounts the discussion concerns that which will be only if it would be. Schelling notes,

> The present question is not about whether there may be original being but how it might be able to arise . . . If that which will be is merely that which can immediately be, then we would only encounter blind being in reality . . .[21]

If there would be anything at all, thus an original or archical something – which is not to be asserted from the an-archical view prior to being – then there must be conditions or, more precisely, determinations that make it possible. The first of these determinations is the contingency to be or not-be. Should this will be without limit, then it would immediately, without mediation, pass into being from a state of possibly being. So long as nothing comes between the possibility to be and actual being, nothing restrains this movement *a potentia ad actum*, nothing limits this will. The first determination would blindly or im-mediately pass into being. Spinozism, in which the attributes and modes eternally ensue from infinite substance,[22] would reign! It would no longer be a question of if being emerges or not, because it could not have done otherwise. Without something inserting itself in the middle between capacity (*Können*) to be and being (*Sein*), the first determination of that which can be (*das Sein Könnende*) is not actually the contingency of being and not-being, but only the possibility, and hence necessity, of being.[23] It would spell the necessity of being because it would lack the counter-possibility of not-being. Without something which interjects itself between possibly being and actually being, the first determination – and, concomitantly, that which will be as such and as a whole – is not what can be and can not-be. The first determination cannot, therefore, be thought in isolation; it demands a second, apart from which it is not even what it is, namely the possibility of both being and non-being. Spinozism, which holds whenever movement *a potentia ad actum* follows with necessity, errs by failing to begin 'behind being'[24] but rather beginning with infinite substance, with what is already in being.

It is impossible to remain with the first determination alone, because the point of departure is before being, a moment instantaneously lost if one posits only the first. Schelling implores,

> We want to preserve it before the transgression into being: we want for it to remain as *pura potentia*, as sheer capacity, as that which is capable apart from being. As that which can be, however, it can only remain as it is if it accepts a replacement for being, which it could accept, and it is therefore only something contingent, a possible being . . . it can only remain as potency insofar as it, in and for itself, is already that pure being before which no possibility precedes.[25]

The only way for the first determination of that which will be to preserve its contingency is for it to sacrifice its potency to the second determination, namely to pure being without potency. If that which will be, as the contingency of being itself, is that which can be and can not-be (*das Sein und Nichtsein Könnende*), then it is both pure *Können* (capacity to be) and *reines Sein* (pure being). Only in this way is it 'a being without transition, without a pre-given potency';[26] only in this way can it be without also losing its potency. The issue concerns the possible co-belonging of *actus* and *potentia*, being and not-being. Only in the identity, the virtual contradiction, between being and the capacity to be can the capacity or possibility of being remain as it is, namely within the power of that which will be as a mere determination of it rather than as the whole of it. Only in this way does the first remain a determination of that which will be, instead of immediately positing itself as the totality of substance itself. Spinoza, as it were, knows only the first determination of that which will be and, therefore, is unable to preserve it as something futural. He only knows it as what is, as an eternal present, eternal actuality. In isolation, apart from its contradicting the second determination, the first cannot be restrained. In isolation from the second, it is without borders or, rather, without determination altogether: ἄπειρον. One cannot help but to posit ἄπειρον as the first, which means one can only posit πέρας or that which provides limit, boundary and determination as the second. A thesis common to each of the previous two chapters is again affirmed: number or quantification is only second (or two is the first number),[27] only something that follows being *qua* being, namely the unmeasured and unquantified, pure contingency as pure quality without boundary.

With these two determinations, the question of what comes between these disjuncts remains. The third determination, as that which comes to stand 'in the middle'[28] of these two, is 'free from both'.[29] It is only in this equipollence or stabilisation of the contradiction between two wills, between willing and not-willing, being and not-being, that the third and final determination of that which will be emerges. It emerges, contrary to the Hegelian dialectic and contrary to traditional interpretations of Schelling, not as a sublation of the prior determinations into a higher synthesis[30] but as a middle that differentiates as much as it unifies. Rather than being thought principally as a both/and, the third is a neither/nor. Only as neither/nor is the third free[31] from both, that which neither has to be the one – possibility to be – nor the other – being. The virtual contradiction between the prior two determinations is not cancelled by being mediated into a higher unity. It is not sublated, but the prior two determinations, *qua* contradictory, exclude each other in a positive sense, positing the third outside their tension. The contradictories are neither cancelled nor synthesised, but in antithesis the third is extained. Extainment[32] is a technical term that indicates exclusion as the act of positing something outside a contradictory relation rather than the negating of one of the disjuncts and rather than the suspension of one or both by elevating them to a higher synthesis that 'includes' or 'contains' both. Extainment is thus the counter-concept of inclusion and containment. The third determination is an extained third, which becomes important for the sense in which it is also an excluded third, an excluded middle, which will be discussed later when the nature of contradiction is the issue.

The contingency of reason

Schelling, after elucidating the three merely virtual determinations, which cannot not be thought, of that which will be, if it will be, insists that the question remains as to whether this dialectic actually is. The entire train of thought was executed conditionally, only if there is to be something rather than nothing. That this is so, however, had been systematically bracketed. Schelling reminds his readers, 'But, this entire succession is based on this presupposition: if there is being ... but just this presupposition is itself doubtful ... It can be asked: Why is there not rather nothing?'[33] Schelling presses the point: 'We asked, *if* being arises, then it can only arise in this series. But, it is now to be wondered, how and why does being in fact arise? Only insofar as there is a first actuality.'[34]

One should be careful when treating this 'first actuality'. This, *actus purus* or sometimes *actus purissimus*, is not a first entity or first *actualitas*. Schelling's argument cannot be understood as a relic of Thomism or onto-theology because this 'first actuality' has 'not been conceived as absolute necessity but only hypothetically. Further, it is obvious that we have not inferred it from reason, as I can always still ask: Why is there thus reason and not unreason?'[35] The inference to a first actuality is not an inference to an absolutely necessary entity but to a hypothetical necessity that is, with respect to itself, the being of contingency as such. The being of contingency, its essence, consists in the three necessary determinations of that which will be, but that these three determinations constitutive of the essence of reason actually are is utterly contingent. If these three determinations constitute the figure of reason, the question remains whether this figure, reason itself, at first constituted merely for thought, actually is. If yes, then the figure of reason is also the figure of being, the 'house of being' if one will. What demands explanation, at any rate, is the being, the *actus*, of reason itself and not its determinations, hence the impossibility of inferring the necessary actuality of this figure from its essence. The ontological argument cannot be applied to reason itself (and nor to God). Reason can exist only if *actus purus* exists, while the inverse inference, according to Schelling, would be a form of Hegelianism, which is predicated on the presumed success of the ontological argument. Even if it is admitted that *actus purus* is, it is not there for the sake of reason. It is indifferent to reason. As the *prius* of reason, as that which will be if it would be, *actus purus* names the utter contingency between reason and unreason. It is without reason, 'groundless' and 'without a foregoing necessity',[36] which, nevertheless, does not exclude a proceeding or consequent necessity.[37]

Truths of reason, in contradistinction with matters of fact, are indeed necessary, that is, if reason is. Reason, however, is not itself a truth of reason. It is not self-grounding but a groundless, reasonless matter of fact.[38] Schelling infers, 'By this means the foundation of all philosophical rationalism is destroyed. Reason is not something necessary in itself.'[39] Of the absolute *prius*, *actus purus*, it can only be said that '*it is because it is*'.[40] This is not unlike Angelus Silesius' rose, which has drawn Heidegger's attention, who states, 'The rose is without why. It blooms because it blooms.'[41] This *actus* without why is not, however, the 'without why' of the mystics. It is rather that which is reason – as reason is that which will be if only something is it – and so it admits of an a posteriori rationality, that is, a science or method ensues from it even if no a priori approach to this *actus* is possible. An empiricism that is not sensibilism is required: narrative empiricism.

Further remarks on the methodology of narrative empiricism must wait until the following chapter. Here one should simply note the difference with the Hegelian viewpoint as an instance of negative philosophy. The absolute *prius*, the absolute a priori – which can only be known through its *posterius*, that is, a posteriori or, more properly, *per posterius* – is not, as for Hegel, an empty logical construction or reason itself, a thinking that has only thinking as its content, a mere dialectic of the determinations of thought, but it is antecedent to reason, thought, conceptuality, intelligibility and the like. If, however, that which will be subsequently reveals itself as reason, then thought or the truly logical would now bear a necessary relation to being, to that which is it. Thought/reason/intelligibility/logic would thus constitute the content, essence or quiddity of being. It would be something a posteriori or empirical, albeit not sensible, a matter of fact. Rightly understood, which means positively understood, rational philosophy is 'a priori empiricism'.[42]

While reason's essence is necessary, its existence is contingent. As the domain of necessary truths but itself consequent upon pre-rational facticity, it is at most a consequent or contingent necessity. Moreover, insofar as its essence consists in the three necessary determinations of thought, the three determinations of that which will be as that which can be (*das Sein Könnende*), it comprises 'all that can', namely Kant's transcendental Ideal as the totality of all possibility. Reason's content consists in the totality of all possible predicates; for, insofar as predicates do not exist in their own right but only if predicated of something which is, all the more so here. As the totality of all possibility, reason is universal. It can thus finally be asserted that reason is the consequent universal of being itself, an eternally contingent and universal consequent. The difference between Schelling's conception of the transcendental Ideal and Kant's, aside from Schelling's affirmation of it as both eternal and contingent – whereas Kant, conflating necessity with universality, is unable to admit eternal facts, eternal contingencies, things which could have not been but in point of fact eternally and universally obtain – is that Schelling does not think of this as Ideal but as Real. In this regard, Schelling proves more Spinozistic than Kantian. As Real the transcendental Ideal is operative as a material rather than logical or formal ground of possibility. The ground of all possibility – which groundlessly eventuates from out of unground – is not to be thought regulatively but constitutively. Moreover, since the determinations of thought are not generic categories but individual powers of being, Schelling does not so much think this ground of possibility as a totality but as a figure of being, not as a pre-given whole but as the figure of the whole. It signifies that which can be, the ability to bring forth all possibilities, but not the pre-givenness of all possibles as a lump sum.

The contingency of the unprethinkable

The counter-effect that the figure of all possibility enacts on its *prius* is fascinating and startling. As moments for thought alone, as something thought in isolation from that *actus* which, as the absolute *prius* or unprethinkable (*das Unvordenkliche*), cannot be thought in advance of being, every potency stood in a necessary relation to each of the others. Everything unfolded for thought necessarily. The potencies were all thought as necessary determinations of that which will be, if only it would be. That which will be, however, is *actus purus* without potency or that which precedes all determination and all possibility. Here, then, is what Schelling calls original. 'We call original . . . only that of which possibility is first given through actuality.'[43] Schelling's aforementioned 'first actuality' corresponds to his notion of originality and not to a first entity or first cause. This is similar to when one views original art, that is, the art of the genius, and is unable to believe that such art is possible were it not that one is now confronted with its actuality. In everything original, actuality is first and possibility second, because where possibility precedes actuality, actuality only follows as a copy and possibility functions as the model. Likewise, if freedom is original or capable of bringing about something original, then this is a very odd sort of 'capability', namely capability without potency, im-potent capacity, *actus* in advance of *potentia*. Originality subsists only where movement *a potentia ad actum* is impossible, only where possibilities are not given in advance.

The question, then, is the following: How does unprethinkable being, in which no possibility is to be found, make itself possible? How is it transfigured, as that which will be, into something that might have a future? How is *actus* supplemented with *potentia*?

Thus far the determinations were not yet properly potencies, as they only become something potent, something capable of bringing forth a future being, if they have unprethinkable being, the futural *par excellence*, as their *prius*. From the perspective of unprethinkable *actus*, the potencies are what will be or can be; they are only its *posterius*. How, then, is the pre-potent supplemented with a consequent possibility and potentiality that it does not contain in advance? Yet Schelling remarks, 'The opposite of blind emergence is only there where the possibility of the deed actually goes in advance.'[44] The opposite of blind, that is, necessary, emergence, however, consists in that in which actuality precedes possibility, thus in that in which possibility does not go in advance; this is the free and original. There would seem to be an impasse here, unless *actus* precedent to *potentia* can be consequently, that is, *post factum*, transformed or transfigured into possibility.[45] The question is how unprethinkable being as blind, as absolutely precedent to thought, vision and understanding, is transformed into free possibility. How is blind ἀνάγκη liberated for the possible or contingent? The consequent, reason, grants possibility and thinkability to what is antecedent to both, transforming ἀνάγκη or necessity into freedom or contingency. In other words, *post factum* or *per posterius* the unprethinkable *prius* is transformed into contingency or absolute possibility for a future being and, in this respect, that which will be first is what it is, something futural, by means of its liberation from itself, from its own ἀνάγκη. *Post factum* it is no longer ἀνάγκη or, rather, ἀνάγκη is more properly understood as absolute contingency than as necessity. If ἀνάγκη signifies only that which 'is because it is', that which does what it does for no reason whatsoever, out of no grounds and without conditions, then it is the contingent rather than the necessary. In this respect, despite rhetoric borrowed from the Middle Ages, namely that *actus purus* precedes *potentia*, one here finds something like Heidegger's assertion that 'higher than actuality stands possibility'.[46] Possibility supplements the unprethinkable both by positing and alleviating its contradiction. Rather than the third determination, which follows necessarily from the prior two, indicating the highest ground and possibility of freedom, actual freedom must emerge from the unprethinkable unground as something antecedent to the contradiction constitutive of its consequent nature. Freedom is not the dissolution, solution or synthesis of the contradiction; it is the groundless positing of contradiction.

The principles of non-contradiction and excluded middle

Until now the analysis has more or less followed Schelling's *Urfassung der Philosophie der Offenbarung*, but now attention will be turned to his most sustained reflection of the nature of contradiction in another untranslated series of lectures, 'Darstellung der reinrationalen Philosophie', particularly the thirteenth lecture. The position Schelling there reacts against, which he associates with Kant and modern logic, is any account that makes the principle of non-contradiction (and logic generally) operative without relation to time, because this reduces logic to a formal law that no longer, as it did for Aristotle, functions as a law of being. Schelling finds that modernity reduces all opposition to contradiction as a way of bracketing its temporal determinations. Schelling insists, however, that not even contradiction is absolutely timeless because contradictions can only emerge if the opposed are posited at the same time, which cannot mean the same thing as timelessly. Obviously, not all opposition is contradiction. Things can also be

> opposed only as *contrarium* . . . which only becomes contradictory, i.e. falls under the law of non-contradiction, when it is posited *at the same time* but not, therefore, when the one precedes and the other follows, in which case the opposed can admittedly be one and the same.[47]

To relate this to Schelling's *Potenzenlehre*, the question is whether the first two determinations relate as contraries or as contradictories? On the one hand, all three determinations are posited at once, while, on the other, all three are posited as three different times.

In distinction from Kant's idea of the perfect or most complete being (*das allervollkommenste Wesen*), which unites all *realitates compossibiles* within itself, Schelling's potencies require each other and are thus *consentes*.[48] They arise together – if there should be being – as, in isolation, they would cease to be, hence why these contradictories cannot simply nullify each other. Yet despite being posited all at once, they are not merely contradictory because in a contradictory statement – the bachelor is married – nothing is actually affirmed because its negation – it is not the case that the bachelor is married – would also say nothing. There is nothing more than analyticity here. All contradictions, for which the imposition of time would mean nothing, are not real assertions and all real assertions that actually affirm something are synthetical rather than analytical. The doctrine of the potencies, however, actually affirms something because its negation or non-existence could also be, and so it is not an analytical proposition and must bear some relation to time. In short, the principle of non-contradiction for Schelling, insofar as it must relate to time in some way, regulates real assertions, that is, synthetical propositions, and not the merely analytical, which can be divorced from relations to time. The analytical is merely formal, but the synthetical is more than a law of formal (or even transcendental) logic; it is also a law of being. Schelling summarises as follows:

> The merely negative law hereby contains a positive meaning and is comprehended, as it is according to Aristotle, as the law of *all* being ... if one fails to understand it in this way, then statements which say nothing would remain in place and emphatic propositions, which actually express something, would be impossible. For, of what does one say that it is bright than that which is dark in itself, of what that it is sick than that which merely can be sick but which is healthy in itself?[49]

If the question is about reason as a matter of fact, as a synthetical or emphatic assertion that actually posits something whose negation could have also been, something that itself could have also not been, then reason can only be asserted of that which is not reason, just as bright or sick can only be asserted of that which is not bright and not sick, namely the dark and healthy. The same child who is healthy remains potentially sick. All that is prohibited is that one asserts sickness and health at the same time (and in the same respect). As long as sickness and health are asserted of that which, in itself, is neither sick nor healthy, both remain possible. Here, then, one again encounters the neutral as a neither/nor, the contingency between two opposites, even when construed as contradictories. One who can be sick is the same as one who can be not-sick; that which can be is the same as that which can also not-be, the neutrality between being and not-being.

Contraries and contradictions alike are both possible so long as they are thought as contingent possibilities, namely as potential predicates of the same, of a common ὑποκείμενον. Although Schelling employs this Aristotelian rhetoric, it is nevertheless the case that this 'same' of which two contradictories are both possible is not a substrate at first identical to itself (*das sich selbst Gleiche*), but it is the non-identical or chaotic, 'the impermanent'.[50] Gabriel elaborates thus: 'Schelling locates *total* inconsistency which is not even a multiple at the basis of consistency by introducing his concept of "that which is unequal to itself (*das sich selbst Ungleiche*)".'[51] This absolute inconsistency signifies chaos. The unprethinkable substrate, chaotic as such, first becomes what it will be, if in fact it will be, only after it has acquired an essence, quiddity, whatness, identity or nature. This only occurs once the unprethinkable *Daß* has been supplemented with a *Was*, once the necessary is transfigured into the possible and contingent, once the unprethinkable has become post-thinkable through its supplementation with thinkability. Schelling exclaims,

> That which *Is das Seiende* cannot, as that which is free of essence or free of the Idea as such (namely for itself and considered outside [the figure] of being), be *the One* right at once but rather only *One*, Ἕν τι, which for Aristotle is equivalent with that which is a *This* (a τόδε τι ὄν) and with that-which-can-be-for-itself, the χωριστόν.⁵²

Prior even to the One, which is equal to itself or a self-same, there is only chaos. Being and thinking belong together but being, as chaos, is the most original, an-archically original, prior to all origins, prior to any ἀρχή. The thinkable, order, is only derivative or consequent. Thinkability is a synthetical, emphatic pronouncement uttered by being, by that chaos which excluded no possibilities, neither thinking/intelligibility/order nor not-thinking/non-intelligibility/caprice. In itself, this 'same' of which thinking or not-thinking, reason or unreason, might be predicated is not a substrate or self-same, not yet a ὑποκείμενον in the proper sense of the term, but chaos. Chaos must be understood not as the admixture and confusion of elements but as the neither/nor, *actus purus*, in which nothing, including the possible advent of *potentia*, has been excluded. Chaos indicates contingency precedent to the demand to choose one thing over another because it even precedes the determinateness of the contradiction. It is the *prius* of the contradiction; for, the contradiction constitutes the essence of reason, but reason too is consequent to the absolute *prius*.

This, of which contradictories could be predicated, is primary and that which is attributed or asserted of it only secondary. Hence, employing Aristotelian rhetoric, Schelling is able to say of the determinations of that which will be,

> Thus, that which precedes simultaneously becomes the subordinated (ὑποκείμενον) against that which follows and the moments of being also comport themselves perfectly as stages, which step forth just as little *at the same time* as they are able to be *in the same position*. Aristotle here says that privation is *also* negation, only not, as he clarifies elsewhere, as unconditioned negation, which denies that which is negated of the object *as such*.⁵³

Although the determinations are posited 'simultaneously' they also 'follow' one another and are thus clearly not posited as the same times. The times under question are qualitatively rather than quantitatively distinguished. That determined as the first – and the fact that terms like 'first' or 'second', namely enumeration, are used (A^1, A^2 and A^3), indicates that sequentiality and hence time is at play – did not precede the second in time, but it is the subjected and subordinated, that without which any talk of the second, the attributed or predicated, would be meaningless. Only in this sense do terms like 'subject' – which designates what bears predicates – or 'ὑποκείμενον' – which designates the bearer of attribution – make sense.

This is true despite the fact that these are the determinations of that which will be, which, prior to these determinations, is without determination and so not even equal to itself, a veritable chaos.

Chaos signifies unprethinkable being in advance of thinkability and *actus* in advance of *potentia*. It is the ἀνυπόθετος, the neither/nor, what has excluded neither this nor that. Accordingly, it has also not yet even posited the contradiction, as that would bring the principle of non-contradiction into play already at the level of chaos, a principle which demands resolution, which demands that a decision be made for one disjunct or the other. Although nothing has been decided, and so nothing has been determinately formed as a potency in chaos, nor has anything, potency included, been excluded or negated from it. Chaos neither contains all possibility as a lump sum nor has it decisively removed the possibility of possibility from itself. For chaos, everything is futural or not yet decided. Schelling contends that

> This is just as that which is simply not positively being is not *non*-being but rather, through negation, becomes only a particular mode of being; it becomes μὴ ὄν . . . What A is not is either that wholly incapable of being A (τὸ ἀδύνατον ὅλως ἔχειν) or that which A can be but is not (τὸ πεφυκὸς ἔχειν μὴ ἔχῃ).[54]

If and only if something is the three determinations so that they are determinations of being rather than just determinations of thought, then they first become potentiated and predicated thereby, while that which is them, which beforehand was that which could be them, first becomes the subject of predication, the receptacle of limit (πέρας) or determination. Prior to that which the receptacle receives, the receptacle is not receptive or not yet the receptacle. As predicates, the determinations of being are not generalities but modalities. Before being attributed to that which is them, they never could have been modalities because modalities are manners of being, that is, *modi operandi*, ways of being operative. These modes can only be attributed to that which is not a mode in itself, modeless ἀνάγκη. This ἀνάγκη, which can just as adequately be understood as primal contingency than as necessity, is all the same not to be understood as the modality of contingency. Whether understood as contingency or as necessity, ἀνάγκη cannot be a modality; it is the modeless, the pre-modal.[55] Should contingency and necessity only be understood as modalities, then Gabriel is correct that unprethinkable being/ἀνάγκη 'is the indifference of contingency and necessity',[56] that to which modalities do not apply.[57] If reason is the domain of necessary truths, the modality of necessity, then reason is only a *modus* of the actual but not actuality itself. Reason cannot be presupposed; the being of rational and logical space is contingent or consequent upon, is but a *modus* of, the modeless. That which is 'attributed' or 'predicated' of the modeless as a 'substance' or 'substrate' is, in fact, only activity *in concreto*, a particular mode of *actus*, while 'substance' is nothing other than activity as such or *actus purus*, but certainly not an entity or *actualitas* that functions as the uncaused cause of the universe.

Chaos, the modeless, being neither the one contradictory nor the other, is able to function as that of which the contradiction is expressed. Returning, then, to the issue of time and its relation to the law of non-contradiction thought as a law of being, Schelling relates his position to Aristotle.

> Aristotle, as often as he mentions the great law [of non-contradiction] (that it is impossible that the same may at the same time be and not be), speaks only of εἶναι καὶ μὴ εἶναι and never of εἶναι καὶ οὐκ εἶναι as he would have had to do if for him the law [of non-contradiction] would merely have a formal meaning, which is the only meaning the moderns know.[58]

The reason the law of non-contradiction is not a formal law is because it does not logically exclude the negated, but it posits the negated; it posits it as the negated, −A. In other words, because negation is not absolute but relative, it does not absolutely exclude something from being but it negates by positing the negated as what potentially could be (or could have been) but is not. The contradiction is between three potencies of being. The excluded is not logically denied but actually extained. If the contradiction is between +A and −A, then ±A is extained, posited as something excluded from both. Contradiction would only exclude in the negative sense rather than in the positive sense of extainment if there were three different beings rather than three different modalities of the 'same'. Extainment does not render the excluded impossible, but it posits it as possible, that is, as potent, because the other potency only has its being in the contradiction as the negated. Each only has its being in relation to its negation, that which it positively excludes. None of the potencies may emerge for themselves in isolation or outside the contradiction. Schelling explains,

> For that which precedes it must be determined that it go in advance, for that which follows that it succeed, for the last that it be the aim and the end. One cannot avoid coming upon '*everything at the same time*', as Aristotle also admits that, according to one point of view, those people are right who let not-being and being exist beforehand in the object . . . Here everything is as in an organic whole, reciprocally determining and determined. That which is not being is the ground (the *ratio sufficiens*) of pure being but, in turn, pure being is the determining cause (*ratio determinans*) of sheer being-*in*-itself and even the third mediates to the preceding that they are, in like manner, moments of being, just as this is mediated to it through them. All must be posited or none of them can be.[59]

Everything is posited at once, but not as the same time.

William F. Vallicella, an analytically trained metaphysician, dealt with the nature of contradiction in a similar way. He contended that

> The inherent contradictoriness of facts shows that they cannot be ultimately real, they must be mere appearances. Thus we are referred beyond them to that of which they are the appearances, the Absolute. I take facts to be inherently contradictory when considered as self-existent, when considered apart from their ontological ground, but free of contradiction when considered in dependence on their ontological ground.[60]

While the intention is not to reduce contradiction to a 'mere appearance' in the sense of not being 'ultimately real', it is the case that unprethinkable being only acquires an essence or thinkability as contradiction. Contradiction is its *modus*, how it is operative. Contrary to Meillassoux, contradiction not only exists but it constitutes the figure of reason itself. Contrary to Meillassoux, instead of everything being possible except contradictions, the contradiction constitutive of reason comprises the totality of all possibility. The contradiction is real and possible, that is, the reality of the possible, because it is the very *modus* of pre-modal chaos, chaos's consequent and contingent universal. In fact, it is only through chaos's supplementation with thinkability/reason that even chaos becomes a selfsame, decidedly chaos rather than not-chaos. Only with this supplementation is something decided. Contrary to Meillassoux, contradictions are indeed possible so long as they are said of the 'same', so long as the relation between contradictories is not extrinsic. Contradictories are but the *modus operandi* of one and the same. This 'sameness' that holds the contradictories together, however, is not the unity of an actual entity, not an essential unity, but the unity of the unprethinkable deed, the free act that posits the contradictories as mutually excluding/extaining. The absolute *prius* is not an entity but a deed, an act, a decision, hence again the meaning of act precedes potency.

If the original deed first posits the determinations, namely the contradiction, this occurs not by synthesising pre-given contradictories but by first severing or separating disjuncts as contradictory. As Vallicella suggests, 'Unity can in no way be construed as a property.'[61] Identity and unity are not properties but the very act of differentiation or disjunction by which synthesis and mediation first become possible, the very act by which truth is made possible, something like Heidegger's truth-event. Contradiction ensues by means of the exclusion/extainment of the middle. In other words, the principle of excluded middle must hold sway before contradictions and the concomitant law that contradictions must be decided, namely the principle of non-contradiction, can come into effect.

The excluded middle is not the disjunction and synthesis of two foregoing contradictories, but the exclusion of the middle occurs through the pre-original deed that precedes the contradictories.[62] In this way synthesis only occurs in disjunction and indifference in difference. If the principle of excluded middle differs from the principle of non-contradiction in that the latter principle demands that everything is either true or false and the former demands that this either/or is exhaustive, then this exhaustiveness is produced only by an act of differentiation or disjunction, the positing of an interstice between the two that first brings them into being at all, namely as contradictories. This act unprethinkably emerges from a chaos that is neither the one contradictory nor the other. The chaotic contingency of neither/nor must first incur a cision, a de-cision, that excludes the middle domain of neutrality, that de-neuters and de-neutralises chaos. This interstice that severs the inexhaustive neither/nor, (trans)figuring it into an exhaustive either/or, is the imperative that de-cision occur, the imperative that neutrality and absolute indifference cannot remain, that the virtual contradiction must be decided. The decision of being will be discussed in the following chapter, but let it presently suffice to suggest that the law of non-contradiction is first operative as a prescriptive rather than descriptive law of being, which presupposes that contradiction indeed exists, but cannot remain. As Schelling notes, 'When it is known that a contradiction cannot be, it must be known that it nevertheless in a certain way is.'[63] The law of non-contradiction does not say that contradiction does not exist; it demands that it ought to exist no longer.

The argument is that the principle of excluded middle is the condition of the operativity of the law of non-contradiction, although neither yet holds in pure chaos or primordial contingency. Primordial contingency's supplementation with the principle of excluded middle occurs only through an unprethinkable de-cision, through the imposition of an interstice. This interstice supplements *actus purus* with possibility; this interstice is the ur-possibility. Once supplemented with this possibility, chaos or the unprethinkable first accrues an identity, because with this its neutrality is first decided. According to this suggestion, one would be able to adhere to all three laws of thought, the principle of excluded middle, the principle of non-contradiction and the principle of identity. None of them, however, have absolute provenance, as none of them hold in chaos. All of them, as laws of thought, as laws of universal and consequent reason, are but matters of fact. If thinking/reason is itself a contingent and consequent matter of fact, so are its laws.

The Law of the World and the copula

This section will explain why possibility must be shown to unprethinkable being, which is antecedent to all possibility, and how this possibility intervenes as an interstice, as a between-space, as the excluded middle, the copulating enactment between two contradictories, thereby permitting the possibility of emphatic propositions rather than the sheer consonance of tautology. The discussion must thus return to the nature of emphatic propositions.

The copula, in Schelling, must be thought transitively rather than reduplicatively, which means that it must be thought (1) verbally, as the act of copulation, and (2) in its relation to time. Consequently, (3) it must be able to bring about novel and unforeseeable consequents, because it is a synthetical rather than analytical relation. Schelling argues of any proposition that actually asserts something, for example, 'A is B', that 'A is something for itself without B . . . It could be otherwise than B and insofar as it is capable of not being B I can say *cum emphasi*: It *is* B.'[64] Analytical statements are not real assertions because that of which the predicate is asserted could not be anything else. The first requirement, then, of emphatic assertions is that they rest upon a basic contingency; that of which the predicate is said could have received a different predicate. Such assertions must be synthetical because the analytical never expresses a predicate whose negation, whose contradictory, would also have been possible. Schelling elaborates by example of the rose.

> That which I see here is a rose, the subject of that which is expressed – matter. This matter is something without the plant; this is indifferent to the form and in itself it is capable even of not being this plant. It is an ἄπειρον and could be a different plant or not even a plant at all.[65]

That of which the predicates are expressed is thus not merely the contingency to be otherwise but also the contingency not to have been at all. That which expresses reason, that which is reason, is something that not only could have been otherwise but something that could have not been at all. Reason, if it is, is synthetically and contingently. Given that it is, it transfigures that which is it into a kind of matter or potency, as, for Schelling, the concepts of matter, subject and potency are nearly synonymous insofar as they all indicate that which is capable of receiving form, predication and determination but which is as such deficient of all these. Schelling explains, 'But it, because it could be otherwise, makes this ability to be otherwise than B into a mere potency.'[66] The 'subject's' supplementation with determination first makes it into a determinate subject by materialising it, by rendering it receptive or potent, capable of receiving any determination possible. Vladimir Jankélévitch helpfully remarks that

> In an emphatic proposition, where the verb is no longer simply copulative, but synthetical, several adjectives are latent, but only one is attributed in act, emphatically, to the free subject that awaits its determination. The subject is by itself indifferent to all forms and qualities of which it will become the bearer. The subject is the ἄπειρον, the indecisive matter of the judgment; this matter attracts the predicates to itself via a type of magic . . .[67]

Actus purus prior to *potentia* is itself 'potentiated' insofar as it is this *potentia*. This indicates what was described before as the liberation of *actus purus* from itself; it is now free against its own being, against its own necessity or ἀνάγκη now rendered contingent. First with a *posterius* is the absolute *prius* revealed as something prior or past – since it was futural with respect to itself – and as the contingency of being itself.

Being is not a pre-given substance with the power to receive attributes, but it is the potentiation of unprethinkable *actus*, the figuration of chaos into temporal determination and order, transitivity as temporalisation. Being is operative as the act of copulation, as a verb, as an *Ereignis*, in the Heideggerian sense, not as the eternal presence and rigidity of a first substance. The act of copulation brings forth its *relata*, the contradictories, as consequents, that is, as accusatives, as opposed to predicate nominatives that would rename something already pre-given.

In the drafts of the *Ages of the World* Schelling expressed this insight by means of the idea that *relata* are what is expressed and the copula the expressing. Schelling there argued that 'the *expressing* (the essence of the copula, as one would have to say in the language of logic) can only be one. However, this does not prevent (the expressed) [*das Ausgesprochene*] from being Two that are opposed.'[68] Here is Schelling's rebuttal of all those who argue that contradictions cannot be. They can and are, so long as the contradictorily opposed are expressed of one and the same.[69] Is there a law, however, that necessitates that something be expressed at all? This question has not yet been definitively answered.

There is something rather than nothing because the unprethinkable was supplemented with thinking, because act without potency was supplemented with possibility. What law necessitates this? Schelling answers that it is 'no other law than that every possibility be fulfilled, that none are suppressed . . . This justice . . . is the most supreme Law of the World . . . Justice and Tribunal, which here means as much as disputation and judgment . . .'[70] Schelling seems to be relating his position back to Anaximander's notion of justice. In any event, this passage does not say that all possibilities must be actualised but that all possibilities must be *revealed*, that all must be presented as possible. Jankélévitch explains, '*Everything possible must arrive* . . . [This phrase] is, understood well, less Spinozistic than it appears: because with Spinoza nothing *arrives* . . .'[71] Not all possibilities must be actualised but all must 'arrive', all must be presented as possible. What is necessitated, then, is not the actualisation of the possible, not a movement *a potentia ad actum*, but that all possibility be decided, that what remains forever unactualised remains so not accidentally but decisively. Contingency is not suspended by the Law of the World, as there could have always been nothing instead of something, but if there would have been nothing instead of something, that would have been because of a decision against being. Nothing is ever actualised by remaining in limbo between being and non-being; chaos must be decided. The Law of the World dictates that an interstice come between possibilities, possibilities which first are on account of this interstice; it demands that one possibility be posited as actual and the other negated, posited as potent. Not everything must be actualised, but everything must be posited, either as actual or as potent. The Law of the World demands that the principle of excluded middle obtains in order that contradictions be decided, in order that the principle of non-contradiction also obtain. If everything must be decided, if everything must emerge from indecision, indifference, ambivalence, duplicity or neutrality, this also means that the principle of identity obtains. The Law of the World dictates that things emerge from non-identity into identity. The Law of the World thus provides all three laws of thought with their fundamentally prescriptive character.

The Law of the World dictates that ur-possibility be presented even to the unprethinkable, in which no possibility is to be found, which liberates it from its ἀνάγκη by revealing its self-ignorance in order that it may come to know and lay hold of its own being. Schelling explains that it

> makes the entire *being* of this moment . . . into a contingent being, in this respect a being that could be otherwise and thus in this regard a being still duplicitous. This duplicity may, so to speak, not remain, it *must* be decided. It *may* not remain, I say, and pronounce thereby a law, as it were, that forbids that something abide in indecisiveness, a law that demands that nothing remain concealed, that everything become manifest, that everything be clear, determined and decided . . . In fact, just *this* is that all-encompassing Law of the World that presides supremely over everything.[72]

Unprethinkable being, the three determinations of which have been designated as three modes of will, does not know itself as will. It lacks all knowledge, including of itself, until the possibility of thinking/knowledge has been shown to it. Only with this, even should it remain in repose rather than incite its will, does it first know itself as that which can will and, thus, also as that which can not-will. Only then does it know itself as free to will or not-will; only then does it know itself as liberated from unprethinkable necessity. Schelling explicates,

> Accordingly, it is, on account of this Law of the World, also necessary that this possibility be shown to the will (for, first, if it . . . has learned of this possibility and does *not* will it, it is that which it is with its own willing and, thus, secured to that place . . . but it is merely contingent in independence from itself, i.e. *relative* to itself). By virtue of this supreme and singular Law of the World that tolerates nothing accidental/contingent [*Zufälliges*], it is, I declare, necessary that . . . possibility be shown to that which can be which has power over itself, to that will that until now remained at rest . . .'[73]

Ironically, the Law of the World, which tolerates that nothing remain ambivalent, is itself ambivalent; its law is double in nature. On the one hand, the Law shows everything all its possibilities – which for unprethinkable being is the total figure of all possibility as such – while, on the other hand, it demands that nothing can remain as a possibility merely but that all possibilities either be actualised or potentiated, affirmed or extained. On the one hand, it potentiates or possibilises unprethinkable being, liberating it from its necessity/ἀνάγκη and rendering it contingent, while, on the other hand, it simultaneously demands that it cannot abide by this contingency or equipollence between potencies. It offers possibility with the one hand while dictating that one cannot abide by possibility with the other. Possibility, when affirmed, transitions into actuality, and possibility, when denied, excludes something once possible but now no longer; thus it offers possibility only to forbid that the ambivalence possibility offers can persist. For these reasons Schelling also refers to the Law of the World as tempter or 'nemesis', although he is careful, in so doing, to note how this remains part of a divine economy. This exceeds the scope of the current discussion, but what Schelling does, in short, is to allot a role to Satan, *qua* tempter, in the divine economy. He intriguingly contends that 'This Law of the World, this power, which is generally adverse to the ignorant, duplicitous and even to the accidental, is *nemesis*.'[74] The Law offers (*Gebot*) the possibility of decision only by first forbidding (*Verbot*) duplicity. The Law that forbids duplicity is itself duplicitous, enacting a double-law, a denying law of temptation that is also the divine imperative to affirm freedom and decisiveness.

The Law of the World creates contradictions by coming between two equally valid disjuncts, by imposing itself as the interstice or excluded middle between two equi-valent possibilities. By excluding the middle, it brings contradiction into being, positing it as the impetus to decisiveness. As Schelling noted in the 1815 draft of the *Ages of the World*, 'Only the contradiction is absolutely not allowed not to act and is alone what drives, nay, what coerces, action.'[75] Contradictions must exist, otherwise there would never be anything to be decided; for, everything but the contradiction permits a both/and rather than an either/or that also excludes the neither/nor, that is, rather than an either/or that exhausts all options, an either/or that is only there because the principle of excluded middle is already operative. For mere contraries, neither/nor remains possible. In other words, contraries can both be false, and even both/and is possible as long as one contrary is determined to precede and the other to follow. Nevertheless, that the one goes first and that the other follows can itself only be the result of a decision, which stems from the fact that both could not be affirmed at once and as the same time. In this respect, contrariety is but a modification of contradiction; for example, cold, insofar as it is not-hot, also holds as a contradiction of hot. Decisiveness accrues only where the middle option is excluded. 'With this [exclusion]', Schelling exclaims,

> the highest contradiction finally emerges. For there are not two inactive wills here, nor is one of the two inactive; rather, both are active. One and the same will is activated as the will that wills nothing and is also activated as the will that wills something (life and actuality) . . . an absolute decision is demanded.[76]

Meillassoux adhered to the principle of non-contradiction but denied the principle of sufficient reason. Schelling, on the contrary, denies efficacy to both with respect to chaos, but once the Law of the World supplements chaos with possibility, it manifests chaos as the original contradiction. The principle of non-contradiction does obtain prescriptively. The principle of sufficient reason is also to be admitted, but only as a consequent, only as a principle that regulates or 'houses' a being that precedes it. Schelling confirms, 'The principle of contradiction should be strictly adhered to, and what this formulation expresses negatively must instead be affirmed, as in the principle of reason.'[77] To think the principle of non-contradiction positively as a law of being rather than negatively as a formal law of thought alone is to think it as that which demands decisiveness. What the decision posits is ground/reason. The decision is what holds logical space or the space of reasons open. The customary view that decisions follow grounds or reasons is thus to be rejected, as it is rather the inverse that is true.[78] All forms of rational choice theory must be opposed. Genuine decisions are those for which reasons can only be provided after the fact, for example, the decision to be the person that one is or the decision to love someone. If one tells one's son that he will be getting a kitten, he immediately decides to love it. Why? It is not because it is cute, as it is not even known what kitten he will be receiving. It is not because he knows that it is healthy. It is not because he knows it will love him. He loves it for no reason except that he has decided to relate to it in this way. Yet if he were to be asked a month later why he loves his kitten, he would have a large list of reasons, all of which materialised only after the fact of loving his kitten. That was a mundane example, but the same account holds for why one loves one's beloved or one's God. Theory and deliberation always lag behind praxis; reason and grounds are being's consequent, not its antecedent. In the beginning was not deliberation or the self-contemplation of Aristotle's God, but the deed, the fact that a decision of being occurred, the reasons for which are only enumerable *post factum*. Reason is being's consequent, its *posterius*.

Decision as event

The positive in positive philosophy is that wherein will decides, as opposed to the merely logical. Logic and reason alone are impersonal, the neuter and neutral, but what results from will, deed and decisiveness is personal. The personal, then, results from no necessity whatsoever. It is something for which one can only narrate that it has so happened, that one has so willed. This indicates that being, occurring as a 'leap' or as something which simply 'bechances', could just as easily not have been and thus occurs as personal, if it occurs. There is no tension in affirming that the deed, the decision, simply bechances and simultaneously affirming that it is also the event of freedom, because freedom and its decision operate in advance of deliberation and conscious reflection, without precedent reasons. Reasons certainly accrue. The deed is not without reason, but only as something consequent to the deed; reasons supplement the decision. Gabriel is correct when he says, 'Freedom is . . . the establishment and differentiation of the modalities.'[79] One must only remember that these modalities constitute reason itself; reason exists only as the modality of unprethinkable *actus*, *actus* thought verbally as the decisive deed itself.

Hutter is correct to surmise that Schelling presents a new relation between reason and history[80] because the deed that brings about reason as its consequent brings it about as a temporal relation.[81] One modality is determined as what precedes, the other as what follows and the third as what completes the series. Reason is thus not thought as timeless but as part of the history of being itself,[82] even if these temporal determinations emerge as an eternal happening. The positive in positive philosophy is not the unprethinkable *Daß*, chaos, but the unprethinkable decision, and is thus connected to the rupture of temporal determination. As Edward Allen Beach has contended, in Schelling there is not Hegel's *Aufhebungsdialektik* but an *Erzeugungsdialektik* in which there is a temporal rather than logical production of new principles, not just the conceptual clarification or parsing of *der Begriff*. In Schelling's *Potenzenlehre* 'the next succeeding level or principle of being is not just logically entailed, but is actually caused by the preceding potencies of the system'.[83] If philosophy's object is temporal rather than logical, then the actual object of philosophy is the de-cision or the event of being.

Van der Heiden insightfully comments, '*Event is a concept that is created to think an alternative to the principle of sufficient reason.*'[84] To repeat, sufficient reason should not be denied all provenance. The being of reason, even sufficient reason, is contingent and consequent, yet eternal, not absolute, yet universal. The event, the decision, which is antecedent to reason, is what is absolute and its consequent is universal. Van der Heiden, while agreeing that the event is absolute, nevertheless argues that 'the event is always the event of pluralizing'.[85] He never considers the possibility that the event, instead of ensuing only in fragmentation and plurality, could contingently bring about a universal, all-encompassing reason. He never considers that not all events are preliminary and necessarily to be surpassed by a future event. He fails to speculate about the possibility that the event, the decision of being, could be once and for all. His absolute thus falls prey to the sectarian. If there is an event like the one proposed by this book, then, as the following chapter argues, this event can properly be designated with the name 'God'.

The following chapter will elaborate the event not in relation to its consequent, reason, but as such, that is, as God. God, antecedent to reason itself, will thus not be subject to sufficient reason and, therefore, not be able to be thought by the ontological argument. The following quote by Schelling provides a helpful preview:

> One says that God is determined to exist through his essence or that God's existence is, for this reason, necessary, because his sufficient reason lies in his essence. This is an expression of which Leibniz makes ample use because he denies that God's *existence* is demonstrable without the principle of sufficient reason, i.e. without this no conclusiveness is ascribed even to the ontological argument. In all these expressions *essence* is posited before existence. The meaning of the Aristotelian concept, however, is that essence itself consists in sheer *actus*.[86]

As this chapter has repeatedly emphasised, sheer or naked existence precedes essence. The same that has been said of reason, then, will be said of God: their *modus essendi* or *modus operandi* is necessary, but their existence or actuality lies in the contingency of the modeless. While this chapter dealt with the ontology of reason, the following deals with the ontological constitution of God as the consequent identity of the decision itself, the meaning of the event of being.

Notes

1. 'Bei Schelling gibt es keine feste Terminologie. Das Sein und das Seiende können ihren gegenseitigen Sinn umkehren; das Übersein kann wieder Sein heißen; das Wort Geist wird für die dritte Potenz gebraucht und für das alle Potenzen übergreifende Übersein; Gott kann das Übersein oder dessen erste Erscheinung bedeuten. Je im Zusammenhang ist die Vorstellung deutlich' (Jaspers, *Schelling*, p. 170).
2. 'Schelling ist Gnostiker . . . weil er das Material der Gnosis aus der Überlieferung der Theosophie aufnimmt und aneignet, – weil er von früh bis spät alles sieht im Raum der intellektuellen Anschauung, ohne den wirksamen Zusammenhang zwischen ihr und dem faktischen Weltwissen und dem endlichen Handeln zu finden . . .' (ibid., p. 212).
3. See Brown, *The Later Philosophy of Schelling*.
4. See Hutter, *Geschichtliche Vernunft*.
5. Beach, *Potencies*, p. 264.
6. Deleuze, *Difference and Repetition*, p. 190.
7. Ibid., p. 277.
8. Schelling, *Initia Philosophiae Universae*, p. 37. Schelling is thus not enamoured by the rationalism that ensues from the a priori alone, remarking in 1830 that philosophy assumes nothing, at least not voluntarily, because it rather begins with experience. This is what permits philosophy to begin without having to postulate hypotheticals (Schelling, *Einleitung*, p. 19). To begin with experience – which is not equivalent with sensibilism, impressionism or representationalism – is not to deduce facts from a presupposed premise but to take facticity as the starting point, which begins before anything one might voluntarily assume.
9. Hegel, *Philosophy of Right*, p. xix.
10. Schelling, *Grundlegung*, p. 161.
11. 'Die Vernunftwissenschaft begründet die Bedingungen der Möglichkeit von Erfahrung, aber nicht die Wirklichkeit der Erfahrung' (Durner, *Wissen und Geschichte*, p. 137).
12. 'Sie enthält eine überwiegende Masse von Unvernunft, sodass man beinahe sagen könnte, das Rationale sei <nur>das Accidens' (Schelling, *Grundlegung*, pp. 99–100).
13. Schelling, *On the History of Modern Philosophy*, p. 147.
14. 'Warum ist Sinn überhaupt, warum ist nicht Unsinn statt Sinn? . . . Die ganze Welt liegt gleichsam in der Vernunft gefangen, aber die Frage ist: wie ist sie in dieses Netz gekommen?' (Schelling, *Grundlegung*, p. 222).
15. Kierkegaard, *Concept of Anxiety*, pp. 9–10.
16. Schelling, *Die endlich offenbar gewordene positive Philosophie*, p. 152.
17. See Tritten, 'Against Kant'. This article shows how Schelling abides by Kant's strictures. Kant forbade the movement from interiority to exteriority, from immanence to transcendence, but Kant never forbade the inverse movement. One can begin on the absolute outside, Meillassoux's 'great outdoors', if one will, and have before oneself the task of how first to construct a domain of immanence, the transcendental. This absolute outside, anterior to all immanence and interiority, is not the outside of any inside; thus the very distinction that separates philosophies of transcendence and philosophies of immanence collapses.
18. Peirce, who admitted Schelling's influence (as well as Hegel's) upon his own thought, also formulates a tri-fold notion of everything thinkable. He writes, 'My view is that there are three modes of being . . . They are the being of positive qualitative possibility, the being of actual fact, and the being of law that will govern facts in the future' (Peirce, 'Lessons', p. 23).
19. 'Denn hat sich dieser Wille einmal entzündet, so ist er nicht mehr Wille – er ist nicht mehr das, was sein und nicht sein *kann*; er ist jetzt das, was sein und nicht sein *konnte*

... dem zufällig Seienden wird sein Sein zur Notwendigkeit ...' (Schelling, *Urfassung*, p. 28).
20. 'Das Zufällige wird zum Notwendigen, weil es, wenn es ist, nicht mehr nicht sein kann' (ibid., p. 29).
21. 'Darüber ist aber jetzt nicht die Frage, ob es ein ursprüngliches Sein gäbe, sondern wie es entstehen könne ... Wäre das, was sein wird, bloß ein unmittelbar sein Könnendes, so würden wir in der Wirklichkeit nur auf ein blindes Sein stoßen ...' (ibid., p. 32).
22. As Hutter has remarked, if a cause or ground proceeds immediately unto its effect or consequent, as in logic, then the temporal and the historical is lost (Hutter, *Geschichtliche Vernunft*, p. 158).
23. Here a difference between Schelling's and Peirce's accounts emerges. For both thinkers, the first determination represents pure possibility; however, for Schelling, the pure possibility of being, if unimpeded, could not resist its inclination and would incite itself without delay, while, for Peirce, the first holds itself in check without the need of the second to constrain it. Peirce writes, 'The first is a *posse* which it has in itself; for the *priman* stops at *can-bes* and never reaches to existence, which depends on interactions, or *secundanity*' (Peirce, 'Categories', p. 351). Peirce's second determination, then, far from prohibiting the incitation of the first, is rather that which grants the first the ability to raise itself to being. Certainly, for Schelling too, the second is an indispensable condition for determinate being, but the apeiratic first operates like an addiction (*Sucht*) for being apart from the limits the second imposes upon it. For Schelling, without the second the addiction or mania of the first never becomes regulated or curbed. Nevertheless, one also finds Peirce affirming that 'The idea of second is predominant in the ideas of causation and of statical force. For cause and effect are two; and statical forces always occur between pairs. Constraint is a Secondness' (ibid., p. 325).
24. 'hinter dem Sein' (Schelling, *Urfassung*, p. 33).
25. 'Wir wollen es vor dem Übertritt ins Sein bewahren: wir wollen, daß es als pura potentia, als reines Können, stehen bleibe, als Können ohne Sein. Als sein Könnendes kann es aber nur stehenbleiben, wenn es zum Ersatz des Seins, welches es annehmen könnte, und das daher nur ein zufälliges, mögliches Sein ist ... Potenz bleiben kann es nämlich nur so, daß es selbst an und für sich schon das rein Seiende, dem keine Möglichkeit vorausgeht, ist' (ibid., p. 34).
26. 'ein Sein ohne Übergang, ohne vorausgegangene Potenz' (ibid., p. 35).
27. Peirce proves to be close to Schelling again in his most speculative endeavours, asserting,

> Time is itself an organized something, having its law or regularity; so that time itself is a part of that universe whose origin is to be considered. We have therefore to suppose a state of things before time was organized. Accordingly, when we speak of the universe as 'arising' we do not mean that literally. (Peirce, 'Objective Logic', p. 214)

> The question of the origin of number, which presupposes succession and so a minimum of two, a before and an after, hence two as the first number, is thus related to the origin of time itself. Time, as succession or seriality, only arises with two or more because there is only time when there is a countable 'before'. There was hence never a first (one) without the succeeding/second (two), because a first without a second is not a first or a before, only the Alone. Number and time both emerge from nothing or from 0; thus Peirce continues,

> We start, then, with nothing, pure zero. But this is not the nothing of negation. For *not* means *other than*, and *other* is merely a synonym of the ordinal numeral *second*. As such it implies a first; while the present pure zero is prior to every first. The nothing of negation is the nothing of death, which comes *second* to, or after,

everything. But this pure zero is the nothing of not having been born. There is no individual thing, no compulsion, outward nor inward, no law . . . As such, it is absolutely undefined and unlimited possibility – boundless possibility. There is no compulsion and no law. It is boundless freedom. (ibid., p. 217)

28. 'in die Mitte' (Schelling, *Urfassung*, p. 58).
29. 'von beiden frei' (ibid., p. 58).
30. Peirce seems to follow the Hegelian dialectic more closely than the Schellingian. He writes, 'Thirdness . . . is the same as mediation. For that reason, pure dyadism is an act of arbitrary will or of blind force; for if there is any reason, or law, governing it, that mediates between the two subjects and brings about their connection . . .' (Peirce, 'Categories', p. 328). Peirce, with Hegel, views the third as synthesis and mediation rather than as a middle that divides the contradiction and thus excludes or extains. He does, however, intriguingly suggest that the third is what first institutes law and order, which are thus first granted as consequents and not as what has priority. In this vein, he suggests that law, reason and order are nothing more than the aptitude of being for continuity and regularity; they are but the habit of being. He writes, 'Thirdly, the categories suggest our looking for a synthesizing law; and this we find in the power of assimilation, incident to which is the habit-taking faculty' (ibid., p. 351).
31. While, for Schelling, freedom is (re)instituted with the third, what he also calls 'Spirit', which is attracted no more by the first determination than by the second, for Peirce, the first determination alone suffices for the use of the adjective 'free.' He asserts that

The idea of First is predominant in the ideas of freshness, life, freedom. The free is that which has not another behind it . . . Freedom can only manifest itself in unlimited and uncontrolled variety and multiplicity; and thus the first becomes predominant in the ideas of measureless variety and multiplicity . . . It is not in being separated from qualities that Firstness is most predominant, but in being something peculiar and idiosyncratic. (Peirce, 'Categories', p. 302)

The rhetoric of freedom aside, Peirce's description of firstness is perfectly compatible with Schelling's, especially when one considers that Schelling also speaks of a freedom that is not the result of the determinations of thought but their *prius*.
32. The term 'extainment' has probably been unconsciously adopted from Iain Hamilton Grant.
33. 'Aber diese ganze Aufeinanderfolge beruht auf der Voraussetzung: wenn es ein Sein gibt . . . Aber eben jene Voraussetzung ist selbst eine zweifelhafte . . . Es kann gefragt werden: Warum ist denn nicht nichts?' (Schelling, *Urfassung*, p. 65).
34. 'Wir sagten, *wenn* ein Sein entsteht, so kann es nur in dieser Folge entstehen. Aber, fragt sich jetzt, wie nach und warum entsteht denn ein Sein? Nur inwiefern es eine erste Wirklichkeit gibt' (ibid., p. 69).
35. 'nicht als absolute Notwendigkeit begriffen haben, sondern nur hypothetisch. Ferner ist es offenbar, daß wir ihn nicht aus der Vernunft abgeleitet haben, denn ich kann immer noch fragen: Warum ist denn Vernunft und nicht Unvernunft?' (ibid., p. 69).
36. 'grundlos' and 'ohne vorausgehende Notwendigkeit' (ibid., p. 69).
37. Emilio Brito remarks, 'The absolute *prius* does not have a *prius*, nor necessity nor precedent. [Le Prius absolut n'a aucun Prius, aucune nécessité ne le devance.]' (Brito, 'Création', p. 316).
38. As Peirce remarked, 'Actuality is something *brute*. There is no reason in it' ('Lessons', p. 24). This is also reminiscent of Meillassoux's insight that what makes a fact a fact is its absence of reason. The determinations of thought reveal only the necessary essence or quiddity of reason, never the contingent quoddity or facticity of reason.
39. 'Dadurch ist allem philosophischen Rationalismus das Fundament zerstört. Die Vernunft ist nicht das an sich Notwendige' (Schelling, *Urfassung*, p. 71).

40. '*er ist, weil er ist*' (ibid., p. 71).
41. Heidegger, *Principle of Reason*, p. 36.
42. 'apriorischer Empirismus' (Schelling, 'Einleitung in die Philosophie der Offenbarung oder Begründung', *SW II/3*, p. 102).
43. 'Ursprünglich nennen wir ... nur das, wovon die Möglichkeit erst durch die Wirklichkeit gegeben ist' (Schelling, *Urfassung*, p. 82).
44. 'Das Gegenteil des blinden Entstehens ist nur da, wo die Möglichkeit der Tat wirklich vorausgeht' (ibid., p. 33).
45. Schelling comments, 'Contingency presupposes that actuality is not determined through possibility, that being is not determined through thinking ... [Zufälligkeit setzt voraus, daß die Wirklichkeit nicht durch die Möglichkeit, das Seyn nicht durch das Denken bestimmt sey ...]' ('System', *SW I/6*, p. 529).
46. Heidegger, *Being and Time*, p. 34.
47. 'nur als contrarium sich Entgegenstehende ... das nämlich nur widersprechend werde, also unter den Grundsatz des Widerspruchs falle, wenn es *zugleich* gesetzt werde, nicht also, wenn das eine vorausgehe, das andere folge, wo Entgegengesetztes allerdings eines und dasselbe seyn können' (Schelling, 'Darstellung der reinrationalen Philosophie', *SW II/1*, p. 305).
48. Ibid., *SW II/1*, pp. 292–3.
49. 'Hiedurch erhält das sonst bloß negative Gesetz positive Bedeutung, und es begreift sich, wie es nach Aristoteles das Gesetz *alles* Seyenden, also das fruchtbarste und inhaltsreichste aller Gesetze ... daß ohne das so verstandene nur nichtssagende Sätze übrig bleiben, und emphatische, d.h. die wirklich etwas aussprechen, unmöglich seyn würden. Denn wovon läßt sich sagen, daß es hell ist, als von dem an sich-Dunkeln, wovon, es sey krank, als von dem bloß krank seyn Könnenden, an sich also Gesunden' (ibid., *SW II/1*, p. 305).
50. 'das Unstete' (Schelling, *System der Weltalter*, p. 132).
51. Gabriel, 'Mythological Being', p. 54.
52. 'Das, was das Seyende *Ist*, kann als das schlechthin Wesen- oder Idee-Freie (nämlich für sich und außer dem Seyenden betrachtet), nicht einmal *das Eine* seyn, sondern nur *Eines*, Ἕν τι, was dem Aristoteles mit dem was ein *Dieses* (ein τόδε τι ὄν) und dem für-sich-seyn-Könnenden gleichbedeutend ist, dem χωριστόν' (Schelling, 'Darstellung der reinrationalen Philosophie', *SW II/1*, p. 314).
53. 'Denn das Vorausgehende wird gegen das Folgende zugleich zum Untergeordneten (ὑποκείμενον), und die Momente des Seyenden verhalten sich vollkommen wie Stufen, die ebensowenig *zugleich* betreten als *an derselben Stelle* seyn können. Beraubung sey *auch* Verneinung, sagt Aristoteles hier, nur nicht, wie er anderwärts unterscheidet, unbedingte, die das Verneinte dem Gegenstand *überhaupt* abspricht ...' (ibid., *SW II/1*, p. 306).
54. 'wie das nur nicht positiv Seyende nicht das *Nicht*seyende, sondern durch die Verneinung nur zu einer besondern Art des Seyenden, zum μὴ ὄν wird ... Was A nicht ist, ist entweder das ganz des Aseyns Unfähige (τὸ ἀδύνατον ὅλως ἔχειν), oder das es seyn kann aber nicht ist (τὸ πεφυκὸς ἔχειν μὴ ἔχῃ)' (ibid., *SW II/1*, p. 307).
55. Heidegger, in the *Beiträge*, indicates that Schelling would have thought the other beginning, would have broken through metaphysics, had he been able 'to ground the question of the "modalities" differently' (Heidegger, *Contributions*, p. 138). The contention is that in his latest thought, which Heidegger never explicitly addresses, this is precisely what Schelling does. He namely thinks the modalities no longer as modes at all.
56. Gabriel, 'Mythological Being', p. 66.
57. In this context, Gabriel is justifiably critical of modal logic, bemoaning that 'another problem with modal logics modelled along the lines of an unclear notion of possible worlds (which, by the way, is closer to science-fiction B movies than to Leibniz's notion of a possible world) is that it is based on a circle. If necessity is understood

as truth in all possible worlds' – a veritable conflation of necessity and universality – 'then possibility and actuality also are tied to possible worlds. Talk of "possible worlds" evidently already presupposes an understanding of the modalities' (Gabriel, *Transcendental Ontology*, p. 120). In short, modal logics fail to support themselves with an ontology that would account for the origin of modality as such; for a *modus* is always the *modus operandi* of something or some event that precedes modal operations. So-called modal ontologies do not uncover this presupposition of modality; they just presuppose that logic is ontology, except not even in the Aristotelian sense where logic is a law of being itself. As Gabriel suggests, 'I doubt that modal logics contributes anything to our understanding of the modals as long as its metaphysical presuppositions are not put under scrutiny . . . what uncritical contemporary analytical metaphysics implicitly assumes – namely, that logical space has always already been there anyway . . .' (ibid., p. 121).
58. 'Aristoteles, so oft er den großen Grundsatz erwähnt (unmöglich ist, daß dasselbe zugleich sey und nicht sey), nur von εἶναι καὶ μὴ εἶναι, nie von εἶναι καὶ οὐκ εἶναι spricht, wie er müßte, wenn der Grundsatz ihm bloß die formelle Bedeutung hätte, von der die Neueren allein wissen' (Schelling, 'Darstellung der reinrationalen Philosophie', *SW II/1*, p. 314).
59. 'dem Vorausgehenden mußte bestimmt seyn, daß es voraus gehe, dem Folgenden, daß es folge, dem Letzten, daß es der Zweck und das Ende sey. Es ist unvermeidlich, auf das *alles zugleich* zu kommen, wie auch Aristoteles zugibt, daß nach Einem Gesichtspunkt die Recht haben, welche nicht-Seyn und Seyn im Gegenstand präexistiren lassen . . . es ist hier alles wie in einem organischen Ganzen gegen sich welchselseitig bestimmend und bestimmt; das nicht seyende ist dem rein seyenden der Grund (die ratio sufficiens), aber hinwieder ist das rein seyende die bestimmende Ursache (ratio determinans) des bloßen *An*-sich-seyns, und auch das Dritte vermittelt den vorausgehenden ebenso Momente des Seyenden zu seyn, wie eben dieses ihm durch sie vermittelt ist; es müssen deßhalb alle oder es kann keines gesetzt seyn' (ibid., *SW II/1*, p. 311).
60. Vallicella, *Paradigm Theory*, p. 244.
61. Ibid., p. 161.
62. The absolute *prius* is neither the determined (πέρας) nor the undetermined (ἄπειρον) but that which posits both and, in this respect, that which even posits chaos as chaos, namely as something indeterminate. Were it not the case that the unlimited and the limited were posited in the same act, it would never be understandable why the first lets itself be subjected to limit and measure. The first deed, as it were, is the positing of the unlimited as unlimited, the positing of chaos as chaos, the positing of the receptacle as receptive of determination.
63. Schelling, *Ages of the World (3rd draft)*, p. 12.
64. 'A ist für sich etwas ohne B . . . Es könnte etwas anders sein, als B, und insofern, als es des nicht B Seins fähig ist, kann ich cum emphasi sagen: Es *ist* B' (Schelling, *Urfassung*, p. 52).
65. 'Das, was ich hier sehe, ist eine Rose, ist das Subject des Ausgesagten – Materie. Diese Materie ist etwas ohne die Pflanze; diese ist gegen die Form gleichgültig, und an sich fähig, auch nicht diese Pflanze zu sein: sie ist ein ἄπειρον und könnte eine andere oder gar keine Pflanze sein' (ibid., p. 52).
66. 'Aber macht es, weil es etwas anders sein könnte, dieses anders sein Können gegen B zur bloßen Potenz' (ibid., p. 52).
67. 'Dans une proposition emphatique, où le verbe n'est plus simplement copulative, mais synthétique, plusieurs adjectifs sont latents mais un seul est attribué en acte, emphatiquement, au libre sujet qui attend sa détermination. Le sujet est par lui-même indifférent aux formes et qualités dont il deviendra porteur. Le sujet est l'ἄπειρον, la matière indécise du jugement ; cette matière attire à soi les prédicats par une sorte de magie . . .' (Jankélévitch, *L'Odyssée*, p. 38).
68. Schelling, *Ages of the World (2nd draft)*, p. 127. Van der Heiden, through Agamben's

reading of Aristotle, artfully shows how contradictions can be rendered inoperative by merely avoiding expression altogether, by ceasing to speak. This is how he argues that the ἀνυπόθετος of Plato's *Parmenides* is achieved. If the principle of non-contradiction prevails over all speech-acts, by remaining silent one renders the principle inoperative. Van der Heiden writes,

> By ceasing to speak, one indeed interrupts one's communication and one's will to communicate, but one does not lose one's potential to speak or to reason ... the potential to communicate is also the *potential not to communicate*. This latter potential not to ... characterizes the realm disclosed by the deactivation of the principle of noncontradiction. (Van der Heiden, *Ontology after Ontotheology*, p. 118)

He suggests that in this way Agamben uncovers a potentiality beyond the negativity of the 'not yet'. This, however, does not mark a break with Schelling's conception of that which will be, because *das was sein wird* does not denote that which necessarily will be but just has not yet. It rather indicates that which will be, if it will be, which it might not. At any rate, the neither/nor of the ἀνυπόθετος can be revealed not just in not-expressing but also in expressing, insofar as the 'subject' of expression is revealed as sheer contingency or potency.

69. In this text Schelling even formulates this in a way that hints at a solution to the mind–body problem.

> One = X is soul and body, which is to say one is the expressing of both ... but to the extent that it is only their expressing – without taking into account the fact that it actually does express them – it is neither the one nor the other ... But if it actually expresses them both, then it is both, though not as the expressing but rather with respect to the expressed, just as it was both before as well, not as the expressing but indeed with respect <to the expressible> [dem Aussprechlichen]. (Schelling, *Ages of the World (2nd draft)*, p. 128)

That which is both soul and body is the one that it is only in the opposition of these two, hence two is the first number. One, identity, is the deposit retroactively visible in the wake of two. Additionally, the expressing of the two is that which is neither the first nor the second, hence both or number as such emerges from nothing. The nothing too, however, the 0, can only appear as the void locus of expressing if, in fact, it expresses rather than remaining silent. Thus, 0 too is first posited *in actu* only after two, only *post factum*.

70. 'kein anderes Gesetz, als daß alle Möglichkeit sich erfülle, keine unterdrückt werde ... Diese Gerechtigkeit ... ist zugleich das höchste Weltgesetz.' 'Gerechtigkeit und Gericht (hier so viel als Auseinandersetzung und Schiedsspruch) ...' (Schelling, 'Darstellung der reinrationalen Philosophie', *SW II/1*, p. 492).

71. '*Tout le possible doit arriver* ... est, bien entendu, moins spinoziste qu'elle n'en a l'air : car chez Spinoza rien n'*arrive* ...' (Jankélévitch, *L'Odyssée*, p. 198).

72. 'macht das ganze *Seyn* dieses Moments ... selbst zum zufälligen, insofern auch anders seyn könnenden und so weit selbst noch zweideutigen Seyn. Diese Zweideutigkeit darf, so zu sagen, nicht bleiben, sie *muß* entschieden werden. Sie *darf* nicht bleiben, sage ich, und spreche damit gleichsam ein Gesetz aus, das verbietet, daß etwas in der Unentschiedenheit verharre, ein Gesetz, das fordert, daß nichts verborgen bleibe, alles offenbar werde, alles klar, bestimmt und entschieden sey ... In der That eben *dieß* ist das alleinige, das höchste über allem schwebende Weltgesetz' (Schelling, *Philosophie der Mythologie*, p. 142).

73. 'Demnach ist es vermögen desselben Weltgesetzes auch nothwendig, daß diese Möglichkeit dem Willen gezeigt werde (denn erst, wenn das ... diese Möglichkeit

ersehen hat und sie *nicht* will, ist es mit seinem eignen Wollen das, was es ist, und also an dem Ort befestigt ... aber unabhängig von sich selbst, d.h. *relativ* auf sich selbst bloß zufällig ist). Zufolge jenes höchsten und einzigen Weltgesetzes, das nichts Zufälliges duldet, ist es, sage ich, nothwendig daß jenem seiner selbst Mächtigen Seynkönnen, jenem bis jetzt noch ruhenden Willen ... die Möglichkeit gezeigt werde ...' (ibid., p. 143).
74. 'Dieses Weltgesetz, die dem Ungewissen, dem Zweideutigen, sowie dem Zufälligen überhaupt abholde Macht ist *Nemesis*' (ibid., p. 143).
75. Schelling, *Ages of the World (3rd draft)*, p. 12.
76. Schelling, *Ages of the World (2nd draft)*, p. 169.
77. Ibid., p. 173.
78. As Gabriel asserts, 'The continued existence of logical space is at every moment the result of the repetition of a decision to see x as F and thus to actively exclude G' (Gabriel, *Transcendental Ontology*, p. 99). Not only does his response relate to the notions of exclusion as extainment, as an actively positing as..., but, more importantly, he affirms that logical space, the space of reasons and deliberation, only comes after and as a consequence of the decision, which means that it can in no way function as a condition of the deed itself. The decision is to let determinacy prevail over indeterminacy, thinkability over unthinkability, which presupposes that something prior to thinkability, the unprethinkable, is affirmed as anterior.
79. Gabriel, *Transcendental Ontology*, p. 94.
80. Hutter, *Geschichtliche Vernunft*, p. 11.
81. Jankélévitch writes, in accord with Hutter, '*The universe is not a system, but a history.* That is why there is a philosophy of Mythology and Revelation. [*L'univers n'est pas un système ; mais une histoire. Voilà pourquoi il existe une philosophie de la Mythologie et de la Révélation.*]' (Jankélévitch, *L'Odyssée*, p. 3).
82. Although he is speaking rather of the inner-historical conditions of rationality and not its emergence as such – which corresponds to his penchant for deflationary readings – Gabriel's remark remains valid:

> The very mythology of modernity is committed to reason as the glue, which is to hold communities together. Yet its apotheosis of reason represses the genealogy of reason not only in order to cover up the irrational and violent origins of modern rationality, but also in order to make it look necessary despite its contingent history. (Gabriel, *Transcendental Ontology*, p. 80)

83. Beach, 'Later Schelling's Conception', p. 41.
84. Van der Heiden, *Ontology after Ontotheology*, p. 6.
85. Ibid., p. 17.
86. 'man sagt: Gott sey durch sein Wesen bestimmt zur Existenz, oder: Gottes Existenz sey darum eine nothwendige, weil der zureichende Grund derselben in seinem Wesen liege, ein Ausdruck, dessen Leibnitz um so mehr sich bedient, weil er leugnet, daß ohne das Princip des zureichenden Grundes Gottes *Daseyn* erweislich sey, also auch dem ontologischen Argument ohne dieses keine Beweiskraft zuschreibt. In allen diesen Ausdrücken wird Wesen vor die Existenz gesetzt, der Sinn des aristotelischen Begriffs aber ist, daß das Wesen selbst bloß im Actus bestehe' (Schelling, 'Darstellung der reinrationalen Philosophie', *SW II/1*, p. 316).

Chapter 5

Decision and Withdrawal: On the Facticity and Posteriority of God

Traditional theology thinks of God as Creator, which does not err by drawing God into a relation with the world *per se*, but does, unfortunately, imply that God is only God because he creates, thus drawing God into a necessary relation with the actual world. It implies that God is unable not to create. Were this so, then it could only be either because God's nature necessarily overflows into creation (corresponding to Neoplatonic notions of procession), which would call God's freedom against his own nature into question, or because, in a Leibnizian fashion, God is constrained to create by sufficient reasons. The previous chapter argued that reason can only be consequent to a decision for creation, which means that if God creates, he must be the *prius* of reason. God cannot thus create out of prevailing reasons, only out of chaos.

To grasp chaos as the absolute point of departure, the absolute *prius*, Schelling exclaims, one must abandon not just reason but everything that is, including God.[1] Chaos is not God, because chaos is duplicitous and without exclusions, something undecided and thus indifferent, neutral and impersonal. Chaos is that in which wheat has not yet been separated from chaff, in which being and non-being are not yet excluded from one another. Neither sensible nor spiritual, chaos is nothing at all. As nothing, however, it is nevertheless the Absolute in the sense of that which is absolved of all relations, both to another and even to itself, lacking even internal consistency and substance. God, who in this sense is not the Absolute, is not void of relation but is rather pure relation, the copula itself or *ex se*. God is not chaos but the deed, the freedom that reigns sovereign over chaos, he who holds sway over the *Abgrund* (abyss) and *Ungrund* (groundlessness and reasonlessness). The task, then, is to narrate the history of how chaos, the absolute *prius*, will be that which *post factum* can be assumed as the anterior being of God, as his substantiality, that without which God could not be God but not that by which God is God in propriety.

God is not chaos, not the Absolute, but this is God's anterior, over which he reigns in sovereignty and freedom, without which God would have nothing over which to exert his sovereignty and express his freedom. God is freedom and sovereignty, but these cannot be without his anterior. The question, then, is how actually to depart from this absolute *prius*. Schelling confirms, 'We must take leave of it, we must get free of unprethinkable being in order to reach the *Idea*. This would only be possible if . . . unprethinkable being itself could again be shown as something contingent.'[2] If the absolutely antecedent *prius* could not be shown to be contingent but were rather, even in respect to itself, necessary, then it would be rigid, incapable of leading to something other and, given that it is nothing, this means incapable of being something, anything at all.

If, however, it is contingent, then the fact that it is nothing – or, more precisely, no more something than nothing, the neutral zone of indistinction that is neither something nor nothing, the undecided ambivalence between being and nothingness – is only an accident (*Zufall*). It turns out, in point of fact, that it can be something other, namely the Idea, which signifies the figure of reason itself. Schelling attests that

> Nothing prevents that precisely this being, which is a priori, after the fact, *post actum*, (as that is here precisely the appropriate expression) is that which can be . . . By this means a not to be excluded contingency is posited in this unprethinkable act of existing.[3]

While this indicates that the possibility of actually departing from the absolute *prius* is not excluded, it also indicates that the opposite, the possibility of not-departing, has not yet been excluded either. This only negatively shows that it is not impossible to break free of unprethinkable being.

If the absolute *prius*, that anterior over which God would sovereignly preside, were something from which he could break free, then and only then is it that which will be God. As that without which he could never be God but not that by which he positively is as God, it is that which will constitute his negative attributes. Schelling explains,

> Eternal is that being in which God is even before *he himself* thinks it . . . Eternity belongs to those attributes of God that the more speculative amongst the theologians have termed negative. If one investigates this more closely, they are throughout those attributes which are thought of God in and of himself, i.e. before his divinity, *those without* which he could not be God but through which he is not yet God. Spinozistic substance, for

example, is also eternal, without any presupposition, eternally groundless, and yet it is not God; inversely, however, God could not be God if he would not be eternal; eternity is a *conditio sine qua non* of his divinity.[4]

The absolute *prius* – although only after having departed from it – proves inextricable and indispensable to the being of God, but it is not God as such. The task, then, is actually to depart from the absolute *prius*, to narrate the eternal decision by which God comes to reign as sovereign over (his own) being, the event by which he brings about a ground (*Grund*) in 'groundless being',[5] in the unground (*Ungrund*). With the unprethinkable, if one recalls from the prior chapter, one begins before being, even before God, as one begins only with what will be and not with what is. This 'before', however, is only a *momentum* and nothing according to actual time, as there is not first the absolute *prius* and afterwards God's coming to gain hold over it. The event of being is an eternal occurrence. As Deleuze has noted, a lot happens in that dark night in which all cows were allegedly black. There was never, at time t, the absolute *Daß* without a *Was*, never A^0 without A^1, A^2 and A^3; or, if there was, then it was only as nothing, as nought. This chapter, then, will show not just that the possibility of leaving naked *Daß* is not logically excluded, but it will also narrate what happens when this possibility, from eternity forth, is actually presented to the unprethinkable.

The Law of the World and the child who plays before God

The Law of the World demands that the duplicity of chaos, which excludes nothing, cannot remain. It demands a decision. Where there is decision there is something excluded and something which remains. In other words, the Law of the World demands a decision by first presenting chaos with a dichotomy: a contradiction. It is thus that which first correlates thinking and being by presenting chaotic will, which finds nothing determinate to will within itself, with something to will, with a contradiction to be decided. For Schelling, will is primal being, as all three potencies of being are forms of will; being is omnipotent, an omni-potency, only because it is omni-volent. The Law of the World enacts its imperative by showing pre-potent and chaotic will the possibility of something outside itself, the possibility of an other being. Only once presented with something to will is primal will actually that which can will and can not-will, as that which now must will or not-will. Only with this ur-possibility is pre-original, an-archical being possibilised, supplemented with something that it can. It is now that which can be (*das Sein Könnende*), being which also can, *actus* supplemented with *potentia*. This is how act precedes potency or how the potencies of being do not pre-determine the absolute *prius*, but are its consequent. In short, chaos is only aware of itself as will or comes to self-knowledge in relation to this possibility of willing something other than itself. The Law of the World, in presenting 'it' with alterity, the possibility of an other being, first gives 'it' to 'itself' so that 'it' can now be some-thing and not no-thing, so that it does not have to endure as the ambivalence between something and nothing.

Presented with the possibility of something other, chaos is determined as that which can be and thus also as that which will be, if in fact this is what it decides. In other words, only with this is it a futural being, that which holds before or ahead of itself the possibility of a future rather than being trapped within a timeless, self-consuming, eternal present that has neither past nor future. The Law of the World enacts itself, therefore, as a law of order, succession and numerability, that is, as the Law of Time. Only on account of this Law is the absolute *prius* something futural, that which will be. Whether it chooses to be or to not-be, it is, all the same, what can be; it relates to a possible future. On account of this, then, it is not simply the Absolute, that without relation, but it stands in relation to something other than itself. Even if it had decided for non-being by excluding the possibility of being, it would have done this decisively, not through an accident of fate but as a destiny for which it itself has decided. Deciding either for or against being, it extricates itself from *Zufall* and gives itself a *Schicksal*. In this respect, the deed extricates itself from its primordial contingency and elevates itself to something necessary, to something which is decisively rather than accidentally. As Jankélévitch confirms, 'It is necessary that everything should be precise, determined, acute . . . Everything equivocal will be sliced up; the thing of God will be open and clear.'[6] Far from *Schicksal* (destiny) being antithetical to freedom, it is posited by the free deed.

The Law of the World, by positing the contradiction, transfigures chaos, indeterminate contingency, into a determinate contingency that must necessarily be decided. It is now more than a neither/nor but, for the first time, an either/or. The Law of the World presents chaos with the imperative, hence the possibility, nay, the necessity, of deciding between this dichotomy, the counterbalance of possibilities. The Law of the World makes chaos into a determinate contradiction by excluding the middle, by coming between possibilities, by inserting itself as an interstice. Schelling speaks of the necessity 'that something be in the middle between the *natura*, the eternal being of God, and the decision of the deed, a middle element without which the world could only be thought as an immediately necessary emanation of divinity'.[7] God is not constrained to create, because the possibility of the creation is given as something other than God, something outside his eternal nature, outside his eternal *prius* or anterior. Creation does not follow as a mere effect of God's nature. The world, contrary to Neoplatonism, does not ensue from the overflowing or abundance of the divine nature. It is a possibility only and not an immanent, and thus imminent, necessity.

The Law of the World, says Schelling, draws a breach, a middle ground, through God's anterior and eternal nature, through the middle of the neutral zone of indistinction, by tantalisingly playing before God. Schelling appeals here to Hebrew scriptures that speak of Wisdom, which plays before God for all eternity, 'before' the creation of the world. As co-eternal, yet as something which God can will, Schelling speaks of this as something which occupies 'that middle between the creator and the creature'.[8] The possibility of the creation, of a future being, mediates not by synthesising but by excluding the middle. It relates God to a possible future, which also makes God something Past with respect to this Future, by drawing a breach, 'an interstice'[9] or 'a between-space',[10] that unifies only by first severing, a veritable chiasmus. Schelling's employment of the Law of the World thus presages Heidegger's truth-event, the opening or trothing of being. Why does trothing occur? Why is being correlated with something thinkable, a possibility that it 'can'? On account of the Law of the World. Beyond this Law, however, no further grounds can be given, as this Law first pronounces the dictate that grounds be supplied, that the equipollence or counterbalance between reasons, between all possibilities, be decided.

The original possibility is not pre-contained in God, it is with God.[11] Its operation is to draw a breach through the middle of eternity, to draw a line between eternity and time by presenting the possibility of a future being and thus the possibility of a temporally determined being, thereby relating eternity to temporal determination. As Manfred Durner depicts it, '"Wisdom", as the spiritual exemplar of the creation is that which, by means of structuration, makes order possible.'[12] By presenting the possibility of a future being, namely temporal being, the Law simultaneously posits eternity itself as something possibly past, an eternal past or eternity as the past, the before, of time itself. The division of times are all posited *simultas* or in concurrence. Durner clarifies:

> Should God be proved as a free creator, then the 'Wisdom'-phase is necessarily to be thought as an integrating moment of the absolute process, which precedes the act of creation itself. If this phase is negated, then nothing else remains except to postulate an 'eternal creation' in the Spinozistic sense. The real world ... appears in such a conception ultimately as a necessary emanation of God.[13]

This would make Schelling not only Spinozistic in just the sense that he wants to avoid, but it would also make him Hegelian, whereby otherness is but the externalisation of the same. The Other, the ur-possibility, is, for Schelling, not how God mediates himself to himself, but it is what prompts God to a decision apart from which only his anterior or negative attribute, the attribute of eternity, would remain.

Wisdom, as the 'whole of possibility',[14] is not God, yet it is also something eternally with God, without which God could never be as God. It is the co-eternal condition of God's potentiation. God was never first *actus purus* without *potentia* and then, at a later time, came to acquire the possibility of a future being. Everything is rather an eternal event. As Schelling expresses it, 'The possibility comes first after being, but it appears to that which is in unprethinkable being from this point forward, namely *that* it Is, thus from eternity.'[15] Wisdom is not God's negative attribute but the positive condition of God's being as God, God in God's propriety. Wisdom or ur-possibility is, as Schelling describes it not dissimilarly to Heidegger at the end of *Der Satz vom Grund* – where Heidegger is appealing not to Hebrew scripture but to a saying of Heraclitus – a child that plays before God from all eternity. It is a child because it is the possibility of future being, that which still has its life in front of it. It plays because it is neither bound by prior rules, by the prior dictates of reason, nor by the dictates of a past. Its appearance, because not pre-contained as a determinate potency in God's anterior being, is sudden, 'something that has not already been, something unforeseen'.[16] In offering the possibility of a future, it shows that eternity can possibly become past, something actually departed from. It shows that time does not flow out of eternity as an overflow of eternity and the moving image of eternity, but that time is a rupture or trothing within eternity, the possibility of something other than eternity.

Possibility, presented to *actus purus*, 'offers an object of the will, so that it is internalised as will, as this appearance in general . . . posits this will in freedom against the necessity of its being . . . by liberating it from holy ἀναγκη'.[17] Ur-possibility, severing its way into the middle, breaks the fetters of necessity. On the one hand, this possibility is with rather than in God, something other than God, but, on the other hand, by potentiating God, by bringing forth the contradiction that is the equipollence of the potencies, which constitutes the nature/essence of God and the stuff of the possible creation, possibility, *qua* potencies, emerges from God himself, out of his consequent nature. In other words, the ur-possibility potentiates God or posits the contradiction between the potencies of being; thus God only has the potentiality to bring about a future being by means of these potencies that are in him, that have constituted his nature. The other being is possible only because a potentiation occurs in the being of God himself by means of the interstice that excludes the middle, thus bringing about the contradiction of the potencies, namely the potencies themselves (for, the potencies have no being apart from one another or outside the act of contradiction). The 'stuff' of the creation, then, is *ex nihilo* in the sense that it is not found in a pre-given matter, but the ur-possibility potentiates and 'materialises' God himself. Potentiation, materialisation and subjection are more or less synonymous concepts. Thus, on the one hand, the possibility of the creation comes from outside God and is for a being other than God, while, on the other hand, it is God himself who is this possibility, who is the potencies. As potentiated, however, he is no longer fixed to and immobilised by his own anterior *actus*, but now bears within himself the possibility of an other being and of being otherwise. He can depart from eternity, from his merely negative attribute; God now has a future.

For these reasons the possibility of an other being is not a threat to God's sovereignty but, as will be seen, precisely what first grants him his sovereignty. This possibility, as Schelling suggests, is welcome, '*Willkommen*', because it makes God aware of himself as will, as something which can; it liberates God from himself. God does not simply tolerate alterity, he welcomes it; it spells his liberation from his own *fatum*. God is, contra Aristotle, not auto-affective, but he only is as God through hetero-affectivity, the fact that he is touched and split down the middle by alterity. God's will, although antecedent to reason, is nevertheless not arbitrarily enacted, as it is evoked as responsivity to a real possibility that affects him, that cuts to the heart of (his own) being.

God's decision, the decision which God is, is a response to alterity. God's decision is the original act of responsibility. Employing the rhetoric of Emmanuel Levinas, possibility as alterity – and as *actus purus* without *potentia* how could possibility be anything but alterior to God, as it cannot be pre-contained in God's being – 'dephases' God's eternal being. This fissure in God's anterior being is a kind of *Entsetzung* or ekstasis, a dispossession or de-occupation, as Schelling describes it in his 1820/21 lectures in Erlangen. It is the cision in God's anterior being, in chaos, that demands the de-cision of the 'same' – which, of course, is not yet the same that it is in advance of this decision. This instituted law of either/or, however, remains indifferent to what is chosen, being or non-being; it is only adverse to duplicity. Its only objective is that everything either be or not-be decisively or in freedom. The ur-possibility equips being with will, which means that it condemns being to freedom, as Sartre might have expressed it. Only as free, then, as liberated from its own anterior ἀναγκη, is the name 'God' actually appropriate. Schelling elaborates that it is now 'no longer just not-necessity' – chaos which has simply not yet excluded any possibilities from itself – 'but it is also the freedom to transition into being or not. First now can he say of himself: "I will be who I will be, namely who I will to be."[18] That which will be what it will be is now, and eternally, he who will be who he will be. The de-neutering of neutrality enacts personhood.

Stated as properly as is possible, God is neither that which can be nor is he who can be. The former is inappropriate because God is not a neuter – the neither/nor – but de-neutered, the decisive – the either/or – and hence something personal. The latter is inappropriate because that which can be designates potential being but, as the act of decisiveness, God is more than what is potential. Even if he is (in the transitive sense) what is potential, he is not reducible to it; he is not reducible to the potencies that constitute his consequent nature/essence. There is only potency because preceded by an act, a de-cision. Potencies operate as principles that blindly ensue unto fruition, as the bud blossoms into a flower without the need of its own volition. God, however, is a free and personal cause, not a potency or principle whose effect is but an outgrowth and eternal consequence of his nature.

The highest concept of God is that he is freedom, free against all being, including and primarily his own.[19] The potencies are determinations of God's nature, of his divine essence, but God is not the necessity of this 'organism'; God is not constrained by his own essence, in which each potency necessarily leads to the following in a necessary structure. God is prior to his determinations. God – in a reinterpretation of the classic medieval doctrine that God's essence is his existence and in anticipation of Sartrean existentialism – exists antecedent to his essence. God is not constrained by his essence any more than he is fixed to his anterior existence. God proper is, as it were, outside himself, the band or act of copulation between his unprethinkable existence and the necessity of his consequent essence. God is free from both, not coerced to be either. That he is them is only the result of God as free deed, as the freedom of the decision. Schelling reinterprets the medieval doctrine that God's essence is his existence to mean that God is not substance, that God is not different from his own doing (*sein Tun*).[20] This is what it means to say that God is he who he will be. He can be whomever or however he pleases, because the only thing he cannot decide not to be is freedom itself. Yet even freedom is nothing, is nought, until it decides, which holds even if the decision is to not-act, to remain in restraint, refrain or repose. Again, what it means to be is to have a consequent – hence why God is properly not whoever he wills to be but whomever he wills to be – which holds even for freedom. The potencies, as God's consequent, constitute his essence, but they are not God as such, not God in freedom. God as such is groundless, nothing more than the execution of the divine decision as the execution of the Law of the World.

To decide to actualise one disjunct of a contradiction, for God, does not mean to nullify the opposed but to potentiate the opposite. When one decides to get married, their potential to get divorced is not nullified but, quite the contrary, this is a potentiality first gained in this act. Likewise, if God decides for being and against non-being, this posits or posit-ions, in the posit-ive sense, non-being as something not chosen; it posits being as what is actual and non-being as what is potential (as potency is not what is; it is either what 'can' or what 'could have been'). If one decides to get married, then one cannot later decide not to have got married; one cannot change the past and neither can God. The question, however, is in what sense, by excluding the possibility of divorce as a live option, one actually preserves and secures it as potentiality all the more. If it is a true decision or, as it were, a 'godly' decision, which makes a cision and cuts away what one has decided against as something never to be actualised, then this is not to be understood in the sense of someone who on her wedding day is without fear and trembling only because she has not excluded the possibility that she will get a divorce once she becomes unhappy in her marriage. On the contrary, something is only truly posited as potency if it is something truly decided against, something genuinely excluded or 'extained'. Only then, as a potentiality never to be recalled or actualised, is it truly secured and preserved as non-being rather remaining in the limbo of neither being nor non-being, for example, being married without having excluded the possibility of divorce, with one foot out the door (and one foot in), as one might say. The divine decision emerges from a zone of indistinction between actuality and potentiality, positing the actual as actual and extaining potency as potency. Potentiality, then, is not nullified in the decision; it is first posited and preserved therein.

God as ex se

God proper is neither his anterior existence nor his accrued essence, the potencies. God is nothing in himself; he is rather 'pure relation'.[21] While everything substantial, everything which has being, is concerned with the preservation of its being, with its *conatus essendi*, God, as *das Übersubstantielle*, is wholly outside himself or *ex se*. God only is God in relation to the ur-possibility that grants him distance, thus a relation, against his own being. God's existence and his essence are both, as it were, but mere *relata*, inseparable from God but still not God in propriety, namely the act of relating – and thereby bringing into being – these *relata*.

If God creates, which is not necessary but only offered as a possibility, then 'he can only make the decision for this process on account of something *outside* himself, *praeter se* ("outside" is equal to *praeter* and *extra*)'.[22] 'Extra' indicates the supplemental, something unnecessary and even superfluous. God creates out of no compulsion and out of no sufficient reason. Only in this way is the cosmos truly a cosmos, an adornment, a superfluity that may very well be good and beautiful, but something which could have been done without. This does not mean that the act of creation does nothing for or to God. It reveals his divinity and glory in addition to, as will be seen, preserving God's withdrawal from being. None of these 'reasons', however, were operative in advance of the creation; for, in the act of creation at least two things happen: (1) God is revealed to Man, who himself would not have been had God not created; and (2) God is withdrawn from being, which also would not have been had God not created, thereby preserving his holiness. Both of these so-called reasons, however, are only accrued *post factum*.

The lone incentive Schelling offers for the creation which would not merely be belatedly accrued after the creation has nothing to do with God's own being, his own *conatus* or drive to ἐντελέχεια, but God creates on account of that other being, which is not but could be. Without the possibility of this other being, Schelling's God would either be synonymous with Spinoza's god, which lacks real distance from, and thus relation to, itself, or with Aristotle's (and Hegel's) god, which relates only to itself and only as an act of knowledge, in which the function of otherness is to mediate the self to the self in perfect self-knowledge as self-thinking thought. Against the god of the philosophers, Schelling claims,

> But, if the activity of the actual God should just consist in this, then we must rather regard this incessant thinking of itself as the most insufferable state. There can certainly be nothing more insufferable than to think only oneself and thus only about oneself interminably.[23]

In opposition to Aristotle's, Spinoza's or Hegel's god – the term remains uncapitalised because capitalisation signifies a proper name, but this god is anonymous and impersonal – Schelling's God does not suffer under the weight of his own being. Schelling's God can depart from himself and think about something other than himself; Schelling's God is not narcissistic. In layman's terms, it is not so much the case that without an Other God is lonely, and so might create for this reason, because God certainly has no need of an Other. Rather, God derives great pleasure, the highest possible bliss, from this possible Other, the child that plays before God from all eternity. This is just as one may have no need of friends to maintain their *conatus essendi* – what kind of person would one be if they only had friends because they met certain needs – but that does not preclude that friends supplement one's life with an excess of joy. So too does God take pleasure in that which exceeds his needs, of which he has none. God's desire surpasses what might be required to fulfill his deficiencies, of which he has none, and to achieve ἐντελέχεια. In short, desire, contra Plotinus, St Augustine and perhaps the entire Western metaphysical tradition, does not originate in lack or privation. God is desirous despite the fact that his anterior being, which is without exclusion, lacks nothing and is without privation (although it also does not yet positively 'contain' anything either). Desire is not the desire to fill in lacunas; it is the desire for the positive, for what surpasses being.

Schelling assures his readers,

> Just for this reason is God the most blissful, as Pindar calls him, because all his thoughts are perpetually in that which is outside him, in his creation. He alone has nothing to do with himself, as he is sure and certain of his being a priori.[24]

Farther from the Aristotelian god one cannot be! Schelling's God is not just capable of thinking of something other than himself, but he and he alone does not think of himself precisely because, contra Hegel, God does not have to come to himself to secure his being. God's unprethinkable anteriority is never in question.

God relates to himself by taking a distance from his existence, by acquiring freedom from and even against his own ἀνάγκη. God relates to future possibility, which relation constitutes the potencies, the being of his own essence. God, however, is bound neither to his anterior existence nor to his consequent essence. That God is *ex se* means 'that he sees *himself* in the middle between both . . . as something free from *both*'.[25] God's abode occurs in the open-space between or at a withdrawal from both his unprethinkable existence and that unforeseeable possibility of what, from this perspective, is still futural. God resides between both the contingency of his existence, chaos, and the necessity of his essence, the contradictory concatenation of the potencies, between both *actus purus* without potency and *potentia pura*. God himself is the cision in being, which means the Law of the World is not an oppressive yoke for God, but the highest instance of his being. The Law is indeed holy and divine. God succumbs, in other words, to no law outside himself but, as Spinoza valorises, only to his own law. This is to be thought along the lines of Spinoza's notion of self-determination and not according to Kantian autonomy, because autonomy is a law of reason, but God is anterior to reason.

God, as *ex se*, as neither his existence nor his essence, is more than being (*seiend*); he is beyond being (*überseiend*). As the decision of being, God is the transitive event operative above and beyond his *relata* in order to copulate between them, in order to appropriate them as his *relata*. God is not a substance, as substances are concerned with their own being, with their own *conatus* and ἐντελέχεια, but God, who is outside himself, is concerned only with alterity.

How does God copulate or hold sway? Should God's anterior existence be designated as the Real and his consequent essence – which is constitutive of reason or thinkability itself, the figure or Idea of being – as the Ideal, then God is the Cause that grants the Ideal prominence over the Real. Had the opposite been the case, had the Real remained predominant over the Ideal, then there would have been nothing instead of something, namely the absence of the cision or interstice in being itself, Heidegger's truth-event. God is not indifference (which is the Absolute) but difference; the Real and the Ideal are only equipollent and, hence, indifferent in chaos, but God decides chaos by granting supremacy to the Ideal over the Real. God is the unity of the Real and the Ideal only insofar as he decides, draws a cision or intercedes between, the Real and the Ideal, breaking their monotony or consonance. He is the Cause of their unity by divorcing them and instituting their disequilibrium. Accordingly, this unity is not substantial, not pre-contained within an infinite substance, but both *relata* are rather extained, excluded one from the other. If this unity were merely substantial, then there could be no 'indivisible remainder' (*nie aufgehender Rest*) that could hold the contradictories together by itself remaining unsubsumed into the contradiction.

God acts as Cause between the Ideal and Real – and the term 'Cause' is capitalised to distinguish it from the four instrumental causes of Aristotle, which can be identified with the potencies themselves (as there is also an A^4), and to distinguish it from one of Kant's categories of the understanding, which are only applicable in the phenomenal domain – but the sense in which he is Cause of each is different. He causes his essence, the potencies, the Ideal, by willing the ur-possibility. His anterior existence, however, is, as absolute *prius*, pre-existent. It admits of no cause. God only causes its exclusion from the Ideal or, said differently, the fact that it is the Real of the Ideal, that which is the Idea. God is the Cause of the fact that unprethinkable *Ungrund* now holds sway as a *Grund*, a sufficient reason, with a consequent.[26] In this sense, then, God cannot act, even as Cause, apart from the fact that his anterior, unprethinkable existence is always already pre-given. God cannot act unless his *Grund*, which in advance of this act is but *Ungrund*, namely something which lacks a consequent and so is nought, is also something which God, in a sense, is.

God, in one sense unprethinkable ground and in another Cause, is only the one insofar as he is also the other. The ground, ungrounded as such, is only brought forth as ground by the Cause.[27] Yet if the unprethinkable were not always already there, as that which could be transfigured into a ground, then God would not be able to act as Cause. This unground, God's anterior, is his absolute *prius*, the always already presupposed, which only becomes a ground, reason or ἀρχή *post factum*, namely with a consequent. In this context, Schelling often appeals to another story from the Hebrew scriptures in which God passes before Moses but only reveals his backside, his *posterius* or consequent, and never his face, his *anterius*.[28] The unprethinkable, the *Ungrund*, is only post-thinkable or only manifest through its consequent, and thus only as *Grund*. In advance of its consequent, however, it is not *Grund* but sheer void.

Schelling criticises Spinoza's god for being substance or ground only and not a Cause also, or, more exactly, he complains that Spinoza's god is only essentially rather than transitively a cause.[29] Its consequents ensue immediately from its essence, hence why it could not refrain from creating. The attributes and modes are necessary entailments of infinite substance. Yet the concept of Cause, Schelling urges, should indicate the counterpart to that of substance or ground, lest everything happen by emanation rather than free decision. Emanationism sees everything flow out of substance as ground, whereas God is the Cause that gives the Ideal prominence over the Real, over the ground; God's Causing posits the Real as the ground of that consequent which the ground transitively is. Unlike substance or ground, which unfolds unto its consequents with necessity, that there is a Cause and that it has acted can only be shown factically and thus only empirically narrated.[30]

A ground that is not also a Cause – Spinozism – entails materialism.[31] Inversely, that God would be Cause but not ground, a Cause without a foregoing *prius* or anterior, entails idealism. God, however, unites the Real and the Ideal – and hence too materialism and idealism – even if only by differentiating them. God only is Cause by positing *Ungrund* as *Grund* and, in this respect, God is the Cause of his own substantiality, at least as a stable ground rather than as chaos. God, as it were, posits his own reason. One can only recognise this, however, if one has first asked the question of God for God's own sake and not simply as a ground or first cause of beings, not simply as the onto-theological god that, not who, is nothing more than the being (*Seiendheit*) of beings, as Heidegger might express it.

God is nothing more than the being of beings if he is only their ground, as in Spinozism, but he is both Cause and ground; God is the freedom that the *Ungrund* acquires when presented with that ur-possibility even to be as *Grund*. Recall that 'God is called God only in accordance with his freedom.'[32] God is the cision in the *Ungrund*, which first makes it possible for God to be the ground or substrate of a future being, a consequent being that retroactively posits God as antecedent. This cision copulates ground and consequent, positing the one as the bearer, the subject, the other as the attributed, the predicate, hence the use of the grammatically derived term 'copulation'. The relation between the *relata* is not an equivalency but a transitive act, thus the need to express everything verbally rather than nominally.

Schelling states, 'In the Arabic language the copula "is" is expressed through a word that corresponds to our German "can".'[33] The verb 'can', functioning in Arabic as more than a modal verb but as the transitive verb *par excellence*, would thus take an accusative rather than a predicate nominative. A bold proposition might thus already be proffered that perhaps ventures to a place Schelling may not prefer to go. It is certainly fair to say that God's existence is thought in the subject-position, God's essence in the accusative position and God himself as the decision, the act of copulation as such. From this perspective, then, God occupies the accusative position as something consequent upon the unprethinkable deed and the following proposition becomes possible: Unprethinkable being 'can' God. This would indicate that God, as it were, is structurally similar, although not equivalent, to reason, insofar as God too is an eternal and contingent consequent, the eternal consequent of copulation. This is the line of thought that will be explored in the following chapter as a possible way of reading – or, perhaps, creatively misreading – Heidegger's passing by of the last God. Heidegger, refusing to equate God with being or with beyng (the copulating/appropriating event), nevertheless specifies the latter as the site of the gods, including the last God. For now, a brief elaboration upon a few passages in which Schelling hints at this reading must suffice.

Schelling writes that the unprethinkable is an 'absolute singularity, which I do not pronounce of God but already presuppose in order to be able to say "God"'.[34] The unprethinkable is the *prius* of God, that which allows God to be expressed. Is it, however, only that without which one cannot say God, or is it, as has been argued, that without which God could not be? If the latter is true, if it is that without which God could not even be while still not indicating that by which God is as such, then it must be something capable of God, that which 'can' God. As Schelling writes in the 'Andere Deduktion der Principien der positiven Philosophie [Another Deduction of the Principle of Positive Philosophy]', where he is arguably the most radical and comes the closest to this line of thought, 'Admittedly, only the eternal, which is from itself (*quod a se est*) can be God . . . *only* the eternal *can* be God, but it *is* not necessarily God, it is merely God a posteriori . . .'[35] In this astounding passage, in which all non-Latin italics are Schelling's own, (1) he clearly demarcates between what 'can' God and God himself; (2) he emphasises the verbal or transitive aspect of 'can'; (3) he attests to the fact that it could have also not been God, to the fact that it is not necessary that it is God; and (4) he admits, therefore, that if it is

God, then it is so only a posteriori, only as consequent or as accusative. The third point can be drawn into relation with the nature of the copula as transitive, because, as transitive, all assertions are emphatic or synthetical, none are analytical. God is not pre-contained in the unprethinkable – hence its designation as unprethinkable – which could have exercised its operativity otherwise than it has or not at all. If the proposition that God exists is emphatic and synthetical, that means that this proposition's negation must also be possible. Atheism too must have been possible. All assertions (*Behauptungen*) have a content which is asserted (*Haupt*),[36] something analytical propositions lack. If the unprethinkable is not necessarily God, if, contrary to the ontological argument, God's existence is not entailed in a pre-given essence, then the unprethinkable is only contingently God, which means it could have not been God, in which case atheism would have been the case. The caveat is that while it is certainly true that atheism was possible, would that also necessarily have coincided with a state in which there was nothing at all instead of something? In other words, maybe God's existence is necessary if and only if there is to be something rather than nothing, which is itself not necessary. God would thus be contingently necessary, necessary in relation to the contingency of the fact that there is something rather than nothing but, absolutely considered, contingent *simpliciter*. As Richard Swinburne has remarked, 'Any terminus to explanation of things logically contingent must be itself something logically contingent.'[37] Or, is there a way to affirm the possibility of atheism even while admitting that there is something rather than nothing?

Sovereignty and personhood

God is not being itself but *überseiend*, which means that he is not a substance, which is first and foremost concerned with its own being, but God relates to his own being by reigning sovereignly above it, free to will against it. His relation to the ur-possibility grants him the freedom to will for or against being, including his own. God, as *ex se*, as pure relation, is the Lord/Sovereign (*Herr*) of being. For Schelling, the concepts of sovereignty (*Herrschaft*) and freedom are indissociable insofar as a sovereign being is coerced by nothing, free against everything that would constrain it and free for everything possible. Being first appears as sovereign, free to will or to not-will, with the ur-possibility. To reiterate: 'By showing it a being . . . possibility gives it something which it can will – something to be willed at all, which it did not have before, namely something it can be and can not-be.'[38] Only as he who can be whom he wills to be, as he who is free to be whomever he wills to be (or to not-be), is God sovereign, and only as such is God God. This means that God is sovereign prior to the creation of the world. He must not reign over the actual world to be sovereign. It suffices for him to be sovereign over the possibility to be. God must not create to be God, he must only be sovereign over the possibility of creation, which means he must be free to create or to not-create.

If freedom and sovereignty cannot be thought apart, then nor can personhood. One who has no control over oneself, one who is subject to their body and not sovereign over it, is not a person but an animal (or an automaton). One is only a person if she relates to herself in freedom and sovereignty. Accordingly, chaos is the opposite of personality. Chaos, prior to its supplementation with ur-possibility, which allows God to emerge as the distance taken from chaos, is the non-personal. That chaos is structured and ordered, that a cision, the de-cision, occurs in it, elevates it to personhood and thus to Godhood. God, *qua* free and sovereign, cannot be the chaotic or a mere substrate, but he presupposes this as that over which he reigns free and sovereign as Person.

In this context, Gabriel offers a few interesting, but also highly problematic, remarks. He correctly notes that the free deed, 'in contradistinction to the Kantian identification of freedom and autonomy, cannot be brought under any rule'[39] and 'to this end, personality as such must be conceived as the meaning of being'.[40] He even indicates that the free deed is only to be thought as personal because it surpasses the Kantian identification of freedom with autonomy. Insofar as autonomy is strictly bound to laws posited by reason this would seem to indicate that he acknowledges that freedom and personality, which are what make God God, which are what constitute his godliness, surpass rule and reason. Yet only ten pages later, he decrees,

> For Schelling it is crucial to note that 'God' refers to nothing more or less than the incessant and polymorphous becoming of intelligibility. God is sense, the almost trivial fact that the ways we access the world (our sense-making practices, which generate fields of sense) belong to the world itself . . .[41]

It is hard to understand how he elevates God above Kantian rule, on the one hand, and reduces God to changing forms of intelligibility on the other. God is antecedent to reason, thinkability or intelligibility. Gabriel, a demythologiser to the end, not only reduces God to intelligibility, but he also makes this intelligibility, insofar as it results from human *praxis*, local and temporal rather than an eternally universal consequent of being. Additionally, by equivocating God with an intelligibility reduced to the product of humans' 'sense-making practices', he also makes God consequent to humans. He reads Schelling as Feuerbach. God is now something consequent to the world rather than sovereign over the possibility of the world, free to posit it or not. God is now subject to the vicissitudes and temporal alterations of the world, subject to human convention and projection. But Schelling is not a post-modern and not a Foucauldian; reason is universal and not the result of merely local crystallisations of power and social commerce. How could Gabriel's view be squared with the assertion that personality is the meaning of being? At any rate, God is not to be equated with intelligibility/thinkability, but this is to be posited only as God's consequent essence, while reserving the abyssal event of this essence's taking-place for God proper. God is thus an event that can only be named, only be identified, post-eventally or *post factum*, which corresponds perfectly to how one comes to know another person.

To know a person is to know their will. Will, however, is something only knowable if revealed by means of one's words and deeds. A will in repose remains mysterious and concealed, while the action of the will is the revelation of the mystery (although one cannot collapse the distinction between will and deed, lest deception become impossible). All revelation is thus the result of will and not reason; hence if one admits that revelation and religion are inextricably related concepts, then one must also admit, contra Kant, the impossibility of religion within the limits of reason alone. Revelation is only revelation if it reveals something that could not possibly have been known apart from the revelatory event, thus not through reason, just as a person can only be known through their manifestations, through their words and deeds. Revelation presupposes the concept of freedom; revelation thus presupposes the personal. Once another person becomes entirely predictable they become boring and nothing more than putty in the other's hands. They are always at the disposal of others and thus become disposable. Here is the reason, if one will, why women are said to be uninterested in nice (predictable and disposable) men; these men are, in a sense, less than persons. A person must be able to deviate from law, from what reason and social niceties dictate. A perfectly autonomous person is not a person at all but much closer to Descartes' animal, an automaton. Just as the greatest acts of human freedom go above and beyond reason, surpassing what would be considered rational, for example when somebody jumps in front of a moving bus to save a stranger or when a monk sets himself on fire for a cause or when good Samaritans love their enemies, so too, contra Gabriel, must God, in order to be God, in order to be personal, surpass reason. It impugns and belittles God to reduce him to rationality or intelligibility, which makes him less than a person. The God of revelation is not the god of reason, not the god of the philosophers. God is not confined to religion within the limits of reason alone, a god who could be nothing more than the perfect exemplar of autonomy and morality or the postulate of practical reason. Religion has suffered under its misconception as nothing more than morality – and bad morality at that – long enough.

God is neither the God of morality nor the God of the epistemologists, namely the limit-term of intelligibility and rationality. God must be conceived in his ontological domain. God is the God of being, the Sovereign over being, free to posit it or not to posit it. This freedom, however, is only accrued by virtue of that ur-possibility which, playing before God for all eternity, potentiates God, liberating him from his unprethinkable *actus*. Schelling shows exactly what this liberation entails.

> Imagine he who is Sovereign over the not yet, but possible, being, which, *if* it is, is a contingent being. Imagine this contingent being as something that has emerged, then it will encounter that which does not emerge, that which has always already been there, primordial being, which now first even appears *as* eternal.[42]

This is the inverse reaction that the consequent, which is perfectly contingent, which could have never been, exerts upon antecedent ἀνάγκη. With the possibility of the consequent, ἀνάγκη is transfigured into the freedom of being, that which will be whomever he wants to be, the Sovereign of being. With the actual emergence of this consequent, namely with the actual creation, God's unprethinkable futurity is transformed into an eternal past. Eternity itself is posited as the inexhaustible depth or indivisible remainder of being. Schelling comments, 'This (previously immoveable) being is itself turned into something else . . . into *a* being (since it was originally being *itself*).'[43] By this means, being, or – if anticipation of Heidegger might already be permitted – 'beyng', becomes a being, the determinacy of being, being that has eventuated or been decided. Schelling continues,

> In this way we see how he . . . insofar as he is Sovereign, [free] to *posit* or *not* to posit contingent being, how he has through this means become Sovereign even over his *Urseyn* . . . and thus can transform his necessary act of existing itself into something contingent.[44]

Nothing exists with absolute necessity, not even God's existence. The very concept of necessary existence is problematic. Accordingly, having been transformed into a being, *Urseyn*, primordial or an-archical being, the absolute and unprethinkable *prius*, is itself transformed into a contingent being that could, alternatively, never have been. In short, God's existence, the fact that the absolute *prius* is God, is also utterly contingent. Sovereign over and above his own act of existing, God's anterior – his negative attribute, his *conditio sine qua non* – no longer comports itself as *fatum*, *Verhängnis* or ἀνάγκη. Its liberation therefrom corresponds to nothing more than its potentiation, the fact that it is posited as the contingency to be or not-be. It is free to relapse into the necessity of *fatum* or to actualise a contingent being, thus free from contingency and necessity both. It had always been contingent with respect to itself,[45] without regard to its possible consequent, but now it has been transformed into a contingency even in relation to its consequent. Even God – or perhaps primarily and exclusively God – must ask himself why even he exists, only to be greeted with no response and no reasons, only to be confronted with the brutality of his own unprethinkable act of existing. One must acknowledge 'the contingent in the *actu* necessary act of existing',[46] that '*through* the appearance of the potency of an *other* being, that which is antecedent to this potency, the merely *actu* necessary act of existing itself, appears as something contingent and capable of being suspended, that which can also *not* be'.[47]

The unprethinkable act of existing is contingent to the degree that that to which it comports itself as ground is also contingent and, inversely, the consequent has emerged from an unground contingent with respect to itself. There is a reciprocal play of contingency here. On the one hand, the ground is necessary with respect to the consequent but, given that the consequent did not have to be, so too does the ground not have to ground it, which means that, in not acting as ground, it is actually, in itself, nothing more than unground. On the other hand, given that the being of the ground is at bottom the contingency of the unground, for this reason the consequent is a contingent rather than necessary consequent. Necessary consequents could only emerge through the necessity of their ground, which is always lacking. If the consequent is contingent just to the degree that the unground is contingent, then all consequents are only to be narrated as facts rather than as something pre-contained as entailments within the (un)ground. Concerning the actual affirmation of the actualisation of the ur-possibility, the affirmation of the act of creation, Schelling contends, 'We can now also only say of the deed, which we in no way acknowledge a priori but only a posteriori, that it *has* happened.'[48] Although it cannot be addressed in any detail, it is noteworthy that the same is said of the Fall of Man.

> We have with all this hypothetically presupposed the *factum*; for, it is not proved a priori. It is a fact and indeed the fact κατ' ἐξοχην, the original fact of history, of which one can only say that it has bechanced.[49]

The Fall, just like the act of creation, is an unprethinkable act, without which there would be no history. Original deeds, namely revelatory decisions, manifest something that never would have or even could have been known otherwise. The consequent or posterior constitutes the nature of the antecedent *post factum* just as the consequent words and deeds of a person reveal that person not by exposing something pre-given but by first manifesting the personality and identity of the person. One is sovereign over one's acts just as one's acts, in turn, constitute the identity and meaning of the will as their anterior.

Monotheism and withdrawal

God's anterior is the chaotic or that without identity, which, however, does not exclude the possibility of a future identity. God is not chaos, which is antithetical to all personality. God is the enactment of decisiveness, identity and personhood. Merely to affirm God's anterior, which is only a negative attribute, cannot, Schelling argues, constitute the position of monotheism, as this recognises only that without which God could not be, but not God himself. Such is not monotheism but only theism or atheism. Schelling declares, 'Theism acknowledges God merely according to substance, but not according to divinity.'[50] Mere theism, which Schelling equates with Spinozism, is actually nothing more than atheism. He bluntly declares, 'Theism = atheism'.[51] (Not only is this Spinozism, but he also refers to it as the God of Muhammad, whose monotheism so strictly prohibits plurality that it not only restricts that 'outside of God is no other God'[52] but also 'through this formula nothing is posited in God himself, nothing positive is posited *in* him, but only something *outside* him is negated.')[53]

For the 'mono' in mono-theism to mean something emphatic, Schelling rightfully contends that it must presuppose the possibility of its opposite, namely multiplicity, the non-one or non-identical as that which emphatically is that which is the One. The being of the One, in other words, is not antecedent but consequent, not *prius* but *posterius*, not *antecedens* but *consequens*. Monotheism does not mean that there is only one God rather than eight, twenty-four or zero, but it means that that which is God is so because it is the One. Schelling specifies, 'whether the *monas* is already to be found with unprethinkable being, *that* is the question'.[54] If God only is if he is one rather than chaotic, the question is whether God is already to be found from all eternity, whether chaos has always already been decided from all eternity. To speak of monotheism is not to deny something outside of God, namely other Gods, but it is to affirm something about that which is God, which, in itself, is a foregoing multiplicity or lack of identity: chaos. God is only God if he is the Person who freely and sovereignly decides chaos, which means that there is something apart from God or, at least, something anterior to God, a chaos which he himself must overcome. God cannot be without a resistant, otherwise why could God not just have snapped his fingers to accomplish all his acts? Why would God, for example, not just remove evil in an instant? Why would, for example, the death and resurrection of the Christ not just be a sham, given that God could have granted forgiveness through a simple wave of his hand? Such things only make sense and are not laughable if there is something antecedent to God that offers genuine resistance. God's very being is thus a theodicy, because God's being is the overcoming of that which ought not to remain, the deciding of prior ambivalence and duplicity, the separation of wheat from chaff: Justice. To affirm this is emphatically to affirm a real event that could have not been. It is to admit that atheism could have been possible, which mere theism – which is actually equivalent to atheism – in proposing that there can be no other Gods or nothing apart from God, refuses to admit. If a proposition's negation is impossible, then that proposition asserts nothing; it is an analytical proposition at best and tautological at worst. Monotheism, however, is not an analytical proposition; God could be as many – as indeed he was manifest, Schelling claims, in mythological religion – or not at all rather than as the One. Monotheism emphatically asserts something about being that could have been otherwise. The μονάς in monotheism is not superfluous; or, it is only superfluous when monotheism is conceived as the mere rejection of all other Gods. The only way that conception of monotheism could still contain an emphatic assertion is if it were actually polytheism at heart, except a polytheism that says of all the Gods that only one of them actually exists. This God would thus be no more than a polytheistic God who just happened to find himself alone, like one stranded on a desert island. The question is what would actually make this solitary entity a God. What would constitute its Godhood?

Chaos – once confronted with the ur-possibility – can operate as a unity, as One, or as many. From chaos, neither atheism, polytheism nor monotheism are excluded as future possibilities. Schelling argues 'that there cannot be monotheism without the possibility of polytheism . . . monotheism can only be a dogma insofar as its opposite is possible . . .' – note that the contrary of monotheism is not atheism but polytheism – 'what *cannot* be contradicted can also not be asserted'.[55] In saying that 'what cannot be contradicted can also not be asserted', Schelling is already showing that the ontological argument for God's existence is wrong because it does not assert anything for which the negation would also be possible. God would only emphatically be a necessary being if atheism had also been a possibility. Atheism had to be possible, says Schelling, for monotheism actually to have something to say in a positive or exclamatory sense. In other words, in order for God's existence possibly to be an emphatic assertion, both atheism and 'theism', so-called, had to be possible and so God's existence is contingent.

Chaos or the absolute *prius*, that which will be God, can only be named God *post factum* or after the event. As Schelling argues, 'the divinity of this a priori *being* is only proven a posteriori'.[56] This indicates what Levinas has termed the 'posteriority of the anterior'.[57] Only after chaos has been decided is chaos even what chaos is, hence the earlier discussion of the inverse effect the consequent enacts on the *prius*. The Law of the World, which indicates nothing more than the efficacy of the principle of excluded middle as a law of either/or, enacts its influence first and foremost on chaos itself, demanding that it either remain non-identical, in which case it would ironically be decisively unequal to itself, or that it be supplemented with an identity, in which case it must exclude – in the positive sense of extainment – from itself everything that it is not. It therefore excludes or posits outside itself the determinations of its being, the potencies – A^1, A^2 and A^3 – in order that it emerge as A^0, as *actus purus* without *potentia*, in a decided and indicative sense. Even though pure act has acquired potency, this potency, which constitutes its essence, is extained or posited outside itself. In Heidegger's language, God, as the unprethinkability of the decision, withdraws from his essence, which is the determinations of his own being and of all being. God withdraws from being in order decisively to be secluded as the Sovereign and Free beyond being. God truly is without being in the sense that he withdraws from it or in the sense that his being, his essence, is something with which he is not equivalent or to which he is not reducible, but free against.

The transition from the merely (a)theistic moment to mono-theism happens through the event of God's withdrawal; God is One by excluding/extaining all plurality outside himself. God proper is not the potencies but their *prius* in withdrawal. God is that being who truly exists apart from his essence or nature, hence his freedom, sovereignty and personhood, hence his Godhood. If the positing of the potencies is the act of creation, then one here sees how God only acts once. The decision by which God is God, by which he creates, by which he enacts salvation history, is incarnate, resurrected, hears the prayers of the saints, loves grandmothers and so forth are all one and the same act. To suggest otherwise would be to posit more than one decision, with one occurring before and another only after. God would thus be diachronically dispersed across time instead of all times being posited concurrently by God.

In the withdrawal, which is but the act of creation itself, God ceases to be merely what is nought by excluding the subjunctivity or, as Meillassoux would have it, virtuality of chaos. God is thus he who indicatively is not; he is decisively not being. Only from the subjunctivity of the μή ὄν, however, is the indicative οὐκ ὄν possible. God reigns sovereign above his own anterior being, but he can never lay aside his own pre-condition. God withdraws from being, which requires the preservation of the being outside him from which he withdraws. God's creation and God's withdrawal into the realm of the Holy of Holies are one and the same act.

Recall that God, insofar as he is not originally a substance, never concerns himself with his own being but only with that other being, the possible creation. It is as if God could decide for himself or for the creation, and his withdrawal into non-being, in the indicative sense, is the proof of his self-sacrifice, the fact that he decided in favour of that other being and against his own. God only exists *per contrarium*, or God exists only through not being his contrary. God rejects, that is, extains, being for/from himself in order to bequeath it to the world. To return to the earlier discussion of how potentiality is preserved as potentiality, Agamben's account of potentiality proves homologous or structurally similar. According to Agamben, to actualise means to set the potential not-to to the side, just as it has been argued that the de-cision cuts away the possibility not chosen and extains it, sets it outside itself or posits it as *praeter deum*. This is not a nullification of potentiality so much as its preservation as potential. The decision of God is enacted by withdrawing into the holiness of *actus purissimus*, which, ironically, is non-being (οὐκ ὄν), *actus* removed from all *potentia* (μή ὄν). Potentiality is excluded, in the positive sense of the term, set outside God. This, in fact, is its very positing as potency, as the figure of all possibility. To decide for potency is to decide against its being *in actu* and thus to posit it *in potentia*;[58] potentiality is the *modus* of this being. God always acts *per contrarium*. This too is arguably similar to Agamben's claim that to set 'im-potentiality' to the side, for example to choose not to speak, is not to destroy the potentiality to speak, as one could break one's silence later, but to preserve it as potentiality. The crucial difference is that, for Agamben, potentiality is preserved precisely for the sake of reserving the possibility of actualising it later, whereas for Schelling, the decisiveness of God, should it prove to be a divine decision, must be once and for all, a decision that will never be revoked. Is there a 'proof' of the finality of this decision? In other words, is there a proof for God, for monotheism?

A running proof

There is no argument for God's existence – God's anterior and unprethinkable being is beyond proof, the *prius* that, given that there is something rather than nothing, one cannot fail to presuppose. There is, consequently, only an argument for godliness. The question is not whether some entity exists, but whether the event/decision of being proves to be final, whether the decision is superseded by another, and what the *modus operandi*, namely the meaning, significance and identity, of the decision proves to be. Is the decision operative atheistically, polytheistically, monotheistically or in some other way altogether? The fact of being, which is a given, is not to be proved, but what or who that fact reveals, the manner or the identity with which being reveals itself. As Schelling writes, 'It is not it itself (the absolute *prius*) that ought to be proved, but the *consequent* of this, that must be proved *factically*, and, concomitantly, the *divinity* of that prius – that it is *God* and thus that *God* exists.'[59] There is no proof for the fact that the event or de-cision has taken place, only for the meaning revealed by the de-cision, what it indicates. Schelling explains,

> That it is God is not a *res naturae*, something understandable from itself; it is a *res facti* and can therefore also only be factically proven. 'It is God.' This proposition does not contain the following meaning: the concept of that *prius* = the concept of God. Its meaning is: that *prius is* God, not according to the concept but according to actuality.[60]

If the *prius* is God in the transitive sense, namely that which can God, then it is the consequent, the accusative in the proposition – 'It is God' – that requires proof. How is that which is? Is it as God, as many Gods or as void? It is not a question of what is existing, but how is being/existing operative . . . monotheistically, polytheistically, atheistically . . .?

Schulz argues that Schelling has nothing to do with the empirically based cosmological and teleological arguments, at least as classically construed.[61] While this is true, Schelling's position is nevertheless closer to those kinds of arguments than to the ontological argument based in reason alone. The problem with the ontological argument is that it places possibility in advance of actuality, essence in advance of existence. By arguing that God's existence is contained in his essence, it argues that God necessarily exists because his existence is first made possible by his essence. An essence, a concept, delimits possibility. It is, for example, possible for a bachelor to be single, a male, swarthy or sensuous, but it is impossible for him to be a she or to be married. To infer from essence to existence, as the ontological argument does, is to commence with the possible and then to see that, if a certain possibility's negation is not possible, that said possibility is in fact not not possible, that is, necessary. This is the way analytical 'proofs' operate, although, as Schelling has persuasively argued, they emphatically assert nothing. If God, however, is operative as the decision of *actus purus*, then it is impossible to find any pre-given essence in God. If God has an essence, that is, if it is God that has eventuated, then this essence accrues only as a contingent consequent or as God's *posterius*.[62] All a priori arguments for God are thus excluded in principle. Vallicella, an analytic philosopher by trade, also pinpoints the pertinent issue:

Note also that from the fact that the essence of the Paradigm is (identically) its self-identity, there is no quick ontological argument to the existence of the Paradigm. If the Paradigm exists, then it necessarily exists (where its necessity is grounded in its self-identity); but *that* it exists cannot be shown by showing *how* it exists if it exists.[63]

One might also note a renowned analytic theologian, Swinburne:

> To say that 'God exists' is necessary . . . is to say that God does not depend for his existence on himself or on anything else . . . His existence is an ultimate brute fact. Yet being the sort of being which he essentially is, everything else in the universe depends on him, and must do so – for he is by his nature the ultimate sources of things. Hence his existence is not merely *an* ultimate brute fact, but *the* ultimate brute fact. All other logically contingent facts depend on this one . . . It is logically contingent that this is how the world works. But it is the ultimate principle of its operation . . . The necessary proposition, the theist must then claim, is not 'God exists' but rather 'there does not exist a moment before which God was not'.[64]

Even if the consequent essence of God were necessary, just as the necessary essence of a unicorn is that it has one horn, just as God's essence, the determinations/potencies of his being, consists in a necessary concatenation, this does not mean that it is necessary that this essence, this concatenation of the potencies, exists. One must distinguish, as Schelling does, the 'manner of existence',[65] which is necessary, from 'existence as such',[66] which is contingent. God may not necessarily exist, but he might exist necessarily, where the placement of the adverb after the verb is meant to indicate only the modality/manner of existing and not the fact of existing. God's essence may be necessary even if the facticity of this manner of existing is contingent. Schelling confirms,

> That God is determined to exist through nothing else in or outside himself, what more does this mean than that he exists groundlessly? Do we not name such existence contingent and must we not consequently say of God, according to this assumption, that he is a being existing with the utmost contingency since no reason is seen in his being?[67]

Schelling thus concludes, 'For this reason nothing more is said, however, than that God, if he is, can only necessarily and not contingently be.'[68] If God exists, which is not necessary, he exists necessarily, that is, with a necessary essence or *modus*, but only if he exists. God is thus a contingent necessity, where contingency refers to the non-necessity of the fact that a necessarily determined *modus* exists. This and nothing more is all that the running proof for God can show.

If being is operative with a Godly *modus*, this is a *vérité de fait*, not the necessary conclusion of the analytical parsing of a pre-given essence, not a *vérité de raison*. The task is to prove that the manner of existence, the *modus operandi* of the unprethinkable *actus* of existing, is, as a matter of fact, Godly and not ungodly – and here, where *modus* is the discussion, adverbs must be used. God's existence is contingent, as there could have been nothing at all, inclusive of the essence of God. Chaos could have held sway, the modeless and essence-less. The question is whether being is in fact operative with a divine *modus*, with a decisive and necessary *modus*. Schelling writes,

> The necessary act of existing (namely the merely-necessary act of existing) *is* – not necessarily, but *factically* it is the necessary necessarily-existing being or God. This is proved a posteriori in the manner already indicated, in that one says: if the necessary act of existing is *God*, then certain consequences will follow – we want to say, so will a, b, c and so forth be *possible*. Now, according to our experience, however, a, b, c and so forth exist in fact, thus – this is the necessary conclusion – the necessary act of existing is *in fact* God.[69]

God is proved through his consequents but, contrary to the cosmological and teleological proofs, contrary to Thomism, not as something necessarily existent, but only factically existent and only factically necessary, something contingently existing necessarily. God's *modus* is necessary or the unprethinkable *actus* of existing is operative in a necessarily structured manner – the necessary sequence of the potencies – just as unicorns exist necessarily as one-horned, if they, in fact, exist. The necessary *modus* of existing exists only factically, only contingently. God exists necessarily as the *natura necessaria*, if and only if he exists, if and only if a *natura necessaria* exists. In short, necessity only exists factically, hence contingently. God's *modus operandi* is necessary and so if God exists, he exists necessarily as this *modus*.

Schelling shows that the event or decision of being could not possibly be known apart from its factical occurrence, apart from its actual revelation. In this regard the decision proves to be something personal because it is elevated above truths of reason, which can be known a priori, in advance of the deed through reason alone and thus apart from historical revelation. Only the deed is historical and personal. God holds sway or eventuates as the *modus operandi* of this deed, its meaning and identity. God, contrary to the opinion of Gabriel, is not the taking-place and limit-term of rationality and intelligibility, but he is both the *prius* of and the withdrawal from the determinations of reason. This is the manner by which being acquires its identity and oneness, its *monas*-character. This, however, does not mean that God necessarily exists, which means that it is not necessary that being hold sway as *monas* and that reason be consequent upon being. It is not necessary that being is supplemented with thinkability/intelligibility. The event of being itself, the fact that there is something rather than nothing, and everything that has happened to ensue in its wake, is ultimately contingent. Schelling, well before Heidegger, attempted to think contingency and necessity as more than the modalities of some entity, some *actualitas*, but as such, as the modeless, as the operativity or eventuation of the decision of being itself.

Notes

1. Schelling, *Initia Philosophiae Universae*, pp. 18–19.
2. 'Wir müssen von ihm hinweg-, von dem unvordenklichen Seyn loskommen, um zur *Idee* zu gelangen. Dieß wäre bloß möglich, wenn . . . jenes unvordenkliche Seyn doch selbst wieder als das zufällige zu zeigen wäre' (Schelling, 'Andere Deduktion', *SW II/4*, p. 337).
3. 'Nichts verhindert, daß eben dieses, welches a priori das Seyende ist, nach der Hand, post actum (wie hier recht eigentlich zu sagen ist) das Seynkönnende sey . . . Dadurch aber ist gerade in diesem unvordenklichen Existieren eine nicht auszuschließende Zufälligkeit gesetzt' (ibid., *SW II/4*, p. 338).
4. 'Ewig is das Seyn, in dem Gott ist, sogar ehe *er selbst* es denkt.' 'Die Ewigkeit gehört mit zu den Attributen Gottes, welche die Speculativeren unter den Theologen die negativen genannt haben. Untersucht man diese genauer, so sind sie durchgängig solche, die von Gott an und vor sich, d.h. vor seiner Gottheit, gedacht werden, *die ohne* welche er nicht Gott seyn könnte, aber durch die er noch nicht Gott ist. Denn z.B. auch die Spinozische Substanz ist ewig, ohne alle Voraussetzung, grundlos ewig, und doch ist sie nicht Gott; hinwiederum aber könnte Gott nicht Gott seyn, wenn er nicht ewig wäre, die Ewigkeit ist eine conditio sine qua non seiner Gottheit' (ibid., *SW II/4*, p. 342).
5. 'jenes grundlose Seyn' (ibid., *SW II/4*, p. 342).
6. 'Il faut que tout soit précis, déterminé, aigu . . . Toute équivoque sera tranchée; la chose de Dieu sera franche et claire' (Jankélévitch, *L'Odyssée*, p. 200).
7. 'daß zwischen dem natura ewigen Sein Gottes und zwischen dem Entschluß zur Tat etwas in der Mitte sei, ohne welches Mittelglied die Welt nur als unmittelbar notwendige Emanation der Gottheit gedacht werden könnte' (Schelling, *Urfassung*, p. 131).
8. 'das Mittel zwischen Schöpfer und Geschöpf' (ibid., p. 134).
9. 'ein Interstitium' (ibid., p. 137).
10. 'ein Zwischenraum' (ibid., p. 137).
11. Emilio Brito warns,

    > This Wisdom . . . is not for Schelling the second person of the Trinity, the Word . . . The *Urpotenz* is not the co-substantial Word, but the *latent* presence in God of an Other than His own. [Cette Sagesse . . . n'est pas pour Schelling la deuxième personne de la Trinité, le Verbe . . . L'*Urpotenz* n'est pas le Verbe consubstantiel, mais la présence *latente* en Dieu d'un Autre que Lui-même.] (Brito, 'Création', p. 321)

    Whether ur-possibility is identifiable with the Word is a debatable point, a debate which might even obscure the point here, namely that the possibility of creation is God's confrontation with alterity and not a possibility found within his own nature.
12. 'Die »Weisheit« als geistiges Urbild der Schöpfung ist dasjenige, was durch Gliederung Ordnung ermöglicht . . .' (Durner, *Wissen und Geschichte*, p. 220).

13. 'Soll Gott als freier Schöpfer erwiesen werden, so ist die »Weisheits«-Phase notwendig als integrierendes, dem Schöpfungsakt vorausgehendes Moment des absoluten Prozesses zu denken. Wird diese Phase negiert, so bleibt nichts anderes übrig, als eine »ewige Schöpfung« im spinozistischen Sinne zu postulieren. D.h. die reale Welt . . . erscheint in einer solchen Konzeption letztlich als notwendige Emanation Gottes' (ibid., p. 223).
14. 'Allmöglichkeit' (Schelling, 'Die Philosophie der Offenbarung: Erster Theil', *SW II/3*, p. 302).
15. 'Die Möglichkeit kommt erst nach dem Seyn, aber sie erscheint dem im unvordenklichen Seyn Seyenden von da an, *daß* es Ist, also von Ewigkeit' (Schelling, 'Andere Deduktion', *SW II/4*, p. 341).
16. 'etwas zuvor nicht Gewesenes, Unversehenes' (ibid., *SW II/4*, p. 342).
17. 'einen solchen Gegenstand des Willens gibt, wird er sich selbst als Wille inne, sowie überhaupt diese Erscheinung . . . ihn zuerst in Freiheit gegen die Notwendigkeit seines Seins setzt . . . indem sie ihn von der heiligen ἀνάγκη befreit' (Schelling, *Urfassung*, p. 87).
18. 'nicht mehr bloß Nicht=Notwendigkeit, sondern auch Freiheit ist, ins Sein überzugehen oder nicht. Jetzt erst kann er von sich sagen: »Ich werde sein, der ich sein werde, d.i., der ich sein will«' (Schelling, *Urfassung*, p. 88).
19. Schelling, *Grundlegung*, p. 334.
20. Schelling, *System der Weltalter*, p. 105.
21. 'lautere Beziehung' (ibid., p. 105).
22. 'Er kann sich also zu diesem Processe nur entschließen wegen etwas *außer* sich, praeter se ("außer" ist = praeter und extra . . .)' (Schelling, 'Andere Deduktion', *SW II/4*, p. 351).
23. 'Wenn aber eben darin auch die Aktivität des wirklichen Gottes bestehen soll, so müßten wir dieses immerwährende sich selbst Denken vielmehr als den peinlichsten Zustand ansehen. Peinlicher kann es gewiß nichts geben, als ohne Aufhören nur sich selbst und also an sich selbst zu denken' (ibid., *SW II/4*, p. 352).
24. 'Gerade darum ist Gott der große Selige, wie ihn Pindar nennt, weil alle seine Gedanken immerwährend in dem sind, was außer ihm ist, in seiner Schöpfung. Er allein hat mit sich nicht zu thun, denn er ist seines Seyns a priori sicher und gewiß' (ibid., *SW II/4*, p. 354).
25. 'daß er *sich* in der Mitte zwischen beiden und als ein Drittes, von *beiden* Freies sieht' (ibid., *SW II/4*, p. 354.).
26. Isabelle Stengers, commenting on Alfred North Whitehead's philosophy, recently wrote, 'the slippage of the present into the past always comes first, ready to be mobilized in terms of a cause or reason' (Stengers, *Thinking With Whitehead*, p. 73). The *Ungrund*, supplemented with a possible future, becomes the past of this future, the ground or reason of that which follows. The *Ungrund* first becomes *Grund* through its consequent and, given that something only is if it has a consequent, this means that the *Ungrund* only is at all as *Grund*.
27. Schelling, *System der Weltalter*, p. 126.
28. Exodus 33:18–23.
29. Schelling, 'Vorrede', *SW I/10*, p. 222.
30. Schelling, 'Darstellung des philosophischen Empirismus', *SW I/10*, p. 255.
31. Schelling, *Grundlegung*, p. 332.
32. Schelling, *Ages of the World (3rd draft)*, p. 31.
33. 'In der arabischen Sprache wird die Kopula »ist« durch ein Wort ausgedrückt, welches unserem deutschen »kann« entspricht' (Schelling, *Urfassung*, p. 53).
34. 'absolute Einzigkeit, die ich nicht von Gott aussage, sondern schon voraussetze, um »Gott« sagen zu können . . .' (ibid., p. 111).
35. 'Allerdings nur das Ewige, das von selbst Seyende (quod a se est) kann Gott seyn . . . nur das Ewige *kann* Gott seyn, aber es *ist* nicht nothwendig Gott, es ist bloß a posteriori Gott . . .' (Schelling, 'Andere Deduktion', *SW II/4*, p. 349).

36. Schelling, 'Einleitung in die Philosophie der Offenbarung oder Begründung', *SW II/3*, p. 133.
37. Swinburne, *Existence of God*, p. 93.
38. 'Indem sie ihm ein Seyn zeigt . . . gibt sie ihm überhaupt etwas, das es wollen kann – etwas überhaupt zu Wollendes, was es zuvor nicht hatte, nämlich ein bloßes Seyn- und Nichtseyn-Könnendes' (Schelling, 'Andere Deduktion', *SW II/4*, p. 342).
39. Gabriel, *Transcendental Ontology*, p. 71.
40. Ibid., p. 72.
41. Ibid., p. 82.
42. 'Denken *Sie* sich jenen Herrn des noch nicht seyenden, aber möglichen, und *wenn* es ist, zufälligen Seyns, denken *Sie* sich also dieses zufällige Seyn als entstanden, so wird es dem unentstandenen, dem zuvor dagewesenen, dem Urseyn begegnen, welches nun erst *als* ewige auch erscheint' (Schelling, 'Andere Deduktion', *SW II/4*, p. 343).
43. 'Dieses [zuvor unbewegliche] Seyn wird selbst auch ein anderes . . . selbst zu *einem* Seyenden (da es uranfänglich *das* Seyende war)' (ibid., *SW II/4*, p. 344).
44. 'Auf diese Weise sehen wir, wie der . . . indem er Herr ist, dieses zufällige Seyn zu *setzen* oder *nicht* zu setzen, wie er eben dadurch auch seines *Urseyns* Herr geworden ist . . . und so sein nothwendiges Existiren selbst in ein zufälliges verwandeln kann' (ibid., *SW II/4*, p. 344).
45. Note:

    According to its *nature*, the necessary act of existing, the merely *actu* necessary act of existing, must be something indifferent, a contingent being in regard to itself. [Dem seiner *Natur* nach nothwendig Existirenden muß das bloß actu nothwendige Existiren ein gleichgültiges, ein in Ansehung seiner selbst *zufälliges* seyn.] (Schelling, 'Andere Deduktion', *SW II/4*, p. 346)

    Schelling continues further, 'The unprethinkable act of existing is . . . to be sure, only contingently necessary, i.e. something blind. [Das unvordenkliche Existiren ist . . . doch nur zufällig-nothwendiges, d.h. ein blindes.]' (ibid., *SW II/4*, p. 347).
46. 'in dem actu nothwendigen Existiren das Zufällige' (ibid., *SW II/4*, p. 348).
47. '*Durch* die Erscheinung der Potenz eines *anderen* Seyns erscheint das ihr zuvorgekommene bloß actu nothwendige Existiren selbst als ein Zufälliges, Aufhebliches, auch *nicht* seyn Könnendes' (ibid., *SW II/4*, p. 349).
48. 'Wir können nun auch über die Tat, die wir keineswegs a priori, sondern nur a posteriori erkennen, nur sagen, daß sie geschehen *ist*' (Schelling, *Urfassung*, p. 135).
49. 'Wir haben bei all diesem das Faktum hypothetisch vorausgesetzt; denn a priori läßt es sich nicht beweisen. Es ist Tatsache, und zwar die Tatsache κατ' ἐξοχην, die Urtatsache der Geschichte, von der man nur sagen kann, daß sie sich begeben hat' (ibid., p. 223). Here too Schelling appeals to the Law of the World as that which first sets Man upon the summit of either/or, demanding that he either eat of the Tree of the Knowledge of Good and Evil and fall or refrain from eating and remain in Paradise. What the Law excludes is that Man can remain in Paradise indecisively, that is, by accident, by *Zufall* rather than by *Schicksal*. The Fall of Man is not necessary, but it is necessary that the possibility of the Fall and therewith the imperative to decide for or against it be shown to Man. In this respect, Schelling's discussion of Nemesis as the embodiment of the Law of the World, that which executes the divine economy, finds further application. The Law tempts Man. Nemesis is allowed to tempt Man because God wants Man to be in Paradise freely and not by chance. The imperative – 'Do not eat!' – first reveals the opposite possibility. When a child playing peacefully is told not to scream this first incites the possibility of screaming. As the Apostle Paul might wonder, is the law, insofar as it tempts one and incites sin, then bad? By no means. For what is good is only known by means of the law, even though, inversely, one also only knows of all the bad one can possibly do by means of the same law. To paraphrase

Paul, who would not know what sin was had the Law of the World not first forbade it? In this context, Schelling relates the term 'nemesis' to 'νόμος' or law (Schelling, 'Die Mythologie', *SW II/2*, p. 145).
50. 'Der Theismus erkennt Gott bloß der Substanz nach, nicht aber der Gottheit nach' (Schelling, *Urfassung*, p. 115).
51. 'Theismus = Atheismus' (ibid., p. 115).
52. 'außer Gott kein anderer Gott ist' (ibid., p. 103).
53. 'Denn durch diese Formel ist nichts in Gott selbst, nichts Positives *in* ihm gesetzt, sondern nur etwas *außer* ihm negiert' (ibid., p. 103).
54. 'ob also die Monas schon mit dem unvordenklichen Seyn gefunden sey, *ist* eben die Frage' (Schelling, 'Andere Deduktion', *SW II/4*, p. 337).
55. 'daß es ohne Möglichkeit des Polytheismus keinen Monotheismus geben könne ... Monotheismus kann nur Dogma sein, inwiefern das Gegenteil von ihm möglich ist ... Was nicht widersprochen werden *kann*, kann auch nicht behauptet werden' (Schelling, *Urfassung*, p. 123).
56. 'die Gottheit dieses a priori *Seyenden* läßt sich allerdings nur a posteriori beweisen' (Schelling, 'Andere Deduktion', *SW II/4*, p. 350).
57. Levinas, *Totality and Infinity*, pp. 54, 170.
58. Marcela García, an excellent reader of the later Schelling, draws Schelling's notion of decisiveness into relation with the Greek notion of crisis.

> *Krisis*, from the Greek κρίνω: separating, distinguishing; deciding a dispute or a contest, choosing, picking out, preferring; judgment; the turning point of a disease. This complex of meanings is reproduced by Schelling's expressions: cision [*Scheidung*], decision [*Entscheidung*], excision [*Abscheidung*], elimination or expulsion [*Ausscheidung*] (García, 'Schelling's Late Negative Philosophy', p. 151, n. 13)

In conjunction with the present rejection of a dialectic of synthesis that raises contradictories to a both/and in favour of a logic of extainment, she also adds,

> What has been called sublation [*Aufhebung*] is now seen more clearly as *crisis*: elimination (*Ausscheidung*) of what is relative non-being and *decision* (*Entscheidung*) for what is being in the primary sense. Indeed, if the rational philosophy only consisted of a progression from potentiality to actuality, even if it meant to separate them, it would end up connecting them through the progression itself as its two ends. (ibid., p. 157)

Actuality, in Schelling, is not an entity, an *actualitas*, hence why it has nothing to do with *conatus* and ἐντελέχεια. Actuality is not the end term of a movement *a potentia ad actum*, but is the deed by which it purifies itself of potentiality, by which potentiality is excised and extained. Ironically, then, the potential fills the domain of what is and *actus purissimus* the domain of what is not, but in the indicative rather than subjunctive sense.
59. 'nicht es selbst (das absolute Prius) soll bewiesen werden, sondern die *Folge* aus diesem, diese muß *faktisch* bewiesen werden, und damit die *Gottheit* jenes Prius – daß es *Gott* ist und also *Gott* existirt' (Schelling, 'Einleitung in die Philosophie der Offenbarung oder Begründung', *SW II/3*, p. 129).
60. 'Daß es Gott ist, ist nicht eine res naturae, ein sich von selbst Verstehendes; es ist eine res facti, und kann daher auch nur faktisch bewiesen werden. – Es ist Gott. Dieser Satz hat nicht die Bedeutung: der Begriff jenes Prius ist = dem Begriff Gott; seine Bedeutung ist: jenes Prius *ist* Gott, nicht dem Begriff, sondern der Wirklichkeit nach' (ibid., *SW II/3*, p. 128).
61. Schulz, *Vollendung*, p. 324.

62. Recalling that Schelling's method, which operates *per posterius*, is an a priori empiricism, note the following explication:

> positive philosophy is empirical *a priorism*, or it is the empiricism of the a priori, insofar as it proves that the *prius* exists as God *per posterius*. With respect to the *world* positive philosophy is an a priori science, a science derived from the absolute *prius*. With respect to *God* it is an a posteriori science and knowledge. [ist die positive Philosophie empirischer *Apriorismus*, oder sie ist der Empirismus des Apriorischen, inwiefern sie das Prius per posterius als Gott seyend erweist. In Ansehung der *Welt* ist die positive Philosophie Wissenschaft a priori, aber vom absoluten Prius abgeleitete; in Ansehung *Gottes* ist sie Wissenschaft und Erkenntniß a posteriori.] (Schelling, 'Einleitung in die Philosophie der Offenbarung oder Begründung', *SW II/3*, p. 130)

63. Vallicella, *Paradigm Theory*, pp. 7–8.
64. Swinburne, *Coherence*, p. 277.
65. 'Art der Existenz' (Schelling, 'Geschichte', *SW I/10*, p. 16).
66. 'Existenz überhaupt' (ibid., *SW I/10*, p. 16).
67. 'daß Gott durch nichts anderes in oder außer sich zur Existenz bestimmt sei; was heißt dies mehr, als daß er grundlos existiere? Nennen wir nicht gerade eine solche Existenz eine Zufällige, und müßten wir nicht konsequenterweise von Gott dieser Voraussetzung gemäß sagen, er sei ein höchst zufällig existierendes Wesen, da sich ja von seinem Sein kein Grund einsehen läßt?' (Schelling, *Einleitung*, p. 23).
68. 'Damit ist aber nicht mehr gesagt als Gott, wenn er ist, kann nur das notwendig, nicht zufällig Seiende sein' (ibid., p. 23).
69. 'das nothwendig Existirende (nämlich das einfach-nothwendig Existirende) *ist* – nicht nothwendig, aber *faktisch* das nothwendig nothwendig-existirende Wesen oder Gott; und dieß wird a posteriori auf die schon angezeigte Art bewiesen, indem man nämlich sagt: wenn das nothwendig Existirende *Gott* ist, so wird diese und jene Folge – wir wollen sagen, so wird a, b, c u.s.w. *möglich;* nun existirt aber unserer Erfahrung zufolge a, b, c u.s.w. wirklich, also – der nothwendige Schluß – ist das nothwendig Existirende *wirklich* Gott' (Schelling, 'Einleitung in die Philosophie der Offenbarung oder Begründung', *SW II/3*, p. 169). One should compare this with the following:

> We thus want to say: the *prius*, whose concept is such and such (the concept of what is beyond being), will *be able* to have a consequence of a certain *sort*. (We will not say: it will necessarily *have* such a consequence, as then we would again relapse into a necessary movement, i.e. one determined through the mere concept. We will only be permitted to say: it can have such a consequence *if it wills*. The consequence is independent from its will.) Now, however, this consequence actually exists (*this* proposition is one based on experience); the existence of such a consequence is a *factum*, a factual matter of experience. This *factum* shows itself to us thus – the *existence* of such a consequence shows us that the *prius* itself *exists* in this way, just as we have *conceived* it, such that God exists. [Wir werden also sagen: das Prius, dessen *Begriff* dieser und dieser (der des Ueberseyenden) ist, wird eine *solche* Folge haben *können* (wir werden nicht sagen: es wird nothwendig eine solche Folge *haben*, denn da fielen wir wieder in die nothwendige, d.h. durch den bloßen Begriff bestimmte Bewegung zurück, wir werden nur sagen dürfen: es kann eine solche Folge haben, *wenn es will,* die Folge ist eine von seinem Willen abhängige). Nun existirt aber diese Folge wirklich (*dieser* Satz ist nun der auf Erfahrung beruhende Satz; die Existenz einer solchen Folge ist ein Factum, eine Thatsache der Erfahrung. Also zeigt uns dieses Factum - die *Existenz* einer solchen Folge zeigt uns, daß auch das Prius selbst so *existirt*, wie wir es *begriffen* haben, d.h. daß Gott existirt.]' (Schelling, 'Die Philosophie der Offenbarung: Zweiter Theil', *SW II/4*, p. 129)

Chapter 6

Event and De-cision: Towards an Appropriation of Heidegger's Last God

This chapter aims at a creative confrontation between the later Schelling and the later Heidegger insofar as it concerns their respective reflections on the nature of the event and the decision(s) of being, as well as the question of Godhood. Before commencing, however, it will prove beneficial first to sketch Heidegger's persistent, from early to late, criticism of logic, eventually showing how he attempts to account for the emergence of these cardinal laws of thinking historically – the law of identity, the law of non-contradiction and the law of excluded middle (as well as the principle of reason itself) – from the operativity of the event of being itself. This will help to relate Heidegger's project to some of the issues that dominated the thought of Meillassoux and Boutroux, for example the question of the origin of the principle of reason and the contingency of the basic laws of logic. Ultimately, Heidegger will confirm that both reason/thinking, even in the guise of formal logic, and the existence of God, if he exists, are contingent rather than necessary. Heidegger also argues that the fact that there is something rather than nothing is to be regarded as factical and not as a metaphysical necessity. For him, this Leibnizian question, as it did for Schelling, acutely problematises the question of God, a question, however, which Heidegger, unlike Schelling, is more reticent to broach as a philosophical question. Ultimately, the task is not to gentrify one thinker or the other, namely to make Heidegger compatible with Schelling or Schelling compatible with Heidegger, but to let a third interpretation creatively emerge, even if this may unintentionally produce both a Heideggerised Schelling and a Schellingianised Heidegger.

On the question of logic

This subheading is meant to suggest that logic itself, its philosophical grounding as a discipline, can be put in question. As Heidegger remarked in a lecture series on Kant just prior to the publication of *Sein und Zeit*, 'Nowadays logic has become the stepchild of philosophy, is dragged along in its old forms with occasional corrections, and is the most retarded science in that it has never yet been genuinely grounded philosophically.'[1] In a series of lectures delivered in 1937–38, at the time he was completing the *Beiträge*, which is thought to mark the 'turn' to his later thought, he concludes, 'It should at least now be clear that the question of truth is no longer a "problem of logic".'[2] *Per* Heidegger, for logic to have a properly philosophical use, it must be more than formal or, as he refers to it, scholastic logic. As he scathingly remarks in a way that would include present-day courses in Critical Thinking,

> Scholastic logic is a form of sloth tailor-made for instructors. All they have to do, year after year, is parrot the same old stock of unchanging, shopworn propositions, formulas, rules, and definitions ... It would be easier and more expeditious for [students] – not to mention quicker and cheaper – to just read the stuff on their own in any logic manual ... It is beneath the dignity of the university as a place of questioning and searching.[3]

According to Heidegger there are a few exceptions who have attempted to ground logic philosophically. Kant avoided logical scholasticism by creating a transcendental logic and Hegel a speculative, dialectical logic. (Heidegger would also recuse Aristotle's analytics.)

Another way to avoid the philosophical sterility of logic would be to uncover the very grounds of logic and its basic laws. For Heidegger, it is not obvious of its own accord that logic just is valid and that, therefore, nothing more is to be said about its justification as a discipline. Gabriel rightly comments, 'As Schelling, Heidegger, and Wittgenstein agree, reflection is inevitably bound to a set of finite, discursive expressions of itself generating imaginary frameworks, mythologies.'[4] While this unfortunately whitewashes these three authors, as Schelling clearly does not abandon the project of a purely rational philosophy, namely a universal logic, even if he does show how it is a contingent consequent, it does indicate that all forms of thought, inclusive of merely formal logic – if logic can really be formal merely – are based upon propositions that are not yet grounded. In logic, such truths, which are universally accepted but, Heidegger contends, not yet philosophically grounded, are the law of identity, the law of non-contradiction and the law of excluded middle. Moreover, Heidegger will also attempt philosophically to ground the principle of sufficient reason itself. In accord with Schelling, Heidegger's questioning of the basic laws of logic, the presumed laws of thought itself, even calls into question the necessity of the existence of reason itself or, as Gabriel prefers to phrase it, logical space itself. Explicating Schelling by means of Heidegger, Gabriel writes,

> The existence of logical space is contingent, because no ground can be given for the fact that it exists. Unprethinkable being [in Schelling] cannot therefore be understood as the *ground* of logical space, because the concept of ground already presupposes the successful constitution of logical space. Unprethinkable being is consequently the paradoxical 'ground of ground' in the full-blooded Heideggerian sense, what Heidegger also speaks of as the 'abyss'.[5]

Grund, in German, means both ground and reason, thus avoiding a separation of the ontological and the logical. If Gabriel is right that the notion of ground presupposes logical space or that logical space constitutes the notion of ground itself, then this could also be reformulated to say that the question of the 'ground of ground' is the question of the 'reason of reason'. The question, as Heidegger formulates it, would be: Why is there a domain of whys and becauses? Presupposing an understanding of his account of truth, Heidegger states, 'The question of *why* there is at all truth as clearing-concealing presupposes the truth of the "why". But both, truth and the "why" (the call for a grounding), are the same.'[6] For Heidegger, then, as much as for Schelling, the question concerning the ground and existence of logical space as such as well as the efficacy of the principles of reason and causality cannot be answered with a 'because', but this emergence of reason/logic from unreason can be historically narrated. One cannot even appeal to God as the ultimate 'why' of reason, as one side of the Euthyphro Dilemma attempts to do insofar as it says that eternal truths of reason, for example A ≠ ~A, only exist because God eternally thinks them. Heidegger, extending his point beyond the existence of logical space to the Leibnizian question of why anything exists at all, rhetorically implores:

> Why beings? Because a highest being causes them, produces them? . . . the highest being, *summum ens*, belongs all the more to beings. How is the 'why' supposed to be answered on that basis? Why beings? Why? Wherefore? To what extent? Reasons! Ground and origin of the 'why'.[7]

When Heidegger, in *Satz vom Grund* (*Principle of Reason*) in 1955–56, discusses Leibniz,[8] who answered the question as to why there is something rather than nothing by appeal to the principle of sufficient reason, he emphasises the different tonalities, the different ways, one can hear the principle *nihil est sine ratione*. In accord with the epistemo-ontological task of this book, the most informative way to hear this principle is nihil *est sine ratione*. Emphasising the *nihil* as an abyss, as chaos, which is without reason – but also, therefore, as that which can be (with) reason – this says that the nothing or chaos alone is without reason. Consequently, whatever is something, rather than nothing, does succumb to the principle of reason; only what is nothing does not come under the influence of this principle. That from which the principle of sufficient reason can emerge, then, that wherein the principle of sufficient reason originates, is nothing. If reason does not emerge from something, as all such somethings already presuppose the efficacy of the principle of reason, it must emerge from nothing. The ground of ground/reason itself can only be the groundless, what Heidegger has called *Abgrund*, Schelling *Ungrund* and what Meillassoux insists could only emerge *ex nihilo* or from out of unreason: Hyper-Chaos. This way of broaching the ground of reason or the reason of ground takes seriously Heidegger's contention that 'the principle of reason is without reason'.[9]

That the facticity of reason is without reason turns out to corroborate the fact that reason and its laws are not just laws of thinking or formal laws of logic, but laws of being. If, as Heidegger contends, the principle of reason 'is the ground/reason for all principles and that means for what a principle is per se . . . the principle of reason . . . is the ground/reason for what a principle is . . .'[10] The principle of reason is a principle that emerges from pre-principled, pre-rational being. More explicitly, Heidegger pronounces,

> *To being there belongs something like ground/reason. Being is akin to grounds, it is ground-like.* The sentence 'Being is ground-like' speaks quite differently than the statement 'beings have a reason.' 'Being is ground-like' thus in no way means 'being has a ground'; rather, it says: *being in itself essentially comes to be as grounding.*[11]

Like Schelling, being and reason/thinking belong together or, to put it in the terms Schelling utilises to explain the transitive nature of the copula, that which is being is the same as that which is reason. It is not the case that being is there because reason/thinking is there. Both Heidegger and Schelling reject this tenet of Hegelianism. Heidegger criticises that 'according to the rules of ordinary logic. According to these "being and ground/reason: the same" amounts to saying: being = ground/reason.'[12] This gives predominance to reason/ground over being/unground, but, on the contrary, it is not because reason/ground is that being is, but vice versa. Rather, being is reason, whereby the 'is' must be understood not as an equivalency but transitively as a bringing about of the essence and principle of being as something not already contained in being (albeit also not yet excluded). In Heidegger's own words, 'Insofar as being essentially comes to be as ground/reason, it has no ground/reason ... Being: the *a*-byss'[13] and

> Ground/reason receives its essence from its belonging together with being qua being. Put in the reverse, being reigns qua being from out of the essence of ground/reason. Ground/reason and being ('are') the same – not equivalent ... Being 'is' in essence: ground/reason. Therefore being can never first have a ground/reason which would supposedly ground it. Accordingly, ground/reason is missing from being ... Being 'is' the abyss in the sense of such a remaining-apart of reason from being. To the extent that being as such grounds, it remains groundless.[14]

'Being reigns qua being from out the essence of ground/reason' means that being proves itself 'sovereign' by holding sway over its own being, over its ground, which it proves always to outstrip and into which it can never be subsumed or sublated. 'Ground/reason and being ("are") the same – not equivalent' explicitly pronounces a rejection of the equivalence of the two. 'Being "is" in essence ground/reason' says that rather than an equivalency, the 'is' expresses a transitivity: that which is being is not other than that which is reason. That which is being is the same as that which is reason, except that reason always occupies the place of *consequens*/accusative and never that of the *antecedens*/nominative. 'Being can never first have a ground/reason' means that there is ground/reason because there is being and not vice versa. 'Accordingly ground/reason is missing from being.' This says, again, that the 'same' which is ground/reason is the same which is being, but this 'same' is not being-as-ground but being-as-unground, as abyss. 'Being "is" the abyss in the sense of such a remaining-apart of reason from being' indicates that the reason there can never be an equivalency between being and reason/ground is because being is never subsumed into the latter, as being 'withdraws' or is 'set-apart' as an 'indivisible remainder', as Schelling would state the matter. Heidegger's setting the copula in parentheses conveys the sense of bracketing its meaning as equivalency and as merely reduplicative, as re-constative, in order to stress its transitivity and operativity. Finally, 'to the extent that being as such grounds, it remains groundless' specifies that only that which is not a ground as such is capable of grounding, just as only that which is not sick, but healthy, can become sick or can 'be' sick. Here too, then – despite Meillassoux's claims to the contrary – is evidence that Heidegger is not a correlationist, at least if correlationism indicates that it is impossible to affirm being apart from its entanglement with reason/ground/thinking. Heidegger even hints towards thinking of this in terms of Plato's *Timaeus*, writing of the emergence of reason/ground from out of being, 'As what is to be thought, it becomes, from out of its truth, what gives a measure.'[15] Might one even say, then, that for Heidegger too reason/ground is that which provides limit, quantifiability, mathematisability and thinkability to that which antecedently is unlimited, non-quantified, non-mathematised and unprethinkable?

If, for Schelling, the law of excluded middle operates as the condition of the law of non-contradiction and the law of identity, Heidegger, although expressly denying that any of the three take precedence over the others, surely privileges the principle of identity. Nevertheless, Joan Stambaugh, in the introduction to her translation of Heidegger's *Identity and Difference* (1957), remarks that Schelling is closer than anybody to Heidegger's problem of identity, where identity must be thought prior to the basis of the ground, appealing in particular to Schelling's account of the identity of *Grund* and *Existenz* in his 1809 *Freiheitsschrift*.[16] Noting that this identity signifies the groundless rather than a synthesis or indifference of already established antitheses, she grants that this thought of Schelling is certainly closer to Heidegger than to German Idealism.[17] The principle of identity in Heidegger is also not an identification or unification of pre-given disjuncts; it is not the indifference of all differences. Deleuze explicates (or rather pushes his own interpretation of) the meaning of identity and difference, which are not counterparts or dialectical opposites, in the following way:

> In accordance with Heidegger's ontological intuition, difference must be articulation and connection in itself; it must relate different to different without any mediation whatsoever by the identical, the similar, the analogous or the opposed. There must be a differenciation of difference, an in-itself which is like a *differenciator*, a *Sich-Unterscheidende*, by virtue of which the different is gathered all at once rather than represented on condition of a prior resemblance, identity, analogy or opposition.[18]

If indifference is neither the synthesis nor opposition of two things already neatly differentiated from one another, then difference is fundamentally never the difference between two givens, but only the differenciation – as Deleuze insists on writing this non-representational and non-dialectical account of differentiation with a 'c' rather than with a 't' – of a 'same' that is not even equal to itself, at least not prior to its differenciation. This account of difference is operative without medium because, insofar as it does not first begin with the two that are different, it does not require a third or mediating term. The middle – what Heidegger sometimes names *Lichtung*, the clearing or opening – is, prior to the event of differenciation, something not yet excluded, a breach or clearing not yet opened. The middle, at any rate, is not a mediator but disjunction. Its opening, its exclusion, is one and the same with the act of differencing itself. Nevertheless, Deleuze also grants that

> There is no doubt that *there is* an identity belonging to the precursor . . . This 'there is', however, remains perfectly indeterminate. Are identity and resemblance here the preconditions of the functioning of this dark precursor, or are they, on the contrary, its effects?[19]

The very being of the pre-cursor is indeterminate and undefined; it is unequal to itself, what has been called ἄπειρον. The 'identity' of the precursor, at least as Deleuze speaks of it, is only an effect of the difference that ensues or, better, that will ensue from 'it'.

In 'Basic Principles of Thinking', lectures delivered in 1957, Heidegger offers the following description of what Deleuze has termed a self-differencing pre-cursor.

> Identity is itself nothing that lies before, but it co-constitutes what lies before as such. What appears to lie at the ground of the basic principle A is A . . . is nothing that lies before, nothing that lies at ground, and in this sense it is no longer ground. But because it is no longer a ground, we speak in a rigorous and sober sense of an abyss [*Ab-grund*].[20]

The principle of identity, in other words, is not a law descriptive of a primordial identity at the basis of things, a description of something that already 'lies before', but it is a prescriptive law that demands that identity and ground be constituted, that identity and ground come to be. Accordingly, when Heidegger says that this which 'appears' to lie at the ground is 'no longer' ground, he is speaking from an epistemological point of view. It is not the case that it was already a ground but now no longer is, but it now only no longer 'appears' as ground because it is now known as it really is, as *Ab-grund*. He specifies this *Ab-grund* by proposing, 'Indeed this abyss is neither the empty nothing nor an obscure confusion, but rather the event of appropriation.'[21] Although it is not yet something, it is also not nullity. It is chaos. In line with the account of chaos already given, Heidegger too is quick to warn, even if he does not use the term 'chaos' but rather 'abyss (*Abgrund*)', that this does not signify a confusion or mixture of elements, but it is prior to everything elemental and thus to all possible confusion and mixture. It is *das Gähnen*, the yawning of the abyss,[22] the differencing event. The differencing event, however, is also an event of appropriation, an event of correlation, given that what is set apart, being and thinking/reason, *Ab-grund* and *Grund*, are also united or made to belong. Only insofar as they are first differenced can it be said that they are identifiable or, more precisely, that the 'same' which is being/unground is the same that is reason/ground. Only thus can it be said that being is reason or that the unground is the ground/principle of being. In short: 'Principle of identity now says: a leap that achieves the event of appropriation, i.e. the essence of identity.'[23] For both Schelling and Heidegger, identity is something posited as a result of the event and not as pre-condition of the event.

Before advancing to a more developed discussion of the event in Heidegger, which follows from his account of the principle of identity, let a couple of consequences this has for the law of non-contradiction and the law of excluded middle first be drawn. First, regarding the law of non-contradiction, he, contra Meillassoux but in line with Schelling, is not willing to admit that contradictions are absolutely impossible and thus non-existent. He rather affirms that, in some sense, they are real. He writes, 'Ever since Hegel's *Logic* it is no longer immediately certain that where a contradiction is present what contradicts itself cannot be real.'[24] Second, he is willing to grant the law of excluded middle unlimited efficacy neither before, in nor after the event, but he does grant its role as the event itself. Heidegger's reluctance to grant the law of excluded middle unconditional sway is because he is not willing to admit what follows from this, namely that truth would be bivalent, that something must henceforth be either true or false. As Lee Braver explains, 'Even if we concede bivalence to correspondence truth' – which Heidegger rejects as original – 'we should not immediately apply it to Unconcealment Truth' – truth as the event of appropriation. Unconcealment Truth 'not bivalent, since a being's unconcealment is naturally a matter of degrees'.[25] Bivalency holds where the law of non-contradiction holds, since to affirm that something is both true and not true at the same time (assuming that this could also be done in the same respect) would be contradictory. The law of non-contradiction, however, is only operative, A or ~A, true or not-true only exhaust all possible options, if the principle of excluded middle is in effect first. Given that Heidegger wants to avoid truth as bivalent, since he sees this as one of the hallmarks of truth as correspondence, he must delimit the efficacy of the principle of excluded middle. Braver correctly concludes, 'Heidegger rejects bivalence because truth and untruth, conceived as unconcealment and concealment, are inextricably linked rather than mutually exclusive or simply opposed to one another.'[26] This will all make more sense if one bears in mind that Heidegger's event is a truth-event, the event of unconcealment or, better, an event that both unconceals and conceals.

Reading Schelling and Heidegger together

This subheading is as ambiguous as the first. First, it can refer to a justification for why this pair of authors can be brought into conversation by showing how they are not incommensurable and are even complementary. This would implicate the historical claim that the earlier author functions as a historical precedent for questions and concepts received by the later author (even if or, perhaps, particularly when the later thinker is not always aware of this influence) and that the later thinker's philosophy is in some way dependent upon and retroactively illuminating of the earlier thinker's philosophy. Second, the subheading can refer to the promise of the interpretation. To think two authors together is to think their concrescence, to let their philosophies coalesce into one, not as an abhorrent compromise but as a novel third forged by their confrontation. The result may look like a conflation of two philosophies and two thinkers, but the hope is creatively to appropriate each just as every philosophical reading is also a creative appropriation. Before embarking upon this audacious project, however, let a few historiographical and comparative remarks be made.

For both Schelling and Heidegger, philosophy's principal, and perhaps sole, occupation is with the question of being. Assuming that this is already well established in Heidegger scholarship, Schelling then sounds quite proto-Heideggerian when he declares, 'One can also distinguish philosophy in this manner: The other sciences are concerned only with this or that being of things; however, philosophy is concerned only with being itself.'[27] As will be seen, their joint preoccupation with the question of being also extends as far as their mutual, albeit differing, affirmation of ontological difference.

Concerning the presumed connection between Schelling and Heidegger, be it historical, thematic or both, one finds a host of testimonies, often full of hyperbole. Jason M. Wirth admits that Heidegger recognised Schelling's importance but kept him at bay by overemphasising the desire for a system in Schelling, 'otherwise he would have already been Heidegger'.[28] In the same collection of essays devoted to Schelling's relevance for contemporary thought, Joseph Lawrence argues that Schelling, first conceived as a link in the chain to Hegel, should now be thought as the link in the chain to Heidegger[29] and that Heidegger's *Ereignis* (event of appropriation) parallels Schelling's historical understanding of being, grounded as it is in temporal ages of the world rather than in logic.[30] Peter Warnek argues that Heidegger's debt to Schelling has still not yet been fully elaborated with clarity and depth.[31] Even Gabriel Marcel, elsewhere, wonders if 'Schelling, completely otherwise and much less directly than

Kierkegaard, has prepared the terrain – must it be said for the philosophy of existence? . . . Amongst contemporary thinkers it is Heidegger and apparently he alone . . . who appears authentically related to Schelling.'[32]

Concerning the sticky question of whether Schelling suffers under the spell of ontotheology, which Heidegger too often hastily equates with the history of metaphysics as such, Gabriel highlights Heidegger's own ambivalence towards Schelling. 'It seems difficult for Heidegger to unequivocally align Schelling to the tradition of ontotheological metaphysics.'[33] He elsewhere explains,

> Heidegger's judgment of Schelling's thought oscillates between, on the one hand, the high approbation of Schelling as the first philosopher to overcome onto-theology and, on the other hand, the opprobrium of Schelling as a necessary station on the onto-theological path from Hegel's idealism to Nietzsche's will to power, the latter of which Heidegger sees as an explication of Schelling's famous formulation 'Will is primal Being [*Wollen ist Urseyn*].'[34]

It is not just that Heidegger's indecisiveness with respect to Schelling is striking, but that his indecision always occupies an extreme position. Either Schelling is the first decisively to inaugurate a new beginning in the history of Western philosophy or he is the pinnacle of the ontotheological tradition, although it must be admitted that for Heidegger both positions would be a testament to Schelling's greatness.

Heidegger himself, in 1941, deemed Schelling's famous 1809 essay on human freedom the '*pinnacle of the metaphysics* of German Idealism',[35] although pages later he also attributes this dubious distinction to Nietzsche. Just five years earlier, however, in a seminar devoted exclusively to Schelling's 1809 text, Heidegger had praised Schelling for moving German Idealism past its fundamental position,[36] commenting that Schelling's period of silence after 1809, rather than being due to the premature death of his wife, resulted from the fact that he was on the precipice of something completely new but was unable to bring it to fruition. Whoever might be able to provide the reason for this breakdown, Heidegger speculates, would be in a position to become the founder of a new beginning in Western philosophy,[37] what he termed at this same time in the *Beiträge* 'the other beginning'. He refers to a similar breakdown in Nietzsche, whom he believes to be the only other essential thinker after Schelling. (It is worth mentioning that this would either apparently exclude Hegel from the list of 'essential thinkers', or it would appear that he views Schelling as one who surpassed Hegel rather than merely being a forerunner of Hegel, as is too often thought. One might also add here that this would not necessarily exclude Kierkegaard, but Kierkegaard, for

Heidegger, is not a philosopher, but presumably just a religious thinker.) Finally, Philipp Schwab has helpfully written an informative article detailing Heidegger's various validations and disaccreditations of Schelling's thought. It was not only in 1936 and 1941 that Heidegger gave lectures on Schelling, but also in 1927/28. Schwab tracks the change in Heidegger's estimation of Schelling from 1927/28 to 1936, concluding, 'Schelling's treatise [of 1809] and its failure is no longer considered in an "*affirmative*" sense as the "heat lightning of a new beginning," but instead reveals only *ex negativo*, as it were, the difficulties of the first and the *necessity* for a second beginning.'[38] Although Heidegger's opinion is again oscillating, one sees that Schelling, whichever way he might fall, marks a watershed moment in the history of philosophy for Heidegger. Schelling either commences with the 'other' beginning or he terminates the first beginning, but not without stressing the imperative, the need, for the other beginning. By 1936 and still in 1941 Heidegger has decided that Schelling has not yet made the leap into the other beginning; however, this may be due in part to Heidegger's suppression of certain elements of Schelling's philosophy. Jean Grondin, for one, affirms in full assurance, 'That Schelling played an essential role in shaping [Heidegger's] "official" turn in the 1930s is, as is known, easily documented through the Schelling lectures of 1936.'[39] Also, Schwab points out that by 1936 'the central term in Schelling's presentation of the Absolute is not mentioned even once, it *drops out* completely – the concept of *nonground*'.[40]

An immediate problem that arises if one wants to discuss notions like beginnings, decisions and events in Schelling and Heidegger is that Schelling talks only of the beginning, the origin and the decision of being, never seriously entertaining the possibility of an 'other' decision and thus the possibility of an 'other beginning' in philosophy. Schelling, always a thinker of origins, remains in this respect a metaphysician. Heidegger seems to suggest that being can incur a second and, in principle, an unlimited number of decisions; being can, so to speak, reset. As Robert Crease has argued,

> Unlike the a priori of Dasein's *Seinsverständnis*, for instance, the character of the *Lichtung* is not constant but changes over time . . . Even such an apparently permanent fixture of our world as Newtonian physics is something that *became* true and, by implication, could become false.[41]

Should this interpretation prove tenable, it would seem to place Heidegger much closer to Meillassoux and his belief that laws of nature can change than Meillassoux would like to admit, but it would also place him at a certain remove from Schelling. While both Schelling and Heidegger are preoccupied with the Leibnizian question as to why there are beings at all rather than no beings whatsoever, Schelling consistently pursues this as a question of origins; he tries again and again to provide a response to this question. Heidegger rather only asks what the fact that there is something rather than nothing means, how the posing of this question is relevant to the question of who man is in relation to being and beings, but he does not attempt to formulate an actual answer. Much of the reason for this difference is due to the fact that, for Heidegger, God (and the gods) is never a God who is the creator of being, although this may not preclude that God could become the sovereign (*Herr*) of being, while Schelling, as has been seen, holds it to be of utmost importance that God, in order to be God, must be free to create or not-create. Here Schelling proves to be more 'metaphysical'. Concerning methodology, as Heidegger himself argues in his 1927 article entitled 'Philosophy and Theology', theology should not be speculation about the existence of God or ruminations on his nature, but it should rather faithfully describe the experience of faith as it occurs in the life of the believer. In other words, *per* Heidegger, theology should not be an ontology of God but only a phenomenology of the life of faith, probably something like what he did in his very early 1920/21 lectures, *The Phenomenology of Religious Life*. There are, then, at least three (and probably many more) crucial differences that distance Heidegger from Schelling: (1) it seems that no decision of being is final so that future decisions can follow and supersede foregoing ones; (2) God is not required to be a God who can create, let alone actually create, in order to be God; and (3) for this reason, at least earlier in his career, Heidegger also thinks it is possible and preferable to account for God without regard to his existence or ontological determinations – theology without the word 'being' – although this becomes fuzzier in the *Beiträge*. Despite these points of divergence, one may nevertheless operate under the assumption that these differences do not preclude real congress between the two thinkers.

Concerning whether a decision of being must be preliminary or whether it could also be both originary and final, Daniela Vallega-Neu, in her commentary on Heidegger's *Beiträge*, insightfully writes,

> Since originarily the deciding encounter of the first and the other beginning is not a linear event, we must be careful how we originarily understand the words 'beginning,' 'first,' and 'other.' It is not clear, at the outset, if we are dealing with one or two beginnings, or if we should even make this differentiation. Interestingly, Heidegger never speaks of a 'second beginning' . . . there is one beginning, articulated into first and other.[42]

Contrary to appearances, there may be but one decision of being. In other words, the other beginning is a new beginning not in the sense of a 'second' beginning, of which Heidegger never speaks, but in the sense of a new and more original questioning of the first and only beginning, of the one and only event of being. Schelling tends to speak of the happening/event (*das Geschehen*) as the decision of being, whereas for Heidegger event and decision are not synonymous. The decision is about how the event is taken into question, that is, in terms of the first or the other beginning of philosophy, but not in terms of a second inception or origination of being itself. Any changes in being, the way it holds sway (*west*) are then nothing like a resetting of being, but rather only the playing out, the further execution or enactment, of the first and only event of appropriation. The other beginning is but a return, a new approach, to this event, this one and only inception. The decision, then, is whether or not more original questioning, which, as will be seen, will also foreclose or open the passing by of the last God, will take place. Vallega-Neu further explains,

> In understanding more originarily the first beginning, thinking finds the other beginning to be already intimated and decided for thinking. It is in the light of the more original understanding of the first beginning that the other, in its possibility, begins.[43]

The event of being is a singular occurrence. The first and other beginnings are possibilities for philosophy, possibilities yet to be decided, not by philosophers but by being itself. Being, in other words, has not yet unveiled its decision. Heidegger seems to corroborate this reading, writing that 'precisely as the other beginning it is essentially related to the first, and only, beginning . . . in the other beginning the first is experienced more originarily and is restored to its greatness'.[44]

Historical philosophy and the question of time and being

For both Schelling and Heidegger, the event of being or, in Schellingian parlance, the decision of being is temporal and historical, but not exactly in the same sense. Noting their similarities first, Gabriel observes, 'Unlike [Platonism]' – which thinks of true being as eternal – 'Schelling thinks *being as time*: with this move he comes into direct contact with Heidegger.'[45] For both thinkers, time is more than the horizon of being, but it is being, or, more precisely, being is time. Time is that event by which being is thinkable and ordered. Heidegger can thus say: '"being and thinking" and "being and time." In the first formula, being is understood as the beingness of being; in the second, as that whose truth is interrogated.'[46] Unlike in *Sein und Zeit*, it is not the timelessly temporal existentials of Dasein that make being intelligible, it is the historically temporal sendings of being (or beyng) (*Geschick des Seyns*) that afford being its thinkability. Despite this change, however, the question of time, either as an existential of Dasein or through the sendings of being, is constitutive of being's thinkability; the question of being and time is the question of being and thinking.

> The questioning of being in the sense of the formula 'being and time' makes it possible to grasp more originarily (i.e. to grasp in terms of the historicality of being) the history of the question of being in the sense of the formula 'being and thinking'.[47]

By questioning being in terms of time, being is questioned historically. A '*seynsgeschichtliches Denken*' is enacted that now encompasses the question of being and thinking by historicising the relation between being and thinking. Is this also what being-historical thinking means in Schelling?

Schelling's thinking is historical in the sense that it is a positive rather than negative or purely rational philosophy. His thinking is historical insofar as its object, the freedom of being, is something which cannot be known a priori, that is, purely rationally, but only if historically revealed, which also distinguishes it from the merely a posteriori. It is only known *per posterius* or abductively. One must thus distinguish between being a *prius* and being known a posteriori or *per posterius*. That which is to be known must be known from itself as absolute *prius*, but only through the *posterius*. This can only be accomplished historically by a narration of the history of the *prius* itself from its unprethinkability unto its posterior thinkability. This progressive history, rather than the rationalistic regression to the *prius* that occurs in negative philosophy, this directionality of thought, constitutes Schelling's positive philosophy, his brand of being-historical thinking. Is this, however, commensurable with Heidegger's approach?

Vallega-Neu also depicts Heidegger's being-historical thinking in terms of directionality. She writes,

> Whereas in *Being and Time* Heidegger exposes the question of being in a way that leads *toward* the origin . . . in *Contributions* Heidegger attempts to think *from* the origin . . . this shift in the directionality of thought has been thematised and much discussed as the 'turning' (*Kehre*) . . .[48]

Not only is a nearly identical rhetoric employed, but she even draws this into relation to Heidegger's 'turn'. If Schelling is indeed a link in the chain to Heidegger, then it is certainly not the Heidegger of *Sein und Zeit*, but the post-turn Heidegger. The *Kehre* also caused Heidegger to reconsider the significance of ontological difference. As Vallega-Neu explains,

> Thinking in terms of the ontological difference obstructs a more original understanding of being because it is a difference that originates in questioning being as such . . . what is required for a more original understanding of

> being is to find the more original unity of the ontological difference... The task is not to think *toward* the origin, toward the opening of be-ing[49] in its truth (temporality), but rather *from* the origin, from be-ing in its truth.[50]

When thought begins with beings, ontological difference lies at hand as a distinction between two already established domains, between being and beings, which attempts to regress back to being as that from which beings have emerged. Alternatively, to think forward from being, namely progressively and historically, corresponds to the direction of positive philosophy. In this sense, Heidegger's turn is pre-figured in Schelling's positive philosophy.

Schulz, who wrote what has come to be the canonical interpretation of the late Schelling, has commented that the difference between Heidegger and Schelling is that Heidegger understands being from existence, while Schelling understands existence from the ground of being. Schulz concludes on behalf of Heidegger that only by moving from existence to being can one attain being as something other than a subject for beings.[51] Schulz is wrong on multiple counts. Not only does the later Heidegger at least attempt to think from be-ing/beyng to beings, towards and not from Dasein, but it is also the case that only by progressing this way can one avoid positing being as a subject, substance or substrate. In other words, only in this way can one avoid 'metaphysical' determinations of being. Heidegger confirms, 'To think Being without beings means: to think Being without regard to metaphysics.'[52] Freeing the thinking of being from metaphysical determinations allows being to be thought on its own accord instead of simply as a ground for beings or as the subject of being, or, as Heidegger would say, the beingness of beings.[53] A ground is not free because it stands in a necessary relation to its consequent. Thought as a ground, being is not free to be without beings; it is not, as Schelling would say, 'sovereign' over beings, but bound to them as their ground, reason or cause. The later Heidegger too finds it to be of utmost significance that being can be thought freely apart from a necessary bond to beings as their mere ground, as the mere being of beings. This renders being not just free from beings, but free as such, without prior condition and without regard to a necessary consequent or entailment. This allows Heidegger to pronounce propositions like the following: 'Thinking is historical in the peculiar sense that beyng itself as appropriating event bears all history and therefore can never be calculated. In place of systematics and deduction, there now stands historical preparedness for the truth of beyng.'[54]

One possible incommensurability between Schelling and Heidegger with respect to time and being-historical thinking remains. Schelling temporalises being, but still admits that all times are eternally posited.

Being is thoroughly historical, but this historicality does not coincide with inner-historical occurrences. Heidegger too wants to avoid a coincidence between the history of being (*Geschichte*) and inner-historical occurrences (*Historie*), but he would, seemingly at least, also want to reject all talk of eternity (save as an altered Kierkegaardian notion of repetition), even if, as Deleuze delights, Schelling's eternity is temporally filled and populated by all sorts of happenings rather than a night in which all cows are black. Yet one is able to find Heidegger, in 1936, offering a defence, although a very rough one, of what he unfortunately terms timelessness in Schelling. He writes, '"Independence of time" cannot speak against *Being and Time* ... (Being is "dependent" upon ecstatic time as an essential character of the "truth" of Being, but this "truth" belongs to the presencing of Being itself.)'[55] If time as the truth of being belongs to the presencing of being itself, then perhaps Heidegger is also willing to admit a time-independent or eternal positing of time, so long as this is not conceived from a reified eternity or reified being operative from a *nunc stans*. In a pre-*Being and Time* lecture series, one can find Heidegger proclaiming, 'The primal fact, in the metaphysical sense, is that there is anything like temporality at all. The entrance into world by beings is primal history [*Urgeschichte*] pure and simple';[56] and he continues, connecting this problematic, as does Schelling, to a possible philosophy of mythology, 'From this primal history a region of problems must be developed which we are today beginning to approach with greater clarity, the region of the mythic.'[57] Are beings, even the Gods, to be taken as facts in the sense of a brute givenness, or is there an 'entrance' into time and primal history? If so, then from where and at what time? Perhaps from a place before or in front of being, from the futural *par excellence*, which has in this book been called the timeless positing of future times? Does time emerge from the event as the very being of the event? In what sense is the event the emergence of time?

Being and event

The event is the de-cision of being, the inception from which future trajectories of being not yet known, because not yet revealed, take their impetus. Van der Heiden contends,

> in every situation in which thought's reasoning does not offer a passage and in which it is therefore possibly placed for a decision, thought encounters, experiences, and is confronted *first* with the task to think an *undecidability* ... If there is a necessity or urgency to decide or to pass, it is grounded in thought's encounter with the undecidable.[58]

This account could pass as Heideggerian so long as one adds that the decision is not thinking's decision, not the decision of autonomous agents, not a decision that follows upon a rational choice theory. The decision is taken by being because the de-cision, which decided the undecidability of being itself, must have been made in advance of the space of reason(s). The de-cision was for thinking and reason, the event of appropriation as the appropriation of thinking by being. Van der Heiden is perfectly right, then, to undermine Meillassoux's thesis that Heidegger is from beginning to end a correlationist, a philosopher who never fails to think being outside or before its correlation with thinkability.[59] Van der Heiden declares,

> Rather than a form of co-belonging, it is the experience of abandonment and the absolution it demands that are at stake in his turning to the event. As long as the event is thought as co-belonging *alone*, a speculative reading only scratches the surface of Heidegger's understanding of the event.[60]

The event is, to employ Schelling's term, an unprethinkable rupture in being. This means that being does not have to co-belong or be in correlation with thinking. The event cannot be thought as co-belonging alone, because co-belonging emerges – even if eternally so, though Heidegger would never speak of it this way – from not-belonging. This is what it means to think not from ontological difference but rather to think the emergence of ontological difference itself. Positive or incipient thinking must commence from a place before the decision in order properly to think this decision. Van der Heiden astutely comments, 'but for [Heidegger] thought does not depart from a decision' – contrary to the decisionism of Badiou, who begins only from what he has first militantly decided to presuppose – 'rather, it first needs to think where the necessity of such a decision comes from. It needs to think the de-cision (*Ent-Scheidung*) that precedes every actual decision.'[61] This is something that both Kierkegaard and Heidegger learned from Schelling. It is not sufficient to begin with the decision as such, but one must begin from that which makes decisiveness necessary in the prescriptive sense (which, for Schelling, was the Law of the World). The undecidable, as that which must be decided, rather than the actual decision itself, is where thought must begin if it wants to begin before beings and free from arbitrary presuppositions and decisions.

Should thought begin from a decision merely as an arbitrary axiom, then its task would only consist in carrying out the consequences that follow from the decision. Thought's task would be finished once it had resolved the decision into its consequences that render it transparent without remainder, with nothing left unthought. On the contrary, because the decision is the de-cision of being that, as a decision for thinkability, emerged from a zone of undecidability antecedent to thinkability, thought is never able to exhaust the last grounds (*ergründet*) of the decision of being. In this way, the decision, *qua* event, is a gift and not a deduction, not a carrying out of a postulate to its last consequence. Heidegger expounds upon this gift, the *es gibt*, writing, 'A giving which gives only its gift, but in the giving holds itself back and withdraws, such a giving we call sending.'[62] This giving is a sending and not a deduction because that which has sent the gift is not delivered along with it, but remains withdrawn and concealed. Giving only occurs through what is given without itself consisting in givenness, or giving is only given *per posterius*, only given as withdrawn, which means more than simply ungiven, but a giving that has abandoned its gift, hence why it must be 'sent' and not 'presented'.

The task is not to elaborate upon the dynamics of the gift but to pave the way for forthcoming discussions of the withdrawal, the contingency of the gift and the question whether God passes by in the gift itself, the withdrawal from the gift, or neither. This event of appropriation, which Heidegger prefers to name the truth of being, Schelling names freedom. This designation, however, is not foreign to Heidegger himself, as Vallega-Neu explains: 'Freedom names the swaying of truth itself which opens as the abyss out of which enowning [event of appropriation] occurs . . .'[63] Were one pressed to distinguish truth and freedom, one might say that truth names the abyss, the *Abgrund*, as the open-space itself, while freedom names the 'swaying of truth', the opening of the open, the yawning of the gape.

A thinking of the de-cision or event commences not from the inception of being, not from the decision as such or the open-space as such, but before the inception, where the imperative to decide must be thought. Thought must commence from the undecidability of the opening, before a ground/*Grund* has yet been laid. Only in this way is metaphysics, in its beleaguered sense, overcome and the leap into the 'other' beginning accomplished. As one commentator remarked of Schelling,

> The path into the unground leads to the surpassing of metaphysics as such. It now no longer transcends *beyond nature* (μετὰ τὰ φυσιχά) to a supreme ground of being (θεός); it rather returns *behind* nature into that which is antecedent to the existence of things as much as it is to its own founding [*Ergründung*]. In this path or 'step back' lies that which Heidegger called the 'turn'.[64]

If, as mentioned earlier, metaphysical determinations of being can only be avoided if one does not begin with beings and regress to being as their ground, instead progressively commencing with being itself, then this is tantamount to commencing, as Schelling has said, 'behind being [*hinter dem Sein*]' or before the beginning, which means before beings, even God.

The 'step back' is not a regression, but it is appropriate to situate oneself for a real, historical progression from the absolute *prius* forth, to situate oneself at that vantage point from which everything, even the inception of being and the God(s), is still futural. As the Schellingian commentator just cited adroitly illustrates in anticipation of the discussion of the last God,

> Heidegger's exegesis of the Schellingian teaching on time ties immediately onto this *pre*-inception. *Prior* to his own inception God is neither existent nor ground. He first *becomes* the ground by deciding for this and thereby positing his own pre-inceptual not-yet-being as past.[65]

The event of appropriation is also being's decision about Godhood. While Schelling says that God must emerge from the unground as both Cause and ground, Heidegger repudiates all such determinations, exclaiming, 'Beyng never runs through a causal network of effects. As beyng, the way that beyng sends itself neither precedes anything effected, nor follows upon anything causative.'[66] Not only, in Heidegger's mind, would this be 'metaphysical', but it would also make God religiously inadequate, a *causa sui* before whom one can neither praise, sing or dance, as he remarks in 1957 at the end of *Identity and Difference*. If God existed within a causal network, then this would bring God into a necessary relation with consequents, with beings. God does not exist in this manner, however, because as what 'passes by' in the eventuation of beyng itself God is never annexed into the causal arrangement of beings. Yet 'being must remain inexplicable, the venture against nothingness . . .' because 'beyng . . . [is] . . . the denial of every possibility of explanation'.[67] Because God is not explicable by reason, he escapes the chain of causality. As Heidegger reiterates, 'The Principle of causality belongs within the orbit of the principle of reason'[68] and 'all effecting requires a cause. But the first cause is God. So, the principle of reason holds only insofar as God exists. But God exists only insofar as the principle of reason holds. Such thinking moves in a circle.'[69] God's comings and goings, the God who only passes by through the incalculable sendings of being without cause, ground or reason, are therefore just as enigmatic as the sendings of beyng. This is precisely why Heidegger chooses a word like 'sending [*Geschick*]', which has also been translated as 'destining' or 'fate'. Lee Braver thus complains, 'Heidegger often calls these epochal understandings of Being "destinings" or "fate." These seem like exactly the wrong words to use, given their connotations of necessity and planning by an intelligent agent.'[70] Heidegger's whole point, however, is to avoid agency and to choose a word that occurs anonymously or without agency, signifying both something sent from nowhere and something sent simply because it is sent, something which only happens because it happens: fate. This is the meaning of the event in Heidegger. Can it, then, as in Schelling, be personal?

The actual passing of the God of possibility

Heidegger's God, the 'last God', occurs – if it will eventuate, that is, pass by – as Godhood itself, ensuring its finality. Its passing by would mark the surpassing of all its intimations in the previous gods. Concerning the connection to Schelling, Gabriel bluntly states: 'the "last god" – this philosophy of future is concerned with "what will be" . . . and thus undeniably echoes the late Schelling'.[71] An apparent difference, however, is that Schelling finds personality to be the mystery of being, while Heidegger seems to cling to anonymity. Yet each moves closer to the other in their own way. For Schelling's part, he, in a proto-Heideggerian fashion, conceives of Man as the site where the essence of the divine as well as the essence of being hold sway. As one commentator properly elucidates the dynamic, 'Far from humanizing God, Schelling "divinizes" the human, raising it to the importance that it properly and uniquely possesses: as the there of the occurrence of being, as the place where the human stands in being and reveals the decision in being.'[72] In other words, anthropomorphism, rightly understood, is not unbefitting of God. The true purpose of anthropomorphism is not to drag God down to the level of humanity, but to elevate the human being, as the site or 'there' of the decision of being and the decision of God(s), to her properly divine locus. Heidegger, for his part, draws closer to Schelling insofar as the anonymity of being is not definitive or, at least, this is what will be argued. Does the last God, *qua* last, indicate that Heidegger too can think the event as personal and final, a decision not to be surpassed by another?

Even if the sendings of beyng occur anonymously, without agency, this does not preclude the passing by of the gods, the passing by of the personal, through these sendings. It may even require it. Heidegger proclaims, 'Beyng attains its greatness only if it is recognized as that which both the god of gods and all divinization *need*.'[73] This obviously cannot mean that there are first gods and that the event of beyng occurs in order to expose them as something already existent, just not yet known. This rather means that the gods can only pass by because beyng first holds sway. Why does beyng hold sway? Not because of the gods as such, although perhaps because of the 'need'? What could this mean? Surely, the need cannot be the impetus to the event if the need is only the need of the gods who are not yet existent. It is not the need of the gods, however, but the need of divinisation, by which the gods first are. Beyng holds sway as divinisation.

> Beyng never *is* more fully than beings but also never less fully than the gods, because these latter 'are' not at all. Beyng 'is' the 'between' amidst beings and the gods, utterly and in every respect incomparable, 'needed' by the gods and withdrawn from beings.[74]

Beyng, as the 'between', is not merely an empty space, but it 'is'. It 'is' in the sense of a transitive act of copulation that lets beings emerge; beyng withdraws and the gods pass by. But, beyng does not withdraw and then the gods pass by, as if these were two different events. Rather, the event, *qua* opening of the between, is the very passing by of the gods. The passing by of the gods is the very spacing of the between itself, the traversal by which this space is drawn. In other words, space is not the condition of motion, but motion, the passing of the gods, namely divinisation, is the condition of space, its spac-ing, what draws the breach in be-ing. Divinisation is the exclusion of the middle. This interpretation, however, makes the spacing and opening of beyng as needful of the passing by of the gods as the gods are needful of beyng. Without the opening of being the gods cannot pass by, but should the gods not pass by, should divinisation not eventuate, then the gaping would have remained closed and chaos would have remained undecided. Beyng does not open in order that gods spill out, but the outpouring of the gods is the very opening of beyng. According to this interpretation, divinisation needs beyng as much as beyng needs divinisation. Need, then, expresses the impetus and demand that the event of appropriation occur as divinisation. When Heidegger says something like the following, then, it must be interpreted to mean that the advent and absconding of the gods is a motion as constitutive of the space of de-cision as the decision decides the fate of the gods: 'beyng is the realm of the decision for the battle among the gods. This battle is waged over their advent and absconding; it is the battle in which the gods first divinize and bring their god into a decision.'[75]

What can it mean to say that the gods bring their god to a decision, that they are themselves the occurrence of this deciding about the god? Vallega-Neu comments, 'Heidegger conceives the plurality of gods, which occurs through manifold ways of sheltering the truth of be-ing, as ways in which the "one" last god sways . . .'[76] The gods are the battle site where the decision about the last God is enacted, who, in opposition to the gods, is 'one' rather than multiple. Structural similarities abound with Schelling's expositions of polytheism and monotheism. God can only be one by affirming a preceding multiplicity of gods. The many gods are only divine, only partake of Godhood, because they are 'ways in which the "one" last god sways' or, as Schelling would implore, they are the divine itself but not yet in propriety, not yet as One, not yet as God. Divinity or Godhood occurs in the gods to be sure, but in a dissembling or false form, not as the true

God. To attribute this to Heidegger would be unfair; however, there are structural similarities. Whether divinisation has eventuated in the passing of the gods, whether they were intimations of the passing of God(hood), is something not yet decided until the last God.

The epithet 'last God' is not so much intended in a chronological sense, but, more significantly, 'last' hearkens to notions of ultimacy and decisiveness: finality. As Heidegger suggests,

> What if the last god must be so named, because the decision about the gods ultimately leads under and among them and so raises to the highest the essence of the uniqueness of the Godhead? . . . 'last' . . . in the sense of the most extreme and most compendious decision about what is highest.[77]

The 'last' God is last because the most extreme decision, the finality of resolve about the gods, about the question of the divinisation and Godhood of beyng. If 'the god is neither a "being" nor a "nonbeing" and is also not to be identified with *beyng*',[78] it is because it is the identity of the de-cision which being is, the way being is identified. Beyng eventuates or is operative as de-cision. The de-cision of beyng is a decision about the divinisation of beyng. The decision about beyng's divinisation is a decision about the gods. The advent and absconding of the gods is the play-space or battleground – depending on whether one wants to emphasise the severity of the decision or the fact that it occurs without rules as play – in which the decision is enacted and executed. The last God is the finality and ultimacy of this de-cision of beyng. The last God, then, is not a being, but the meaning, truth and identity of the de-cision that is the event of beyng. The last God is not a being but nor is the last God equivalent to beyng itself. 'This essential occurrence of beyng is not itself the last god; instead, the essential occurrence of being grounds the sheltering, and thereby the creative preservation, of the god, who *pervades* beyng *with divinity*.'[79]

It is here that one of the most significant points of contact between Schelling and Heidegger becomes apparent. For neither thinker is God fundamentally an existent, an *actualitas*, but for both God is the manner of holding sway that 'pervades' beyng, the *modus operandi* of beyng itself. Divinity or divinisation indicates, in a sense to be qualified later, the *modus* of beyng, the fact that being holds sway divinely or Godly rather than vacuously, anonymously, mechanistically or atheistically. For both thinkers, God, even if not the Creator of being for Heidegger, holds sway sovereignly, as more than beyng but not as a hyper-being or the supreme being of beings. For both authors, (the last) God announces the end of the succession of the gods. Given that this God also does not appear as a being the way that the succeeding gods do, so does the God always remain set apart (*Absonderung*), as Schelling would say, or in withdrawal (*Entzug*), as Heidegger would say. Heidegger asserts, 'The divinities are the hinting messengers of godhood. From the concealed reign of these there appears the god in his essence, withdrawing him from every comparison with what is present.'[80]

Mythological gods are forebears of (the last) God, neither God as such nor divine apart from their anticipation of the God. In mythology the decision about God is dramatised before human consciousness. Both Schelling and Heidegger would agree on this point, except that the former says that the gods of mythology have yielded to the true God, while the latter is not as ready to close the book on the age of mythology (or, at least, on *mythos* as a form of poetry). Both agree, however, that the decision about the gods and God is a question only approached historically, in a *seynsgeschichtlich* manner. As Heidegger contends,

> Refusal [withdrawal] is not nothing, it is the highest secret of beyng ... Whether the God lives or remains dead is not decided by the religiosity of humans and even less by the theological aspirations of philosophy and natural science. Whether God is God, this takes place from and within the constellation of beyng.[81]

The decision is beyng's not humanity's. Nobody can force beyng and nobody can force God concerning the question 'whether God is God'. The question concerning God's existence, namely the existence of unprethinkable being or the existence of beyng, is beyond proof. The question is whether this exists as God, whether beyng is divine and free or vacuous and opaque.

The last God eventuates as the finality of the decision about the meaning of the event of beyng. It is the response to the question about how beyng is. What is the *modus operandi* of beyng? There is a respect, despite acute differences, in which God is the God of the possible for both Schelling and Heidegger, who each in their own way assert that possibility/contingency is higher than actuality/necessity. Yet even if beyng is as possible, even if this is its *modus operandi*, it is also an operativity or effectivity. Possibility must be real and effectual. Contingency must be real, not just logical. The relationship between actuality and possibility must be questioned anew.

To think the event of being, not from beings back to their ground but from beyng forward, is to think the eventuation of ontological difference itself. Although employing the rhetoric of freedom, grounding, de-cision, clearing and the like, Heidegger's favourite characterisation of the event is truth. Truth, however, not only unconceals beings, but it also, by withdrawing, conceals itself. That which gives, as it were, is concealed (and constituted) in the very event of giving. What can be said of that which remains concealed, that which first finds a veil for itself, in the truth-event? Van der Heiden glosses,

> The concealment at the core of the event is not so much concerned with giving or nongiving as such but, rather, with the event as the *possibility* of giving ... the event is also always the possibility of nongiving or giving differently.[82]

Instead of thinking being as the being of beings, the actuality of the actual, instead of thinking from an already constituted ontological difference, by thinking the event as the origination of the difference between being/the unconcealed and beyng/the concealed one learns to think the event on its own terms. The event, considered with regard to itself, is not an event of unconcealment, but the event of concealment. Or, more properly, thought stumbles upon the event as that which is no more necessitated to unconceal as to conceal, to give as to not-give. It is the possibility and, thus, contingency of both. In Van der Heiden's words, 'In thinking concealment, the thought of the event thinks the giving as well as the nongiving of the event as the event's pure potentiality: it can no more give than not give.'[83] Undetermined by any 'reason', neither compelled nor inclined to give than to not-give, that from which the event is thought, that view 'behind' or 'before' the inceptive event, proves to be the possibility of both. Beyng can both send or not send, hence again why the sending (*das Geschick*) of beyng, far from the necessity of fatality, expresses the contingency of beyng as the possibility to be or to not-be. *Per* Van der Heiden, 'The event is the potentiality to take place and not to take place',[84] where potentiality does not here refer back to the power of some *actualitas* but to pure potentiality.

It has been observed that although Schelling employs the classical rhetoric of *actus purus* and *actus purissimus*, this is all intended to indicate the unaccountable, unprethinkable inceptuality of beyng or, as Schelling prefers, the 'originality' of beyng. 'Original is that of which one first admits possibility when one sees the actuality before one's eyes.'[85] To affirm actuality in advance of potency is a way of reckoning absolute possibility as an actuality for which nothing relates to it as impossibility. Accordingly, Gabriel can claim, 'Unprethinkable being should thus be understood as the actuality of all possibility, that is, all determinability prior to its becoming anything determinate as such.'[86] The actually possible, the possible which *actus purus* is, is only determinately something, only actually something, consequently. Indeterminacy is thus higher than determinacy, possible determinability higher than actual determination, and undetermined contingency higher than all determinisms and necessitarianisms.

Heidegger, too, who first explicitly stated that 'higher than actuality stands *possibility*',[87] also confirms in his later thought: 'what the Greeks thought even then in the *esti* . . . which we can paraphrase by: "It is capable."'[88] Heidegger's understanding of the Greek notion of 'it is' as 'it is capable' hearkens to Schelling's transitive understanding of the copula and the Arabic 'is' as '*Können*' or 'it can', which, once potentiated, becomes 'that which can [*das Sein Könnende*]'. It also calls for comparison with Meillassoux, for whom being *qua* being is Hyper-Chaos as the *peut-être*, the ultimate perhaps, the 'can-be'. For all authors, albeit in varying senses, being/beyng indicates first and foremost possibility, because being/beyng indicates transitivity. It bears repeating, however, that transitivity is a kind of pure operativity, *actus* operative as the being of all possibility.

In the Introduction, the programme of this book was distanced from the possible-God theologies of Meillassoux, Caputo and Kearney. Yet Kearney's approach was regarded as more favourable than Caputo's, because his possible-God theology contained a desirable ambivalence. It is not always clear if Kearney is talking about a God who might possibly begin to exist on Wednesday or if he is talking about God as the God of the possible, God as the being or *actus* of all possibility. The latter possibility would fall in line with the term he borrows from Nicholas of Cusa, *possest*, which could be rendered as 'being-possibility' or, in a more cumbersome manner, as 'possibility that can be operative'. Kearney comments, 'Playing on the latent etymological affinities between the German verbs for loving (*mögen*) and making possible (*vermögen*), Heidegger invites us to rethink Being itself as the power that possibilizes the authentic being of things.'[89] He adds that, for Heidegger, 'Being is thus reinterpreted as "that which is capable of being".'[90] To be affirmed, at all costs, is that, for Heidegger, beyng is never necessitated but 'essentially occurs as venture [*Wagnis*]', because 'the *possible* essentially occurs in beyng alone and as its deepest fissure, so that in the thinking of the other beginning beyng must first be thought in the form of the possible'.[91] The first beginning, the tradition of 'metaphysics', subjects the possible to the actual and subordinates contingency to necessity. The first beginning thinks possibility and contingency as modalities of actuality and necessity. The other beginning inverts this order, conceiving of *actualitas* and necessity as modalities of pre-modal possibility and pre-modal contingency. Before turning attention to the question of the modalities and the relationship between contingency and necessity, the analysis of the last God should culminate in an alternative notion of the God's withdrawal born from the *Auseinandersetzung* between Schelling and Heidegger.

That Heidegger employs a notion of withdrawal as one of the primary concepts of his late philosophy is well known, but that Schelling did something similar in his later thought is mostly unknown. Lore Hühn informatively writes of the connection between the two authors' conceptions: 'The Heideggerian impetus ... has, in any event, more to do with Schelling's late philosophy than is to be assumed at first glance. The later Schelling eventually knowingly unfurls the central figures of withdrawal and concealment ...'[92]

Heidegger states,

> Beyng is the trembling of divinization ... This trembling expands the temporal-spatial playing field in which the trembling itself comes into the open as refusal ... For beyng is never a determination of the god as god; rather, beyng is that which the divinization of the god needs so as to remain nevertheless completely distinct from it.[93]

The event of beyng is a divinisation, as has already been seen. It has also already been noted that Heidegger has remarked that God (and the gods) needs beyng, although this reading also showed how this need is reciprocal. This is the case, at least, if it is feasible to read the passing by of the gods as the movement constitutive of the spac-ing of the clearing, the spatio-temporal playing field itself. It has also already been noted that beyng withdraws and, for Heidegger, that God is not to be identified with beyng itself. What is new in the quote just offered is the explicit mention that the event is needed by the gods not so much to be unconcealed and to stand in beyng, but in order to conceal themselves. The event is needed as a way of withdrawing even from beyng. Beyng is a divinisation, which means that Godhood needs beyng not in order to appear, but in order to withdraw from beyng, to secure and protect its divinity, its holiness. The divinisation of beyng relates not so much to its unconcealing effect but to its inner concealment, and the unconcealment of beings is precisely the cover by which the concealed is concealed. For Heidegger, Godhood only is what it is just as beyng only is divinisation if and only if the last God is destined only to hint towards a future and pass by as a trace, but never abide as an enduring presence. The 'need' of Godhood is the need to remain distinct from beyng and beings. The passing by is not a passing through a pre-ordained space but a transitive passing that first draws space by means of its traversal, leaving the open-space as the very trace of its passing. This trace is, in short, God's backside, his consequent or *posterius*. In this way, too, beyng also proves to have needed the passing of Godhood. God proper, Godhood in its propriety, is not the event as such but its withdrawn character, the fact that it is already always just passed by, neither present nor that which presents. It is neither what endures in the open nor the open itself, but what remains indivisibly and essentially unopened in the opening of the open. It is the meaning of the open-ing, giv-ing and withdraw-ing. Beyng is divinisation because the passing by of Godhood – and not its abiding presence – is how beyng holds sway, the divine manner in which it holds sway. It is the meaning of the event or decision of being: holiness, setting apart.

If a human acts, she loses the power not to have acted, she passes from a state of potentially acting to an irrevocable state of having already acted. She loses her prior potency to not-act. God, however, acts in such a way as to stay away, to have passed through without stopping, thereby preserving his potency to act or pass by despite having always already done so. The act of the God is, so to speak, a refrain, restraint or refusal. For a human to act is the opposite of refrain, but God acts, as it were, without losing his restraint. God acts *per contrarium*. Herein lies the necessary co-belonging of unconcealment–concealment, giving–refusal, procession–withdrawal and passing by–staying away. As Heidegger states, 'The refusal is the highest nobility of bestowal.'[94] Refusal–bestowal, adding another set of contraries to the list, 'is the basic trait of the self-concealment *whose* manifestness constitutes the originary essence of the truth of beyng. Only in this way does beyng become estrangement itself, the stillness of the passing by of the last god.'[95] The emphasis on 'whose' here is quite striking, because it would seem to emphasise that this self-concealment is now not anonymous or impersonal, but personal. One will certainly not find Heidegger explicitly claiming, as Schelling had done, that personality is the meaning of being, but it does seem that if divinisation has a personalising effect and is necessary for beyng, then this way of thinking through Heidegger's thought may prove plausible and fruitful. Heidegger's God, even if neither the God of the metaphysician nor of the religionist, is the God of the poets as well as, one presumes, a God to which one can sing, dance and pray. One can at least safely affirm that he does not want God to be thought impersonally.

For Heidegger, Godhood passes by or becomes manifest neither for the philosopher (metaphysician) nor for the religionist, but for the poets, the future ones, the creators of a new comportment to beyng. The concealment of beyng and the withdrawal of Godhood is preserved and safeguarded in poetry. Schelling too refuses to privilege the philosopher; yet, despite his valorisation of art, he privileges neither the artists nor the poets. Schelling also does not allocate a special supremacy for the religious practitioner, but he does find that the passing by of the gods is vouchsafed in religious consciousness – and, in fact, all consciousness is god-positing (*Gott-Setzendes*) for Schelling. As Gabriel writes,

> Unlike Heidegger, Schelling locates the primordial withdrawal of the event in *mythology*. The indispensability of a mythology constitutive of

intelligibility as such can never be rendered fully transparent by reflection, thinking, or poetry. For Schelling, being thus turns into the fragmentary history of mythological images and narratives.[96]

Schelling's philosophy is being-historical because it is a 'narrative philosophy (*erzählende Philosophie*)', a narrative empiricism.

Beyng is thoroughly historical, but for Heidegger it is still poetry rather than history that exhibits insight into the mystery and meaning of the whole. In Schelling, insight is never granted to any particular group, even the poets. The passing by of the gods occurs in consciousness to be sure, but never as the reflective product of consciousness itself but only as something unconsciously generated. Beyng's intelligibility, in Schelling, is always, shall one say, deferred. Schwab, discussing Schelling's 1809 text, relates this deferral not just to Heidegger but also to Derrida, writing,

> Both [Heidegger and Derrida] see a motif, (pre-)formulated in Schelling's text, that is central to the development of their own philosophical conceptions. This motif might best be described as an 'unrealisable or original withdrawal' [*uneinholbarer oder ursprünglicher Entzug*]; as a movement which 'unprethinkably' [*unvordenklich*] precedes but at the same time conveys, carries and latently structures thought and knowledge.[97]

The 'ground' of knowledge and thinkability is an unprethinkable 'unground',[98] something which can never be situated as the master key of all intelligibility. Rather, the meaning of being, *qua* historical, is always deferred, hence Schelling's historically determined 'proof' of God, his open-ended or 'running' proof. Beyng itself is 'unrealisable', hence why its powers and possibilities are never exhausted.

Turning around modality

'Higher than actuality stands possibility.' The exact meaning and justification of this proposition is different, but espoused all the same by both Schelling and Heidegger. Heidegger, however, maintains his reservations about Schelling in just this regard. Heidegger is convinced that Schelling, although on the precipice of the other beginning, could not have said that possibility is higher than actuality, not because of his persistent utilisation of the rhetoric of *actus* as such, but rather because he is convinced that Schelling thinks of modality only as the modality of a pre-given actuality. He elaborates,

> The history of the first beginning is in this way completely delivered from the semblance of futility and sheer errancy; now for the first time a great illumination comes over all previous works of thought. The 'historical' lecture

courses belong in the sphere of this task . . . to work out *Schelling's* question of freedom but to ground the question of the 'modalities' differently.⁹⁹

The contention is that Schelling's merit lies in the fact that he did ground the modalities differently than the tradition, and that in two ways. First, Schelling turns the modes around so that actual entities are only possible on the basis of a pre-modal chaos in which no possibilities had yet been excluded. Second, this means that rather than possibility representing the modality of a necessary actuality, necessity becomes a possibility, namely a possible modality, of modeless or pre-modal chaos.

This, however, is not Heidegger's interpretation of Schelling, which may be due to the fact that he did not read Schelling's later thought as seriously as the famous 1809 *Freiheitsschrift*. Heidegger complains, in the *Beiträge*,

> If one wanted to attempt the impossible and grasp the essence of beyng with the help of the 'modalities' of 'metaphysics', then one might say: refusal (the essential occurrence of beyng) is the first necessity . . . this 'clarification' of beyng tears it from its truth (the clearing of Da-sein) and degrades it to a pure and simple objectively present thing in itself.¹⁰⁰

One can plainly see that Heidegger, here at least, thinks of actuality as an entity, a thing objectively present, an *actualitas*. However, had Heidegger rather conceived of the actual otherwise than as an entity, otherwise than the necessary ground for modal determinations like possibility, then he would have been able to see in Schelling a forerunner to his claim that possibility is higher than actuality, higher than the necessity of the actual. For Schelling, to say that possibility is higher than actuality is to affirm pre-modal contingency as the basis of all necessity and the basis of second-order contingency, namely contingency as a modal concept rather than the pre-modal itself.

Heidegger, referring to the Greeks, rhetorically asks,

> Does the ὅτι ἔστιν include only 'actuality' or also possibility and necessity? Are the latter 'modalities' modalities of *actuality*? If actuality itself is but one modality among others, then of what are these the *modalities*? . . . it can be said that every 'quiddity' has its modality and every modality is that of a quiddity. Thus both belong together.¹⁰¹

Schelling, however, does not presuppose quiddity, but naked quoddity. Schelling then asks what the *modus operandi* of naked quoddity is. This turns the modalities around because it does not ask about the modality of an actual entity, but it asks about the manner of operativity of pure quoddity, of pure transitivity. There is not a thing which acts, a substance which is operative, but operativity as such must first seek out its own essence; it must produce its own way of be-ing. Pure operativity becomes habituated with a manner of operating, a *modus operandi*, which means that the operation only is the operation that it is on account of this posterior *modus*, hence the posteriority of the antecedent. The habituation of the *modus* is the condition of the quiddity of operativity. Quiddity, far from being hypothetically presupposed, is consequent to quoddity. Naked quoddity is not another name for something which is actual, but it signifies the actuality, the actually taking place, of the event of beyng itself. Heidegger, then, is simply wrong when he tries to delimit philosophy by claiming that 'the essential occurrence of beyng will remain closed to philosophy, as long as philosophy maintains that being could be known and, so to speak, assembled together by working out the various modal concepts'.[102] The modal concepts can remain, but they must be re-conceptualised apart from the actual and instead be thought as the adverbial aspect of beyng, which is itself to be thought verbally, that is, transitively as pure operativity, as the *actus* of the event of being as a copulating event.

One must, then, indeed follow Heidegger's suggestion to ask about 'the problematic origin of the modalities themselves'.[103] One must historically and progressively think the modeless origination of the modalities themselves. Heidegger laments that 'The "modalities" pertain to beings (to beingness) and say nothing at all about the fissure of beyng itself.'[104] On the contrary, the question of the origination of the modalities is precisely that project by which the modalities are thought apart from beings (beingness) and in relation to beyng itself. The modalities thus undergo a reorientation that views them in their very origination from the fissure of beyng itself.

Heidegger's presentation of beyng occurs through

> that history whose 'events' are nothing other than the strokes of the event of appropriation itself. We can say so much only by saying *that* this eventuates . . . the thrust of beyng itself. This thrust cannot be deduced and is to be captured in its purest 'that' . . .[105]

Heidegger, too, thinks beyng first in terms of quoddity and not quiddity. Quoddity, however, is not the necessity of the actual, but the actuality of a possibility never to be 'deduced' and only occurring in 'strokes' or, elsewhere, 'sendings'. Beyng, then, is indeed the possible rather than the actual and/or necessary, but this possibility is not a modal concept in the traditional sense. It is the contingency of beyng, pre-modal contingency. The contingent is without explanation; it cannot be explained in terms of 'why' and 'because'. As Heidegger declares, 'The *appropriating event* and the possibility of the *why*! Can the "why" still be made into a tribunal before which beyng is to be haled?'[106] Beyng is without why, which means it is only to be historically narrated. As Heidegger affirms, 'History means ... *the happening [Ereignis] of a decision about the essence of truth.*'[107] Being, the essence or identity that pervades the decision, can only be known in its contingent sending, thus only a narrative empiricism is appropriate. The possible and contingent, now no longer based on the necessity of law and calculation, are no longer modalities, no longer simple deviation from a foregoing necessity, but the heart of beyng itself.

Beyng is without reason, without ground or an unground, 'which Schelling, in his later philosophy, thinks as the contingency of being itself'.[108] Heidegger, unwilling to apply modal concepts to beyng, even if in a non-modal manner, is more ambivalent and non-committal, noting, '[t]he sequence of epochs in the destiny of Being is not accidental, nor can it be calculated as necessary',[109] denying both contingency and necessity as appropriate concepts. Nevertheless, given his elevation of the possible over the actual, he seems more comfortable elevating contingency over necessity. As he states at the end of *Satz vom Grund*, 'The *Geschick* of being: a child that plays. Why does it play ... it plays, because it plays. The "because" withers away in the play. The play is without "why".'[110] Heidegger does not here make reference to the 'without why' of the mystical tradition, but he is appealing to Fragment 52 of Heraclitus in referring to the child who plays. Schelling also appeals to the child at play, but by invoking the Jewish tradition, namely the depiction of Wisdom in the Hebraic scriptures as a child who played before God prior to the creation of the world. This child, in Schelling, personifies possibility as such. Heraclitus' and Heidegger's child embodies the absence of necessity and rule. Both would agree, then, that this play signifies more than the mere 'necessity' or 'fatality' of 'it is so because it is so', but also the 'and so it could have just as easily not been so'.

The other beginning, which had arguably already been inaugurated in Schelling (and perhaps other pre-Heideggerians as well), proceeds, unlike the first beginning, from the groundlessness of why there is givenness at all, of why there is something rather than nothing. 'The other question proceeds from the terror before the groundlessness of beings: that no ground has been laid for them, indeed that grounding itself is held to be superfluous.'[111] This is not nihilism. It does not implicate the absence of meaning and it does not spell the abandonment of questions of ontology. It can also spell liberation from the fetters of necessity in all its forms, metaphysical, physical, transcendental, logical, moral and even theological. Contingency is antecedent to necessity even in God himself. As Gabriel claims,

> The necessity of the absolute origin must consequently be compatible with the contingency of that which originates. The necessity of the origin,

however, thereby becomes, for its part, contingent, because it depends upon the existence of contingent being, which cannot be excluded *a priori*.[112]

Necessity is not excluded, but it is consequent to contingency, itself a modality of pre-modal contingency. Nihilism does not rule the day because order, which was not excluded in chaos, reigns as a matter of fact and, in turn, order is not oppressive and tyrannical because it is consequent upon foregoing chaos. The possibility of disorder and evil is not something that God created but something within or antecedent to God himself, something even he must overcome. The possibility – not actuality – of evil is thus something that God cannot suspend without extinguishing his own unprethinkable existence.

In Schelling and Heidegger (and Boutroux as well), thinking does not consist in a series of interconnected propositions that is each necessarily entailed by the preceding, but thinking consists in free speculation. 'Speculation', as Schelling explains, 'means to look around for possibilities by which a certain aim in knowledge can be attained. These are admittedly immediately only possibilities that must be proved through the success of knowledge as actualities.'[113] Philosophy speculates because genuine thinking begins before the inception of actual beings, before the eventuation of beyng, from a domain of pure contingency and pure possibility. All of philosophy's proofs and deductions are but subsequent possibilities posited through the free ventures and adventures of thought itself, only corroborated – and never verified or falsified – historically. Thinking can only meet the measure of being if thought learns to mimic being by learning to play without foregoing rules.

Notes

1. Heidegger, *Phenomenological Interpretation*, p. 123.
2. Heidegger, *Basic Concepts*, p. 172.
3. Heidegger, *Logic*, p. 10.
4. Gabriel, 'Mythological Being', p. 19. Gabriel elsewhere adds, 'Schelling and Heidegger identify the historical concept of being as a presupposition or condition of the logical concept of being' (Gabriel, *Transcendental Ontology*, p. 62). This is true, but, as will be seen, the sense in which being is historical is slightly different in Heidegger and Schelling. Schelling, while granting being a fundamental historicality and temporality, permits that multiple times can be posited at once, that the times themselves are eternally posited. Consequently, he is able to permit what Heidegger cannot, the possibility that logic or purely rational philosophy is itself eternal and yet with temporal determination. Eternity cannot here mean lack of time but the positing of temporal differentiation from eternity. Nevertheless, Schelling would still concur that apart from the historical occurrence of mythology, the purely rational doctrine of the potencies could never have been known.
5. Gabriel, *Transcendental Ontology*, p. 70.

6. Heidegger, *Contributions*, p. 203.
7. Ibid., p. 400.
8. Heidegger, like Jaspers, remarks, 'Schelling initiated the first and truly metaphysical conversation with Leibniz . . .' (Heidegger, *Principle of Reason*, p. 21).
9. Heidegger, *Principle of Reason*, p. 17.
10. Ibid., p. 18.
11. Ibid., p. 49.
12. Ibid., p. 111.
13. Ibid., p. 111.
14. Ibid., p. 51.
15. Ibid., p. 111.
16. Heidegger, *Identity*, p. 10.
17. Ibid., p. 11.
18. Deleuze, *Difference and Repetition*, p. 117.
19. Ibid., p. 119.
20. Heidegger, *Bremen*, p. 105.
21. Ibid., p. 120.
22. Note Schelling on the connection between chaos (χαως) and abyss: 'I will just briefly remark that the word that corresponds in German to the Greek χάω and χαίνω is also used by the poets [Homer and Hesiod] in order to speak of a yawning, according to our pronunciation a *Jähnen* (gaping), abyss, or to say that the depths yawningly gape before us. [Ich bemerke noch kürzlich, daß das Wort, welches im Deutschen dem Griechischen χάω und χαίνω entspricht, von Dichtern ja auch gebraucht wird, um von einem gähnenden, nach anderer Aussprache einem jähnenden Abgrund zu sprechen, oder zu sagen, die Tiefe gähnte uns an.]' (Schelling, 'Die Mythologie', *SW II/2*, p. 614). Schelling explains that the birth of the gods is their emergence from the yawning of the abyss and their death retreat back into abyss/chaos.
23. Heidegger, *Bremen*, p. 120.
24. Ibid., p. 18.
25. Braver, *Thing of This World*, p. 298.
26. Ibid., p. 299.
27. Schelling, *Urfassung*, p. 47.
28. Wirth, 'Introduction', p. 7.
29. Lawrence, 'Philosophical Religion', p. 13.
30. Ibid., p. 16.
31. Warnek, 'Reading Schelling', p. 169.
32. Marcel, 'Schelling', p. 86. 'Schelling, tout autrement et beaucoup moins directement que Kierkegaard, a préparé le terrain – faut-il dire pour la philosophie de l'existence? . . . Parmi les penseurs contemporains, c'est Heidegger et vraisemblablement lui seul . . . qui apparaît comme relié authentiquement à Schelling.'
33. Gabriel, 'Unvordenkliches', p. 81.
34. Gabriel, *Transcendental Ontology*, p. 61.
35. '*Gipfel der Metaphysik* des deutschen Idealismus' (Heidegger, 'Metaphysik des deutschen Idealismus', p. 83)
36. Heidegger, *Schelling's Treatise*, p. 4.
37. Ibid., p. 3.
38. Schwab, 'Nonground', p. 10.
39. Grondin, 'Die späte Entdeckung Schellings', p. 71.
40. Schwab, 'Nonground', p. 11.
41. Crease, *Heidegger*, p. 180.
42. Vallega-Neu, *Heidegger's* Contributions to Philosophy, pp. 65–6.
43. Ibid., p. 70.
44. Heidegger, *Basic Concepts*, p. 171.
45. Gabriel, *Transcendental Ontology*, p. 73.

46. Heidegger, *Contributions*, p. 341.
47. Ibid., p. 342.
48. Vallega-Neu, *Heidegger's* Contributions to Philosophy, p. 7.
49. The term 'be-ing' is equivalent to a term already seen: 'beyng'. These are simply different translations of *Seyn*. Heidegger, beginning from the time of the *Beiträge*, began to write *Sein* in the old-fashioned way with a 'y' instead of an 'i'. While 'beyng' alerts the reader to this difference without having to make an interpretive choice, 'be-ing' already risks a philosophical interpretation in the translation. The '-' in 'be-ing' designates the clearing, opening or spacing by which being is now thought. In this respect, although riskier, 'be-ing' is a more provocative translation.
50. Ibid., p. 28.
51. Schulz, *Vollendung*, p. 295.
52. Heidegger, *On Time and Being*, p. 24.
53. Hans-Joachim Friedrich, discussing the distinction Schelling makes between *Grund* and *Existenz* in his 1809 essay, offers the following take on Schelling's 'breakdown', the following period of silence and Schelling's relation to the metaphysical tradition:

> The distinction of ground and existence is here led back to an origin that is itself no longer a ground. With this Schelling's philosophy comes to its breaking point. And not only that. Finally, with this the history of philosophy *as* a history of metaphysics comes to its breaking point. Ever since it has at least become questionable whether the distinction between ground and existence can still be conceived as a relation between ground and what is grounded. [Die Unterscheidung von Grund und Existenz wird hier auf einen Ursprung zurückgeführt, der selbst kein Grund mehr ist. Damit kommt es zum Bruch in Schellings Philosophie. Und nicht nur das. Letzlich kommt es damit zum Bruch in der Geschichte der Philosophie *als* Geschichte der Metaphysik. Seitdem ist zumindest fraglich geworden, ob die Unterscheidung zwischen Grund und Existenz noch als Verhältnis zwischen Grund und Gegründetem begriffen werden kann.] (Friedrich, *Ungrund der Freiheit*, pp. 28–9)

54. Heidegger, *Contributions*, p. 191.
55. Heidegger, *Schelling's Treatise*, p. 171.
56. Heidegger, *Metaphysical Foundations*, p. 209.
57. Ibid., p. 209.
58. Van der Heiden, *Ontology after Ontotheology*, p. 277.
59. On a related note, Gabriel Marcel states,

> What we can say is that here and there subjectivity is situated as something opened by its Other: with Schelling, the *Daß*, with Heidegger, the *Nichts*, that I am a little disgusted to have to translate as *néant* (non-existing) . . . The *Daß* of incomprehensibility separates God as pure mediation of himself from reason . . . It is all the more so with the role that the *Nichts* plays between being and beings. [Ce qu'on peut dire, c'est que ici et là la subjectivité se trouve comme médiatisée par son Autre : chez Schelling, le *Das*, chez Heidegger, le *nichts*, que je répugne un peu a traduire par néant . . . Le *Das* de la non-compréhensibilité sépare Dieu comme pure médiation de soi de la raison . . . Il en est de même du rôle que joue le *nichts* entre l'être et l'étant.] (Marcel, 'Schelling', p. 81)

60. Van der Heiden, *Ontology after Ontotheology*, p. 238.
61. Ibid., p. 277.
62. Heidegger, *On Time and Being*, p. 8.
63. Vallega-Neu, *Heidegger's* Contributions to Philosophy, p. 109.

64. 'Der Weg in den Ungrund führt als solcher zur Überwindung der Metaphysik. Er geht jetzt nicht mehr *über die Natur* (μετὰ τὰ φυσιχά) hinaus auf einen höchsten Grund des Seins (θεός); vielmehr führt er *hinter* die Natur zurück in das, was sowohl der Existenz der Dinge als auch ihrer Ergründung vorausgegangen ist. In diesem Weg oder "Schritt zurück" liegt das, was Heidegger die "Kehre" nennt' (Friedrich, *Ungrund der Freiheit*, p. 29).
65. Ibid., p. 201.
66. Heidegger, *Bremen*, p. 69.
67. Heidegger, *Contributions*, p. 375.
68. Heidegger, *Principle of Reason*, p. 21.
69. Ibid., p. 28.
70. Braver, *Thing of This World*, p. 289.
71. Gabriel, 'Heidegger's "Turn"', p. 60.
72. Clark, 'Heidegger's Craving', p. 27.
73. Heidegger, *Contributions*, p. 192.
74. Ibid., p. 192.
75. Ibid., p. 192.
76. Vallega-Neu, *Heidegger's* Contributions to Philosophy, p. 104.
77. Heidegger, *Contributions*, p. 322.
78. Ibid., p. 207.
79. Ibid., p. 206.
80. Heidegger, *Bremen*, p. 16.
81. Ibid., p. 72.
82. Van der Heiden, *Ontology after Ontotheology*, p. 237.
83. Ibid., p. 236.
84. Ibid., p. 238.
85. 'Original ist, wovon man die Möglichkeit erst zugibt, wenn man die Wirklichkeit vor Augen sieht' (Schelling, 'Andere Deduktion', *SW II/4*, p. 342).
86. Gabriel, *Transcendental Ontology*, p. 70.
87. Heidegger, *Being and Time*, p. 36.
88. Heidegger, *On Time and Being*, p. 8.
89. Kearney, *God Who May Be*, p. 92.
90. Ibid., p. 93.
91. Heidegger, *Contributions*, p. 374.
92. Hühn, 'Heidegger–Schelling', p. 30.
93. Heidegger, *Contributions*, p. 189.
94. Ibid., p. 321.
95. Ibid., p. 321.
96. Gabriel, 'Mythological Being', p. 26.
97. Schwab, 'Nonground', p. 1.
98. Note Schwab again:

> The paradoxical constellation of an 'inexpressible' and 'transcendent' or 'exterior' ground, which in itself is *not* a ground and at the same time groundless, is neither 'pure' presence nor 'simple' absence, a nonground which 'unprethinkably' precedes any *specific* difference, but is at the same time its 'impure origin', without already containing it archetypically, no doubt marks a systematic parallel with Derrida's own notions of *différance* and supplement. (Schwab, 'Nonground', p. 30)

99. Heidegger, *Contributions*, p. 138.
100. Ibid., p. 192.
101. Ibid., p. 213.
102. Ibid., p. 219.

103. Ibid., p. 219.
104. Ibid., p. 219.
105. Ibid., p. 365.
106. Ibid., p. 400.
107. Heidegger, *Basic Concepts*, p. 17.
108. 'den Schelling in seiner Spätphilosophie als Kontingenz des Seins selbst denkt' (Gabriel, 'Unvordenkliches', p. 82).
109. Heidegger, *On Time and Being*, p. 9.
110. Heidegger, *Principle of Reason*, p. 113.
111. Heidegger, *Basic Concepts*, p. 170.
112. 'Die Notwendigkeit des absoluten Ursprungs muss folglich mit der Zufälligkeit des Entsprungenen kompatibel sein. Dadurch wird die Notwendigkeit des Ursprungs aber ihrerseits zufällig, weil sie von der Existenz eines zufälligen Seins abhängt, die nicht *a priori* ausgeschlossen werden kann' (Gabriel, 'Unvordenkliches', p. 90).
113. 'Speculiren heißt, sich nach Möglichkeiten umsehen, durch welche ein gewisser Zweck in der Wissenschaft erreicht werden kann' (Schelling, 'Andere Deduktion', *SW II/4*, p. 345).

Part III
Application and Concluding Remarks

Chapter 7

A Response to Old Riddles and a New Typology: On the Euthyphro Dilemma and Theomonism

This chapter has three objectives. First, it will apply a number of the concepts and theses of this book to the Euthyphro Dilemma, to the question whether eternal and necessary truths are eternal and necessary because eternally (and presumably also necessarily) thought by God, or whether God thinks them because they are eternal and necessary as such. This question will be broached through a reading of one of Schelling's very last lectures, entitled 'A Tract Concerning the Source of Eternal Truths' [*Abhandlung über die Quelle der ewigen Wahrheiten*]. Second, this chapter will employ many of the book's basic concepts in an attempt to outline a new typology: theomonism. Third, the logic of Badiou's subtractive ontology will be explicated as homologous to theomonism, as structurally parallel even if materially antithetical. The connection between the objectives of this chapter consists in the fact that the ontological position of monism can only avoid atheism and polytheism (in favour of theomonism) if the decision of being is a divinisation that eventuates as reason, namely as a consequent universal, the domain of eternal and necessary truths. Reflection upon the Euthyphro Dilemma, then, functions as a way of exposing the internal connection between this book's two main theses: the contingency of the existence of reason and the contingency of the existence of God.

The Euthyphro Dilemma as a problem of universalism and individualism

Schelling's *Abhandlung über die Quelle der ewigen Wahrheiten* was read at the Academy of Sciences in Berlin in 1850, shortly after he gave his last semester-long lecture series and only four years prior to his death. This tract treats a problem that stems at least as far back as Plato's dialogue *Euthyphro*, although he does not explicitly discuss this dialogue itself. He rather frames his thoughts in regard to John Duns Scotus (and the Scotists) and Leibniz. This is because the particular formulation of the problem that concerns him is not, as Plato formulated it, about whether something is good, just and holy because approved by the gods or approved by the gods because good, just and holy. He rather asks whether eternal truths are eternal because eternally thought by God or whether God thinks on these truths because they are eternal. These are two of many possible variations of the same question, but what is at stake for Schelling is the relation between being and thinking as the relationship between the singularity and individuality of God's existence and the universality of his essence. The question concerns how God's existence relates to his essence, but this also means that it is a question of the relation between the individual and the universal generally, hence its implications for the debate between nominalism and realism. Finally, one will also see that this becomes a question of how God's singular will can will something universally intelligible, hence it also has ramifications for the relation between voluntarism and intellectualism.

Schelling's tract really begins in earnest once he states the impetus behind the Scholastic formulations of this question. He writes, 'The motive was thus that eternal, that is, necessary, truths were *not* able to have acquired their sanction from the divine *will*. Established merely by divine *liking*, they would be contingent truths, which could just as well be non-truths.'[1] Simply basing these truths in the *ens necessarium* does not actually guarantee their necessity. The question is how they are based in the *ens necessarium*: as something dependent on God's will or on his intellect? The implication is clear: eternal truths must contain a root outside divine volition. Moreover, insofar as whatever is contradictory to these eternal truths is impossible, this means that the domain of necessary truths – if, in fact, they turn out to be necessary – also constitutes the domain of what is possible. Hence, the possibility of all things must not result from divine will merely, but also be related to intellect. If the divine will is that power by which certain possibilities are actualised, the possibility of whatever is actualised must contain a source independent of divine volition in order to be more than a matter of divine caprice.

If the possibility of all things must have a root independent from the mere whims of the divine, then perhaps the possibility of things is contained in the divine essence or nature, particularly the divine intellect. St Thomas Aquinas espoused this intellectualist position, which, Schelling asserts, lasted at least until Nicolas Malebranche in the 1600s. This position, while granting that the possibility of things stems from a source independent from divine volition, does not actually grant that the possibility of things is independent from God as such. Possibility is still rooted in God's nature. However one might attempt to ground possibility in nature, the ultimate conclusion, for Schelling, is unavoidable. By this means the possible existence of things is ultimately pre-contained within the essence of the actual God. This means (1) that what he eventually terms Spinozism is already efficacious insofar as the existence of things would already be pre-contained in a pre-given essence, whereby all movement is a merely immanent movement *implicitum ad explicitum*; (2) that all possibility is ultimately rooted in God's necessary actuality, hence, as the tradition has always affirmed, it means that possibility is but the attribute or modality of necessity; and (3) even though possibility is based in the essence or nature of a necessarily actual entity, which delimits possibility merely to what is not contradictory to this nature, that all movement is nevertheless only accomplished by means of a movement *a potentia ad actum*.

Schelling points to Duns Scotus as a possible departure from this traditional view that locates the root of all possibility within God's nature itself. 'Scotus spoke,' says Schelling, 'of an *ente diminuto, in quo possibile constitutum sit*.'[2] This suggests that the seat of possibility is to be found not within God's nature but in something which accompanies or supplements God's nature, something accessory to God's nature. With this, however, the opposite and equally problematic side of the Euthyphro Dilemma announces itself.

> What is unresolved, and remains unresolved into our own time, does not lie in the constitution [of possible and eternal truths] but in the fact that what according to its nature is simply that which can be must nevertheless have some sort of relation to God.[3]

If possibility, which by its nature is a kind of diminutive (*diminuto*) because its being consists only in possibility, in 'can-being' but not in actual-being, is no longer posited in or as a part of God's nature, then what precisely is its relation to God? It (*potentia pura*) must relate to God (*actus purus*) in some way, otherwise this *diminuto* would have no relation to actuality at all. It is Descartes and Leibniz, Schelling argues, that make the domain of eternal truths as the domain of all possible truths, which, for the Scotists, 'would subsist even if there would be no understanding at all',[4] into the product of God's understanding, God's intellect. Unlike in Neoplatonism and many strands of medieval thought, modern subjectivism demands that the Intellect or, simply, intelligibility can never have an ontological standing of its own, for example, as a hypostasis, but must always be located in or be the intellect of some subject. With the modern conviction, by the way, that Intellect or the Intelligible-domain can never be self-subsistent, not only is the transition to a particularly debased form of crude nominalism actualised, but the division of the subject itself into competing faculties and sources of knowledge is firmly established. This faculty psychology not only resulted in the modern divide between the Rationalists and the Empiricists, but this division of the faculties remained unresolved at least through Kant, who was never able adequately to reconcile the unity between intuition and understanding as the two sources of knowledge,[5] even in his attempts to reconcile the two in the imagination and its schematism, which he occasionally referred to as a third source, as a third faculty of knowledge. This is worth mentioning if only to show that the modern problematic was not shot out of a cannon by Descartes, but has its precedent in late Scholasticism and the nominalism of Scotism, not to mention the intervening rise of Renaissance science.

The real question, says Schelling, is not about the constitution of possibility as such but about its relation, which it certainly must have, to God. He writes, 'Something is in the middle between "being completely independent from God" and being determined through God's capriciousness.'[6] For Leibniz (and perhaps the moderns generally), this was the divine understanding. For Leibniz, it is the divine understanding that mediates between God as such and the domain of all possibility as the domain of eternal truths; but how? Does it do so as a faculty of God's nature, as divine intellect, or as something independent from God's nature? Schelling ultimately argues that the Leibnizian solution is no solution at all, levelling the following critique:

> But now how does this understanding *relate* to the eternal truths? Either the understanding determines what should be necessary and eternal in things from out of itself and without being bound to anything else, in which case one is unable to see how the understanding is distinguished from the will ... If it is the understanding of God which, without being determined or delimited by anything at all, [establishes] the possibilities of things ... then one will also not be able to avoid arbitrariness. Or is the meaning the following: the understanding does not bring these possibilities into being, but comes upon them, discovers them as something already existing there. In this case, it must be something different from this understanding and something presupposed by the understanding itself wherein these possibilities are grounded and wherein the understanding beholds or takes sight of them.[7]

Simply to assert that the understanding mediates between the domain of eternal truths as the domain of all possibility and divine volition as that which can actualise all possibilities merely by its will neither explains why this act of volition is no longer capricious, nor explains whether the understanding mediates these truths to the will by producing them or by catching a glimpse of them as something that passes before the understanding but not as possibilities contained within or determined by the understanding.⁸ As has been detailed in Chapter 4, not only does the understanding view something, a possibility, other than its own fabrication, but this other which is beheld by the understanding is the very thing that determines the understanding as understanding. The understanding only is understanding, only is the divine intellect, if it is the understanding of something other and precedent to itself as understanding. Thinking or understanding, even for God, only comes on the scene belatedly or *post factum*, never constituting its subject matter in advance. Being and thinking belong together but being takes priority over thinking because thinking only has something to think because the being, at least the possible being, of that to be understood precedes its actually being thought and comprehended. Volition and intellect both, voluntarism and intellectualism both, are dependent upon that which presents itself as something to be willed (or not willed) and to be known.

The understanding of God is the understanding of an individual, but, insofar as this understanding knows, catches sight of, the whole of what is possible, the domain of eternal truths, it knows what is universally binding; hence God's understanding is not a particular understanding but the understanding of things. That which the understanding knows is universal, but understanding as such, even if it is the understanding of things, is something individual. There is thus the individual act of knowing the universal, but this presents a problem, because 'the source of the *universal* and *necessary* in things can itself be nothing individual, as we must think the understanding'.⁹ This was more problematic for the moderns than for medievalists, because for the moderns the intellect or understanding is always only a faculty of a subject, an individual, thus precluding that that which knows, the intellect, could itself be something universal. In other words, the relation between knower and known, at least for modern thought, is a relation between individual and universal.

What, however, is this universal? It is, formally considered, the domain of necessary and eternal truths, which itself delimits and circumscribes the whole of what is logically possible and thinkable. In short, the universal is nothing other than reason itself. Schelling writes,

> Independently from everything individual, even in opposition to this, itself the universal and the seat of universal and necessary truths, all of this can only be said of *reason*. We would thus be pointed to reason as something eternally existing in independence from the divine will, the borders or laws of which the divine intellect could not bypass in its own productions and designs.¹⁰

Reason, as the eternal *ente diminuto*, as encompassing of the eternal possibility of things and the domain of necessary truths, contains an eternal subsistence as something possible, as the universal whole of possibility, which is necessarily related to but also necessarily not determined and produced by the intellect/understanding itself. It is *Urmöglichkeit* or ur-possibility. Ground has been gained insofar as it has at least been clarified that this is something independent from both the will and the intellect of God, while still maintaining that it must, somehow, relate to God all the same. It relates to God, then, not by means of God's faculties, if it even makes any sense to apply a psychological division of faculties to God. It still does not yet answer, however, in what precisely this relation consists.

If it cannot be mediated by the supposed faculties of God, then one way of explaining the relation between God and reason, a solution which Schelling will reject in one sense but accept in another, is to affirm that God is reason. As Schelling proposes,

> Why not therefore say that God himself is nothing else than this eternal reason, an opinion which has at some time been adopted amongst diverse peoples as incontestable and self-evident, relieving infinite problems and removing everything difficult to understand with a single blow?[11]

Despite the dismissive connotations, a variation of this position will ultimately be espoused by Schelling, but not in the reductionistic sense in which it is currently formulated. While it may be, properly understood, possible to say that God is reason, it is not to be said that 'God himself is nothing else than this eternal reason.' In this case the copula indicates equivalence merely and has the effect of sublating God into reason itself, as if God were reason and nothing besides, capable of nothing else. This cannot be the proper understanding.

On the one hand, if things were dependent upon God's will, then instead of being necessary and universal they would be nothing more than individual products of caprice. On the other hand, if things are dependent upon God's intellect or proceed from reason alone, then it becomes impossible to explain the contingency and actuality of things, permitting only an explanation of the necessary and essential. The eternal possibility of things must have a basis independent from both God's will and intellect. Nevertheless, this independence cannot be absolute, because things must also relate to God in some way. Pitting himself against the Leibnizian position that remains caught up in a division of faculties in God, Schelling argues,

> In order to avoid what is equally impossible, perfect dependence and complete independence, Leibniz accepts two different faculties in God, but would it not be simpler and more natural to seek the cause of the different relation to God in the nature of that *nescio quod* itself . . . which is itself only

> possibility and can thus only be the *potentia universalis*, which is as such *toto coelo* distinct from God, something that must, according to its essence and thus merely logically considered, be distinct from *he* who, as *all* teachings pronounce in accord, is *pure actuality*, actuality in which there is no potency at all?[12]

The relation between God, as knower, and reason itself, as that which is unknowing, *nescio quod*, because what is known, is a relation between *actus purus* as the absolutely individual and *potentia universalis*, namely that which is only possible and universal. Their relation is such that neither is contained within or determined by the other, but they relate as things perfectly distinct, *toto coelo*, from one another. This is not to say that either can be without the other, but it does mean that they relate as two distinct things, that the relation is not one of *implicitum* and *explicitum*. In fact, Schelling explicitly denies that the *potentia universalis* or ur-possibility, distinct as it is from God, could actually subsist apart from its relation to God.

> That which encompasses all possibility, itself something merely possible, will be something incapable of *self*-subsistence, only able to be in the manner by which it relates as sheer matter to another which is its being and against which it appears as that which cannot be for itself.[13]

While the relation may appear Aristotelian, and is in certain respects, it is also fundamentally Platonist in the sense described in Chapter 3. The relation of matter to that which is matter is, in a sense, external, namely insofar as matter is not merely the attribute or potency of some actuality, but exists apart, as χωριστόν, although never in an ab-solute or unrelated manner. It relates to actuality indeed, but it is not borne by actuality. In the statement 'God *is* ur-possibility; God is *potentia universalis*', the predicate is not a logical predicate that merely makes explicit something already implicit in the subject, but it is a novel accusative, something different than the subject, something outside God himself, independent from his nature and his faculties.

This, as has been seen in Chapter 5, transfigures God himself; it potentiates *actus purus*; it possibilises God. *Potentia universalis* does not relate to actuality as its ground and, therefore, as something grounded, but possibility relates to its 'other' and

> this other, which *is* this which is incapable of self-subsistence, this would have to be the self-subsistent and indeed *self-subsistent* in the highest sense – God. The real relation would thus be that God *is* that which cannot be of its own accord, which now, insofar as it is – namely, *Is* in the manner that only it can be – will thus appear as the *ens universale*, as the essence in which all essences, namely all possibilities, are.[14]

It is now in an external, but, with respect to its own subsistence, still necessary relation to God. It is Kant's transcendental Ideal, except no longer regulatively as a mere Ideal, but as Real, as a material and not just logical or formal ground of possibility. The being or *actus* of reason is now established, with the result that the provenance of reason extends beyond thought alone and now expresses the boundaries of being itself. In this relation, the universal which was only possible is now actualised by the absolute individual, and the absolute individual, in whom there is originally nothing universal but only *actus*, is potentiated and universalised. The Aristotelian dictate that only the individual and not the universal exists thus holds. 'Stated generally, nothing universal exists but only something individual, and the *universal* essence exists only if the *absolute singularity* is it.'[15] To say that God is reason is not a reductive equivalency, but it means that God is the actuality of the being of the possible, which God did not cause but only elevates from a state of sheer potency to actuality. This movement, which can only now first be said to occur *a potentia ad actum*, is not caused, as the 'effect' is something independent from God's faculties or powers, but it is something that eventuates only if God is *potentia universalis*, the *ens universale*. God is this prior to his will and prior to his causing, as it is the condition of his will insofar as this is what first reveals to God that he can will (or not-will), and thus not capriciously so. This does not mean that it is necessary that God wills, that God eventuates (*west*) as this essence, but it does mean that he did not fabricate the possibility of doing so through mere whim and fancy. That which God could be shows itself as a possibility to God and for God, not as a product of God's intellect but as something (Wisdom) objectively beheld by God, which demands that he either be it or not be it. This decision, that which God must decide, does not spring from God's fancy – hence the rejection of all decisionism and its corresponding fideisms – even if both alternatives, willing or not-willing, are without sufficient reason and thus contingent. As Schelling explains, 'The relation is now certainly determined in such a way that God is the universal essence, but he is it still neither as nor in consequence of any necessity';[16] yet God's despotic capriciousness has also been obviated. He is obliged to decide; even God cannot be Buridan's Ass without withering away in atrophy as a non-entity.[17]

Whether God is or is not the ur-possibility, both express a relation – and God is relation – either an affirmative relation or a negative relation. God is 'condemned' – a term Sartre may prefer in this context – to relate to this ur-possibility, even if he decides against it. This thus exemplifies, although Schelling never uses the term in this tract, the Law of the World because it demands a relation between being and reason, but also because it demands that the ambivalence of this relation, the either/

or, be decided. The middle has been excluded. The Law of the World necessitates decisiveness by letting ur-possibility pass by or pass before the sight (*Sicht*), countenance (*Ansicht*) and face (*Gesicht*) of God as something which he must decide for or against. The Law of the World demands 'that whatever *Is* must also bear a relation to the *concept* and that whatever is *nothing*, namely whatever does not have any relation to thinking, is also not what *truly Is*'.[18] The Law of the World, then, dictates that the domain of the principle of sufficient reason be delimited. Either the principle of sufficient reason will be, in which case being eventuates as *Grund*, or the principle of sufficient reason is not and will not be, in which case nothing eventuates or nullity holds sway. If, however, there would be something rather than nothing, then it must relate to thinking/ intelligibility. That which is nought remains unthinkable and that which is must be thinkable, although the fact that it is will always lead back to a zone of undecidability prior to reason/*Grund* that remains mysterious. This is, as it were, a way of thinking before Heidegger's event of appropriation in order to think the event's law, the law of truth or unconcealment, the law of trothing and appropriation, as the law of decisiveness. As Schelling indicates,

> As the pure *Daß* of his own being God contains nothing within himself, but this, the fact that he Is, would not be a *truth* if he would not be *Something* – admittedly Something not in the sense of a being, but in the sense of all being – if he would not have a relation to thinking, not a relation to a *concept* but to the *concept of all concepts*, to the *Idea*. *Here* is the true place for the unity of being and thinking . . . In this unity, however, priority is not on the side of thinking; *being* is the first, thinking the second or consequent. It is at once this opposition of the universal and the simply individual, but the path does not go from the universal to the individual, as one nowadays generally seems to hold.[19]

It is not the case that there must be something instead of nothing, but if there would be something, then and only then is a positive relation to thinking, reason, ground, essence or possibility necessary. Had the absolutely individual negatively related to thinking, reason, ground, essence or possibility, this would mean that there is nothing instead of something. It means that *das was seyn wird* will be as nothingness instead of as something, that the unprethinkable will be as un-thinkable instead of as post-thinkable. The only option that the Law of the World excludes is the ambivalence of the middle option, that being/*actus* bears no relation, neither positively nor negatively, to thinking/*potentia*. There is, then, contrary to Meillassoux, a necessary relation indeed between being and thinking, but this relation is not necessarily one of correlation or co-belonging; it may remain a simply virtual or possible correlation. Although stretching well beyond the scope of this book, it is difficult to refrain from adding that Meillassoux might be right, however, to associate correlationism first and foremost with Kant and the post-Kantian tradition, namely with German Idealism and early phenomenology, with the grand tradition of German philosophy. As Schelling intriguingly contends,

> The certified predominance of thinking over being, of whatness over thatness, seems to me not to be a special but a general affliction of the entire German nation, which has felicitously been provided with unflappable self-contentment by God. The German nation appears to be in a position, unconcerned with thatness, to busy itself with the whatness of a constitution for a long, long time . . . which appears to me also to be the cause of Germany's lack of political productivity.[20]

The Euthyphro Dilemma as impetus to a new conception of divinity

Part and parcel of Schelling's solution to the Euthyphro Dilemma, which primarily consists of sweeping away its artificial basis in a false psychology of faculties applied to a divine psyche, is the recognition that any actual connection between being and thinking is contingent. This includes the being of God, as God too only properly and truthfully is in his Godhood or propriety in the co-belonging of being and thinking. A few remarks should thus be made concerning the connections between the contingency of reason/thinking and the requirement for a new typology not of divine existence but of divine being.

God is God because he is sovereign over the possibility of things, sovereign over the possibility to create and the possibility not to create. God is thus not, in the first instance, the God of the actual, otherwise there would be an order of knowledge that could necessarily derive all actuality from God. Accordingly, all natural theology, when taken in the strictest sense as purely rational theology, is precluded. God is the Idea, but not because the Idea is contained within his nature. God is the Idea, but not because his actuality is granted thereby. Rather, the actuality of the Idea (the Idea which God is) is granted from God as he who is also more than this Idea. Here, then, is a veritable inversion of the ontological argument, because reason or thinking alone as absolutely a priori is capable neither of generating nor even acknowledging actuality. As Schelling argues in his Erlangen lectures of 1820/21, thinking is not the same thing as knowing, or διάνοια is not the same thing as ἐπιστήμη. This is why those bodies of knowledge which presumably operate by means of reason alone, formal logic and geometry, are unknowing. Said differently, geometry 'knows' only what a triangle would be, if triangles actually exist; it would 'know' that triangles necessarily contained 180 degrees even if nothing existed at all.

As has been repeatedly mentioned, instead of a purely rational philosophy, Schelling endorses a new empiricism, an a priori or metaphysical empiricism, which this book has attempted to elaborate as a narrative empiricism. This corresponds to the approach of positive philosophy and is thus also a historical approach, hence Schelling's valorisation of Plato's transition from a dialectical to a historical or narrative presentation in the *Timaeus*. The problem with reason alone with respect to God, and thus with natural or rational theology, Schelling argues, is that it results either in atheism or in pantheism, and in both cases fatalism.[21] Both are systems of necessity. Either rational theology leads to nothing more than mere theism, as has been argued in Chapter 5, which is equivalent to atheism because it only admits blind, unprethinkable being and is incapable of departing from it, or rational theology leads to pantheism, which results when the potencies are regarded merely naturally and not as determinations of freedom, in which case the first potency necessarily transitions into actuality, precluding the procession of the other potencies and thus occupying the place of the whole of being, hence pantheism. In opposition to rational theology's arguments for the existence of God, Schelling offers an empirical, that is, *per posterius*, and running, that is, historical, proof. The steps of that argument will not be repeated here, but it should be stressed that it rejects the ontological argument and retains the best of the cosmological and teleological arguments. If the cosmological argument argues from experience in general and the teleological argument from experience in particular, then Schelling's open-ended proof argues from the particular character of experience as a whole, the meaning of being as such and as a whole, while still admitting that the whole, hence the argument's open-ended character, can never be acquired by the experiential road. The task is not to prove the anterior existence of God but rather that the posterior is Godly or is a divinisation that retroactively constitutes the Godhood of the antecedent. This is the logic of the posteriority of the anterior. In arguing from the particular character of experience in general, it argues for the identity of the anterior not just on the basis of but even as that which first constitutes the identity of the anterior, constituting it both as anterior, as eternally past, and as a self-same with some specific identity rather than just the vacuity and anonymity of unprethinkable being, of pure quoddity.

If the anterior proves itself through its posterior or consequent, it must prove itself continually, consistently and regularly. In other words, the character of the anterior must prove itself habitually. The anterior is constituted by means of habituation as an acquired law. One could say that the Euthyphro Dilemma is resolved by the fact that being takes delight in an eternal form, that in which it finds consistency or acquires a habitude. The eternal truths are true and eternal on their own accord, hence why God thinks them, but only because God delights in thinking them are they actual rather than merely possible. God habitually thinks on these eternal truths, on eternal possibility, which, in turn, alleviates God's modeless ἀνάγκη. The eternal truths operate as a divine grace, granting God a divine *modus* and divine *habitus* that breathes a moment of aspiration (vowel) into him, liberating him from blind consonance (consonant).

Félix Ravaisson, who attended Schelling's lectures in Munich in the 1830s, wrote, 'Habit is the dividing line, or the middle term, between will and nature . . . Habit is an acquired nature, a *second nature* . . . It is, finally, a *natured* nature.'[22] Alluding to Spinoza's distinction between *natura naturans* and *natura naturata*, Ravaisson distinguishes between first nature and second nature. In this context, that would indicate a distinction between antecedent nature, which is chaotic and without essence, and consequent nature, which is regulated, consistent and habitual. Habit thus names that which enacts the transition from the chaotic to the ordered, from the unregulated to the regulated, from inconsistency to consistency, from consonance (self-asphyxiation and self-consumption) to aspiration and liberation, from the arbitrariness and capriciousness of will to the lawfulness of understanding. This all also coheres perfectly well with the Boutrouxian thesis that necessity follows upon contingency and not vice versa. As Ravaisson, a contemporary of Boutroux, wrote,

> The lower limit is necessity – destiny, as might be said, but in the spontaneity of Nature; the higher limit is Freedom . . . Habit descends from one to the other; it brings these contraries together, and in doing so reveals their intimate essence and their necessary connection.[23]

Necessity ensues from freedom, from lawless spontaneity; yet this spontaneity is not really freedom until it is habituated by something permanent and lawful, even something eternal. Habit is the name that refers to the binding of these contraries – freedom and necessity, spontaneity and lawful regularity – that relation which habituates the chaotic, which fixes the will upon something unchanging and, ideally, eternal. Once God's gaze catches sight of the ur-possibility, of that domain of eternal and necessary truths, the antecedent nature, chaotic as such, is habituated and finally formed into a definite identity, a stable character and *habitus*. This habituation, which, as Boutroux argued, appears as necessity when viewed from without, is always the consequence of spontaneity, not its condition. Ravaisson agrees, arguing that 'in every thing, the Necessity of Nature is the chain on which Freedom unfolds itself'.[24] Freedom is not a deviation from necessity, but necessity is the habituation of non-habituated spontaneity. Likewise, the *clinamen* is not a deviation from a necessary movement, but necessity is the habituation or directing of spontaneous movement into a determinate trajectory, towards a specific destiny.

Ravaisson adds that habit 'has for a limit and final end the imperfect identity of the ideal and the real, of being and thought . . .'[25] Habit also names the co-belonging of being and thought, because it marks the connection between the individual/real and the universal/ideal. The running proof for God aims to prove God's habitude, hence its open-ended character. One can never definitively state that God's *modus essendi*, his habitude, will never be interrupted, since this *habitus/essendi* does not follow from his being with necessity but only as a matter of fact. Habit is, in this sense, not second nature, but first nature, that which first constitutes the identity of a nature as such. Or, if one persists in calling habit second nature, then it must be said that even for God, in whom unprethinkable being precedes his nature/essence, there is nothing other than second nature to be found in him. God's nature, if there is one, is nothing more than the formation of an eternal habit. Should God kick this habit, he would prove not to be God. The proof, then, is something that God himself executes, as he never tires, at least if he is God, of proving and reproving himself. God too has undergone the liberating effects of grace in catching sight of that co-eternal ur-possibility, which, as should be recalled, is pleasing to God and 'welcome (*Willkommen*)'. God's antecedent 'nature', his unprethinkable ἀνάγκη, is liberated by this grace. God is pardoned from his own being, graced with clemency from his own antecedence, free to form his habitude, his own *modus essendi*, however he sees fit. He will be whomever he wills to be. This brief section, which is meant only to relate the problem of the Euthyphro Dilemma to the need for a new typology of Godhood, might best be brought to a close with a citation from Kierkegaard on repetition – a term which may mean as much as 'free habituation' – as repetition is the link between the radical flux of non-identity posited by Heraclitus, who never stepped in the same river twice, and the stability of Parmenides. Kierkegaard writes, approximately only one year removed from attending Schelling's Berlin lectures,

> Repetition is the new category that will be discovered. If one knows anything of modern philosophy and is not entirely ignorant of Greek philosophy, one will readily see that this category precisely explains the relation between the Eleatics and Heraclitus, and that repetition proper is what has mistakenly been called mediation.[26]

If repetition can fairly be defined as free habituation, namely the same which is always novel and novelty which is always only the novelty of the same, then it becomes plausible to argue for the link between chaos and order, discontinuity and continuity, freedom and necessity, the Real and Ideal, and being and thinking as habit or, more precisely, to emphasise the verbal and transitive aspect of their relation as habituation. Yet what precisely is the habit of being? Is it a divine or a profane *habitus*?

Theomonism as the history of being

Theomonism begins from monism. Monism here names not the givenness of a substance, as in Spinozism, but that which is anterior to givenness, namely the futurity of the absolute *prius*, of unprethinkable being, which is never in question and beyond possible proof. Monism simply indicates the facticity of unprethinkable being and the fact that this facticity is the facticity of all that is. Monism thus names a radical effort at a philosophy of immanence understood as the conviction that whatever is impossible for being is impossible absolutely. Everything which comes to be, even though not pre-contained within being as a storehouse of potencies, nevertheless did not come into being from a locus transcendent to being. Theomonism thus points towards God as the most extreme possibility and most decisive moment of unprethinkable being: the fact that it 'can God'. The immediately following will offer an extremely condensed historical narrative of the emergence of God from out of unprethinkable being or chaos. In other words, the emergence of *theos* from *monism* will be empirically narrated in order to illustrate the being-historical ground of theomonism as the proper typology for conceiving the being of God.

Before the inception, as the an-archical origin of things, is chaos, which is but nothing. As the inception, as that which first makes a beginning, origin or ἀρχή by letting ground emerge from unground, is the clearing (*Lichtung*), as Heidegger named it, or 'the having been made open, the standing open'[27] of chaos, as Schelling expressed it. Schelling further narrates the opening of chaos as '*empty space as such*' and as 'sheer potential'.[28] This opening, as the potentiation of being, is also, in this respect, prime matter, so long as one always understands that the term 'matter' does not express physicalism or somatism, but the potency of the receptacle to accept form and determination. Matter thus expresses the openness or receptivity of the indeterminate to possible determination. This is not, then, a corporeal concept of matter but a speculative concept. Within mythology, even though only something named very late in the history of mythology, chaos occurs as Janus. In Janus the order of the times has not yet been separated, Schelling argues, as Janus is two-faced, indecisive and duplicitous, facing both forwards and backwards, towards the past and the future, without a real direction. The ensuing potencies are not contained in chaos as pre-existent but confused elements; they are rather not yet even determinately formed within indeterminate chaos. Yet Janus, as Schelling explains, is chaos already on the precipice of determination, on the verge of a 'dispersal (*Auseinandergehen*)'[29] of determinate potencies. Chaos, as 0, once it ensues as the determinations A^1, A^2 and A^3, is first supplemented with the identity of A. Only now, in other words, does A = A or does the principle of identity first obtain.

The question is whether this A names God. Certainly, it is not God prior to the ensuing multiplicity of the potencies, at which point it was nought. This multiplicity which follows is the condition of the identity and oneness of the anterior. This identity is not one and not equal to itself in advance of this multiplicity. In advance of this multiplicity, one does not even find the unity of the whole of the potencies, the All-One (*das All-Eine*), but simply the Alone (*das Alleine*). The position that recognises not that God is One nor even that there is only one God, but simply that there is only God, the Alone, is theism. Theism is equivalent to atheism, because it does not acknowledge God but only the absolute *prius*, that *terminus a quo* without which God could not be, but not God as such, not God in propriety. Schelling, despite equating theism with atheism, still grants the rhetoric of θεός purchase prior to the identification of unprethinkable being with God. It is perhaps advisable, however, that one rather name this moment of the simply Alone 'monism'. This, too, is problematic, because monism, as a term, stems from μονάς, and there is not yet expressly μονάς until retroactively posited as the withdrawal from the multiplicity that ensues from 'it'. Nevertheless, monism, as defined above, does not yet indicate that one and only one substance exists; it only indicates a philosophy of immanence that says whatever is impossible for unprethinkable being is impossible absolutely, that nothing is or can become actually possible apart from unprethinkable being. Used in this way the term 'monism' is more appropriate than any pre-mature reference to θεός. The simply Alone, prior to any multiplicity and thus also prior to any possible identity, indicates monism.

From the Alone, the absolutely Unique or, as it might best be rendered, sheer Unicity (*Einzigkeit*)[30] multiplicity or plurality springs. The gods spill forth from chaos. If chaos is the 'pre-concept (*Vorbegriff*)' of God,[31] which must be posited in order ever to be able to posit God, then the multiplicity that follows names the posterior condition of the identity of the anterior. Only with the emergence of the plurality of the gods is the Alone properly divinised, except that here Godhood passes by as many and not yet as One, theo-polystically and not yet theo-monistically. The pre-concept of God only acquires the concept of Godhood consequently.

The correlating of being and thinking is, as it were, the conceptualisation of pre-conceptual being. If conceptuality designates God's essence and the unprethinkability of the Alone designates sheer existence, then their unity designates the old theological dogma that in God being and essence are the same. This holds, except that, in an inversion of the ontological argument, this does not mean that God's existence is contained in his essence, but that God's existence is presupposed and his essence is accrued as an unforeseeable supplementation that first determines the identity of previously naked existence. The most originary name of God is he who will be whom he wills to be. Does 'he', a personal pronoun which can only be said *post factum*, will Godhood and, if so, as many or as One?

Only to posit the monistic moment of the Alone as the *a quo* without which God(hood) could never be is to posit only the negative attribute of divinity. This, to repeat, is atheism. It is to equivocate chaos with Godhood. God is not the God of chaos, however, but of order. With the unprethinkable emergence of the potencies, God, who is not the potencies or any of the plurality of gods as such, but the *prius* in its eventuation as this *modus essendi*, is removed or withdrawn, set apart (*abgesondert*) from them (the potencies and plurality of gods) as A^0. The transition, then, is a being-historical transition from chaos as 0 to God as A^0. Identity and oneness is accrued even if God is best potentiated with the numeral '0' instead of '1', because he is removed from his potencies or essence as pure *actus*. The reason for this is because the transition is from nothing, 0, as that chaos in which no possibilities have been excluded, even if not yet determinately formed, to that which is nothing because positively, namely indicatively or emphatically, excluded from everything which is something. The transition is from subjunctive nothingness, which although not yet what 'can' nevertheless indicates what 'could' be something, to indicative nothingness. God is now decisively excluded (*ausgeschieden*) from being. Heidegger prefers to speak of this as the withdrawal of being, while Schelling speaks of the exclusion (*Ausschließung*) and setting apart (*Absonderung*) of God. The de-cision (*Ent-scheidung*) is also the primordial exclusion and separation (*Aus-scheidung*) of God from being. The de-cision of being is thus one and the same as the divinisation of being. As the plurality of gods emerge from chaos, the One God retreats into exclusion, into the abode of the Holy. This God cannot pass by in the manner of the other gods, yet without the passing by of these gods the One God could never retreat into the Holy of Holies, hence the essential role the gods of mythology play in the history of the truth of being. Godhood passes by as the unconcealing of the plurality of the gods in order to safeguard the concealment of the most extreme God, the God who bears Godhood in the most ultimate sense possible. The meaning of being, *qua* divinisation, consists not in its unconcealing but in its concealing.

The simply Alone is a false monotheism, nothing more than theism, which is but atheism. True monotheism, theomonism, only eventuates through the passing by of the mythological gods of theo-polyism. In Schelling's own words,

> The opposite of [true monotheism] was also possible, but this opposite had to emerge in order to be overcome . . . in order [for false monotheism] to be overcome through polytheism, on the basis of which, then, true and actual Oneness can emerge. This is the true mystery of all mythology and of the entire mythological process.[32]

Why is there a history of mythology? Why were there 'false' gods? They passed by because 'sent' for the sake of the divinisation of being, for the sake of the utmost God, the last God, the One God. This God is not Alone but One, and this on account the inner meaning of the many gods and his opposition to them who were sent on behalf of his concealment. The monism of being thus proves itself as One and as Godly: theo-monism.

Mythology and narrative empiricism

The philosophy of mythology and revelation is not a rational dialectics; it is narratival and being-historical. Mythology, even if only the exhibition of false gods, is not a false process or a false history.[33] Mythological history, the passing by of 'false' gods, eventuates as a truthful divinisation of being and as the decision of the true God to withdraw. Drawing on a distinction that Heidegger and Schelling both make, one could say that historiographically (*historisch*) considered the mythological gods were false gods, but according to the history (*Geschichte*) of being the process is true.[34] The history of mythology as such and as a whole, however, can only be taken as true if the particulars, as they originally occurred in their historical context, were also taken as true. In other words, the many mythological gods must truly have passed by. They did not pass by as allegories intended to depict poetic invention, truths of nature or philosophical doctrine. They passed by truly, truly as gods with true religious and historical significance.

Narrative and historical empiricism accepts things as they are given and the mythological gods were given as true; they were to be taken literally. That one, a modern, could even ask what a myth could mean already shows that the questioner stands outside of the grasp of myth. Who asks about the meaning of a fact (aside, perhaps, from strange philosophers who are not even convinced that the hand in front of their face actually exists)? To treat myths, as is now customary, as mere stories expressive of some other meaning, hence as allegories, already presupposes that they are not treated as facts and that the questioner has already bracketed (ἐποχή) their truthfulness. For the consciousness that was contemporary with these myths and with these gods, however, there is simply no space in which to ask whether these gods are true or false. Something's verity is only called into question on the basis of a prior doubt, but where doubt has not yet made its entry, there is also no room for the question of whether something is to be judged as true or false. It is, *qua* fact, simply accepted as prior to every question and judgement of truth or falsity. So long as it is not doubted and just accepted as fact that I am typing on this computer right now, the very question of whether I am truly doing this is not even raised and, if raised, should really be heard as an absurd question. Only if one were a neurotic Cartesian, or later had the experience of awaking from a dreamy slumber, could one legitimately pose the question of whether their experience of typing was true or false, dream or not dream, matrix-typing or real typing. In other words, scepticism, far from avoiding ontological commitments, is itself an artificial stance that only follows upon artificially and unjustifiably accepted ontological commitments.

Originally, myths were not interpreted as allegories indicating some other doctrine; they were not products of reflection and invention and so were not in need of interpretation at all, but instead everything was received as 'fact (*Faktum*)' and 'the thing itself (*die Sache selbst*)'.[35] Schelling elsewhere elaborates, 'According to our explanation . . . everything is a fact: everything is based on what is carried forward from beginning to end as in a tragedy, an event.'[36] Mythology is a happening, an event, and not a doctrine, philosophical or otherwise. Accordingly, Persephone, for example, does not allegorically depict or represent the principle of consciousness, but Persephone is the principle of human consciousness. In lieu of allegory and the representationalism on which allegory is based, tautegory is the only adequate 'interpretation' of the factuality of myth. According to tautegory, as Jankélévitch succinctly states, 'The image is not one thing and the sense another.'[37] The image, contrary to representationalism, does not represent a thing that would be different from the image, the mythical form. The image is not the image 'of' something, but the original and only sense of the myth. This is the consequence of taking the mythic as a fact instead of as a mere form intended to express some other truth than the religious one, some other truth than the fact that a god is present here. The myth, then, manifests the intimate co-belonging of the materiality of expression, the material signifier, the non-conceptual element, and its significance, the conceptual element. As Grant describes it, 'Myth is of course preconceptual, but precisely in the sense that the potentiation of the *autophysis* generates concepts.'[38] The gods of mythology, the theo-polystic gods, are truly the passing by of Godhood, although not of Godhood as such and in propriety, not in truth. The polytheistic gods and the myths in which they are present bear a genuine religious significance and are not mere fabrication intended to convey some other doctrine to the populace. As the passing by of Godhood, however, they are simultaneously the immediate result of the potentiation of being, given that the potentiation of being corresponds to being's pluralisation, the transition from $(A)^0$ to A^1, A^2 and A^3. The potentiation of being, as is known, is also the event by which being enters into its co-belonging with thinking or conceptuality, with reason. The passing by of the gods, as the event of being itself, what Grant terms *autophysis*, is inseparable from the supplementation of being with thinkability. Both of these, the divinisation of being and the truth of being, name the same event of appropriation.

The question of mythology – and of all religion – is only properly understood when understood in a genuinely historical manner. It remains incomprehensible when understood rationally or, as Kant would have it, 'within the boundaries of reason alone'. Even when Schelling speaks of a 'philosophical religion', this never means the sublation of historical religion into rational discourse and explanation. Philosophical religion would thus name only the consequent comprehension of a religion that it recognises has emerged in complete independence from reason, both in terms of theoretical ratiocinations and in terms of the moral teachings of practical reason. Philosophical religion only comprehends the actual and historical, but it erects no doctrines of its own that it might subsequently 'clothe' or 'dress up' in mythic form as a way of feeding it to the populace, which would be ideology of the crudest kind. Schelling thus indicates the limits of dialectical and conceptual presentations of the history of mythology. He rather hopes to recapture, as David Farrell Krell has argued, the 'protoreal' as it was originally narrated, carved, painted and the like, that is, as it originally passed by within mythic consciousness, within early *Dasein*.[39] Axel Hutter, instead of phrasing the transition from the dialectical to the historical, speaks of Schelling's move from his earlier philosophy, in which immediate knowledge was possible through intellectual intuition, to his later middle period, in which knowledge of the whole was reconstructed through the history of consciousness itself, to the latest period, in which the history of being finally gains priority over natural history and transcendental history.[40] Xavier Tilliette, focusing on Schelling's latest thought in comparison with his middle writings on the deities of Samothrace, argues that

> the writing of Samothrace still seems impregnated with the atmosphere of the *Ages of the World*, of the transcendental theogony . . . Schelling is still

attached to the idea of the *Ursystem* (distinct from the *Uroffenbarung*) . . . This idea will be slowly abandoned for the sake of a conception much more 'historical' than the theogonic process.[41]

Finally, Schelling himself even argues that insofar as his approach to mythology is not conducted from the viewpoint of reason, enacting historical rather than conceptual critique, his viewpoint also opposes all philosophical critique.[42] He, in fact, concludes his final Munich lectures on mythology by claiming that he has shown, by means of a philosophy of mythology, how the borders of philosophy itself must be broadened, brought out of thought alone,[43] thus enacting, in his mind, a critique of the entirety of philosophy itself as it has been traditionally practised.

Mythology is a history and thus not a doctrine; it is theogony, the divinisation of being itself. Accordingly, then, when polytheism begins to die out in the later Greek mystery religions or when henotheism is surpassed in the prophets of Judaism, none of this occurs in favour of mere theism as the rational belief that only one God exists. As Schelling argues, 'The content of the mysteries was not able to be a purified theism, according to which everything historical has been stripped away . . .'[44] in order to be understood merely rationally, in which case much will thereby be understood as irrational. Theogony is quite different from rational theology. Subjectively considered, mythology is a history of actual gods and not mere allegories. Objectively considered, the history of mythology is a theogony, the history of the divinisation of being, the passing by of Godhood. All of this precludes comprehension through reason alone as well as comprehension of the whole. Historical philosophy precludes a view of the whole in contradistinction to intellectual intuition, the transcendental history of consciousness or the insight of Heidegger's poets. All knowledge is partial and fragmentary, even if it asymptotically advances towards an understanding of the whole; or, as Gabriel argues, relating his argument to a few of Meillassoux's false remarks concerning Schelling, all knowledge is relative, albeit not in the sense of relativism.

> The indispensability of constitutive mythology does not preclude thinking the absolute, as Meillassoux claims, but rather allows us to absolutize relativity . . . it asserts that everything is relative to an absolute, to something which cannot be relativized, not even to the relation of knowledge. Meillassoux is therefore mistaken when he ascribes 'correlationism' to [Schelling], i.e. the claim that nothing can precede the circle of reflection's identification with being.[45]

Knowledge can never be absolute because the Absolute itself is historical and, as an unground, never closed up into a finished whole, even if the effort of the Absolute is to strive towards its constitution as a whole.

Count-as-one

The foregoing has shown how God becomes One by means of the passing by of the multiple gods of polytheism. This theogonic process or this typology was termed 'theomonism'. It is not merely God, however, that emerges as One from out of and only on the basis of multiplicity, but being itself emerges as One and as ground through this history. The following will thus briefly sketch Badiou's operation count-as-one as found in the first meditation of *Being and Event*. The structure of this operation homologously, rather than analogously, parallels Schelling's account. The difference, however, is that Schelling (and Heidegger as well) is not describing a logical operation, a formal operation of counting in set theory, but ontological construction. For Schelling, unlike Badiou, ontology is not mathematics (or set theory), but is the account of the historical construction of being's own identity, its divine identity or oneness. Gabriel argues that

> Any similarity between Schelling and Badiou comes to a definite end once we consider Badiou's thoroughly Platonist identification of mathematics and ontology. Indeed, in opposition to Badiou's idea of an absolute discourse (which is based on set theory) Schelling argues for a mythological heteronomy of reflection.[46]

There is an insuperable difference between Badiou's formal operation of the count and Schelling's historical-ontological construction, but the structural similarity between their two presentations is striking and illuminating. Schelling, Badiou and Meillassoux all return to the philosophical tradition as a search for the absolute; however, Schelling, unlike Badiou and Meillassoux, denies that the absolute can ever be achieved as an item of knowledge, but only as the absolute presupposition that historically relativises but also historically grounds all knowledge. It is the ontological condition of the epistemic, an unconditioned epistemo-ontological condition, that nevertheless can never become at item of knowledge itself, but only its absolute presupposition and indivisible remainder. Contra Badiou, the absolute is never the result of the process of knowledge but only a presupposition, although one without a presupposition of its own, an absolute rather than an arbitrary, preliminary or relative presupposition, even if the knowledge grounded upon it is relativised thereby.

The subtitle of the first meditation of Badiou's *Being and Event* announces that it will formulate the '*a priori* conditions of any possible ontology'. What is to be found within this meditation is an explication of the operation count-as-one, which is itself apparently not to be taken as a piece of ontology but only the a priori operation that would govern any possible ontology. This reading will push Badiou beyond this operation until it becomes an actual ontology, no longer a mere operation to be effected by thought upon being, but a construction of being itself.

Badiou's opening move consists in the following: 'The One *is not*'[47] because the One 'solely exists as *operation*'.[48] The One, Badiou argues, can only exist as operation, because all that there is, all that is 'presented', is multiplicity, a point on which both Parmenides and Heraclitus might actually agree, even if Parmenides would judge the presentation of multiplicity to be mere appearance. What is presented is multiple and not one. The question is whether multiplicity is being *qua* being or whether being *qua* being is One and multiplicity merely its mode of presentation. Badiou axiomatically rejects the latter option. Yet he does not thereby side with the former, also rejecting the idea that being *qua* being is multiple, arguing instead that the multiple is simply the mode of being's presentation, of which a situation is then 'any presented multiplicity'[49] or, better, the site or the 'there' at which presentation takes 'place', namely where presentation is situated. The reason being *qua* being is neither properly one nor multiple is because both of these are already subject to the count. Being *qua* being, however, is not reducible to a count – or this is, *prima facie*, what Badiou wants to argue – the count being merely the operation by which being, or its presentation, is structured. This, then, is what Badiou means when he claims to be a Platonist: being is mathematisable. To be mathematisable, however, is not the same thing as already being mathematised. Being *qua* being, Badiou hopes to argue, is not number, but it can be subjected to number or the count. This, then, indicates the nature of an operation, which is not descriptive of being, but axiomatically regulative of the way in which any discourse of being, any onto-logy, must operate: every site/situation, despite the multiplicity of its presentation, must be counted as one, as if one.

In this respect, Badiou, formulating the a priori conditions of any possible ontology, is still Kantian, except that this condition, *qua* operation, is not transcendental but axiomatic. Badiou has made a (militant) decision about how discourse about being must operate in order to avoid the conclusion that 'the One is' and in order to fulfil his opening decision that 'the One is not'. The operation count-as-one constitutes the a priori condition without which the thinking of presentation and the being of that which is presented (or, in the case of being itself, that which is not presented) in the presentation is possible. Even the multiple – which is not the same thing as a plurality, which is something countable – although it precedes the operation, is only 'retroactively legible as *anterior* to the one, insofar as the count-as-one is always a *result*'.[50]

That which has been subjected to the operation count-as-one is, in itself, what is multiple, something not yet countable but something that can be made countable by means of an operation that renders it consistent. In other words, what has been subjected to number is itself without number. Multiplicity thus functions in two senses: there is the multiplicity which is retroactively counted, multiplicity subjected to number, and multiplicity as properly anterior to the count as such, a not yet numerated multiplicity. One might be inclined to call this latter multiplicity chaos (although this already has an ontological ring to it); it is being *qua* being before it has been subjected to the operation count-as-one. Badiou terms the counted multiplicity 'consistent multiplicity' and the not yet numerated 'inconsistent multiplicity'.[51]

The One, then, which is not, governs over multiplicity (both consistent and inconsistent) as an operation or law. Badiou, given that he is not yet doing ontology, but merely elucidating the a priori conditions of any possible ontology, can only think this law as a law of thought, but not as a law of being *qua* being. To think this law ontologically would be to think of it as the imperative that being itself construct itself as one rather than remaining chaotic or inconsistent. Badiou, however, thinks this law only as an axiomatically instituted operation of thought. Badiou's philosophy is mere formalism, a mere theory of the set, the axiomatically imposed strictures of how being can be theorised, how it can be thought, namely counted, but not an account of being as such. The experimental task proposed here is to attempt to read Badiou not as a formalist, not as an *ontologist*, but as veritable *onto*-logist. The task is to read Badiou's law of the one not as an operation of thought, an operation of the count, but as the auto-construction of being itself by means of an ontological understanding of the law of identity: construct-as-one.

Even Badiou's so-called materialism is not really an ontological thesis, but a mere formalism, a linguistic materialism. He claims to be a materialist because 'there is nothing apart from situations',[52] which are the structured/countable sites of presentation. Hence, there is nothing behind, beyond or before the 'material' presentation of multiplicity as subjected to the count. There is, however, no doctrine of ὕλη in the Greek sense, no speculative account of matter, but only the form of modern matter, Cartesian matter as subject to geometrical properties, namely quantification or numerability. One can plausibly argue that Badiou affirms only a countable grid, a thoroughly partitioned receptacle or schematism of presentation, but never the χώρα or the elemental 'stuff', στοιχεῖα, that might obtain as the underside of this set-theoretical grid, that irreducible quality which precedes quantification and the count. At any rate, Badiou's materialism points to a matter, φύσις, unproductive and without its own principle of movement. This, as argued in Chapter 3, is de-substantialised and de-ontologised matter.

Being *qua* being undergoes, to borrow a term from Grant, 'physiocide' in Badiou. All that 'there' is, all that exists, is the partitioning of the multiple into sites or zones, sets which can be counted as one, the mapping of a Venn diagram onto a grid of coordinates. All that 'there' is can be situated 'here' or 'there', presented at a site. If being *qua* being is neither one nor multiple, if the One is not but is only an operation and multiplicity, inconsistent multiplicity, which does not exist but is only subtracted from presentation (at a countable site), then being *qua* being is 'subtracted from every count'.[53] If the multiplicity of presentation is subjected to the structure of the presentation's situatedness, to the count, then being *qua* being, as opposed to being *qua* presentation, must be something radically inconsistent, uncountable or unquantifiable multiplicity. This would not just be the not yet numerated, but it would signify an element that could never be counted, which also means never subtracted. For Badiou, however, given his formalism, the innumerable could not signify, as it were, something which is too much or too inscrutable to be counted, but it can only designate what is too little to be counted: void. Being *qua* being, although it submits to the law of the count, is as such a multiplicity that is supposed to escape the count; it is supposed to evade number but as a deficiency of being rather than as an excess of being. Being *qua* being, for Badiou, is void. As he explains, the law count-as-one structures the multiple by rendering it consistent or countable, but concerning being *qua* being 'there is no structure'.[54]

It would seem that if being *qua* being is the subject matter of ontology, then there is nothing that can be said. Yet Badiou – and here is the consequence of his materialism – rather argues that 'it is the wager of this book, that *ontology is a situation*'.[55] What Badiou calls a wager is an axiomatic decision; or, the wager is simply the belief that if the axiom that 'ontology is a situation' is carried to its conclusion, then it will confirm, nay, guarantee, his decision that the One is not. Badiou's 'wager', which risks nothing but guarantees everything, is admittedly not the claim that ontology's domain is only that of situations, the countable presentation of multiplicity; but it does argue that, as a wager for formalism, being *qua* being, which escapes structure as such, lets itself be structured, counted and mathematised without remainder. The remainder, the void, as will be seen, is itself something that is counted by means of subtraction, but subtraction is still an arithmetical operation, an operation of the count. The void too, as being *qua* being, is only accessible not in but by means of the presentation of a situation. Mathematics is ontology, Badiou famously claims, because mathematics is the universal situation. More exactly and more fairly, mathematics is the structure of the count, a structure universal in all situations and operative in all sets, even the empty set. Badiou seems to be suggesting, then, that being *qua* being – the void – is not that which stands 'outside' of all sets as something uncountable, but it is what is counted or, as he would prefer, 'discerned' as the empty or void set. In this way being *qua* being is mathematisable or thinkable in terms of set theory; mathematics is ontology because, *per* his axiomatic decision, '*ontology is a situation*'. Being never occurs outside of a site/set, but always as a site or set, principally in the empty site, the void set.

Understood in this way the void is not the abyss or *Ab-grund* on the basis of which mathematics plies its labour. It is not the chaotic underbelly of a subsequently partitioned matter, which set theory would make thinkable by exposing as the countable construction of being itself, but, understood in Badiouian fashion, being *qua* being or the void itself is subjected to the form or grid imposed by the count, by an operation of thought. The void or inconsistent multiplicity, then, is not really anterior to the count at all, but numbered among the count; the number 0, or void as number and as set, is, if one recalls, a 'result' of the count. Badiou's wager is that being *qua* being is formalisable, mathematisable and partitionable. The question at hand is really the Parmenidean question concerning the relationship between thinking and being. Badiou wagers that there is no remainder of being unsubsumed into what is thinkable, no indivisible or non-mathematisable remainder. He wagers that the operation count-as-one is able even to count 0 or the void as one, hence a One that is not. Yet – and this is the wager of this venture to *onto*-logise Badiou – because ontology is a situation, this means that the operation count-as-one is not merely a law of thought, the law by which being is rendered cognoscible, but this operation can be understood as a law of being, because, according to Badiou, being is multiple and the multiple is all that is ever presented in any situation. This means that, for Badiou, one cannot speak of being in advance of its correlation with thinkability, with the countable and situated. Being *qua* being is always situated in relation to thought, but always only as the structure of presentation without what is presented, form without content: the void set. Against Badiou, who tries to argue that 'there is no structure of being',[56] the contention here is that this cannot mean that being *qua* being is recalcitrant to structure, because, again, ontology is a situation and all situations have a structure; but it can only mean, given Badiou's own axioms, that being *qua* being – the void – is empty presentation or the presentation of structure alone, the presentation of a set with parameters but without members, a set with an operation or rule for counting but without anything to be operated upon, without anything to count.

Nevertheless, one must persist in the effort to find a less formalised interpretation of Badiou, an interpretation that suggests that the empty set that is the site of being *qua* being is a set that has been emptied out, an evacuated or devoided set, which at least presupposes a foregoing content that was not merely mathematically subtracted. In this way, being acquires a content, a matter, and is not mere form and partition, which is really the absence of content rather than something devoided of being. It is not to be hastily concluded that the term, which is not a proper name, that Badiou gives to being *qua* being – void – is nullity, but, as Badiou himself never tires of affirming, subtraction. Now, one possibility for avoiding Badiouian formalism is to suggest that subtraction can be thought not just as an operator of counting, but, in Heideggerian language, as the 'withdrawal' of being or, in Schellingian terms, as the 'positive exclusion' of being: extainment. Yet one cannot ignore the fact that Badiou explicitly insists that 'the "subtractive" is opposed . . . to the Heideggerian thesis of a withdrawal of being'.[57] Badiou explicitly rejects the idea that being withdraws its presence, withdraws from presentation. Being *qua* being does not withdraw from presence, says Badiou, but it is subtracted from presentation by the mathematician/ontologist herself. How, then, can one find a way to add some substance, some content, some ontological meat to Badiou's being? For Badiou, being *qua* being is not productive or even disclosive, but it is subtracted; it is only a result. Is it impossible, then, to reconstruct Badiouian subtraction, even if not as a withdrawal, at least as a positive auto-construction of being itself?

To accomplish the assigned task, the law of count-as-one must be thought as a law of being and precisely as a law of ontological distribution. As an ontological law, the law of distribution is understood as something like Anaximander's law of justice, the shaking or distribution of being. This reading also wagers, against Badiou, that the inconsistent multiple is anterior to presentation as its abysmal source rather than something only retroactively enumerated by means of subtraction. Finally, and most importantly, in this way being is not subtracted from presentation in order to be conceived as an empty set, but being *qua* being is excluded, positively posited as the outside of all sets, extained from all sets as a 'plus', a supplement, and not as a 'minus'. It is not an empty set, but it is excluded or extained from any and all sets, even the void set. Contra Badiou, it would then not be a void site, but un-positioned and thus without a site at all. If ontology is the discourse of situations, then this discourse *prima facie* excludes being *qua* being, which is never in a situation. To repeat, 'exclusion' does not signify absence, but it is the positing of being outside all positions and sets, even the void set. Exclusion is a de-positing of being; being constructs itself as de-positioned, as the de-positional positing of positions, discourses and countable domains: sets. If these sites make discourse about being possible, the a priori conditions without which ontology would not be possible, if they are the conditions of being's thinkability and knowability, then being *qua* being names the absolutely unconditioned epistemo-ontological condition, relative to which all sites are de-absolutised, relative to which all sites are local and regional. Mathematics and set theory, namely thinkability, is thus the construction of being *qua* being, which is thus never subsumed into its own construction of positions, into the grid which it itself, as the unpositioned positing of all positions, has constructed. According to this interpretation, which departs quite radically from Badiou's own while still homologously retaining his set-theoretical structure, there is not a withdrawal of presence, but a construction of presentation.

This interpretation, therefore, is at least in agreement with Badiou's contention that there is no access to being *qua* being apart from presentation. It is in disagreement, however, about the reducibility of being to presentation and its law of the count. Being is not just the presentation of presentation, not just the being of beings, but it resists reduction to presentation. There could have been no presentation at all. Badiou, however, states that the ontological situation is '*the presentation of presentation*'[58] and that 'no access to being is offered to us except presentations'.[59] Finally, Badiou concludes his a priori conditions for any possible ontology with the pronouncement that 'if an ontology is possible' – which he has apparently not yet been doing – 'that is, a presentation of presentation, then it is the situation of the pure multiple, of the multiple "in-itself." To be more exact; ontology can be solely *the theory of inconsistent multiplicities as such.*'[60] To invert this, by arguing that inconsistent multiplicity – void – is not subtracted from consistent multiplicity by the operation count-as-one, but that consistent multiplicity must be constructed from out of inconsistent multiplicity, is to save inconsistent multiplicity from empty formalism and its reduction to subtraction from presentation. Inconsistent multiplicity excludes, that is, extains or positions outside itself everything that it is not, everything numerable and mathematisable. Not just the One, but also consistent multiplicity, the countable and presentation as such, is a result, a construction. Being is neither subtracted from presentation nor does it withdraw from presentation, but it constructs presentation. It nonpositionally posits presentation outside itself; it ex-cludes presentation. In this sense, being *qua* being is, as Badiou says, the presentation of presentation, but not reductively so and not by means of the axiomatic operation of the count. Being is not reducible to that which has been subtracted from consistent multiplicity and counted-as-one, inconsistent multiplicity retroactively counted as one or, perhaps better, as none. If ontology is the science of the multiple *qua* multiple, then one must retain the two different senses of multiplicity. Ontology is the science of the inconsistent multiple in its construction, not operation, of consistency rather than the science of consistent multiplicity – which Badiou terms phenomenology – retroactively counting inconsistency.

The wager of this reinterpretation of Badiou's structure of ontology is that being *qua* being is neither mere subtraction nor simple withdrawal from presentation, but that being *qua* being constructs or structures that which is to be presented. Being *qua* being indivisibly 'remains', in the Neoplatonic sense of μονή; it is not subtracted or redacted, but it is an indivisible remainder, a never presencing remainder. It is thus itself constructed as remainder, but it begins not as a result, as the countable remainder of a countable sum, but as the unaccountable, unprethinkable effusiveness of abysmal inconsistency. It is not a formalised remainder, because, contra Badiou, mathematics cannot provide a reckoning of being *qua* being.

What of Badiou's first axiom, then, that the One is not? Given a deformalised, *onto*-logised reading of Badiou, which must accord to the One an ontological status rather than relegating it to a mere operation, it becomes possible to affirm that the One is or rather that it may-be. More precisely, the One itself is perpetually under construction insofar as the inconsistent constructs presentation consistently, which retroactively constructs – not just counts, but constructs – inconsistency as One, as consistent. The One is not, but it will have been once construction, once being itself, has finally rendered the inconsistent consistent. Yet given the indivisibility of the remainder of inconsistency, inconsistency will never be rendered entirely consistent. The construction itself is the law of identity as the law of distribution that is impotent definitively to distribute itself within any site, even the site of the void.

Against Badiou, this book has wagered that the void remains always inviolable, to be presupposed as *prius* rather than as result, but ultimately left unmediated by sufficient reason and unpartitionable by set theory. Mathematics is only the form of ontology, but bereft of any content, any being, that might undergo formation-into-one. Mathematics is the posterior structuration of being, which still tells one nothing about the world as it is; it is not amplificatory of knowledge but merely an indispensable *sine qua non* of knowledge of the world.

Gabriel quite legitimately complains that 'Set theory only appears as the best ontology' – if it is an ontology at all instead of the a priori condition without which 'phenomenology' would not be possible – 'as long as we think of existence in terms of quantifiability, as Badiou does.'[61] This work hopes to have broken with the notion that being is best thought in terms of quantifiability in Chapter 3 with the discussion of the relation between matter/quality and form/quantity in Plato's *Timaeus*, if not already during the discussion of Boutroux in Chapter 2. For his part, Badiou quite justifiably laments that

> It is because the One normatively decides on Being that the latter is reduced to what is common, reduced to empty generality. This is why it must also endure the metaphysical preeminence of beings. Metaphysics can be defined as follows: the *enframing* of Being by the One.[62]

This work has also attempted to avoid deducing being from the One, which, as Badiou argues, would collapse ontological difference. Instead, this book has argued for a way of thinking the very emergence of ontological difference itself and, in this chapter, it has also hinted that Badiou himself may collapse ontological difference insofar as he riskily borders on reducing being to presentation.

Badiou's thought is also atheistic. What he terms 'event', which was not discussed, is always neuter or impersonal, rather than that which de-cides the neutrality of the neither/nor. Badiou argues that while the event is not indiscernible, thanks to set theory, and thus not without meaning or signification, it certainly cannot bear a proper name;[63] being is not personal. Badiou here forestalls any relation between his notion of the event and God, although in resistance to Heidegger rather than to Schelling, whom he never discusses. There are structural or homologous similarities all the same. While Badiou's subtractive ontology posits an empty set, which is still a site but outside the realm of presentation, as that which is subtracted from presentation, Heidegger's God withdraws from being and Schelling's excludes (which as a positing has more to do with addition or supplementation than subtraction) being from itself. The event for Schelling and Heidegger, rather than foreclosing the possibility of the personal and the divine, is rather the very divinisation and, *per* Schelling, personalisation of being. This is only possible, however, if being is not formally and axiomatically analysed by means of mere operation. Schelling already bemoaned such formalisation in his own time, writing,

> [Modern theology] could only avail itself of a God from whose concept all power and force had been removed. This is a God whose highest force or expression of life consists in thinking or knowing and which, besides this, is nothing but an empty schematizing of itself.[64]

If God had been de-potentialised and de-ontologised as empty self-schematisation already in Schelling's own time, then today this schematisation has been made completely anonymous in order that the proper name of God can be dispensed with entirely. Today thinking and knowing have ceased to consist in an encounter with being, but have been neutralised as nothing more than axiomatic operation. In short, it may not just be God who has died but speculative thought as such.

Notes

1. 'Dieser Anlaß also war, daß ewige, d.h. nothwendige Wahrheiten ihre Sanction *nicht* von dem göttlichen *Willen* haben konnten; bloß durch göttliches *Gefallen* festgestellt, waren sie zufällige Wahrheiten, die ebenso gut auch Nichtwahrheiten seyn konnten' (Schelling, 'Abhandlung', *SW II/1*, p. 577).
2. Ibid., *SW II/1*, p. 578.
3. 'Das Ungelöste und bis in unsre Zeit ungelöst Gebliebene lag nicht in der Beschaffenheit, sondern darin, daß jenes der eignen Natur nach bloß Seynkönnende doch irgend ein Verhältnis zu Gott haben mußte' (ibid., *SW II/1*, p. 578).
4. Ibid., *SW II/1*, p. 578.
5. It is not the case, of course, that one can simply reject all distinctions between types of knowledge. As Schelling himself argues, in this same tract, it

   > is certain that there are truths of a *different order* and that *unconditional* certainty cannot already attend truths of arithmetic and mathematics in general, because these sciences approach their task with presuppositions that *these sciences themselves* do not justify . . . moreover because they only know many things according to experience, e.g. the straight and equal as well as the unequal, composite and prime numbers . . . [ist gewiß, daß es Wahrheiten von *verschiedener Ordnung* gibt, und daß den Wahrheiten der Arithmetik und der Mathematik überhaupt schon darum nicht *unbedingte* Gewißheit beiwohnen kann, weil diese Wissenschaften . . . mit Voraussetzungen zu Werk gehen, die *sie selbst* nicht rechtfertigen . . . ferner weil sie vieles nur erfahrungsmäßig Wissen, z.B. von geraden und ungeraden, abgeleiteten und Primzahlen . . .] (Schelling, 'Abhandlung', *SW II/1*, p. 581)

   Interestingly, Schelling attributes neither absolute certainty, insofar as it begins with arbitrary and relative presuppositions instead of with the absolute *prius*, nor strict and absolute apriority to mathematics, claiming that many of its conclusions are learned, at least partially, from experience and so must be discovered rather than strictly deduced and derived, for example, prime numbers. One might argue that were prime numbers known strictly a priori, then it should be possible to know, once the largest prime number has been found, that it is indeed and with certainty the largest possible because it simply could not admit of a larger, yet this is precisely what cannot be known.
6. 'Zwischen "ganz unabhängig seyn von Gott" und bestimmt seyn durch göttliche Willkür ist etwas in der Mitte' (ibid., *SW II/1*, p. 582).
7. 'Aber dieser Verstand nun wie *verhält* er sich zu den ewigen Wahrheiten? Entweder bestimmt er von sich aus und ohne an etwas gebunden zu seyn, was in den Dingen nothwendig und ewig seyn soll; in diesem Fall is nicht einzusehen, wie er sich von dem Willen unterscheide . . . Ist es der Verstand Gottes, der, ohne durch irgend etwas bestimmt oder eingeschränkt zu seyn, die Möglichkeiten der Dinge . . . so wird man auch so der Willkür nicht entgehen. Oder ist der Sinn dieser: der Verstand schafft diese Möglichkeiten nicht, er findet sie vor, er entdeckt sie als schon da seyende, dann muß es etwas von diesem Verstand Verschiedenes und von ihm selbst Vorausgesetztes seyn, worin diese Möglichkeiten begründet sind und worin er dieselben erblickt' (ibid., *SW II/1*, p. 582).

8. Schelling, not dissimilarly to Heidegger, refers to the Platonic Ideas as something that God catches sight of in their passing by before his face, drawing a connection between the Greek ἰδέα, from ἰδεῖν, meaning 'to see', with the German *Gesicht*. See Schelling, 'Darstellung der reinrationalen Philosophie', *SW II/1*, p. 381, and Schelling, 'Die Philosophie der Offenbarung: Erster Theil', *SW II/3*, pp. 292–5.
9. 'Quelle des *Allgemeinen* und *Nothwendigen* in den Dingen kann es selbst nichts Individuelles mehr seyn, wie wir den Verstand denken müssen' (Schelling, 'Abhandlung', *SW II/1*, p. 583).
10. 'Unabhängig aber von allem Individuellen, ja diesem entgegengesetzt, selbst das Allgemeine und Sitz der allgemeinen und nothwendigen Wahrheiten, das alles läßt sich nur von der *Vernunft* sagen. Wir wären also auf eine vom göttlichen Willen unabhängig Existirende ewige Vernunft gewiesen, deren Schranken oder Gesetze der göttliche Verstand in seinen eignen Hervorbringungen oder Entwürfen nicht überschreiten könnte' (ibid., *SW II/1*, p. 583).
11. 'Warum also nicht sagen, daß Gott selbst nichts anderes ist als diese ewige Vernunft, eine Meinung, die einmal als unwidersprechlich und unter gescheidten Leuten sich von selbst verstehend adoptirt, unendlicher Beschwerden überhebt und alles Schwerbegreifliche mit einemmal entfernt?' (ibid., *SW II/1*, p. 583).
12. 'Um das gleich Unmögliche einer vollkommenen Abhängigkeit und einer völligen Unabhängigkeit zu vermeiden, nimmt Leibniz zwei verschiedene Facultäten in Gott an; aber wäre es nicht einfacher und natürlicher, die Ursache des verschiedenen Verhältnisses zu Gott in der Natur jenes nescio quod selbst zu suchen ... selbst nur Möglichkeit, also nur die potentia universalis seyn kann, die als solche toto coelo von Gott verschieden, so weit auch ihrem Wesen nach, also bloß logisch betrachtet, unabhängig von *dem* seyn muß, von dem *alle* Lehren übereinstimmend sagen, daß er *reine Wirklichkeit* ist, Wirklichkeit, in der nichts von Potenz ist?' (ibid., *SW II/1*, pp. 584–5).
13. 'Jenes alle Möglichkeit begreifende, selbst bloß Mögliche wird des *selbst*-Seyns unfähig, nur auf die Weise seyn können, daß es sich als bloße Materie eines andern verhält, das ihm das Seyn ist, und gegen das es als das selbst nicht Seyende erscheint' (ibid., *SW II/1*, p. 585).
14. 'Dieses andere aber, das dieses, des selbst-Seyns Unfähige, *ist*, dieses müßte das selbst-Seyende und zwar das im höchsten Sinn *selbst-Seyende* seyn – Gott. Das reale Verhältniß also wäre, daß Gott jenes für sich selbst nicht Seyende *ist*, das nun, inwiefern es ist – nämlich auf die Weise Ist, wie es allein seyn kann – also das ens universale, als das Wesen, in dem alle Wesen, d.h. alle Möglichkeiten sind, erscheinen wird' (ibid., *SW II/1*, p. 585).
15. 'Es existirt überhaupt nichts Allgemeines, sondern nur Einzelnes, und das *allgemeine Wesen* existirt nur, wenn das *absolute Einzelwesen* es ist' (ibid., *SW II/1*, p. 586).
16. 'Es ist also nun wohl das Verhältniß so bestimmt, daß Gott das allgemeine Wesen ist, aber noch weder wie, noch in Folge welcher Nothwendigkeit er es ist' (ibid., *SW II/1*, p. 586).
17. As Kierkegaard once wrote, 'through the choice the personality submerges itself in that which is being chosen, and when it does not choose, it withers away in atrophy' (*Either/Or, Part II*, p. 163).
18. 'daß was immer *Ist* auch ein *Verhältniß* zum *Begriff* haben muß, was *Nichts* ist, d.h. was kein Verhältniß zum Denken hat, auch nicht *wahrhaft Ist*' (Schelling, 'Abhandlung', *SW II/1*, p. 587).
19. 'Gott enthält in sich nichts als das reine Daß des eigenen Seyns; aber dieses, daß er Ist, wäre keine *Wahrheit*, wenn er nicht *Etwas* wäre – Etwas freilich nicht im Sinn eines Seyenden, aber des alles Seyenden –, wenn er nicht ein Verhältniß zum Denken hätte, ein Verhältniß nicht zu einem *Begriff*, aber zum *Begriff aller Begriffe*, zur *Idee*. Hier ist die wahre Stelle für jene Einheit des Seyns und des Denkens ... In dieser Einheit aber ist die Priorität nicht auf Seiten des Denkens; das *Seyn* ist das Erste, das Denken erst

das Zweite oder Folgende. Es ist dieser Gegensatz zugleich der des Allgemeinen und des schlechthin Einzelnen. Aber nicht vom Allgemeinen zum Einzelnen geht der Weg, wie man heutzutag allgemein dafür zu halten scheint' (ibid., *SW II/1*, p. 587).
20. 'Denn jenes dem Denken über das Seyn, dem Was über das Daß ertheilte Uebergewicht scheint mir nicht ein besonderes, sondern ein allgemeines Leiden der gesammten, glücklicher Weise von Gott mit unerschütterlicher Selbstzufriedenheit ausgerüsten deutschen Nation zu seyn, die sich im Stande zeigt, eine so lange – lange Zeit, unbekümmert um das Daß, mit dem Was einer Verfassung sich zu beschäftigen . . . dasselbe scheint mir auch die Ursache der politischen Improductivität Deutschlands . . .' (ibid., *SW II/1*, p. 589).
21. Schelling, 'Einleitung in die Philosophie der Offenbarung oder Begründung', *SW II/3*, pp. 115–16.
22. Ravaisson, *Of Habit*, p. 59.
23. Ibid., p. 67.
24. Ibid., p. 75.
25. Ibid., p. 77.
26. Kierkegaard, *Fear and Trembling*, p. 148.
27. 'des Aufgethanseyns, des Offenstehens' (Schelling, 'Die Mythologie', *SW II/2*, p. 596).
28. '*den leeren Raum überhaupt*' and 'das bloß Potentielle' (ibid., *SW II/2*, p. 596).
29. Ibid., *SW II/2*, p. 601.
30. Schelling, 'Der Monotheismus', *SW II/2*, p. 25.
31. Ibid., *SW II/2*, p. 25.
32. 'denn es war auch sein Gegenteil möglich; aber dieses Gegenteil mußte hervortreten, um überwunden zu werden. Es tritt hervor im falschen Monotheismus, um durch den Polytheismus überwunden zu werden, auf daß dann die wahre aktuelle Einheit hervortreten könne. Dies ist das wahre Geheimnis aller Mythologie und des ganzen mythologischen Prozesses' (Schelling, *Urfassung*, p. 277).
33. 'One can admit that *everything particular of mythology is false*, but *the process itself [is] not in error* [man kann zugeben, *alles einzelne der Mythologie ist falsch*, aber darum *nicht der Prozeß selbst Irrthum* . . .]' (Schelling, 'Die Mythologie', *SW II/2*, p. 167).
34. For the distinction Schelling draws between *Geschichte* and *Historie*, see Schelling, *Philosophie der Mythologie*, p. 183.
35. Schelling, 'Die Philosophie der Offenbarung: Erster Theil', *SW II/3*, p. 500.
36. 'Nach unserer Erklärung ist . . . alles Faktum: Alles beruht auf einem, von Anfang bis zum Ende, wie in einer Tragödie fortgesetzten, Ereignis' (Schelling, *Urfassung*, p. 357).
37. 'l'image n'est pas une chose, et le sens une autre . . .' (Jankélévitch, *L'Odyssée*, p. 261).
38. Grant, *Philosophies of Nature*, p. 188.
39. Krell, 'God's Footstool', p. 103.
40. Hutter, *Geschichtliche Vernunft*, p. 290.
41. 'l'écrit de Samothrace paraît encore imprégné de l'atmosphère des *Weltalter*, de la théogonie transcendantale . . . Schelling est encore attaché à l'idée de l'*Ursystem* (distinct de l'*Uroffenbarung*) . . . Cette idée sera lentement abandonnée au profit d'une conception beaucoup plus « historique » du procès théogonique' (Tilliette, *La Mythologie comprise*, p. 53).
42. Schelling, *Philosophie der Mythologie*, p. 204.
43. Ibid., p. 210.
44. 'Es konnte also der Inhalt der Mysterien kein geläuteter Theismus, unter welchem . . . alles Historische losgewunden ist . . .' (Schelling, *Urfassung*, p. 357).
45. Gabriel, 'Mythological Being', p. 26.
46. Ibid., p. 21.
47. Badiou, *Being and Event*, p. 23.
48. Ibid., p. 24.
49. Ibid., p. 24.
50. Ibid., p. 24.

51. Ibid., p. 25.
52. Ibid., p. 25.
53. Ibid., p. 26.
54. Ibid., p. 26.
55. Ibid., p. 27.
56. Ibid., p. 26.
57. Ibid., p. 27.
58. Ibid., p. 27.
59. Ibid., p. 27.
60. Ibid., p. 28.
61. Gabriel, *Transcendental Ontology*, p. xxiii.
62. Badiou, *Briefings*, p. 34.
63. Badiou, *Manifesto*, p. 95.
64. Schelling, *Ages of the World (3rd draft)*, p. 106.

Afterword

Against the trend, even compulsion, that impels one to write a book that tackles a specific moral, cultural, social or political problem, this book was decidedly speculative, a-problematic in character, written only out of curiosity. Curiosity, related to the Latin *cura*, cares about the world, indeed is deeply concerned for it, although not in the mode of problem solving but through the comportment of wonder. In short, care can also take the form of the playful and speculative musement of curiosity.

The danger of such a book is that it is willing to follow decisions and arguments wherever they may lead, proceeding without regard for the consequences. In other words, insofar as it did not begin with a problem such as racism, sexism, poverty or the environmental crisis, which everyone already knows are problematic, this book has been written without an agreed upon objective. Its researcher attempted to probe fundamental convictions and to follow decisions to their end without this end already standing as a politically correct agenda with a pre-given audience waiting for the author to tell them how he arrived where they all already are, how he, as opposed to other thinkers, has arrived at this ubiquitous conclusion. This is, of course, dangerous. Such books may be liberal at places and conservative at others, but they should always be radical, willing to go wherever Musement, in the full-blooded Peircean sense, may lead.

Although written without conscious ethical and political agendas, that does not mean that predilections of this kind did not find their way into the book. They did, either as blind spots, prejudices the author is unaware he holds (of which he is sure there are many), or as implications that follow from the speculative ontology, even if the ontology was not constructed with the pre-conceived intention of supporting and justifying them. One such ethical implication, which one can actually find more forcefully and directly in Emmanuel Levinas than in any of the authors treated in this book, is the break with *conatus* as the concern for one's own being and self-preservation as the most basic metaphysical impulse. A possible political consequence of the foregoing may not only be that it is impossible to privilege certain sciences and disciplines, for example the physical sciences, which, for some time now, have enjoyed a certain tyranny, but the arguments of this book also explicitly undermine any and all particular sciences when they make claims to finality, as no science, not even mathematics, proceeds with absolute necessity. Consequently, even if the physical scientist is quick to point to the fallibility and revisionary character of her science, she is still wrong to imbibe any politicisation that says that empirical, particularly physical, sciences merit more consideration and respect, which ultimately means more financial resources. One political implication, then, of this book's ontological thesis is that the physicist decidedly does not come closer to getting reality right than the ontologist or historian (of a certain ilk), even if some merely practise philosophy as if it were nothing more than a handmaiden to the empirical sciences, as when the philosopher of mind adopts the methods of neuropsychology, or the philosopher of science becomes indistinguishable from the theoretical physicist.

The decision of this book was neither to corroborate an ethical or political claim nor to provide a theoretical foundation and justification for other sciences. The decision was to disregard agendas and pre-conceived consequences (which, again, does not guarantee that they are absent, only that they are not present as a conscious agenda, which is too often the crutch of value theory), in order to engage in free speculation, to think without a map rather than towards a pre-given destination.

None of this means that the special sciences are not valuable for the ontologist. They are, but it does mean that the information these sciences provide is not accompanied with rules of interpretation, rules that show how this data fits (or does not fit) a speculative approach. Consider the following:

> An electron . . . will take an upward or downward path through the magnetic field, and if quantum mechanics is correct, no observation of its physical configuration prior to the performance of this kind of experiment can possibly reveal which it will be . . . On this interpretation, two quantum mechanical systems that start with exactly the same intrinsic properties can behave in different ways. This is indeterminism. It is seen as challenging the Principle of Sufficient Reason.[1]

Whether such a phenomenon is to be regarded as an epistemological defect, which would mean that, 'on this interpretation', quantum mechanics is not correct, or whether it is to be regarded as an ontologically informative phenomenon, which would mean that, 'on this interpretation', quantum mechanics is correct, cannot be definitively settled. If the latter is the case and the principle of sufficient reason is indeed challenged, then the question remains as to whether this is an isolated occurrence or if the principle of sufficient reason is undermined all the way down. If it is only a local breach of this principle, then why does this violation of the principle occur here and not elsewhere, and why is it violated in this way rather than in some other way? Or, can one even pose these why-questions if this truly is an instance of the violation of the principle of sufficient reason?

C. S. Peirce, and probably also Meillassoux and Boutroux, would take this to be evidence against the ontological positions of mechanism and determinism, that is, necessitarianism. Peirce muses,

> How would [the necessitarian] explain the uniformity and regularity of the universe, whereupon he tells me that the laws of nature are immutable and ultimate facts, and no account is to be given to them. But my hypothesis of spontaneity does explain irregularity . . . and enables us to understand how the uniformity of nature could have been brought about.[2]

Even if the empirical scientist were to decide to explain away this phenomenon as a non-phenomenon by assuming an epistemic deficiency on the part of quantum physics, it is nevertheless likely that she is still implicitly holding the ontological commitment that laws of nature are unexplainable and, hence, themselves the brute facts of the universe, as well as implicitly holding something that is extremely odd to hold about something that is just a brute given, namely that these same laws are inviolable, that the brute facticity of laws also contain inner principles that ensure their continued uniform operation in the future. Peirce, for his part, prefers the following explanation as both simpler and more adequate: 'mechanical laws are nothing but acquired habits . . .'[3] This position is obviously very close to that of Boutroux. In any event, some of the more significant ramifications of this book's thesis may have to do with the sociology and politics of the sciences. There is no unity of the sciences, no reduction of one science to another; no particular science renders another particular science more understandable than it would be on its own. Empirical sciences, hypothetical in nature and expository of contingent laws, ought never to claim a privileged status. No disciplines come equipped with their own rules of philosophical interpretation, which means that speculative thought cannot simply incorporate 'truths' from other sciences into its system as if they were missing puzzle pieces. There is no system, because speculative thinking plays; it speculates without foregoing rules, even if rules and procedures are consequently accrued. Its methodology does not follow a path; it blazes a path.

Rather than a book with a conscious ethical or political agenda, this is a book on logic, a book that attempts to provide a philosophical and ontological interpretation of the cardinal truths of logic: the principle of excluded middle, the principle of non-contradiction, the principle of identity and the principle of (sufficient) reason. It is not a logic manual, but it does show that the principle of identity is dependent upon the prior operativity of the principle of non-contradiction insofar as this latter principle first demands that something either be self-identical or not, that it either be what it is or something else. The principle of non-contradiction, in turn, can only be operative if the principle of excluded middle is already operative, as this principle first dictates that A or ~A exhaust all options by excluding the middle option between actually being A or actually not being A, namely that which is neither A nor ~A because the possibility of both. The principle of excluded middle, by removing possibility as a third option, thus demands actual decision. Its operativity is, at bottom, prescriptive rather than descriptive, the efficaciousness of the Law of the World, which demands that everything must be decided, that ambivalence or undecidability ought not to remain. Only where ambivalence or equipollence between possibilities has been decided, however, is counterbalance broken and one possibility elevated over its negation. It is here, then, that reasons, and with it the principle of (sufficient) reason, first emerge. Reasons are only operative where one thing is actual while another is only potential. A reason is the account for the predominance of the one over the other. Reason is hence inoperative where counterbalance and indecision hold. This is a book about the ontological foundation of the cardinal laws of logic, which offers a narration of the emergence of these laws of reason from lawless unreason as principles of being.

Arthur Schopenhauer, in *On the Fourfold Root of the Principle of Sufficient Reason*, suggests that Hume was perhaps the first to call radically into question the principle of sufficient reason, thus imputing to Hume an ontological thesis rather than an epistemological thesis merely. He writes of Hume, 'None before this serious thinker had ever doubted what follows. First, and before all things in heaven and on earth, is the Principle of Sufficient Reason in the form of the Law of Causality.'[4] Schopenhauer is right to read Hume this way, even if the historical thesis that Hume was the first ever to have doubted this principle remains dubious. For his part, Schopenhauer acutely identifies this principle as the sole harbinger of absolute necessity, so that if this principle itself is not absolutely necessary – which it is not – then absolute necessity simply is not. Schopenhauer explains as follows:

> The Principle of Sufficient Reason in all its forms is the sole principle and sole support of all necessity. For *necessity* has no other true and distinct meaning than that of the infallibility of the consequences when the reason is posited. Accordingly, every necessity is *conditioned*: absolute, *i.e.* unconditioned, necessity therefore is a *contradicto in adjecto* . . . The conception of an 'ABSOLUTELY' *necessary Being* . . . contains therefore a contradiction . . . it annuls by the predicate '*absolute*' (*i.e.* 'unconditioned by anything else') the only determination which makes the '*necessary*' conceivable.[5]

Although the principle of sufficient reason provides the foundation for all forms of necessity, the lack of absoluteness of this same principle does not nullify all necessity, only absolute necessity, allowing conditional or contingent necessity to remain. Absolute necessity does not simply fail to obtain factically, but it is a contradiction in terms; it is an impossibility and yet this does not culminate in the Meillassouxian position that no necessity exists except the necessity of contingency.

Although finding no points of disagreement in the foregoing quote of Schopenhauer, this work does depart from his analysis on at least two points. First, Schopenhauer's enumeration of possible domains of necessity is incomplete. He finds that the principle of sufficient reason can be operative as logical, physical, mathematical or moral necessity. This book does not explicitly analyse moral necessity, but it adds transcendental and metaphysical necessity to his list. Even with these additions, all forms of necessity prove to be contingent rather than absolute. Second, and more importantly, Schopenhauer could not imagine a method for analysing the emergence of the principle of reason itself. He subjects it to critique, indeed, but since this principle is not self-grounding, an account of its emergence is demanded, which Schopenhauer fails to provide. He declines this task, writing, 'The Principle of Sufficient Reason itself . . . cannot be further explained; because there exists no principle by which to explain the source of all explanation.'[6] Not all accounts, however, must consist in explanation by principle. This book has suggested that historical accounts can pick up where explanatory accounts falter. In other words, narrative empiricism remains a possibility, which is precisely what this book has attempted, namely to let the principle of sufficient reason 'empirically' emerge before one's eyes, to narrate the emergence of this principle from out of chaos in a 'being-historical [*seynsgeschichtlich*]' manner. What is called for, if the term may be permitted, is a new and scientific function of 'myth-telling'.

While there may be some ethical and political implications present in this book after all, and while, as a book on logic, the undermining of the principle of sufficient reason was its explicit theme, none of this provides or can provide a full account for why it was written. It might simply be said that its author is a curious daydreamer who loves free speculation. As Peirce once wrote,

> There is no positive sin against logic in *trying* any theory which may come into our heads, so long as it is adopted in such a sense as to permit the investigation to go on unimpeded and undiscouraged. To set up a philosophy which barricades the road of further advance toward the truth is the one unpardonable offence in reasoning...[7]

Although this may not be the most economical approach, it is the approach that decides for nothing other than truth. It makes no demands that truth must be useful, ethically edifying or politically correct. Its only decision is to remain undiscouraged by consequences, be they beautiful or ugly, in the perseverance for truth. The pursuit of truth, then, is inherently a practice in speculation. Speculation does not begin with an agenda or a problem, but it begins in wonder, in curiosity. To this author's mind, the most wondrous question ever encountered has been: Why is there something instead of nothing at all? Why is there meaning instead of meaninglessness? Why is there reason instead of unreason? Why is there regularity rather than absolute irregularity, lawlessness and chaos? As Peirce writes,

> Irregularity does not prompt us to ask for an explanation. Nor can it be said that it is because the explanation is obvious; for there is, on the contrary, no explanation to be given, except that there is no particular reason why there should be a regular pattern – or rather that there is no sufficient reason.[8]

It is not nothingness, nonsense, meaninglessness, chaos, irregularity, lack of uniformity and lawlessness that require an account, but being, sense, meaning, order, regularity, uniformity and law. These not only demand an account, but they invoke wonder and set the mind at play, and this because none of it can be explained by means of simple recourse to the principle of sufficient reason. Order, law, regularity, necessity and the like are all grounded in absolute contingency bereft of reason. There is no reason for reason, but this does not preclude a speculatively empirical narration of its being-historical emergence all the same.

The truly shocking thing about the world, as Wittgenstein well knew, is the facticity of the world itself. In other words, the most curious and awe-inspiring is the advent of something from nothing, the emergence of things *ex nihilo*. In this respect, one might, for example, find the possible belief in a future, bodily resurrection shocking and incredible, but that fact – if it is a fact – should not be more shocking than one's present existence, which is without precedent and came to be from nothing. At least a future resurrection could point to this world as a substrate that simply requires re-animation; there is at least something pre-given as the indispensable condition of that possibility, which is not the case with respect to the fact that there is, here and now, something rather than nothing. The fact that one now exists should be much more shocking than any belief about a future resurrection could ever be, except that, as Hume well knows, by custom or force of habit one has become psychologically accustomed to this fact. If the facticity of the world is not a truth of reason but a matter of fact, if facticity is all there is, then, in stark opposition to Hume, one might risk suggesting that miracles are all there is, because facticity without precedent, facticity without reason, facticity which has not come to be on the basis of any prior law, is all there is. Yet for all that, there does remain this difference. The facticity of being must perpetually prove itself, it must perpetually prove its divine essence, its divine *modus*; it must perpetually witness against its miraculous quality by proving itself regular, consistent and lawful.

The hope of this book – and so maybe it did have an agenda after all – was not to present an ontology of contingency but an ontology of the fact, insofar as the latter does not just present possibilities but affirms that some of them are actual. An ontology of the fact does not just point to the Absolute as the sphere of absolute possibility, but it progresses from this, which is nothing more than a *momentum*, in order to affirm which possibility of being has been actualised. It does not just say what it would be like if being were divine rather than atheistic, but it affirms that this, in fact, is the case. If, as one author has suggested, 'Classical philosophy's characteristic way of dealing with contingency is to . . . replace contingency by necessity wherever possible',[9] then contemporary philosophies of contingency have oscillated to the other extreme, positing contingent possibility only, fearful of affirming any as actual. One only need recall the possible-God theologies of Caputo, Kearney or Meillassoux mentioned in the Introduction, which zealously posit God as a possibility but, as a matter of principle, refuse to affirm God in fact. An ontology of the fact represents an alternative both to possible-God theologies as well as to the now fashionable militantly materialist and atheist ontologies of contingency.

In this context, perhaps the most important conclusion to be drawn from this book is that it affirms both the universality of reason as well as the reality of God, while yet remaining post-ontotheological. On the one hand, ontotheology names the consonance of these two: God exists as the first cause and thus as the basis of the principle of sufficient reason, the ground of all grounds, and the reason God exists is because his sufficient reason is indistinguishable from or contained within his own essence. On the other hand, an ontology of the fact can affirm both that God is and that the principle of sufficient reason is, yet without viewing them as consonant with one another insofar as it regards both as eternal consequents and not as absolutely antecedent and coincident. It is possible to affirm both reason and God without lapsing into ontotheology, because an ontology of the fact thinks the modalities differently than the metaphysical tradition of ontotheology has done. In this respect, Fred Rush offers the following insightful gloss on Schelling's position:

> Actuality as a byproduct of modal thought is precisely not the same as being 'factical' [*faktisch*] or a 'pure act' [*actus purus*]. Necessity . . . has no proper place in being-as-such. Necessity, like the identity expressed in judgments, is relational – 'relative', not 'absolute'. When Schelling feels that he must characterize being-as-such in terms of necessity, it is clearly circumlocution for effect. He calls such being 'simply necessary' in order to make the point that its 'necessity' lies in its *just being* . . . Being-as-such is what one might call 'modally obdurate' then; it is neither 'necessary' nor 'possible' in the standard philosophical senses of these terms.[10]

Heidegger was wrong to say that Schelling failed to think the modalities differently than had been done in the metaphysical tradition of ontotheology, the first beginning, but he was right to note that if Schelling had done so, then he would have already broken through to that other beginning. It is the antecedent of this material implication that Heidegger denied, but that this book affirms; Schelling did think the modalities in a different and novel way.

Finally, this book, espousing an ontology of the fact rather than an ontology of contingency, not only found itself in the unique position of being able to affirm both reason and God without returning to the tradition of ontotheology, but was also able to affirm a God both philosophically and religiously adequate. The God of the ontology of the fact is a God both ontologically ultimate – even if not equivalent with the Absolute – and, because a free God who acts rather than merely moving towards self-achievement according to a principle of nature, a personal God to whom one can sing, dance, pray and worship.[11] This God is religiously adequate because a free individual, a determinate and nameable God who has done certain deeds and not others, and not a generic, indeterminate something 'out there' that might possibly be held in common among all faiths.

Notes

1. Pruss, *Principle of Sufficient Reason*, pp. 160–1.
2. Peirce, 'Doctrine of Necessity', p. 196. Peirce also argues that mechanism is wrong because 'exact law obviously never can produce heterogeneity out of homogeneity . . .' and 'because the law of the conservation of energy is equivalent to the proposition that all operations governed by mechanical laws are reversible; so that an immediate corol-

lary from it is that growth is not explicable by those laws, even if they be not violated in the process of growth' (Peirce, 'Architecture of Theories', p. 163).
3. Peirce, 'Man's Glassy Essence', p. 264.
4. Schopenhauer, *On the Fourfold Root*, p. 23.
5. Ibid., p. 181.
6. Ibid., p. 184.
7. Peirce, 'Note', p. 136.
8. Peirce, 'Logic of Drawing History', p. 189.
9. Grube, 'Introduction', p. 1.
10. Rush, 'Schelling's Critique of Hegel', p. 231.
11. Note Heidegger's comment: 'The god of philosophy. Man can neither pray nor sacrifice to this god. Before the *causa sui*, man can neither fall to his knees in awe nor can he play music and dance before this god' (Heidegger, *Identity*, p. 72).

Bibliography

Aristotle, *Metaphysics, Books 1–9*, Loeb Classical Library 271 (Cambridge, MA: Harvard University Press, 1933).
Aristotle, *Metaphysics, Books 10–14. Oeconomica. Magna Moralia*, Loeb Classical Library 287 (Cambridge, MA: Harvard University Press, 1935).
Badiou, Alain, *Being and Event* (London: Continuum, 2007).
Badiou, Alain, *Briefings on Existence: A Short Treatise on Transitory Ontology* (Albany: State University of New York Press, 2006).
Badiou, Alain, *Manifesto for Philosophy* (Albany: State University of New York Press, 1992).
Beach, Edward Allen, 'The Later Schelling's Conception of Dialectical Method, in Contradistinction to Hegel's', *Owl of Minerva* (Fall 1990), pp. 35–54.
Beach, Edward Allen, *The Potencies of God(s): Schelling's Philosophy of Mythology* (Albany: State University of New York Press, 1994).
Beierwaltes, Werner, 'The Legacy of Neoplatonism in F. W. J. Schelling's Thought', *International Journal of Philosophical Studies* 10.4 (2002), pp. 393–428.
Beierwaltes, Werner, 'Plato's *Timaeus* in German Idealism', in Gretchen J. Reydams-Schils (ed.), *Plato's Timaeus as Cultural Icon* (Notre Dame: University of Notre Dame Press, 2003), pp. 267–89.
Bloechl, Jeffrey, 'Christianity and Possibility', in John Panteleimon Manoussakis (ed.), *After God: Richard Kearney and the Religious Turn in Continental Philosophy* (New York: Fordham University Press, 2006), pp. 127–38.
Boutroux, Émile, *The Contingency of the Laws of Nature* (Chicago: Open Court, 2012).
Boutroux, Émile, *Natural Law in Science and Philosophy* (New York: MacMillan, 2012).
Bowie, Andrew, *Schelling and Modern European Philosophy: An Introduction* (New York: Routledge, 1994.)
Braver, Lee, *A Thing of This World: A History of Continental Anti-Realism* (Evanston: Northwestern University Press, 2007).
Brito, Emilio, 'La Création «ex nihilo» selon Schelling', *Ephemerides Theologicae Lovanienses* 60 (December 1984), pp. 298–324.
Brown, Nathan, 'The Speculative and the Specific: On Hallward and Meillassoux', in Levi Bryant et al. (eds), *The Speculative Turn: Continental Materialism and Realism* (Melbourne: re.press, 2011), pp. 142–63.
Brown, Robert F., *The Later Philosophy of Schelling: The Influence of Böhme on the Works of 1809–1815* (Lewisburg: Bucknell University Press, 1977).
Buchheim, Thomas, *Eins von Allem: Die Selbstbescheidung des Idealismus in Schellings Spätphilosophie* (Hamburg: Felix Meiner, 1992).

Caputo, John D., 'Richard Kearney's Enthusiasm', in John Panteleimon Manoussakis (ed.), *After God: Richard Kearney and the Religious Turn in Continental Philosophy* (New York: Fordham University Press, 2006), pp. 309–17.

Caputo, John D., *The Weakness of God: A Theology of the Event* (Bloomington: Indiana University Press, 2006).

Caputo, John D., and Vattimo, Gianni, 'Spectral Hermeneutics: On the Weakness of God and the Theology of the Event', in Jeffrey W. Robbins (ed.), *After the Death of God* (New York: Columbia University Press, 2007), pp. 47–85.

Chlup, Radek, *Proclus: An Introduction* (Cambridge: Cambridge University Press, 2012).

Clark, David L., 'Heidegger's Craving: Being-on-Schelling', *Diacritics* 27.3 (1997), pp. 8–33, <http://www.jstor.org/stable/1566331>

Clark, Tim, 'A Whiteheadian Chaosmos? Process Philosophy from a Deleuzean Perspective', in Catherine Keller and Anne Daniell (eds), *Process and Difference: Between Cosmological and Poststructuralist Postmodernisms* (Albany: State University of New York Press, 2002), pp. 191–207.

Crease, Robert Poole, Jr, 'Heidegger, Leibniz, and the Principle of Sufficient Reason', dissertation, Ann Arbor: University Microfilms International (UMI), 1987.

Deleuze, Gilles, *Difference and Repetition* (New York: Columbia University Press, 1995).

Deleuze, Gilles, *The Logic of Sense* (New York: Columbia University Press, 1990).

Desmond, William, 'Maybe, Maybe Not: Richard Kearney and God', in John Panteleimon Manoussakis (ed.), *After God: Richard Kearney and the Religious Turn in Continental Philosophy* (New York: Fordham University Press, 2006), pp. 55–77.

Durner, Manfred, *Wissen und Geschichte bei Schelling: eine Interpretation der ersten Erlanger Vorlesung* (Munich: Johannes Berchmans, 1979).

Ejsing, Annette, *Theology of Anticipation: A Constructive Study of C. S. Peirce* (Eugene, OR: Pickwick Publications, 2007).

Frank, Manfred, *Auswege aus dem deutschen Idealismus* (Frankfurt a.M.: Suhrkamp, 2007).

Frank, Manfred, *Der unendliche Mangel an Sein: Schellings Hegelkritik und die Anfänge der Marxschen Dialektik* (Frankfurt a.M.: Suhrkamp, 1975).

Franz, Albert, *Philosophische Religion: Eine Auseinandersetzung mit den Grundlegungsproblemen der Spätphilosophie F.W.J. Schellings* (Würzburg: Königshausen Neumann, 1992).

Friedrich, Hans-Joachim, *Der Ungrund der Freiheit im Denken von Böhme, Schelling und Heidegger* (Stuttgart–Bad Canstatt: Frommann-Holzboog, 2009).

Gabriel, Markus, 'Is Heidegger's "Turn" a Realist Project?', *Meta: Research in Hermeneutics, Phenomenology, and Practical Philosophy*, special issue (2014), pp. 44–73.

Gabriel, Markus, 'The Meaning of "Existence" and the Contingency of Sense', *Speculations* IV (2013), pp. 74–83.

Gabriel, Markus, 'The Mythological Being of Reflection – An Essay on Hegel, Schelling, and the Contingency of Necessity', in Markus Gabriel and Slavoj Žižek, *Mythology, Madness and Laughter: Subjectivity in German Idealism* (London: Continuum, 2009), pp. 15–121.

Gabriel, Markus, *Transcendental Ontology: Essays in German Idealism* (London: Bloomsbury, 2011).

Gabriel, Markus, 'Unvordenkliches Sein und Ereignis', in Lore Hühn and Jörg Jantzen (eds), *Heideggers Schelling-Seminar (1927/28)* (Stuttgart: Frommann-Holzboog, 2010), pp. 81–112.

García, Marcela, 'Schelling's Late Negative Philosophy: Crisis and Critique of Pure Reason', *Comparative and Continental Philosophy* 3.2 (2011), pp. 141–64.

Grant, Iain Hamilton, *Philosophies of Nature after Schelling* (London: Continuum, 2008).

Gratton, Peter, 'Meillassoux's Speculative Politics: Time and the Divinity to Come', *Analecta Hermeneutica* 4 (2012), pp. 1–14.

Griffin, David Ray, *Whitehead's Radically Different Postmodern Philosophy: An Argument for Its Contemporary Relevance* (Albany: State University of New York Press, 2007).

Grondin, Jean, 'Die späte Entdeckung Schellings in der Hermeneutik', in István M. Fehér and Wilhelm G. Jacobs (eds), *Zeit und Freiheit: Schelling – Schopenhauer – Kierkegaard – Heidegger* (Budapest: Éthos Könyvek, 1999), pp. 65–72.

Grube, Dirk-Martin, 'Introduction: Contingency and Religion – A Philosophical *Tour d'Horizon*', in Dirk-Martin Grube and Peter Jonkers (eds), *Religions Challenged by Contingency: Theological and Philosophical Approaches to the Problem of Contingency* (Leiden: Brill, 2008), pp. 1–45.

Gschwandtner, Christina M., *Postmodern Apologetics? Arguments for God in Contemporary Philosophy* (New York: Fordham University Press, 2013).

Hägglund, Martin, 'Radical Atheist Materialism: A Critique of Meillassoux', in Levi Bryant et al. (eds), *The Speculative Turn: Continental Materialism and Realism* (Melbourne: re.press, 2011), pp. 114–29.

Harman, Graham, *Quentin Meillassoux: Philosophy in the Making* (Edinburgh: Edinburgh University Press, 2011).

Hegel, G. F. W., *Philosophy of Right* (New York: Cosimo, 2008).

Heidegger, Martin, *Basic Concepts* (Bloomington: Indiana University Press, 1993).

Heidegger, Martin, *Basic Questions of Philosophy: Selected 'Problems' of 'Logic'* (Bloomington: Indiana University Press, 1994).

Heidegger, Martin, *Being and Time* (Albany: State University of New York Press, 1996).

Heidegger, Martin, 'Beiträge zur Philosophie', *Gesamtausgabe Bd. 65* (Frankfurt a.M.: Klostermann, 2003).

Heidegger, Martin, *Bremen and Freiburg Lectures: 'Insight Into That Which Is' and 'Basic Principles of Thinking'* (Bloomington: Indiana University Press, 2012).

Heidegger, Martin, *Contributions to Philosophy (Of the Event)* (Bloomington: Indiana University Press, 2012).

Heidegger, Martin, 'Die Metaphysik des deutschen Idealismus: Zur erneuten Auslegung von Schelling', in Günter Seubold (ed.), *Gesamtausgabe II. Abteilung: Vorlesungen 1919–1944. Band 39* (Frankfurt a.M.: Vittorio Klostermann, 2006).

Heidegger, Martin, *Identity and Difference* (Chicago: University of Chicago Press, 2002).

Heidegger, Martin, *Logic: The Question of Truth* (Bloomington: Indiana University Press, 2010).

Heidegger, Martin, *The Metaphysical Foundations of Logic* (Bloomington: Indiana University Press, 1984).

Heidegger, Martin, *On Time and Being* (Chicago: University of Chicago Press, 2002).

Heidegger, Martin, *Phenomenological Interpretation of Kant's Critique of Pure Reason* (Bloomington: Indiana University Press, 1977).

Heidegger, Martin, 'Phenomenology and Theology', in William McNeill (ed.), *Pathmarks*, (Cambridge: Cambridge University Press, 1998), pp. 39–62.

Heidegger, Martin, *The Phenomenology of Religious Life* (Bloomington: Indiana University Press, 2010).

Heidegger, Martin, *The Principle of Reason* (Bloomington: Indiana University Press, 1996).

Heidegger, Martin, *Schelling's Treatise on the Essence of Human Freedom* (Athens: Ohio University Press, 1985).

Hodges, Michael, and Lewis, John, *Thinking in the Ruins: Wittgenstein and Santayana on Contingency* (Nashville: Vanderbilt University Press, 2000).

Hogrebe, Wolfram, *Prädikation und Genesis: Metaphysik als Fundamentalheuristik im Ausgang von Schellings 'Die Weltalter'* (Frankfurt a.M.: Suhrkamp, 1989).

Hühn, Lore, 'Heidegger–Schelling im philosophischen Zwiegespräch', in Lore Hühn and Jörg Jantzen (eds), *Heideggers Schelling-Seminar (1927/28)* (Stuttgart: Frommann-Holzboog, 2010), pp. 3–44.

Hutter, Axel, *Geschichtliche Vernunft: Die Weiterführung der Kantischen Vernunftkritik in der Spätphilosophie Schellings* (Frankfurt a.M.: Suhrkamp, 1996).

Jankélévitch, Vladimir, *L'Odyssée de la conscience dans la dernière philosophie de Schelling* (Paris: Librairie Félix Alcan, 1933).

Jaspers, Karl. *Schelling. Grösse und Verhängnis.* (Munich: R. Piper, 1955).
Johnston, Adrian, 'Hume's Revenge: À Dieu Meillassoux', in Levi Bryant et al. (eds), *The Speculative Turn: Continental Materialism and Realism* (Melbourne: re.press, 2011), pp. 92–113.
Kant, Immanuel, *Critique of Pure Reason* (Cambridge: Cambridge University Press, 1998).
Kearney, Richard, *Anatheism: Returning to God After God* (New York: Columbia University Press, 2010).
Kearney, Richard, 'Epiphanies of the Everyday: Toward a Micro-Eschatology', in John Panteleimon Manoussakis (ed.), *After God: Richard Kearney and the Religious Turn in Continental Philosophy* (New York: Fordham University Press, 2006), pp. 3–20.
Kearney, Richard, *The God Who May Be: A Hermeneutics of Religion* (Bloomington: Indiana University Press, 2001).
Kierkegaard, Søren, *The Concept of Anxiety: A Simple Psychologically Orienting Deliberation on the Dogmatic Issue of Hereditary Sine* (Princeton: Princeton University Press, 1980).
Kierkegaard, Søren, *Either/Or: A Fragment of Life, Part II*, ed. Howard V. Hong and Edna H. Hong (Princeton: Princeton University Press, 1987).
Kierkegaard, Søren, *Fear and Trembling. Repetition*, ed. Howard V. Hong and Edna H. Hong (Princeton: Princeton University Press, 1983).
Krell, David Farrell, 'God's Footstool: A Note on the Source for Schelling's Description of the Olympian Zeus in the 1811 Draft of *The Ages of the World*', in Jason M. Wirth (ed.), *Schelling Now: Contemporary Readings* (Bloomington: Indiana University Press, 2005), pp. 101–21.
Lawrence, Joseph P., 'Philosophical Religion and the Quest for Authenticity', in Jason M. Wirth (ed.), *Schelling Now: Contemporary Readings* (Bloomington: Indiana University Press, 2005), pp. 13–30.
Levinas, Emmanuel. *Totality and Infinity: An Essay on Exteriority.* Trans. Alphonso Lingis. (Pittsburgh, PA: Duquesne University Press, 2012).
Lucretius, *On the Nature of Things Books 1–6*, Loeb Classical Library 181 (Cambridge, MA: Harvard University Press, 1924).
Malabou, Catherine, 'Can We Relinquish the Transcendental?', *Journal of Speculative Philosophy* 28.3 (2014), pp. 242–55.
Marcel, Gabriel, 'Schelling fut-il un précurseur de la philosophie de l'existence?', *Revue de Métaphysique et de Morale* LXII (1957), pp. 72–87.
Meillassoux, Quentin, *After Finitude: An Essay on the Necessity of Contingency* (London: Bloomsbury, 2012).
Meillassoux, Quentin, 'The Immanence of the World Beyond', in Conor Cunningham and Peter M. Candler (eds), *The Grandeur of Reason* (London: SCM Press, 2010), pp. 444–78.
Meillassoux, Quentin, 'Potentiality and Virtuality', *Collapse* II (March 2007), pp. 55–82.
Meillassoux, Quentin, 'Spectral Dilemma', *Collapse* IV (May 2008), pp. 261–76.
Meillassoux, Quentin, 'Time without Becoming', 8 May 2008, https://speculativeheresy.files. wordpress.com/2008/07/3729-time_without_becoming.pdf (last accessed 19 October 2016).
Nichols, Craig, 'The God Who May Be and the God Who Was', in John Panteleimon Manoussakis (ed.), *After God: Richard Kearney and the Religious Turn in Continental Philosophy* (New York: Fordham University Press, 2006), pp. 111–26.
Niemoczynski, Leon, 'Speculating God: Speculative Realism and Meillassoux's Divine Inexistence', in Clayton Crockett et al. (eds), *The Future of the Continental Philosophy of Religion* (Bloomington: Indiana University Press, 2014), pp. 92–108.
O'Connor, Timothy, *Theism and Ultimate Explanation: The Necessary Shape of Contingency* (Oxford: Wiley-Blackwell, 2012).
Peirce, C. S., 'The Architecture of Theories', in Morris R. Cohen (ed.), *Chance, Love and Logic* (New York: Harcourt, Brace, 1923), pp. 157–78.

Peirce, C. S., 'The Categories in Detail', in Charles Hartshorne et al. (eds), *The Collected Papers of Charles Sanders Peirce: Vols. I–VIII* (Cambridge, MA: Harvard University Press, 1931–35), vol. 1, pp. 300–53.

Peirce, C. S., 'The Doctrine of Necessity Examined', in Morris R. Cohen (ed.), *Chance, Love and Logic* (New York: Harcourt, Brace, 1923), pp. 179–201.

Peirce, C. S., 'Lessons from the History of Philosophy', in Charles Hartshorne et al. (eds), *The Collected Papers of Charles Sanders Peirce: Vols. I–VIII* (Cambridge, MA: Harvard University Press, 1931–35), vol. 1, pp. 15–42.

Peirce, C. S., 'The Logic of Continuity', in Charles Hartshorne et al. (eds), *The Collected Papers of Charles Sanders Peirce: Vols. I–VIII* (Cambridge, MA: Harvard University Press, 1931–35), vol. 6, pp. 185–213.

Peirce, C. S., 'The Logic of Drawing History from Ancient Documents', in Charles Hartshorne et al. (eds), *The Collected Papers of Charles Sanders Peirce: Vols. I–VIII* (Cambridge, MA: Harvard University Press, 1931–35), vol. 7, pp. 162–255.

Peirce, C. S., 'The Logic of Mathematics; an Attempt to Develop My Categories from Within' in Charles Hartshorne et al. (eds), *The Collected Papers of Charles Sanders Peirce: Vols. I–VIII* (Cambridge, MA: Harvard University Press, 1931–35), vol. 1, pp. 417–520.

Peirce, C. S., 'Man's Glassy Essence', in Morris R. Cohen (ed.), *Chance, Love and Logic* (New York: Harcourt, Brace, 1923), pp. 238–66.

Peirce, C. S., 'Note on Scientific Philosophy', in Charles Hartshorne et al. (eds), *The Collected Papers of Charles Sanders Peirce: Vols. I–VIII* (Cambridge, MA: Harvard University Press, 1931–35), vol. 1, pp. 126–75.

Peirce, C. S., 'Objective Logic', in Charles Hartshorne et al. (eds), *The Collected Papers of Charles Sanders Peirce: Vols. I–VIII* (Cambridge, MA: Harvard University Press, 1931–35), vol. 6, pp. 214–37.

Plato, *Cratylus. Parmenides. Greater Hippias. Lesser Hippias*, Loeb Classical Library 167 (Cambridge, MA: Harvard University Press, 1926).

Plato, *Euthyphro. Apology. Crito. Phaedo. Phaedrus*, Loeb Classical Library 36 (Cambridge, MA: Harvard University Press, 2017).

Plato, *Republic, Volume I: Books 1–5*, Loeb Classical Library 237 (Cambridge, MA: Harvard University Press, 2013).

Plato, *Republic, Volume II: Books 6–10*, Loeb Classical Library 238 (Cambridge, MA: Harvard University Press, 2013).

Plato, *Statesman. Philebus. Ion*, Loeb Classical Library 164 (Cambridge, MA: Harvard University Press, 1925).

Plato, *Theaetetus. Sophist*, Loeb Classical Library 123 (Cambridge, MA: Harvard University Press, 1921).

Plato, *Timaeus. Critias. Cleitophon. Menexenus. Epistles*, Loeb Classical Library 234 (Cambridge, MA: Harvard University Press, 1929).

Plotinus, *Ennead II, 1–9*, Loeb Classical Library 441 (Cambridge, MA: Harvard University Press, 1966).

Proclus, *Commentary on Plato's* Timaeus, *Volume II* (Cambridge: Cambridge University Press, 2008).

Proclus, *The Elements of Theology* (New York: Oxford University Press, 1963).

Proclus, *On the Existence of Evils* (New York: Cornell University Press, 2003).

Pruss, Alexander R., *The Principle of Sufficient Reason: A Reassessment* (Cambridge: Cambridge University Press, 2006).

Ravaisson, Félix, *Of Habit* (London: Continuum, 2008).

Rush, Fred, 'Schelling's Critique of Hegel', in Lara Ostaric (ed.), *Interpreting Schelling: Critical Essays* (Cambridge: Cambridge University Press, 2014), pp. 216–37.

Sallis, John, 'Secluded Nature: The Point of Schelling's Reinscription of the *Timaeus*', *Pli: The Warwick Journal of Philosophy* 8 (1999), pp. 71–85.

Schelling, F. W. J., 'Abhandlung über die Quelle der ewigen Wahrheiten', in K. F. A. Schelling (ed.), *Sämtliche Werke II/1* (Stuttgart: Cotta, 1856), pp. 573–90.
Schelling, F. W. J., *Ages of the World (2ⁿᵈ draft 1813)* (Ann Arbor: University of Michigan Press, 1997).
Schelling, F. W. J., *Ages of the World (3ʳᵈ draft 1815)* (Albany: State University of New York Press, 2000).
Schelling, F. W. J., 'Andere Deduktion der Principien der positiven Philosophie', in K. F. A. Schelling (ed.), *Sämtliche Werke II/4* (Stuttgart: Cotta, 1858), pp. 335–56.
Schelling, F. W. J., *Clara: Or, On Nature's Connection to the Spirit World* (Albany: State University of New York Press, 2002).
Schelling, F. W. J., 'Darstellung des philosophischen Empirismus: Aus der Einleitung in die Philosophie', in K. F. A. Schelling (ed.), *Sämtliche Werke I/10* (Stuttgart: Cotta, 1861), pp. 225–86.
Schelling, F. W. J., 'Der Monotheismus', in K. F. A. Schelling (ed.), *Sämtliche Werke II/2* (Stuttgart: Cotta, 1856), pp. 3–134.
Schelling, F. W. J., *Die endlich offenbar gewordene positive Philosophie der Offenbarung oder Entstehungsgeschichte, wörtlicher Text, Beurtheilung und Berichtigung der v. Schellingschen Entdeckungen über Philosophie überhaupt, Mythologie und Offenbarung des dogmatischen Christenthums in Berliner Winterkursus von 1841–42* (Darmstadt: Karl Wilhelm Leske, 1843).
Schelling, F. W. J., 'Die Mythologie', in K. F. A. Schelling (ed.), *Sämtliche Werke: II/2* (Stuttgart: Cotta, 1856), pp. 135–674.
Schelling, F. W. J., 'Die Philosophie der Offenbarung: Erster Theil', in K. F. A. Schelling (ed.), *Sämtliche Werke: II/3* (Stuttgart: Cotta, 1858), pp. 177–530.
Schelling, F. W. J., 'Die Philosophie der Offenbarung: Zweiter Theil', in K. F. A. Schelling (ed.), *Sämtliche Werke: II/4* (Stuttgart: Cotta, 1858), pp. 3–334.
Schelling, F. W. J., *Einleitung in die Philosophie* (Stuttgart: Frommann-Holzboog, 1989).
Schelling, F. W. J., 'Einleitung in die Philosophie der Offenbarung oder Begründung der positiven Philosophie', in K. F. A. Schelling (ed.), *Sämtliche Werke: II/3* (Stuttgart: Cotta, 1858), pp. 3–176.
Schelling, F. W. J., *The Grounding of Positive Philosophy: The Berlin Lectures* (Albany: State University of New York Press, 2008).
Schelling, F. W. J., *Grundlegung der positiven Philosophie: Münchner Vorlesung WS 1832/33 und SS 1833* (Turin: Bottega D'Erasmo, 1972).
Schelling, F. W. J., *Historical-Critical Introduction to the Philosophy of Mythology* (Albany: State University of New York Press, 2008).
Schelling, F. W. J., 'Historisch-kritische Einleitung in die Philosophie der Mythologie', in K. F. A. Schelling (ed.), *Sämtliche Werke II/1* (Stuttgart: Cotta, 1856), pp. 3–252.
Schelling, F. W. J., *Initia Philosophiae Universae: Erlanger Vorlesung WS 1820/21* (Bonn: Fuhrmans H. Bouvier, 1969).
Schelling, F. W. J., *On the History of Modern Philosophy* (Cambridge: Cambridge University Press, 1994).
Schelling, F. W. J., *Philosophie der Mythologie: Nachschrift der letzten Münchner Vorlesungen 1841* (Stuttgart: Frommann-Holzboog, 1996).
Schelling, F. W. J., 'Philosophische Einleitung in die Philosophie der Mythologie oder Darstellung der reinrationalen Philosophie', in K. F. A. Schelling (ed.), *Sämtliche Werke: II/1* (Stuttgart: Cotta, 1856), pp. 253–572.
Schelling, F. W. J., 'Philosophische Untersuchungen über das Wesen der menschlichen Freiheit und die damit zusammenhängenden Gegenstände', in K. F. A. Schelling (ed.), *Sämtliche Werke: I/7* (Stuttgart: Cotta, 1860), pp. 331–416.
Schelling, F. W. J., *Schelling's Treatise on the Essence of Human Freedom* (Athens: Ohio University Press, 1985).

Schelling, F. W. J., 'System der gesamten Philosophie und der Naturphilosophie insbesondere', in K. F. A. Schelling (ed.), *Sämtliche Werke I/6* (Stuttgart: Cotta, 1860), pp. 131–576.

Schelling, F. W. J., *System der Weltalter: Münchner Vorlesung 1827/28 in einer Nachschrift von Ernst von Lasaulx* (Frankfurt a.M.: Vittorio Klostermann, 1990).

Schelling, F. W. J., 'Timaeus (1794)', *Epoché: A Journal for the History of Philosophy* 12.2 (2008), pp. 205–48.

Schelling, F. W. J. *Urfassung der Philosophie der Offenbarung: Bände I–II* (Hamburg: Felix Meiner, 1992).

Schelling, F. W. J., 'Vorrede zu einer philosophischen Schrift des Herrn Victor Cousin', in K. F. A. Schelling (ed.), *Sämtliche Werke I/10* (Stuttgart: Cotta, 1861), pp. 201–24.

Schopenhauer, Arthur, *On the Fourfold Root of the Principle of Sufficient Reason and On the Will in Nature* (London: Georges Bell and Sons, 1897).

Schulz, Walter, *Die Vollendung des deutschen Idealismus in der Spätphilosphie Schellings* (Pfullingen: Neske, 1975).

Schwab, Philipp, 'Nonground and the Metaphysics of Evil. From Heidegger's First Schelling Seminar to Derrida's Last Reading of Schelling (1927–2002)', *Analecta Hermeneutica* 5 (2013), pp. 1–30.

Shenefelt, Michael, and White, Heidi, *If A Then B: How the World Discovered Logic* (New York: Columbia University Press, 2013).

Smith, Anthony Paul, and Whistler, Daniel (eds), *After the Postsecular and the Postmodern: New Essays in Continental Philosophy of Religion* (Newcastle: Cambridge Scholars Publishing, 2010).

Sparrow, Tom, *The End of Phenomenology: Metaphysics and the New Realism* (Edinburgh: Edinburgh University Press, 2014).

Stengers, Isabelle, *Thinking With Whitehead: A Free and Wild Creation of Concepts*, (Cambridge, MA: Harvard University Press, 2011).

Swinburne, Richard, *The Christian God* (Oxford: Clarendon Press, 1994).

Swinburne, Richard, *The Coherence of Theism (Revised Edition)* (New York: Oxford University Press, 1993).

Swinburne, Richard, *The Existence of God* (Oxford: Clarendon Press, 1979).

Tilliette, Xavier, *La Mythologie comprise: Schelling et l'interprétation du pagisme* (Paris: Librairie Philosophique J. Vrin, 2002).

Tritten, Tyler, 'After Contingency: Toward the Principle of Sufficient Reason as *Post Factum*', *Symposium: Canadian Journal of Continental Philosophy* 19.1 (2015), pp. 24–38.

Tritten, Tyler, 'Against Kant: Toward an Inverted Transcendentalism or a Philosophy of the Doctrinal', *Angelaki: Journal of the Theoretical Humanities* 21.4 (2016), pp. 143–55.

Tritten, Tyler, *Beyond Presence: F. W. J. Schelling's Criticism of Metaphysics* (Boston: De Gruyter, 2012).

Tritten, Tyler, 'Christ as Copula: On the Possibility of Religious Exclusivism', *Analecta Hermeneutica* 6 (2014), pp. 1–21.

Tritten, Tyler, 'On Matter: Schelling's Anti-Platonic Reading of the *Timaeus*', *Kabiri: The Journal of the North American Schelling Society*. Inaugural Issue (2017).

Tritten, Tyler, '*Per Posterius*: Peirce and Hume on Miracles and the Boundaries of the Scientific Game', *Argument: A Bi-Annual Journal for Philosophy* 4.2 (2014), pp. 247–66.

Vallega-Neu, Daniela, *Heidegger's* Contributions to Philosophy*: An Introduction* (Bloomington: Indiana University Press, 2003).

Vallicella, William F., *A Paradigm Theory of Existence: Onto-Theology Vindicated* (Dordrecht: Kluwer Academic, 2002).

Van der Heiden, Gert-Jan, *Ontology after Ontotheology: Plurality, Event, and Contingency in Contemporary Philosophy* (Pittsburgh: Duquesne University Press, 2014).

Warnek, Peter, 'Reading Schelling after Heidegger: The Freedom of Cryptic Dialogue', in Jason M. Wirth (ed.), *Schelling Now: Contemporary Readings* (Bloomington: Indiana University Press, 2005), pp. 163–83.

Whistler, Daniel, *Schelling's Theory of Symbolic Language: Forming the System of Identity*, (Oxford: Oxford University Press, 2013).

Wirth, Jason M., *The Conspiracy of Life: Meditations on Schelling and His Time* (Albany: State University of New York Press, 2003).

Wirth, Jason M., 'Introduction', in Jason M. Wirth (ed.), *Schelling Now: Contemporary Readings* (Bloomington: Indiana University Press, 2005), pp. 1–12.

Žižek, Slavoj, *The Abyss of Freedom* (Ann Arbor: University of Michigan Press, 1997).

Žižek, Slavoj, *The Indivisible Remainder* (London: Verso, 1996).

Index

Absolute, 41, 92, 120, 136–7, 139, 147, 177, 224, 245–6
absolute *prius*, 4, 51, 105–7, 112–13, 117, 120, 123, 131n, 133n, 136–9, 147–8, 153, 157, 159, 165n–6n, 180, 185, 218–19, 234n
absolutism, 7, 21–2
actuality
   actus, 63–6, 110–14, 118–19, 123, 127–8, 139, 142, 153, 158, 161, 191, 194, 196, 212–13, 220
   actus purus, 106, 111–14, 117, 119, 121, 123, 141–2, 146, 157–9, 165n, 190, 207, 211, 246
   ἐντελέχεια, 63, 145–7, 165n
Agamben, Giorgio, 133n–4n, 158
Anaximander, 123, 230
ἀνυπόθετος, 105, 107, 118, 134n
ἄπειρον, 70, 77–80, 83, 95n–7n, 106, 110, 122–3, 133n, 173
Aquinas, Thomas, 63, 89, 98n, 206
   Thomism, 111, 161
Aristotle, 2, 31, 38, 55, 64, 78–9, 81–2, 85–6, 95n–6n, 115–17, 119, 127, 134n, 142, 145, 147, 168
   Aristotelianism, 64–5
atomism, 56–8
Augustine, 84, 164

Badiou, Alain, 2, 11, 13, 19, 34, 41n, 47–8, 96n, 99n, 183, 205, 225–33
Beach, Edward Allen, 127
Beierwaltes, Werner, 77–8, 91–2

beyng, 13, 149, 153, 179, 181, 185–98, 200n; *see also* event
Boutroux, Émile, 2, 11, 39, 44–50, 55–71, 73n, 75–6, 81, 92, 96n, 167, 198, 216, 233, 241
Braver, Lee, 174, 185

Caputo, John, 6–9, 191, 245
causality, 59, 61, 66–8, 70, 73n, 90, 169, 185, 242
   causa sui, 6, 185, 247n
   cause, 39, 57–9, 65–70, 83–5, 88–91, 96n, 119, 130n, 143, 147–8, 163n, 181
   Cause, 147–8, 185
   first cause, 6, 10, 19, 65, 88, 91, 113, 148, 185, 245
chance, 29, 34, 41n, 97n–8n, 164n
chaos, 3–4, 9, 11–13, 18, 20, 23–4, 26, 28, 30–3, 35, 37–8, 40, 45, 49–50, 57–8, 66–8, 73n, 82–4, 94, 116–21, 123–4, 126–7, 133n, 136–9, 142, 146–8, 151, 155–7, 161, 170, 173, 187, 195, 198, 199n, 216, 218–20, 227, 229, 243–4
   Hyper-Chaos, 18, 24, 26–7, 29–38, 41, 73n, 170, 191
clinamen, 56–8, 217
copula, 40, 122–3, 136, 149–50, 170–1, 191, 210
   copulation, 122–3, 143, 149, 187
correlationism, 4, 18, 20–1, 41n, 52, 72n, 171, 214, 224

correlate, 21–3, 25, 40, 51, 67–8, 138, 140
creation, 88–9, 136, 140–2, 145–6, 151, 153–4, 157–8, 162n, 197
    ex nihilo, 20, 37–9, 42n, 142, 170, 244

Damascius, 89
de-cision (decision), 3, 8, 10–13, 35, 37, 43n, 45, 50, 60, 99n, 103, 118, 120–1, 124–8, 135n, 136, 138–9, 141–4, 146, 148–9, 154, 157–9, 161–2, 165n, 167, 177–9, 182–9, 193, 197, 205, 212, 220–1, 226, 228–9, 242
    either/or, 121, 126, 139, 142–3, 157, 164n
    see also freedom
Deleuze, Gilles, 19–20, 58, 94n, 98n, 104–5, 138, 172–3, 182
Derrida, Jacques, 18, 20, 94n, 194, 201n
Descartes, René, 75, 152, 207–8
    Cartesianism, 1
dialectics, 107, 221
Durner, Manfred, 106, 140

emanation, 76–8, 87–8, 91–3, 139–40, 148
empiricism
    a posteriori, 48, 50, 55, 65, 112, 149–50, 154, 157, 161, 166n, 180
    a priori empiricism, 112, 166n
    empirical apriorism, 4, 166n
    induction, 55, 59
    metaphysical empiricism, 4, 215
    narrative empiricism, 4, 18, 60, 112, 194, 197, 215, 243
    sensibilism, 112, 129n
    synthetic, 47, 51, 58–9, 65–70, 115–17, 122–3, 150
Epicurus, 56–9
epistemology, 1, 17, 107
eternity, 24, 37, 65, 89, 137–8, 140–2, 145, 153, 155, 182, 198n
Euthyphro Dilemma, 13, 169, 205, 207, 214, 216–17
event, 8–10, 12–13, 20, 39–41, 52–3, 66–7, 94, 107, 113, 127–8, 138, 141, 146, 149, 152–3, 156–9, 161–2, 167, 172–5, 177–9, 181–90, 192–3, 196, 198, 205, 212–13, 220–3, 233
    between-space, 122, 140
    clearing, 169, 172, 189, 192, 195, 200n, 218
    open-space, 146, 184, 192, 194
    opening, 9, 12, 140, 172–3, 181, 184, 187, 192, 200n, 218
    play-space, 188
    spacing (spac-ing), 187, 192, 200n
exclusion
    extainment, 110, 119–20, 131n, 135n, 157, 165n, 230
    positive exclusion, 230
existentialism, 43
    existential, 5–6, 94n

facticity, 6, 18, 20–7, 38, 40–1, 42n, 51, 53, 68, 73n, 94, 104, 112, 129n, 131n, 160, 170, 218, 241, 244–5
    factial, 24–7, 36, 40, 64
    factical, 20, 23–6, 32, 36, 40, 51, 64, 72n, 94, 161, 167
    factual, 23–5, 41n, 65, 104, 166n
    factum brutum, 1
    matter of fact, 5, 7, 10, 22, 42n, 53, 57–8, 68, 103, 112, 116, 121, 161, 198, 217, 245
fate, 97n, 139, 185–7
    ἀνάγκη, 62, 97, 114, 118, 123–5, 141–2, 146, 153, 216–17
    destiny, 139, 197, 216–17
    sending, 179–80, 184–6, 190, 196–7
fideism, 39–40, 212
freedom, 3, 44, 56–7, 60–2, 103, 108, 113–14, 125, 127, 131n, 136–7, 139, 141–3, 146, 148, 150–3, 157, 180, 184, 195, 215–16, 218

Gabriel, Markus, 2, 41n, 45–7, 52, 71n–2n, 116, 118, 127, 132n–3n, 135n, 151–2, 161, 168–9, 176, 179, 186, 190, 193, 197, 198n, 224–5, 232
German Idealism, 21, 41, 75, 97n, 172, 176, 214
God
    cosmological argument, 215
    divinisation, 13, 186–8, 192–3, 205, 215, 220–1, 223–4, 233
    ens necessarium, 5, 17, 22, 37–8, 206
    ens realissimum, 22, 33
    essence, 1, 7, 18, 38–40, 128, 141, 143–4, 146–7, 149–50, 152, 157, 159, 160–1, 186, 188–9, 206–7, 211–12, 217, 220, 245
    existence, 1, 5, 7, 13, 13n–14n, 18, 39, 40, 63, 128, 143–4, 146–7, 149–50,

God (cont.)
    153, 156, 158–61, 167, 178, 189, 198, 205–6, 214–15, 220
    last God, 13, 14n, 149, 179, 185–9, 191–3, 221
    ontological argument, 111, 128, 150, 156, 159–60, 214–15, 220
    running proof, 158, 160, 217
    teleological argument, 159, 215
    withdrawal of, 3, 193
Good, 84–8, 90–1, 93, 99n
Grant, I. H., 4, 50–1, 54, 72–3n, 79–82, 93, 95n, 97n, 131n, 222–3, 228
ground (*Grund*), 3–4, 11, 20, 23, 33, 36, 42n, 51–3, 66–8, 77, 91, 95n, 105, 107, 113–14, 119–20, 126–7, 130n, 138, 140, 147–8, 154, 163n, 168–74, 181, 184–5, 189, 194–5, 197, 200n–1n, 211–13, 218, 225, 245
    abyss (*Abgrund*), 136, 152, 169–71, 173, 184, 199n, 229
    groundless, 53, 105, 112–14, 136, 138, 143, 160, 170–2, 197, 201
    nonground, 177, 201n
    unground (*Ungrund*), 51, 104–5, 107, 113–14, 136, 138, 147–8, 154, 163n, 170, 173–4, 184–5

habit, 11, 44, 50, 55, 60–2, 73n, 131n, 196, 215–18, 241, 245
Harman, Graham, 22, 27–9, 64
Hegel, G. F. W., 2, 4, 9, 53, 63, 72n, 75, 94, 104–5, 112, 131n, 146, 168, 175–6
    Hegelianism, 64, 72n–3n, 104, 111, 170
Heidegger, Martin, 2–6, 12, 13n–14n, 18–21, 41n–3n, 47, 97n, 112, 114, 120, 123, 132n, 140–1, 147–9, 153, 157, 162, 167–89, 191–8, 198n–200n, 213, 218, 220–1, 224–5, 230, 233, 235n, 246, 247n
Heraclitus, 19, 41, 141, 197, 217, 226
hermeneutics, 6–7
Hume, David, 13n, 29, 41, 58–9, 73, 242, 245
Husserl, Edmund, 20–1

Iamblichus, 82
idealism, 22–3, 148, 176
    Idea, 79–80, 106, 117, 137, 147, 213–14

indivisible remainder, 68, 90, 99n, 147, 153, 171, 225, 232
intellectualism, 206, 209
    Intellect, 76, 78–9, 92, 207
interstice, 121–2, 124–5, 139–40, 142, 147; *see also* wisdom

James, William, 60, 73n, 95n
Jankélévitch, Vladimir, 123–4, 135n, 139, 222
Janus, 218–19
Jaspers, Karl, 5, 42n, 103–4, 199n
justice, 8–9, 123, 156, 230

Kant, Immanuel, 2, 4–5, 41n–2n, 47–8, 51–3, 55, 71, 72n–3n, 79, 107, 113, 115, 129, 152, 168, 208, 214, 223
    Kantianism, 61–2, 73n–4n, 77–8, 81, 95n, 104, 113, 146, 151, 226
    post-Kantian, 5, 41n, 52–3, 94n, 214
Kearney, Richard, 6–10, 191, 245
Kierkegaard, Søren, 106, 176, 182–3, 217, 235n

law
    Law of the World, 123–6, 138–40, 143, 146, 157, 164n–5n, 183, 212–13, 242
    natural law, 55
    physical law, 34, 55–6
    regularity, 1, 12, 28–9, 50, 62, 78, 80, 130n–1n, 216, 241, 244
    uniformity, 11, 36, 38, 44, 241, 244
Leibniz, G. W., 20, 42n, 128, 132n, 136, 167, 169, 177, 199n, 206–8, 210
Levinas, Emmanuel, 94n, 142, 157, 240
logic
    contrariety, 35, 126
    logical space, 3, 17, 45–6, 52, 68, 118, 126, 133n, 135n, 169
    modal logic, 132n–3n
    principle of excluded middle, 7–8, 18, 25–8, 30, 33–6, 46, 66, 73n, 120–1, 124, 126, 157, 174, 242
    principle of identity, 28, 35, 46, 121, 124, 172–4, 219, 242
    principle of non-contradiction, 11, 17–18, 24–8, 30–6, 46, 73n, 115, 120–1, 124, 126, 134n, 242
    space of reasons, 52, 126, 135n, 183
Lucretius, 56, 58

Malabou, Catherine, 53, 72n
Malebranche, Nicolas, 206

Marcel, Gabriel, 175, 200n
materialism, 148, 227–8
　materiality, 79, 81, 222
　matter, 76–93, 95n–9n, 122–3, 142,
　　211, 218, 227–30, 233
　receptacle, 77, 80, 87, 95n, 118, 133n,
　　218, 227
mathematics, 11, 34, 44, 46–50, 54–6,
　71n, 96n, 105–6, 225, 228–9,
　231–2, 234n, 240
　set theory, 13, 34, 46–7, 50, 225, 229,
　　231–3
Meillassoux, Quentin, 6–8, 11, 17–41,
　41n–3n, 45, 47–8, 51–3, 57, 62, 64,
　70, 72n–3n, 96n, 104, 120, 126,
　129n, 131n, 157, 167, 170–1, 174,
　177, 183, 191, 213–14, 224–5, 241,
　243, 245
Merleau-Ponty, Maurice, 20
metaphysics, 4–5, 18–21, 23, 34, 37,
　39, 47, 64, 81–2, 86, 93, 94n–5n,
　132n–3n, 176, 181, 184, 191, 195,
　200n, 233
　ontotheology, 3–4, 10–11, 19, 111,
　　176, 245–6
　post-metaphysical, 4, 6, 18, 40,
　　94n
miracle, 13n, 29, 245
modality, 10–11, 62, 118, 127, 133n,
　160, 194–5, 198, 207
　modal, 133n, 195–7, 246
　modus, 12, 62, 118–20, 133n, 158,
　　160–1, 188, 196, 216, 245
　modus essendi, 62, 128, 217, 220
　modus operandi, 12–13, 29, 36, 38–9,
　　62, 94, 120, 128, 133n, 158, 161,
　　188–9, 195–6
　pre-modal, 62, 118, 120, 191, 195–6,
　　198
monism, 52, 206, 218–19, 221
　philosophy of immanence, 218–19
mythology, 135n, 189, 193, 198, 218,
　220–4, 236n
　allegory, 84, 98n, 222
　philosophy of mythology, 4, 75, 91,
　　135n, 182, 221, 224
　tautegory, 222
　theogony, 9–10, 223–4

naturephilosophy, 76–7, 95n
necessitarianism, 3, 44, 190, 241
Neoplatonism, 11, 69–71, 76–82, 84–6,
　88–94, 95n, 98n–9n, 136, 140, 207,
　232

neutrality
　neither/nor, 35, 105, 110, 116–18, 121,
　　126, 134n, 139, 143, 233
　neuter, 108, 121, 127, 143, 233
Newton, Isaac, 59, 177
Nicholas of Cusa, 8, 191
Nietzsche, Friedrich, 12, 19, 86, 98n,
　176

occasionalism, 29
One, 13, 19, 41n, 66, 76–8, 80, 82–3,
　86–93, 97n–9n, 117, 155–7, 187,
　219–21, 225–9, 231–3
ontology, 1–2, 4–6, 8, 11–12, 22, 34,
　39–40, 46–50, 58, 70, 76, 96n,
　106–7, 128, 133n, 178, 197, 205,
　225–33, 239, 245–6
　epistemo-ontology, 52–3, 72n, 80
　ontology of contingency, 4, 11, 70,
　　245–6
　ontology of the fact, 4, 11, 245–6

Parmenides, 217, 226
Peirce, C. S., 2, 5, 38, 55–6, 60, 73n,
　94n–6n, 129n–31n, 239, 241, 244,
　246n
per posterius, 12, 112, 114, 166n, 180,
　184, 215
　post factum, 9–10, 12, 18, 23, 40, 65,
　　87, 114, 127, 134n, 136, 145, 148,
　　152, 154, 157, 209, 220
　posteriority of the anterior, 157,
　　215
πέρας, 70, 78–80, 96n–7n, 106, 110, 118,
　133n
Persephone, 222
personhood, 143, 150–1, 155, 157
phenomenology, 19, 41n, 52n, 178, 214,
　232
philosophy
　critical, 4, 53, 106
　historical, 40, 91–3, 97n, 107, 180–1,
　　194, 198, 215, 221, 223–4
　of immanence, 41n, 52–3, 129n,
　　218–19
　of mythology, 4, 75, 91, 135n, 182,
　　221, 224
　narrative, 40, 60, 194, 221
　negative, 75–6, 91, 97n, 106–7, 112,
　　180
　positive, 75–6, 91–3, 97n, 106–7, 127,
　　166n, 180–1, 215
　of revelation, 4, 75, 91, 135n,
　　221

Plato, 77–85, 91, 93, 95n–6n, 206, 225
  Euthyphro, 206
  Parmenides, 66, 105, 134n, 217, 226
  Philebus, 79, 96n
  Platonism, 12, 79, 81–2, 84, 90, 93, 97n, 179, 211, 225–6, 235n
  Sophist, 77
  Timaeus, 11, 71, 76–9, 82, 85, 90–1, 93, 95n–6n, 171, 215, 233
Plotinus, 81–2, 84–7, 92–3, 96n–9n, 146
Porphyry, 82
possibility
  a potentia ad actum, 31, 63–4, 109, 113, 124, 165n, 207, 212
  dense-possibles, 32–4, 37, 67
  δύναμις, 77, 81, 85, 92
  may-be, 6, 24, 31–3, 35–7, 64, 66, 108, 232
  possest, 6, 8, 191
  potentia, 63, 65, 109, 113–14, 117–18, 123, 139, 141–2, 157–8, 213
  potentia pura, 109, 146, 207
  potentia universalis, 211–12
  potentiality, 31, 96n, 99n, 114, 134n, 141, 144, 158, 165n, 190
  totality of, 12, 34, 112, 120
  ur-possibility, 121, 124, 138, 141–2, 144, 147–8, 150–1, 153–4, 156, 162n, 210–13, 216–17
  virtual, 26, 31–8, 43n, 67, 73n, 103, 110–11, 121, 213
probability *see* chance
Proclus, 2, 11, 71, 76, 80, 82–93, 97n–9n

quality, 12, 22, 44, 47, 49, 56, 59–60, 68–71, 74n, 76, 96n, 110, 227, 233
quantity, 12, 49, 56, 59–60, 68–71, 74n, 76, 96n, 233
  quantification, 11, 44, 47, 59, 70–1, 71n, 96n, 106, 110, 227

rationalism, 4, 11, 17–18, 24, 26, 32, 70, 73n, 104, 129, 180, 208
  a priori, 4–5, 17–18, 22, 26–7, 35, 38, 45, 48, 50–1, 53, 55, 65, 70, 91, 112, 129, 137, 146, 154, 157, 159, 161, 166n, 177, 180, 198, 214–15, 225–7, 231–2, 234n
  analytic, 47, 58, 65–7, 103, 115–16, 122, 150, 156, 159–60
  deduction, 48, 53, 72n, 107, 181, 184, 198
Ravaisson, Félix, 60, 216–17
realism, 6, 21–2, 52–3, 58, 72n, 206

Real, 49, 54, 58, 63, 113, 147–8, 212, 218
reason
  as consequent, 1, 3, 6, 11–12, 17–18, 26, 54, 66–7, 107, 112–14, 117–18, 121, 126–8, 136, 147–9, 168, 205, 246
  facticity of reason, 6, 18, 22, 131n, 170
  principle of (sufficient) reason, 4–6, 11, 17, 19–20, 23–4, 26–9, 34, 36, 38, 41n–2n, 66, 106, 126, 128, 167, 169–70, 185, 213, 240–5
  principle of unreason, 26, 34–6
  as universal, 1, 18, 24, 47, 94, 112–13, 121, 128, 152, 205, 209, 245
repetition, 19–20, 98n, 182, 217; *see also* supplement
revelation, 91, 152, 154, 161

Sallis, John, 80, 95n
Sartre, Jean-Paul, 20–1, 142–3, 212
Schelling, F. W. J., 4–5, 11–12, 14n, 31, 42n–3n, 45–6, 68, 70–1, 74n, 75–94, 94n–9n, 103–19, 121–8, 129n–32n, 134n, 136–43, 145–6, 148–62, 162n, 164n–6n, 167–72, 174–95, 197–8, 198n–200n, 205–25, 230, 233, 234n–6n, 246
Schopenhauer, Arthur, 242–3
Schulz, Walter, 75, 97n, 159, 181
Scotus, John Duns, 206–7
sovereignty, 108, 136–8, 142, 150–3, 155, 157, 171, 178, 181, 188, 214
  Godhood, 12, 151, 156–7, 167, 185–9, 192–3, 214–15, 217, 219–20, 223–4
speculation, 1, 4–7, 10–11, 18, 20–1, 24–5, 39–40, 50, 92–3, 128, 130n, 198, 218, 227, 234, 239–41, 244
Spinoza, Benedictus de, 65, 110, 124, 145–6, 148, 216
  Spinozism, 57, 109, 113, 124, 137, 140–1, 148, 155, 207, 218
substance, 19, 22, 57, 64–5, 70, 78, 80–2, 109–10, 119, 123, 136–7, 143, 147–8, 150, 155, 158, 181, 195, 218–19, 230
  substantiality, 22, 78–9, 81–3, 96n, 137, 144, 147–8, 162n, 228
  substrate (*substratum*), 10, 37–8, 65, 77, 80–3, 89, 93, 95n–6n, 99n, 116–17, 119, 148, 151, 181, 244
supplement, 1, 3, 8–12, 17, 26–8, 37, 50, 53, 57–8, 66–8, 71, 87, 90, 99n, 103, 114, 116, 120–3, 126–7,

138–9, 145, 151, 157, 161, 163n, 201n, 207, 219–20, 223, 230, 233; *see also* repetition
Swinburne, Richard, 150, 160

theodicy, 156
theology
  apophatic, 86
  cataphatic, 86
  possible-God, 6–7, 9–10, 191, 245
  rational, 214–15, 224
  speculative, 4
  weak, 6–8
time, 18, 36–40, 41n, 52–3, 73n, 78, 81, 83, 89, 94n, 115, 117, 119–20, 122, 130n, 138–41, 157, 179–82, 198n, 218
  temporalisation, 123, 181
  timing, 40
  tychistic time, 38
transcendental, 11, 19–21, 44, 46, 50–5, 65, 67, 71, 72n–4n, 77, 81, 97n, 116, 129n, 168, 197, 223–4, 226, 243
  transcendental Ideal, 12, 33–4, 53–4, 63, 112–13, 212
  transcendentalism, 4, 48, 51–4, 58, 74n
truth, 31, 35, 52, 65–6, 70–1, 120, 133n, 168–9, 172, 179, 206, 213–14, 221–3, 234n, 241, 244
  bivalency, 8, 35, 174
  correspondence, 174
  eternal truth, 13, 205–9, 216
  necessary truths, 1, 7, 11, 43n, 112, 118, 205–6, 209, 216
  truth-event, 120, 140, 147, 169, 174, 181–2, 184, 187–90, 193, 195, 197, 213, 220, 223; *see also* event
  truth-value, 35

truths of reason, 1, 7, 17, 22, 53, 65, 112, 118, 161, 169, 241–2, 245
tychism, 56, 58
typologies of God
  anatheism, 7
  antitheism, 8
  (a)theism, 157
  atheism, 6–7, 150, 155–6, 159, 188, 205, 215, 219–21, 233, 245
  henotheism, 224
  monotheism, 13, 155–9, 187, 221
  pantheism, 215
  polytheism, 156, 159, 187, 205, 221, 222–5
  theism, 7–8, 155–6, 160, 215, 219, 221, 224
  theo-polyism, 221
  theomonism, 13, 205, 218–19, 221, 225

unprethinkable, 36, 77, 94n, 113–14, 116, 118, 120–5, 127, 135n, 137–8, 141, 143, 146–50, 153–5, 157–8, 161, 164n, 169, 180, 183, 189–90, 194, 198, 201n, 213, 215, 217–20, 232

Van der Heiden, Gert-Jan, 3–4, 11, 34, 36, 128, 133n–4n, 182–3, 190
voluntarism, 206, 209

Whistler, Daniel, 74n, 93
Whitehead, A. N., 5, 73n, 163n
Wirth, Jason, 94n, 175
Wisdom, 140–1, 162n, 197, 212; *see also* interstice
Wittgenstein, Ludwig, 20, 71n, 168, 244

Žižek, Slavoj, 72n, 94n, 99n